T0193032

RELIGIOUS DELUSIONS

DELUSIONS

American Style

CONVERT TO BORN-AGAIN CHRISTIAN BEFORE DOOMSDAY: SUDDEN DESTRUCTION!

DANDY THE DIVINE

MANIPULATIONS OF THE PUBLIC'S MIND

BLAIR ALAN GADSBY

Published by:
Trine Day LLC
PO Box 577
Walterville, OR 97489
1-800-556-2012
www.TrineDay.com
trineday@icloud.com

Library of Congress Control Number: 2020931392

Gadsby, Blair Alan.
Religious Delusions, American Style—1st ed.
p. cm.
Epub (ISBN-13) 978-1-63424-284-4
Kindle (ISBN-13) 978-1-63424-285-1
Print (ISBN-13) 978-1-63424-283-7
1. Religious Studies 2. American Religious History. 3. Religion and Politics. 4. Religion, U.S. Government, Conspiracies. I. Title

FIRST EDITION
10 9 8 7 6 5 4 3 2 1

Printed in the USA
Distribution to the Trade by:
Independent Publishers Group (IPG)
814 North Franklin Street
Chicago, Illinois 60610
312.337.0747
www.ipgbook.com

For those who've lost their lives by the hands of officials' injustice.

And for students.

CONTENTS

PREFACE

I insist upon clarifying what this book is *not* prior to venturing into the historical delusions detailed in the following pages. This is not a work in the vein of a recent spate of books challenging the intellectual veracity of religious belief and/or exposing the weaknesses or malfeasance of religious institutions. Nor is it interested in the bad behaviors of explicitly or self-avowed religious individuals in our social and civic life. There is a list of books current to the past decade-to-thirty years that do just these: *The End of Faith* (2004) by Sam Harris, *God is Not Great: How Religion Poisons Everything* (2007) by the now-late Christopher Hitchens who also anthologized *The Portable Atheist: Essential Readings for the Non-Believer* in the same year. Richard Dawkins has long had an esteemed voice in the debate as well with, initially in 1986, *The Blind Watchmaker: Why the Evidence of Evolution Reveals a Universe Without Design,* and more recently in *The God Delusion* (2006) which is a rather scathing assault on religious belief.

Let the reader be aware that the use of the word "*Delusion*" in Dawkins' book is not at all what I mean by "*Delusions*" in my title.

The issues raised by these authors are serious and all well worth their ink. And even if the debate about God's existence or lack thereof and religion's proper place in society has been acrimonious, it has nevertheless been mostly *ongoing* within many societies. Questions of divine metaphysics have persisted down through the millennia giving us no reason to believe this line of reasoning will end any time soon. And so, without doubt, much more ink will be spilt on the topic.

In fact, I, too, enjoy that debate from my vocation as a community college Religious Studies instructor in a large urban setting. It is a challenge taking these deeply engrained cultural traits, *memes* as they have more recently been called, and to mold them into something morally instructive, intellectually nourishing and socially uniting, rather than allowing them to be used in ways that are morally destructive, intellectually dishonest and socially divisive – *partisan*, in other words.

Alas, the delusions I draw attention to are perpetuated consciously and with ulterior motives at work. These ulterior motives can be exposed through historical research and by providing a context for those motives.

Stripped of demagoguery the facts present themselves.

What I term "delusions" are eight areas of American history where the topic of religion has been purposefully distorted and/or used for a particular end or goal which is very often political but sometimes profit-seeking. However, as the reader will quickly find out, these delusions come with deep costs to human dignity and welfare, and to the much-cherished American way of life.

Quotes over the Centuries

*For many a day and year, even from our first beginnings hath this word of the Lord been verified concerning us in the Wilderness; The Lord hath said of New-England, Surely they are my People Children that will not **lie**, so hath he been our Saviour.*
– William Stoughton, 1668

We hold these Truths to be self-evident, that all Men are created equal, that they are endowed by their Creator with certain unalienable Rights, that among these are Life, Liberty, and the Pursuit of Happiness.
– Declaration of Independence, 1776

Neither slavery nor involuntary servitude ... shall exist within the United States or any place subject to their jurisdiction.
– Amendment XIII to the Constitution, ratified 1865

And we should ... guard ourselves against falsifications of the faith by national religiosity, as against a falsification of national piety by Christian trimmings.
– Rudolph Bultmann in *The Task of Theology in the Present Situation*, 2 May 1933, three months after the burning of the Reichstag, Berlin; thereafter Hitler would seize extensive political powers.

"... the pagans, abortionists, feminists, gays, lesbians ... the ACLU, People for the American Way ... all of them who tried to secularize America, I point the finger in their faces and say you helped this happen." Robertson, "I totally concur."[1]
– Jerry Falwell on the *700 Club* television program, September 13, 2001

---

1   https://video.search.yahoo.com/search/video;_ylt=AwrTHQpDw-WBaUnQAnHVXNyoA;_ylu=X3oDMTEzOWU0ZnFhBGNvbG8DZ3ExBHBvcwMxBHZ0aWQDVUkwMkM0XzEEc2VjA3Nj?p=transcript+700+-Club+Sept+13%2C+2001&fr=tightropetb#id=1&vid=70a9562d308298-542ba1e1de192b1cfc&action=view (accessed January 2019).

INTRODUCTION

> *de·lu·sion* n. 1. The act of deluding. 2. The state of being deluded or led astray. 3. A false belief especially when persistent. 4. Psychiatry A false, fixed belief, held in spite of evidence to the contrary.
> – Funk and Wagnalls Standard College Dictionary

The topic of religious delusions in American public life emerged as the result of the past ten years' worth of effort attempting to decipher what I found to be a shocking and troubling truth: that is, *the intentionally-obscured and distorted role of religion in national and world events, as told to us by educational systems, news media, and politicians.*

Fully, it's not only that religion is used as a tool to achieve some goal or other, which on one level makes a certain amount of obvious sense. Instead, fabrications are deliberately told in its name in order to deceive people as to what to believe about religion generally, or a particular religion, or about a particular religious group that may be in question or at the center of some "affair" or controversy.

Furthermore, the social consequences for populations holding religious delusions can range from *benign* (by being ignored and therefore un-influential), to *bad* (by inciting stereotypes and phobias about individuals or groups), to *worse* (by encouraging or extolling actions based in those stereotypes and phobias by means of discrimination, exclusion and persecution), and even to *disastrous* (by fomenting genocidal physical conflicts and wars).

In fact, it can be surprising, if not shocking, to learn the depths to which we, the public at large, have been manipulated. The result is a certain control over the popular imagination as it pertains to religious topics in American life, and therefore a measure of control over how we respond both individually and as a society to any given event or crisis. To be sure, this control will be seized-upon if the population is not wary.

In short, the thesis of this book is that *we have been deliberately fed delusions about religion* by the mass-mainstream and corporatized media at the behest of government officials and their policies (specific officials are relevant to particular cases and will be named in the respective chapters with no intent to accuse, but rather to seek explanations from those best-positioned to provide direct evidence or insight; the term "government officials," after all, casts a very wide and meaningless net over a humungous bureaucracy).

As a result, Americans carry-about many more than one or two delusions regarding religion – these delusions are espoused both from *within* religions and from *without* – and these are what this book strives to address in eight topics which unfold in a roughly chronological narrative of historical-religious delusions championed since the founding of the nation. They are in this sense uniquely *American delusions*, but they are based upon patterns that have existed since the organization of societies and civilizations. A word about such precedents will be made, but only after a brief remark about the nature of the genesis of the inquiry itself.

The CONSTRUCTION of a DELUSION

With the onset of September 11, 2001 attacks, like so many souls, I was held captive to the unfolding of events live, in real-time, as the morning progressed from one tragic scene to another. It was an exercise in the "shock and awe" of the entire viewing audience. The images were arresting: two huge buildings with smoking-gaping holes where the aircrafts entered, the hapless people falling and/or jumping from the towers, and ultimately the two World Trade Center towers exploding into dust and debris across lower Manhattan. The balance of the day was a series of dizzying events culminating in the President's speech from the Oval Office later in the evening at 8PM Eastern time … 5PM in Arizona, where I reside.

The rest is history, as they say.

But on that evening of the attack, the President, having been away from Washington, D.C. much of the day, had arrived back at the Oval Office to address the nation. And he had an explanation for what happened:

> *America was targeted for attack because we're the brightest beacon for freedom and opportunity in the world and no one will keep that light from shining. Today our nation saw evil, the very worst of human nature, and we responded with the best of America…*

In essence, we were told the attackers hated America for freedoms enjoyed here that they found offensive to their religious beliefs. To be sure, the attackers' beliefs are representative of only a fraction of their co-religionists as theirs is merely an *interpretation of religion* embedded within a much larger religion with a worldwide following, Islam. This interpretation would come to be more precisely known as *jihadi Islam, radical Islamic extremism* or *Islamism* in academic circles. The meaning of the President's message, however, was that the attack was motivated by a belief about *what we are*, ostensibly <u>not</u> for *what we had done*.[1]

The President's statement seemed disingenuous to me, even at that time, and I was vaguely suspicious. He seemed to ascribe the cause or motive to religious fanaticism, and only *secondarily* was Americans' behavior (the practice of our freedoms) wrongly identified as the issue. This seemed something of a cover-story and came as a surprise to me that the audience would be misled in this way.

There ought to be nothing domestically-politically wrong, I thought at the time, with admitting some genuine disagreements and interactions with others in foreign lands that may cause backlash. The American people are capable of understanding cause-and-effect in the conflicts of national and regional interests around the world. We realize the USA is a large country with complicated and far-reaching interests and influences; this is bound to create resentment in certain quarters. This honesty would be appreciated by the public.

But instead, the demagoguery began, and was ratcheted-up to a fever pitch, a war-generating pitch, for which the costs endure.[2]

With these words of the President, the façade of *religion as cause* rang hollow as I strived to comprehend the day at hand and the terror that was befalling the country.

Worse still, his words were in direct contradiction from what was previously known to be true from statements made by Osama bin Laden (Lawrence, xx: 58-62). While he certainly *did have grievances* against the USA and had stated them clearly, and even though American freedoms and the lifestyle perpetuated here and in Hollywood movies were among his criticisms, *these were not* what he cited when he gave his speeches and reasons to attack American interests. Bin Laden was most explicit in his rationale for injuring Americans, and it was essentially threefold:

---

1   Again, if the reader lived in North America on that day, you no doubt experienced how this felt. On this continent we were given a *generally uniform presentation* of the events through the news media and so the relative impact upon us is resultantly uniform. This effect is further heightened in the US media with excited visual graphics in news presentations and the excessive use of retired Pentagon analysts and commentators on the FOX, CNN, MSNBC cable stations and across the broadcast networks too. (For another observation of the day's events by a Religious Studies researcher, see McCutcheon, 2).

2   As the world would later come to learn, the subsequent war in Iraq was predicated upon yet a separate set of misleading statements about weapons of mass destruction (WMDs) and their danger to the West.

1) U.S. support for corrupt and oppressive regimes such as the Saudi monarchy or any number of Arab governments including Saddam Hussein whom the U.S. had once supported (1980-1988) only to then turn-on him later in the game (1990-91). In other words, U.S. involvement and interference in Arab-Muslim countries were unacceptable to bin Laden as it caused untold misery and suffering to his fellow Muslims who were victimized by their oppressive "puppet regimes" and the vagaries of U.S. foreign policy.

2) The U.S. implementation of a no-fly zone over parts of Iraq and the continued presence of U.S. troops within Saudi Arabia in the aftermath of the first Gulf War in late 1990 to early 1991. Bin Laden blamed these sanctions for the deaths of over a million Iraqis over the span of a decade. The land of the "two holy shrines" of Islam was, furthermore, and in his religious opinion, being subjected to infidels so long as American (presumably Christian and most certainly non-Muslim) troops remained in Arabia.

And finally,

3) U.S. support for the state of Israel and Zionism over-and-above the human rights of Palestinians. The historically strong support the U.S. has given Israel over its nearly-seventy years of existence has resulted in an ever increasingly desperate set of circumstances for the Palestinians who are preponderantly Muslim.

These three reasons would be repeated after 9/11 by bin Laden (Lawrence, 117) yet remain obscure to the vast majority of Americans who never had it thoroughly and honestly explained to them the full mindset of the accused attackers.

But alas, this distortion about their motives turned out to be one of the more benign elements of the deception – distracting to be sure, but not wholly sinister. To mislead to protect genuine interests, or even incompetence or negligence, or foreign policies that have not been fully disclosed yet but are being implemented, are wholly understandable motives, even if unjustified. I personally chalked-it-up to our dependence upon oil[3] and the subsequent need for cover reasons to maintain some type of military presence in the region – hardly a conspiracy theory.

---

3   This fact should be elaborated upon. It is not for US consumption needs that Middle Eastern oil is sought as only 10-15% of US demand comes from the region. Instead, it appears that it is the wide profit margins stemming from relatively cheap extraction and production costs for sale to third parties, particularly a growing Asia, that could explain the willingness of US and UK-based capital interests to commit itself to an oil war.

However, rendering us victims rather than targets of retribution for wrongdoing would possess greater political capital for an offensive military response. And ultimately, that's precisely what happened. The U.S. was mobilized for a war that, nearly two decades on at the time of this writing, it has still to fully extricate itself from. There is no clear end in sight for a U.S. presence there, despite what we are told by officials about our "military deployment," namely that it has ended, and we are there simply in an advisory role. In fact, our involvement in the Middle East continues to evolve in complexity as recent U.S. relations with Pakistan and Iran (and most recently Syria) show increasing signs of pressure and tension.

This huge gulf between the knowledge and perceptions of the American people on the one hand, and the stated grievances of bin Laden on the other, was masterfully exploited by the political-media apparatus in the US, even internationally, and the groundwork for a war on terror was established, and with the war being swiftly implemented within a month on 7 October 2001.

These are no small consequences.

What is most significant about the maintenance of this gulf in knowledge is that the American people cannot be expected to change what we are as a culture and a people, and so we need look no farther than these claims nor take any remedial actions – the reasoning goes – because it was *not what we had done* that was the attackers' grievance, but *who we are*. This gulf in knowledge undermines all self-examination, reevaluation, and negotiation in their tracks. Much in the same way the "myth of the lone gunman" (see the Terms of Delusion after the Conclusion) puts to rest any need for further inquiry – any need for questioning the involvement of others, or to look for motives beyond a single individual. This is a very convenient and efficient veil to hide behind for those either directly involved in the crime or in the subsequent cover-up.

However, should the cause be rooted in something we have done, then we may be able to easily (or perhaps not-so-easily) undo it; or, going forward, we can pledge to stop doing what we've been doing. We would at least have the opportunity to ask ourselves such questions as part of a national (and rational) self-reflection on events. In other words, the American people may demand that a political solution be sought in order to address the grievances of bin Laden, rather than embark upon a war of questionable necessity and outcome. Instead a delusion was peddled, and the American political system was activated.

But first, these delusions must be forensically and accurately understood, exposed, and swept-aside before any such process of self-reflection can begin, and certainly before any political rectifications be crafted as these same delusions have done enormous damage to the American political psyche (see Postscript to chapter eight). This outcome is advanced in no small part by the 9/11 terror event. Getting to the heart of that event was the first step and, as it turned-out, the last chapter of this book. Indeed, it was because upon closer scrutiny the very attack itself was not what it seemed to be. There was, it now appeared, a far more active role on the part of certain U.S. officials complicit in the operation itself, and who were not merely spinning a tale as to causes but concealing their own direct involvement in the perpetuation of the event.

This was the point (by now it was 2007) at which my understanding was taking a turn and where I became convinced that delusions can be *disastrous*, not simply *bad* or *worse*, as suggested at the outset. What's more, the evidence is straight forward and unimpeachable if one has adequate access to the information and images. The Soliloquy inserted between chapters six and seven presents this evidence and my investigative approach dealing with this evidence. As the reader will see (stress the *see*), the obfuscating of motives and causes became most benign in the light of evidence of direct U.S. participation in the murder of American citizens on American soil.[4]

At this juncture it came into focus that a delusion had been deliberately constructed (and played-out on live TV) and implanted in a traumatized and bewildered nation. The political capital was enormous.

In time, the terrorist attack of 9/11 exposed itself as the latest example of a nation-state performing a *false flag* military operation, and the awareness of a *religious delusion* being perpetuated in its name (Muslims were blamed after all), coupled with an emerging understanding of a shadowed history in the first place, this study was set in motion. Though 9/11 was the topic that first broke through my oversight and provided an awareness of this pattern in history, it would not be the only incident of this nature to challenge long–held assumptions. Beginning with this shadowed element of the 9/11 attack, a line of inquiry would open up that resulted in a new, for me at least, understanding of religion's roles in American history, and it includes a very unpleasant history indeed. It is a history in which religious deception is an instrument of power.

---

4   In the parlance of the literature of 9/11Truth, the acronyms LIHOP and MIHOP are appropriate here. These stand for "Let It Happen On Purpose" and "Made It Happen On Purpose" regarding the US intelligence and military roles in the attack. More will be stated on these concepts in chapter eight.

A NEED for DECEPTION?[5]

We can all appreciate the need for secrecy, even deception. Anyone who is a parent certainly understands the concept. One can't tell the children everything too soon, and sometimes "white lies" are necessary to bide one's time, and in the case of a child it requires time in order for it to grow-up and mature before processing certain information of an adult nature. This is hardly deception; it is common sense.

Perhaps nations are similar, and I intend to demonstrate that at least some people think that national populations are candidates for this kind of deception.

What if nations, too, like children, require time to mature in outlook and cohesion before they can stand the pummels of history – factionalism, racism, religious tumult, and war among them? Therefore, it's not uncommon to hear citizens claim that higher-ups know things that we don't, and probably we shouldn't, so a degree of deception is tolerated and even expected.

However, a common assumption accompanying such claims is that, though deception may be a necessary ingredient in public administration, our leaders would not "conspire." But what is meant by "conspire" is that no one in that decision-making apparatus would harm the American public directly, or conspire (against us, the general population) for profit, or lie to start a war, etc. These are dismissed as "conspiracy theories," a term that's use warrants some critical examination. And conspiracy theories, we are led to believe, are *prima facie* false.

The idea, therefore, that political leaders would use religion as a cover in order to accomplish some specified goal goes back even further than the notorious example of the much-despised Roman leader Nero (54-68 AD/CE). In his case, the emperor, rumor stated (accurately or not), had himself organized to have a fire set in the city of Rome. He would subsequently blame the Christians who were living in Rome at that time and Nero set about to persecute them, going so far as to set some Christians on fire while still alive! A wretched act of terror indeed. This was both nefarious and duplicitous – compounded by the cunning ingenuity that he was able to accomplish two goals: secure the land for his expanded palace grounds; and he was able to quell a hated social group whom he believed, rightly or wrongly, had potential to cause him governance problems by siphoning-off allegiance to his rule. None among his motives is hidden.

---

5   According to *A Theory of Religion's* Def: 79 Deception is any interaction strategy that intentionally leads other people to accept explanations which one privately rejects (Stark and Bainbridge, 1987: 173/329). The dual page numbers used in ATOR citations refers to the Axiom/Definition/Proposition's appearance first in the text and then in the Appendix.

But what is nearly equally horrifying was the response to Nero's activities by Tacitus and recounted by Henry Chadwick in his book *The Early Church*:

> There seemed no necessary reason the Christians should not also achieve toleration. They came into conflict with the State in the first instance by accident, not on any fundamental point of principle. In 64 a great fire destroyed much of Rome. Nero had made himself sufficiently unpopular to be suspected of arson, and turned to the Christians to find a scapegoat. The historian Tacitus, writing about fifty years later, did not believe that the Christians were justly accused of the arson, though he saw no harm in the execution of a contemptible, anti-social group hated for their vices – for by his time, if not by Nero's, the Christians were vulgarly thought to practice incest and cannibalism at their nocturnal meetings. (These charges probably arose from language about universal love and the eucharist.) The Neronian persecution was confined to Rome and was not due to any sense of deep ideological conflict between Church and State; it was simply that the emperor had to blame somebody for the fire (25-26).

The utility of religion is much broader than the above example reveals but it does make us keenly, if painfully, aware of the potentially exploitable nature of religious groups. That's probably why leaders find it such an easy instrument for their deceptions, and why I felt the desire to write this research narrative upon understanding 9/11 in such a light.

A religious delusion told in the name of the 9/11 attack was personally unbearable. I could see no benign element to it. No possible need in America's interest (including oil) that could justify such an atrocity compounded by a huge, indeed global, lie leading ultimately to a second war (first Afghanistan then Iraq) and an increasing number of atrocities in the form of terrible human pain and suffering directly resulting from the wars.

What I can and will accept criticism for, is naïveté; though I doubt much naïveté applies in what you are about to read here. And the question may be fairly asked: *Could there really be factual information that would warrant the need for a 9/11-style operation?* We are coming upon twenty years after the event now and it seems unlikely that it could ever be justified, and as this book argues academically and politically, the 9/11 delusion is an example of one of the more damaging deceptions foisted upon an unsuspecting society. It is a lie that is damaging for the many, and in the interests of only the few, and with the costs being far greater than the benefits. Furthermore, it is a lie that cannot be justified when brought into the full light of examination.

But whatever the existential answer as to *why* the domestic perpetrators of 9/11 believed it was in the country's interest to orchestrate the attack, it appears that such deceits are not uncommon and perhaps it is an axiom of governance: *societies are routinely and systematically lied to by their ruling elites.*

In light of such reasons (rationalizations) the reader can evaluate on a case-by-case basis as to the justifiability of the delusions and determine for him or herself just how grievous each incident is. There is no reason to believe we would each of us find these religious delusions equally unjustifiable. Quite the contrary, there are, evidently, individuals who believe there is a need for such actions based upon delusions (since the latter cannot exist without the former – delusions require deluders).

Further, delusions are done at some risk and cost to those perpetuating them – especially when they are of the criminal sort. Concealment and working from the shadows are the norm and the principal *modus operandi* of those involved in these deceptions. Short of outside and independent scrutiny into the deeper workings of these events there is unlikely any mechanism by which to bring forth these evidences into the full light of day. The political system currently seems unable to combat these delusions using the traditional means of leverage: the Congress and its power to commission investigations. But this is another effort.

For purposes of the thesis presented here, it is sufficient to understand that there is nothing new under the sun and that delusions are routinely perpetuated in the name of religion for some end or other. What we all innately recognize, however, is that delusions undertaken in the name of religion pose a unique philosophical conundrum. What is supposed to be a tool used for honesty and noble purposes suddenly becomes a tool for intentions *most people* would deem ignoble – wealth extension, war for expansion, wasteful use of resources resulting in the neglect and social deprivation of segments of society, or even worse, the murdering of innocents.

But by whom are these decisions calculated? Those in power are the only ones capable of executing these social-engineering projects, which is ultimately what such efforts are tantamount to – steering society in the direction of their goals and ends.

This is the dilemma: *who is to decide when deception is necessary?* Who is to decide what is good and what is evil? Here is where morality becomes relative, if not conveniently then out of necessity, for the ruling powers. The survival of the group may depend upon it, we are frequently told, most assuredly, the established political order may be under threat. This then becomes the basis for political action.

Friedrich Nietzsche warns that the origins of good and evil are rooted in the ruling elites' determination of the very definitions of the terms *good* and *evil* and that there is a *pathos of distance* required[6] between themselves (the political elites) and the masses – words of wisdom, to be sure. Invariably, those defining and applying the terms ascribe to themselves the good/holy and to the *other* the bad/evil.

Our day proves to be no different.

Upon closer examination of the religious language used against us in these delusions, it becomes clear that it is little more than elitists' rationalizations of their lordship over the rest of us. All too often the discourse develops a language that is laden with metaphysical self-justifications of our innocence – again, *hated for what we are, not what we've done.*

But this trick is as old as the Bible itself and was the example I had in mind when stating that such notions go back long before Nero's deviousness.

Indeed, as the Biblical narrators recount, God would take it upon himself to deceive the opposing armies of Israel by making it appear, as in a mirage, that the numbers of Israelite soldiers were far more numerous than they in fact were. Similarly, in the case of the four desperate lepers who made a Syrian army contingent think they were being accosted by "Hittite and Egyptian" kings and their armies hired by the Israelite king (2 Kings 7: 3-7). The Syrians were deceived by God so that the starving inhabitants outside of the city walls could enjoy the spoils of the just-fled Syrian army and then later trample the Israelite king at his own city gates thereby fulfilling prophecy.

The Hebrew Bible's narrative is replete with incidents in which God performs morally questionable acts in order to make some argument to the people of Israel, or to its enemies. In other words, it is an Israel-centric (nationalistic) text with the Hebrew nation-state at the epicenter of God's concerns. As such, it is morally justifiable to demonize (lie about or lie to) a foreign people in order to rationalize attacking or usurping them in some way, typically in a land conquest. Again, a Biblical reference which almost seems a caricature; in the process of demonizing the enemy tribes of Israel, the Hebrew Bible portrays them as offering their sons to Baal in

---

6   Friedrich Nietzsche, 1966: 201 and 1967: 25-26.

burnt offerings (Jeremiah 19:5). Or against the Amalekites, God commanded Samuel to tell King Saul to "destroy all they have; do not spare them, but kill both man and woman, infant and suckling, ox and sheep, camel and donkey" (1 Samuel 15:3, Amplified Bible).

In other words, God did what he felt necessary, including deceiving and brutalizing. Lying to the opponents of Israel or to Israel themselves is simply a means to an end. God would find no moral quandaries in destroying the enemies of His chosen people and using metaphysical deception as his chief weapon.

Alas, since the gods are crafty in their worldly ways, so too must be rulers of men. All *is* fair in love and war, after all, so the saying goes anyway. And it appears that the nations' leaders do in fact indulge in these rationalizations.

As a matter of policy, the judicious use of public religion could be in the best interest of the nation and was used to great effect by the founders of the early American Republic. All men are created equal, or nearly all men at that time. Similarly, the notion often fostered in churches across the land that the founding fathers desired to establish a "Christian nation" based on the morality of the Ten Commandments, when in fact Benjamin Franklin and Thomas Jefferson repudiated the very idea of Jesus as a God-man (referring to the Trinity and Christian orthodoxy more broadly), which was a belief they felt to be superstitious (supernaturalism) and a corruption of the ethical teachings of Jesus. In fact, Thomas Jefferson could arguably be considered an atheist[7] in his personal and practical beliefs and a deist in his public statements. Their verbal assent to deism[8] and approval of Christian ethics is an expression of their belief that there is a certain utilitarian and beneficial effect to religious adherence, namely good behavior and the maintenance of the social order necessary upon which to build the Republic.

But good behavior is hardly predicated solely upon a Christian metaphysic.

Franklin would ruminate that he expected to find decent and upstanding citizens in all sects (chapter one; Kramnick, 166-167). In their own ways, the attitudes of Franklin and Jefferson recognize that religion *does* motivate people's behavior and the sensible use of religious rhetoric

---

7   I am prepared to assert along with Rodney Stark and William Bainbridge that "there can be no wholly naturalistic religion; a religion lacking supernatural assumptions is no religion at all" (3). More on this idea in chapter three.

8   Deism as a religious belief is void of any supernatural content and creedal requirements. Deism is best understood as a compromise philosophy rooted in agnosticism and social morality.

for civilized ends has its honorable place. In a free republic the benefits of religion become obvious and it would have been counterintuitive, if counterproductive, to dissuade all people from all manner of belief. This is the best way to understand certain of the early Republic's legislators' willingness to allow state money to be used to support church activity and ministers' salaries in the overall attempts to reinforce Christian morality (chapter one; Sehat, 36).

We would hardly deem it appropriate today, however, to spend public money in an effort to Christianize Americans' morality in order to "correct the morals of men, restrain their vices and preserve the peace of society" (Sehat, 34).

Or would we?

Certainly, many people today feel this is a most appropriate, if not a necessary, role of government, whether through tax-breaks for religious institutions or by the legislative blocking of public funding or civil sanction for abortion or gay marriage, to name two high-profile topics.

The overall goals may be lofty and the ends desirable – to have a just and peaceful society for all – but the road to get there and the means by which to do so are not so clear and must remain compatible with modern concepts of religious pluralism, as stipulated by the Constitution's First Amendment.[9] Nevertheless, in the late 1700s most Anglos felt that Christian-based morality ought to be the guiding principle of the nation – perhaps with a relaxed enforcement protocol as to creed, but the general outlines of social behavior were certainly predicated on a "good book" mentality. To deny this religious aspect of social development in American political thought is to overlook an important element (and safeguard) of the US's constitutional history.

But let us not romanticize this history either, or worse, allow this historic act by the founders to be interpreted as a signal of state-endorsed religion. It was anything but. Instead, it was a means to an end: managing civil society.

Today we find any number of means (resources) by which to bring about our civil society, most are declarative and straight-forward – rooted in known laws, philosophies and documents. Some means, however, are far more shadowy in their genesis and execution. However society chooses to move – or is moved – forward, the resources of the U.S. federal bureaucracy ranging across its governmental-military-economic spheres

9   Congress shall make no law respecting an establishment of religion, or prohibiting the free exercise thereof; or abridging the freedom of speech, or of the press, or the right of the people peaceably to assemble, and to petition the Government for a redress of grievances.

are enormous and provide innumerable opportunities for power-grabbing individuals and entities. The thesis of this book is to peer behind the veneer of religion which has veiled the activities of certain of those power-grabbing individuals/entities.

More conspicuously, take these two examples of religious motivations deeply influencing politics, yet are political polar opposites: "Liberation Theology" on the one hand and the "Moral Majority" on the other; both represent instances of religious leaders speaking a very political message and trying to achieve some desired political end. Political parties align themselves with one or the other and do so publicly. In these cases, religion is used openly, and both are fair enough examples of religion's efficacy in the social sphere. There's little-to-nothing covert about them, as means of influencing public policy. As citizens we can accept or reject them and/or their respective messages. But such efforts cannot be dismissed as devious; they are the actions of religious people, or "lived religion," as anthropologists like to say these days.

These more-or-less upfront and forthright uses of religion, that is saying and doing whatever it takes to see that one's views prevail, is the basic theme of chapters one through four. The theme of chapters five through eight, on the other hand, take the use of religion a step further. In these chapters, religion's usefulness takes on a more complex, shadowy and far sinister role. Religion is used to deceive. In these chapters, religion assists in accomplishing anything but noble ends. Deception becomes the norm. Only by *seeing* the ways in which we've been deceived can we peer behind the veil. Hence, the importance of viewing suppressed images.

In fact, one option for the reader is to begin at the Soliloquy inserted between chapters six and seven, and then proceed to read chapters seven and eight. If these chapters and the understanding of religion's role in those two events (the Branch Davidian confrontation at Waco in 1993 and the terrorist attack of September 11, 2001) don't bring into sharp, if shocking, focus the political issues raised by our leaders' use of religion against us, then I'm extremely pessimistic for the future political consequences of the role(s) of "religion in society."

A WORD ABOUT the WORD "CONSPIRACY"

Very frustrating due to its intellectual dishonesty is the polemic use of the term "conspiracy theory" so widely used in official discourse, that is, in political discourse, media reports, and most woefully and regrettably, in academe. The selective use of this term does nothing but belie the propagandist nature of what we are being told, and, consequently, *what they are up to*. Whether it is a comprehensively-concerted effort is not the point, nor is it necessary, for a desired effect to be achieved. In fact, having unwitting accomplices in the perpetuating of misnomers like "conspiracy" or "conspiracy theory" is all the better. They willingly and dutifully provide a degree of separation for, and therefore plausible deniability to, those with more active roles and the most to gain from this carefully-crafted and thoroughly deceptive use of the term.

I confess to having been one of these unwitting accomplices thinking of the many times I stood in front of a classroom of students advocating for the conventional understanding of events, and using the term conspiracy theory consistent with that understanding. I no less share the responsibility of misappropriating causes, albeit done unwittingly. There is, it is my contention, greater accountability in the field Religious Studies given that religion is so deeply and thoroughly woven into the official version of events. Given this, if it is not the professional Religious Studies instructor's job to correct the historical distortion of the field, distortions implicating decisively (allegedly) religious actions, then who is to do it? Other academic disciplines[10] have their own responsibilities that may overlap, but it seems principally a Religious Studies task.

There is any number of interests (religious, political, and profiteering opportunists come to mind) who would willingly fill the void left by a distorted understanding, which leads to the next academic issue of concern to this thesis: the highly politically-charged nature of the discourse surrounding the uses of the term conspiracy theory/theories. This biased use in current American political dialogue is so anti-intellectual as to be little more than transparent propaganda that warrants critical examination[11], and should be exposed as such everywhere else, most especially the media. I have included a Terms of Delusion section to illustrate how words are used against an unsuspecting population.

Americans are subjected to propaganda under the guise of "news." And it is done blatantly. Most obviously, and in what conceivable definition of

---

10   Political Science, one would think, ought to have some perspective on the event.

11   Since beginning the writing of this book, Lance deHaven-Smith has published an historical account of the use of the concept and term "conspiracy theory" in America. His book represents a most unbiased coverage of the topic. In it, he presents evidence that the CIA (Central Intelligence Agency) was behind the implementation of the term in popular media in a propaganda program begun in 1967, just around the time questions were arising regarding the John F. Kennedy assassination and the implausibility of elements of the Warren Commission report. This fact clarifies the bigger context for the thesis of this book, as readers will encounter the CIA at various points in the deceptive use of religion in public opinion and the religious delusions expounded upon herein, most especially in chapters five, six and eight.

the word "conspiracy," is the federal government's own version of events contained in the *9/11 Commission Report (9/11CR)* <u>not</u> a conspiracy theory? This is demagoguery, pure and simple. There is no academic or newsworthy usefulness to the term "conspiracy" used in this context.

Conspiracy, by law, means that individuals agree and collude to break the law in order to profit or gain in some way, or worse. The charge of conspiracy is routinely made in legal cases and the selective designation of "conspiracy theory" to those providing alternative explanations for events that implicate parties *within* the command and/or political structure of the United States, but not for the "official story," is neither academically honest nor is it sound reasoning. In fact, such selective use of terms is itself a tool of deception and most useful in perpetuating delusions.

What is even more obfuscating of the facts is that the specific charge brought against the individuals named by the Department of Justice and FBI is "conspiracy to commit terrorism." In other words, the establishment uses the same terms, but expects a different understanding and response from us in *their* use of the terminology.

What lies behind this duplicitous meaning and contradictory use of the word?

Nothing less than what George Orwell called "The Principles of Newspeak," and it is the product of propaganda. Kurtis Hagen applied a very simple test to a policy paper written at the behest of the Obama administration. He revealed that the analysis used to justify government infiltration of "conspiracy" groups applied equally to the government's own "official story." This is particularly true in the phenomenon known as "informational cascades" (i.e., basing one's opinions on that of other people's opinions or information rather than on one's own information, supposedly a characteristic trait of conspiracy groups' thinking due to their crippled epistemology – see footnote 16 in chapter three[page118]), which, Hagen argues, "make more sense as explanations for the success of dubious official stories, since official stories tend to have the crucial advantage of gaining early traction"(6).

There is simply no justification for the use of the term "conspiracy theory" in this uneven and inconsistent manner. It reveals intellectual dishonesty, or worse, intentional manipulation of political narratives and therefore history and the historical record. Also, this must stop within academia if it is to remain relevant to the real world and provide accurate descriptions of events and/or critiques and solutions to critical problems. Currently, this is not happening. Quite the opposite is in effect today. The causes of events are being re-contextualized to predetermined geopolitical ends, academia expounds on the re-contextualized causes, and then these causes are sold in the media to the U.S. and world populations as news and analysis.

One extreme example comes from Michael Shermer of *Skeptic* magazine and most recently from its apparent commercial competition *Skeptical Inquirer*. I will refer to a very recent posting of Shermer's as he has written numerous articles attempting to address the science cited by 9/11Truth,[12] as it has come to be known in the political discourse. He represents an extreme form of rebuttal to the evidence in that his is a form of polemic drenched in conspiracy theory demagoguery.[13]

Michael Shermer has built a career upon providing skeptical evaluations of a whole variety of claims. The vast majority of his work is sound and in keeping with the philosophical tradition found in western history. But turning this very career into a weapon against a perfectly legitimate line of scientific reasoning is most objectionable. Quite simply, Shermer's rebuttals avoid the heart of the forensic evidence. Nowhere in this article or anywhere else does he provide a succinct response to the particular points of controlled demolition raised by *9/11 Blueprint for Truth: The Architecture of Destruction* (chapter eight, Reference). He instead links all kinds of conspiracies together to reveal some type of "mind" that he claims exists within the conspiracy theorist.

What Shermer has done fits the pattern and *methodology of demagoguery*: appealing to people's emotions and prejudices by focusing upon the alleged weaknesses, flaws, or disorders of the individuals who hold the theories in question. No one wants to be associated with intellectual or moral weakness and that is precisely what conspiracy theorists suffer from, according to Shermer. Hence, there is no need to closely examine what these conspiracy theorists are saying – the flaw is with *them*. Curiously, it resonates with the same logic of "they hate us because we are free" which forms the basis of the rationale for the war on terrorism, namely, that we are hated as Americans by these religious fanatics for what *we are* as opposed to something *we had done* to reap their hatred.

---

12   9/11Truth is shorthand for a political viewpoint which challenges the US Government's 9/11 Commission Report (9/11CR, see References). In short, elements embedded with the US Government are blamed for the attack operation, not Muslims who have be falsely blamed for geostrategic reasons.

13   I will use the term conspiracy theory demagoguery when referring to rebuttals to evidence that utilize the rhetoric of "conspiracy theory" because that is exactly what it is, demagoguery, defined as "a pandering to the prejudices and passions of people with the intent to politically agitate." The social outcome of these arguments reveals this to be the case and will be highlighted.

But Shermer's guile does not constitute a rebuttal to forensic evidence, yet it remains a favored and persistent tactic within conspiracy theory demagoguery. This is the type of analysis one expects from the journalism of *TIME* magazine,[14] or perhaps CNN or FOX News, not an academic philosopher.

In the article in *Skeptical Inquirer* by Ted Goertzel the *reductio ad absurdum* of this reasoning takes the form now of a "conspiracy meme." With this, the conspiracy demagoguery now has a metaphysical reality. He simply omits altogether the evidence raised and presented in AE9/11Truth (Architects and Engineers for 9/11Truth) and instead focuses upon a *single* documentary (*Loose Change*) as representative of the entirety of the research conducted by those in the 9/11Truth "movement," as it were. This is but a tactic for dodging the issues and accusing dissenters of the official story with those same intellectual weaknesses that Goertzel is himself demonstrating, namely a single-sourced rebuttal. So, when 9/11Truth states that, for example, molten metal was found in abundance at Ground Zero and must be explained by science, he simply avoids dealing with it.

The social consequences of this demagoguery are nothing short of confusion for the population at large and an unnecessary demonizing of entire groups of people (deHaven-Smith, 26-27). The backlash can bear nothing positive. The results of the failure of investigative journalists, higher educators and intellectuals in general, to properly identify the causes of the religious delusions perpetuated in this American political climate have been catastrophic for the nation as a whole (the wars and their associated costs) and for particular individuals (including both military and Muslim lives) caught in the crossfire of this political confusion.

Of course, the *demagoguery of conspiracy theory* is only a byproduct of the *original deception*. Together their costs are proving to be great, and in the Conclusion I will address further this nexus of scholarship, the media and activism and elaborate more upon the deceptive tactics of those who would seek to infiltrate conspiracy theory groups. This is deplorable and a terrible harbinger for a free society, and we ought to take note, if not stern warning. This will become ever more apparent as the chapters proceed in

14   In 2009 on the 40th anniversary of the moon-landing TIME magazine did a piece of conspiracy theory demagoguery lumping into one group the following topics under the banner of "conspiracy theories": JFK assassination, 9/11 cover-up, Area 51 and the aliens, Paul McCartney is dead, secret societies control the world, fake moon landings, Jesus and Mary Magdalene (having been married), Holocaust revisionism, CIA and AIDS, and the reptilian elite. If these disparate topics qualify as conspiracy theories, then the term is rendered virtually useless and void of meaningful and explanatory content and reveals the demagogical nature of its use in mainstream media discourse. http://www.time.com/time/specials/packages/completelist/0,29569,1860871,00.html (accessed January 2019).

relative severity of malfeasance, and as a decadence seems to be over-taking our political systems, it would appear. In a way we are observing a decaying of the American body politic and the corresponding abuse of the language.

Suffice it here to say, and again referring to George Orwell,

> It is rather the same thing that is happening to the English language. It becomes ugly and inaccurate because our thoughts are foolish, but the slovenliness of our language makes it easier for us to have foolish thoughts. The point is [and this is the key and intent of this book] that the process is reversible (1946: 102).

I offer the argument that the demagoguery around "conspiracy theory" is precisely the type of language decay that enables the political elite to manipulate the public mind. Most assuredly, that demagoguery has ripples through the mainstream-corporate media and the educational systems.

In the case of 9/11, the most recent avatar for conspiracy theory accusations, the original deception was so egregious to compel many American activists to do whatever they could to see it exposed. Awareness of their efforts coupled with my own previously-existing doubts about the government's stated assertions regarding the motives for the attack (they hate us because we are free), are what provided the impetus for this study. It became crystal clear that some of the presumptions we carry around in our heads about religion, its role in this country and its laws, and its *existential* role in particular events was dubious at best, and outright dangerous at worst. These presumptions are tantamount to delusions as there was so much evidence to the contrary. They most certainly qualify for delusions when they cause us to act in irrational ways.

With this in mind, there is little doubt that the information presented herein has already demonstrated for many Americans the potential and capacity to incite the reader to question the legitimacy of government bodies, the officials who govern them, and the Commission Reports these officials produce, especially given their track records.[15] Such an inquiry takes one well beyond the scope of this book, and while this is not the express intent of the current collection of essays, the history presented herein should provide ample reason for a healthy skepticism on the part of the citizenry.

---

15   Think only of the much-criticized Warren Commission Report that produced the official version of the assassination of John F. Kennedy and the myth of the lone gunman Lee Harvey Oswald and his "magic bullet." The same can be said of the commission into the Branch Davidian tragedy and can be seen in the Reference for chapter seven.

FORMAT of the BOOK with ALLUSIONS to METHOD

Each chapter opens with a paragraph containing the principal *delusion* to be addressed, these are in *italics*, and followed by another paragraph consisting of a brief overview of the *correction* to the delusion, also in *italics*; together they constitute the main factors to recognize in unraveling the delusions. I keep these factors to a bare minimum and to easily-verified pieces of evidence that render the delusion just that – a falsehood through-and-through. In the case of the two final chapters (seven and eight) the numbers listed in parentheses can all be confirmed with only *one* REFERENCE that is visually powerful. This is done intentionally as a challenge to fellow scholars, but more importantly to the general public because these issues are not strictly academic. The Soliloquy preceding these final two chapters will explain my reasons for this. I've strived for conciseness in research with this approach.

To begin, the founding fathers, being enlightened thinkers, were well-aware of the utility of religion in forming and enforcing societal norms. James Hutson has collected together some of the notations made by early founders regarding religion's role in governance, which at the time referred principally and overwhelmingly to Christianity. These will be examined in chapter one along with and against the concerns of those who had no representation (natives and slaves) and the variety of religious communities with conflicting and competing beliefs and goals.

In the early twentieth century as science, education and society were still adjusting to the theory of natural selection and the variant offshoot theories of adaptation in the natural world, the concurrently developing human sciences of psychology and sociology were being influenced by their own appropriation of natural selection, commonly called "Social Darwinism." To the degree that it was an ideological battle, which it most certainly was, it centered more upon the uses and abuses of applying Darwin's theories. Interestingly, we are also, with this topic, in the early stages of what will develop to be the program of *eugenics*. A program taken to criminally inhumane levels in Nazi Germany and to which the principled American William Jennings Bryan was portrayed as a Creationist simpleton when in fact he may have been a prophetic voice against an ideology that lingers in some quarters of American governance to this day and to which are connected later incidents recounted in this book. This mythic "battle" of science and religion will be covered in chapter two.

But what if the use of religion for political goals in modern history was not for any such "enlightened" outcome, namely, a peaceable and just society for all? Just as William J. Bryan used religion to curtail potential abuses of Social Darwinism, chapters three, four and five all touch on topics in which the government's own agencies have a vested interest in deceiving the public: whether it was exaggerating the threat of the USSR and its military capabilities coupled with an ideology of malignant atheism as fomented in Reagan's reference to the "evil empire" (chapter three), or courting vast segments of the American electorate by appealing to their Biblical assumptions about Israel's relationship to God and the rest of the world and most directly the Palestinians (chapter four), or by fostering the idea that flying saucers have visited us and that extraterrestrials may be trying to contact us (chapter five), the American population has been systematically subjected to a form of official brainwashing.

This state of affairs in which certain leaders wittingly and many unwittingly delude us, should be named for what it is: *deception and propaganda*. These harsh terms are deserved and appropriate, most especially because the desired end is seldom for the benefit of the entire group (that is, all of society and/or humanity), instead, the benefactors are a particular level of society, namely the ruling classes. Whether we want to admit so or not, there is *a ruling political elite* in American society that has long been recognized as wielding disproportionate power for their numbers. Sociologist C. Wright Mills identified it in the 1950s, the same period in which the military's technological capabilities began to advance by leaps and bounds. Mills identified the condition this way: "Not politicians, but corporate executives, sit with the military and plan the organization of war effort" (276; more comments from Mills are found in the quotes to chapter five and the Conclusion).

Curiously, these motives and ambitions are not difficult to reveal. In fact, they are very often hiding in plain sight and sometimes "leak" into the official stories and may be discerned from piecing together previous policy statements, forensic evidence revealed in the reporting of the event itself, or contradictions made by officials during press conferences and/or official inquiries.

For example, in chapter five I quote Erich von Däniken, who was and remains one of the chief exponents of the alien visitation theory. After over fifty-years in the business, he continues to appear to this day on cable television in the series *Ancient Aliens* on the History Channel. While considering what Däniken refers to as "the new science of futurology," he argued back in the late 1960s that "think tanks are monasteries of scientists of today, who are thinking for tomorrow." These think tanks in combine with government policymakers constantly plan for the future, including war-making plans:

> As early as 1946 Rand scientists evaluated the military usefulness of a spaceship.... There is no end in sight to this research work, and there is unlikely to be one.... Governments and big business simply cannot manage without these thinkers for the future. Governments have to decide on their military plans far in advance (chapter five; von Däniken, 1969: 151-152).

And this, von Däniken informs us, after having taken his reader on a fun, if not-wholly-convincing, tour of the world's "alien" archaeological sites. I predict it may prove alarming to the reader to find out just who those aliens are!

It is here in chapter five where the use of *religion as delusion* takes its ugliest turn and signals America's brush with international fascistic elements in government. These first five chapters bring us up to the current day but have their roots in events in the first half of the last century.

Chapters six, seven and eight are more immediate in that readers may have had a firsthand experience with them – most likely as an observer of the events as they unfolded – and therefore have a memory forged in the reporting of the event itself. As a researcher, this is important and relevant, and I intend to appeal to this experience the reader may possess to elucidate my thesis.

Chapter six covers the Jonestown tragedy of November 18, 1978. If one is old enough to remember Jonestown, then you may also have heard the references to it in the media during the 51-day stand-off that unfolded in Waco, Texas in 1993. This confrontation between, first the ATF, then the FBI, is the subject of chapter seven.

These two American tragedies are covered in two separate and consecutive chapters, but they are separated by a Soliloquy that is intended to act as an investigative tool and as a challenge to scholars and general readers to reinforce why I think it is important (if not to the thesis of this book but to one's own understanding of current events) that *we as observers* be aware that we are susceptible to *brainwashing* in these moments of unfolding crisis.

Yes, that's right, brainwashing!

This term is very emotionally and semantically loaded, but, like the term *conspiracy theory*, it must be confronted as to its precise meaning.

There is a reason for Rahm Emanuel, aide to President Barak Obama, stating "never let a good crisis go to waste."[16] He states quite plainly that

16   Rahm Emmanuel "Don't Waste a Good Crisis!" http://www.youtube.com/watch?v=VjMT-NPXYu-Y (accessed January 2019).

out of crises politicians and social engineers are able to lead society in a particular direction, of their own choosing of course. Crises provide opportunities. This truth became clear as the ripple effect of the event of the final chapter shaped the first decade of the new millennium.

The final topical chapter is eight and covers the September 11, 2001 terrorist attack. This is where the "ten years' worth of effort" journey began that opened this Introduction, and as explained at the outset, immediately, instantly, and with very little doubt, on the very evening of September 11, 2001, I suspected we were being lied to, and religion was being implicated.[17]

Thus, the journey began.

What also began was an exercise in critical analysis of my own vocation and academic field: that is, teaching *about religions* in community college – and in the public (large urban) educational setting where plurality is the norm. How the field of Religious Studies responded to these current events became inextricably implicated within my own research analyses and comments upon the field and its work. It seemed apparent to me that Religious Studies was uniquely positioned and with a certain pre-established academic authority which could go a long way to clarifying the historical record for Americans. Instead, I witnessed in real-time in the case of Islam, from the outset of the attack until this writing, the field of Religious Studies has mostly affirmed the political and war-narrative of jihadi Islam.

The *two cultures* were inseparable – the academic world and the 9/11Truth world – their point of contact was in my *weltanschauung* – worldview – my very mind. Managing the reality that academe was repeating the political myths by situating Islam and Muslims in the seat of culpability for the attack while on the other hand confronting the reality that academe was not factually accurate – *that quite simply, two airplanes*

---

17   As for the President himself and what he knew at that moment of the attack, the reality of it is trivial relative to the scale of the operation and its consequences. There were terrorists on that day, to be sure, and they were threatening the President. The question becomes, who were they? Webster G. Tarpley's *9/11 Synthetic Terror: Made in USA* is the single best reference for an operational understanding of the 9/11 attack. See References in Conclusion.

When public officials at very high levels of government have any number of aids, ministers, advisors, researchers and sponsors of particular interests, they cannot be expected to be personally managing all aspects of decision-making and, most importantly, intelligence-gathering and operational activities. The importance of *plausible deniability* cannot be overstated. This doesn't mean that accountability should not be sought and demanded by the public and any consequent victims. The point for readers is to hold the awareness that much goes on that can be withheld from any specific individual, including a President, perhaps most especially a President. In addition to Tarpley see (see References to chapter three) the 1964 book *The Invisible Government* and the 2011 documentary *Top Secret America: The Legacy of 9/11* as examples of government operations well-beyond the scope of a single individual. The dates of the publications give a sense of how long-ranging and all-encompassing these developments are.

cannot knock straight down three buildings – posed a formidable contradictory reality that I had to navigate. My *weltanschauung* never recovered to
its previous form but was remolded.

Aware of the delusion, I was moved to activism.

The move to activism was the result of recognizing the human suffering as a war consequence that was at stake in the perpetuation of the 9/11
myth. And this not until 2007 and well into the destructive "war on terror." The misery of Syria, the most recent nation-state casualty in the war
on terror as it stands now, was yet to be realized at the time of my activism.
But what was most compelling was the reality that: *deceptive religious-political narratives were the source of immense human suffering.*

Academe is typically not in the business of providing the tools of hu-
manitarianism. But to the degree that knowledge is a tool, then academe's
role in providing the conceptual tools for understanding human suffering
(in this case as it relates to religion, non-religion, or the abuse of religion)
is well within the purview of the academic field of Religious Studies. A
great admiration of the field would develop in me as I found both a crit-
ical-theoretical framework from which to understand human suffering
(*the Critical Theory of Religion*) and, in addition, I would find a sociologi-
cal-theoretical-conceptual framework (in the form of a practical sociological model provided in *A Theory of Religion*) from which to judge human
activities relating to the political dynamics of that same human suffering.

RESEARCH and EMPATHY

Finally, as may or may not be evident or apparent to the reader, certain
Religious Studies students, teachers, instructors and professors come
around to the academic field vocationally as a result of *having been,* and
with many still *being, religious.* Under such circumstances, our research is
touched by, if not saturated with, empathy for that which we study. Aside
from any pitfalls this may potentially (allegedly) bring to social scientific
and humanities research, the positive contribution to social policy, the
health of civil society, and the success of civic pluralism of this empathy
could be considered an intrinsic element of what has elsewhere been
called the *Critical Theory*[18] *of Religion* (as opposed to a *traditional theory
or theories of religion*) and which often, in spite of being an academic

---

18   Born out of the horrors of the Nazi holocaust, *Critical Theory* and the Frankfurt School
were the result of the intellectual revulsion to seeing German history and philosophy reduced to
such animalistic and barbaric tendencies. It sought to reframe all social analysis and philosophy
into a theory/practice model that could meet the demands of social justice and avert human suffering. Knowledge is seen in *Critical Theory* as the product of temporal forces, not least of which is
the state and its agents of power, and so must be critiqued anew.

discipline, has its own stated goal of properly and adequately *understanding* and *combating* human suffering (Siebert, 1994: 1). A goal shared by many individuals of conscience, goodwill, and concern across the planet – not least among whom are the religiously conscious and their representatives/emissaries of various stripes.

So, *Critical Theory* and *empathy* can be found to coalesce around the need for an accurate and honest description of suffering and its source in order that it may be adequately alleviated. When suffering is perceived to be self-inflicted, then some manner of deviance must be the attribution. Here is where the researcher can dissociate from the subject – a potential pitfall in its own right for adequate understanding.

If there were a methodological advantage to the *Critical Theory of Religion*, that advantage has an opportunity to prove its worth in a research assignment such as this: *in examining the mindsets of those who appear to have relinquished their intellect and will to another individual or individuals – in other words, they have become deluded.* These delusions are the source of human suffering and so fall under the eye of *Critical Theory* (of religion), which, in its quest to deal with the *theodicy* problem, the problem of evil, seeks to articulate the roots and nature of human suffering, and in so doing, it must allow its own critical stance to be grounded in human existence – living, loving, losing, confronting honesty, confronting deception, witnessing and responding to corporate and state malfeasance, and the very act of dying – this is *empathy*. The *Critical Theory of Religion* embraces an honest acknowledgement that each and every one of us, the researcher included, will encounter these experiences and that as human beings we will *all* follow a fate contingent upon so many shared variables in life. Along the way, all of us will experience the joys and pains of each of these in varying degrees of intensity. And to live fully we cannot avoid them.

It is my contention that no theoretical model divorced of empathy can cobble-together a meaningful epistemology and coherent cosmology-anthropology if its intent is to build a healthy civil society and successful pluralism. The empathy of *Critical Theory* ought to help get society there (to a state of civic pluralism) by providing a real-world understanding of human suffering and articulate a social science that works toward the extinction of that suffering. Gary M. Simpson also notes,

> This insistence on the real-life contexts and consequences of every philosophy marks Horkheimer's thinking at every turn and remains a hallmark of critical theory [and this] focus on "real life" comes as

no afterthought for him and the other members of the Frankfurt institutes' research team. They were all Jews in a Germany rapidly coming under Hitler's influence. No wonder that their critical theory's aim is the philosophical interpretation of the vicissitudes of human fate … above all … in the context of human social life, to the state, law, economy, and religion (4).

The *Critical Theory of Religion* also notes that "the pathology of modernity consists precisely in the fact that instrumental action was decommunified, while communicative actions were not only deinstrumentalized: it rather fell victim to even more intense functionalization. In this consists the *barbarism* in modernity" (italics mine; Siebert, 1985: 183). In other words, people began to be treated by society's rulers as objects not of worth in their communities, but as functions in a machine. Society (the state) lost its soul with modernity and has arrived at what appears to be an oligarchical-technocracy to which human suffering (i.e., cruelty) is of no consequence (barbarity).

In the shadow of the Holocaust, such a state (both as a set of affairs within society generally and in reference to the nation-state with its "monopoly of cultural means of coercion by a clearly differentiated group of specialists" *ATOR*, Def.41: 80/327) cannot be allowed to persist in society as it will ensure society's degradation and a drift away from democratic and pluralistic tendencies. I would cite the research in this book as principal examples of that national degradation as it relates to religion.

What I offer as American religious delusions can be considered examples of the barbarism attributed to modernity's current pathology of empire. In confronting these delusions, the citizen ought to resist recoiling from them due to the barbarity contained within the truth of the knowledge of the delusion. Because they are painful to confront is not a reason to turn away. Many a citizen simply do not want to confront the idea that, for examples, individuals in the elected government were the perpetrators of some evil event (think JFK assassination) and the citizenry was deceived about it; or, that "9/11 was an inside job." The possibility of American officials' involvement in the terror attack grows more easily believable only as one gets further away from the country (politically). Such ideas are *conspiracy theories within* American political cultural life, and to believe them is a sign of mental weakness[19] or some other character flaw.

---

19   This too is consistent with the sociological understanding offered in *A Theory of Religion*; "Def. 69: *Mental illness* is the imputed condition of any human mind that repeatedly fails to conform to the propositions of the prevailing theory of human action" (Def. 69: 159/329).

Hence, the willingness for distancing – the pathos of distance – is antithetical to empathy.

Similarly, understanding the mindset of those people who, in the parlance of popular political and media discourse, join "cults," especially religious cults, can be hindered by the pathos of distance. No individual, especially in the aftermath of such a horrible event as, for example, Jonestown, would want to themselves feel vulnerable to such evil actions on the part of others.

This poses the age-old research problem of bridging the gap between researcher and subject. In the philosophies of civic life, this is what has been termed the *I-thou* issue, or the problem of the *other*, or *other people's myths* – it has been framed in many ways. In the subject matter of this book, it could be the mindset of those readers who themselves have not been much subject to religious beliefs and their cultural influence upon their own families' and social lives, in contrast to those who have had significant religious influence in those areas. A natural tendency is to distance oneself from those who have been victimized by seemingly their own religious naiveté, even if the evil deeds are attributed to others, or religious coercion of one kind or another. No one wants to believe they could be victimized in such a manner.

It is far too seductive to dissociate oneself from the intellectual stance that would be vulnerable to cult manipulation. It is even easier to believe negatively false characteristics about the victims, somehow blaming them for their own victimhood. Jonestown is one such example. On the surface, being manipulated in such a manner seems a manifestation of profound weakness in an individual's life that no one would care to endure, never mind admit. This intellectual dissociation, though, runs the risk of devaluing the other elements of human nature and circumstance that contribute to this seeming intellectual relinquishment, for example, the personal bonds and emotional attachments formed between people within a group. These can go a long way fulfilling basic human emotional and social requirements such that any religious doctrine maintained by the group is of much less influence.

In the instances of Jonestown, Guyana and the Branch Davidians at Waco, this has been the case – a very lopsided understanding of the members was instrumental in persuading public opinion to agree with the statements, and thereby the actions, of federal officials. Part of the strategy of those who murdered the Jonestown and Waco victims was to cement the image in the minds of Americans and others that the deceased were victims of their own ignorance and intellectual vulnerability and naiveté. In short, that *the victims* were somehow accountable for the predicament in which they found themselves and their fate was due to this ignorance and their compliance to the wishes of another person (brainwashing). We were to conclude that the personal evils of Jim Jones, or the religious excesses of David Koresh combined with over-zealous law enforcement, were not significant factors in the tragedies – no, the victims shared some of the blame. I squarely affirm that these tragedies are not nearly so straightforward and for the public to concur with these conclusions is to add insult to the injury the victims and their families have already endured. Furthermore, such views contribute to the overall political deterioration of civic life.

As a young man who left home to join a group of unknown people in a far-flung region of the world, I approach these issues and the victims involved with a heightened sense of "that could have been me." The responses and concerns of my own family may not have been untypical to those who had loved ones join the Jonestown or Branch Davidian efforts at community living within the framework of a religious ideology. The act of leaving one's family and country to go and join a religious group outside of one's cultural upbringing, requires a worldview and a willingness to step into the unknown that not many people possess. It is very difficult for family members and friends to understand the desire/need to join such a living arrangement. All too often such people are looked-upon disparagingly as weak-minded or gullible, or in some way psychologically damaged goods. This is grossly unfair and is itself a conditioned response that *all of us* as media consumers must become aware of and resist and repudiate. Not least of which because *we, the broader public,* are the ones being victimized by this conditioning and our judgments clouded. We then become susceptible to the distortions of the various actors in a tragic drama such as Jonestown or Waco. We citizens must remain ever wary and vigilant against deception – and this is not easy.

Any cogent theory[20] must also conform to the laws of nature understood by other social scientific disciplines. I therefore use (beginning mostly in chapter three) in addition to *Critical Theory*, the sociological analysis of Rodney Stark and Williams Sims Bainbridge as found in their 1987 collaboration *A Theory of Religion*. In it, are very useful Axioms, Definitions, and Propositions that I find illuminate some of the social-po-

---

20   See Quotes page for chapter eight and Jürgen Habermas' comment regarding describing events and language's role in doing so. Habermas' body of philosophical-sociological-psychological-political work provides the basis for much of Critical Theory of religion's contribution to the applications here.

litical dynamics that are relevant to the delusions discussed in this book. Their theory is grounded in what is called "rational choice theory" and provides a solid theoretical counterweight, I add complement, to *Critical Theory*. Between them I am acknowledging that I recognize human decision-making is a complex set of procedures.

In this research I have strived to take my field of Religious Studies seriously and to implement what it has taught me. One seasoned scholar put it well and meaningfully when he wrote:

> ...this task [of describing people's religious experiences] simultaneously requires sympathetic human empathy. We need that peculiar, almost indefinable quality which enables one individual to have a flash of insight into what it would *really* feel like to be someone else. We need to be able to make a jump from seeing a member of a cult as an intriguing human-sized object "out there" with certain bizarre beliefs and behavior, to saying, "He has the same feelings inside as I do – though he's looking at things with a different pair of spectacles, he could be me and I could be him. By learning about where he is, I'm not just expanding myself intellectually, I'm expanding my *humanness* – my ideas, my feelings, my life style, everything.... How would it feel from within to be part of this religious movement?" (Ellwood, 2).

In my case, I bring the experience of being in a religious movement, a *cult* if you will, to my research. And though Religious Studies may not be in the hardest of sciences since we are dealing with people's lives, and that choices are not entirely predictable or determined by physical instincts alone, we can bring empathy to our work, and push back against the *pathos of distance* Nietzsche described. Let these pages caution that descriptions of other people's religious experiences which exploit the pathos will bring only human degradation constitute their own form of cultural and political barbarity. Let us never be party to and/or complicit with such social degeneration.

This degradation is most insidious and destroys everything humane in its wake. Educators most especially but all citizens generally owe it to the memory of those who have suffered from these degradations and to tread very delicately into the treacherous waters where state crimes have been committed. But we must find courage to follow the evidence wherever it leads so that the memory of the victims remains one worthy of their lives. In the end, and in reality, there is no pathos of distance, there is only *us – citizens of society*.[21]

---

21   The use of the word citizen in this context is not that of political national status but rather a participant in society and its institutions.

Empathy must be an integral part of the research.

Hopefully, this foray into the darker side of the religious history of America finds its place in the narrative and debate over the proper place for religion in the political system and in the country generally. Perhaps, a natural follow-up to this volume ought to be a critical examination of the legitimate role of religion in our national dialogue, and perhaps more crucially, a critical examination of where religion (religious terminology) ought to be *omitted* entirely from the public narrative. This is a fine line to walk considering our Constitutional right to practice our religions and to practice free speech but doing these successfully should reveal a sober-minded approach to a topic that is far too susceptible to the abuses of opportunists, demagogues and profiteers. Instead, we should infuse all our research models, social prescriptions, and civil societies' attempts to foster civic pluralism with a view to the well-being and betterment of all human beings that includes *the other* in the fold of a common good, and where such terminology is appropriate, a Transcendent Common Good.[22]

REFERENCES
Books/Essays

Bookman, John T. (2008). *The Mythology of American Politics: A Critical Response to Fundamental Questions*. Washington, D.C.: Potomac Books.

Chadwick, Henry (1967). *The Early Church*. New York: Dorset Press, 1986.

Cirile, Jim (2011). Skeptical Inquirer Attacks 9/11Truth Movement, Avoids Vast Body of Scientific Evidence. http://www.ae911truth.org/en/news/41-articles/429-skeptical-inquirer.html (accessed January 2019).

DeHaven-Smith, Lance (2013). *Conspiracy Theory in America*. Austin: University of Texas Press.

Ellwood, Robert S. Jr. (1973). *Religious and Spiritual Groups in Modern America*. Englewood Cliffs, New Jersey: Prentice-Hall.

Goertzel, Ted (2011). The Conspiracy Meme: Why Conspiracy Theories Appeal and Persist. *Skeptical Inquirer*. Vol. 35. No. 1. January/February. Pgs. 28-37.

---

22   Throughout this book I will use the term *common good* with the same meaning as the term "Transcendent Common Good"; the former when the religious delusion under critique and the principal actors or parties harnessing religion are secular, capitalist or government enterprises, and the latter when appealing to a religion's or religions' use of a delusion to perpetuate their own social or political goals, e.g., American Christians theologically attacking Islam for apologetic purposes and political capital. The use of the terms common good and Transcendent Common Good is similar in meaning with the terms *health of civil society* and *civic pluralism*, which are advocated throughout the arguments presented here and reflect my own Critical Theory, at least to the degree that I cite government interference as the principal obstacle to achieving such. Similarly, with the word *citizen* as I use it here, which is intended to be more than a political nationality but rather the concept of a person participating in society.

Hagen, Kurtis (2011). Conspiracy Theories and Stylized Facts. *The Journal for Peace and Justice Studies*. Vol. 21. No. 2: 3-22.

Johnson, Roger, ed. (1987). *Rudolph Bultmann: Interpreting Faith for the Modern Era*. London: Collins.

Lawrence, Bruce B. ed. (2005). *Messages to the World: The Statements of Osama Bin Laden*. London: Verso.

McCutcheon, Russell T. (2005). *Religion and the Domestication of Dissent, or, How to Live in a Less than Perfect Nation*. London: Equinox.

Mills, C. Wright (1956). *The Power Elite*. London: Oxford University Press, 1959.

Nietzsche, Friedrich (1967). *On the Genealogy of Morals*. Translated by Walter Kaufman and R.J. Hollingdale. New York: Vintage.

Nietzsche, Friedrich (1966). *Beyond Good and Evil*. Translated by Walter Kaufman. New York: Vintage.

Orwell, George (1949). *1984*. Revised and Updated Bibliography. Afterword by Erich Fromm. New York: New American Library/Signet Classic, 1981.

Orwell, George (1946). *Why I Write: Political Language is Designed to Make Lies Sound Truthful and Murder Respectable, and to Give an Appearance of Solidity to Pure Wind*. New York: Penguin.

Shermer, Michael (2010). The Conspiracy Theory Detector: How to tell the difference between true and false conspiracy theories. http://www.michaelshermer.com/2010/12/the-conspiracy-theory-detector/comment-page-2/ (accessed January 2019).

Siebert, Rudolf J. (1994). *From Critical Theory to Critical Political Theology: Personal Autonomy and Universal Solidarity*. New York: Peter Lang.

Siebert, Rudolf J. (1985). *The Critical Theory of Religion: The Frankfurt School*. Lanham, Maryland: Scarecrow Press, 2001.

Simpson, Gary M. (2002). *Critical Social Theory: Prophetic Reason, Civil Society, and Christian Imagination*. Minneapolis, Minnesota: Fortress Press.

Stark, Rodney and William Sims Bainbridge (1987). *A Theory of Religion*. New Brunswick, New Jersey: Rutgers University Press, 1996.

- In order of appearance in this chapter are the following Definitions and Propositions:

Def. 79 *Deception* is any interaction strategy that intentionally leads other people to accept explanations which one privately rejects.

Def. 41 The *state* is the monopoly of the cultural means of coercion by a clearly differentiated group of specialists.

Def. 69 *Mental illness* is the imputed condition of any human mind that repeatedly fails to conform to the propositions of the prevailing theory of human action.

Stark, Rodney and William Sims Bainbridge (1985). *The Future of Religion: Secularization, Revival, and Cult Formation.* Berkeley: University of California Press.

The 9/11 Commission Report (2004). Final Report of the National Commission on Terrorist Attacks upon the United States. Authorized Edition. No copyright. New York: W.W. Norton.

THE SHERIFF BROUGHT THE WITCH UP THE BROAD AISLE, HER CHAINS
CLANKING AS SHE STEPPED.

1

NATIVES, PURITANS, VOODOO, AND FOUNDING FATHERS: RELIGIOUS FREEDOM IN GOD'S OWN COUNTRY

The delusion: *Beginning in the early 1600s Pilgrims, Puritans and later other dissenting groups fleeing religious persecutions or restrictions by England and mainland European states, as well as fleeing internecine Christian-religious fighting, came to America to practice their religions freely and to establish – more-or-less – a Christian nation. In the next century, the Founding Fathers wrote the laws which would reflect the general religious character of the country, which was dominantly Protestant-Christian, but with some limitations regarding State authority over religious belief and practice.*

The correction: *The goals of the Puritans and their Protestant cousins were hardly the goals of the philosophically, scientifically-minded and Enlightenment-influenced Founding Fathers, whose interests and social standing would have been quite at odds with that of African slaves whom would have experienced religious freedom much differently than Spanish or French representatives of empire, all of whom settled in the New World. And, of course, the Native Americans and their religions cannot be overlooked. This historic reality of widely disparate interests renders the question of "religious freedom idealized in a national creed" answerable by no single voice and is best approached with an awareness of who is inquiring and from which perspective or historical narrative does he/she want the answer.*

PAST MEETS PRESENT, or PRESENT *is* PAST

Of the eight topics covered in this book, the least controversial should be that of challenging the existence of a *singularly legitimate* American view of religious freedoms – if for no other reason than there is no such thing. Nor could there ever really have been one. There were far too many parties, factions and interests involved to elicit a single response in defining so large a project. It was the very founding a nation, after all, and under such weighty circumstances, myths prevail.

Furthermore, there is no fundamental or organic reason that people's views should be substantially different today. Myths play every bit a central role in today's political discourse as they do in the pews and assemblies of houses of worship across the land. As Nicholas Haggar noted, though the vision of the earliest Christian settlers would not win-the-day in the overall contest for the definition of the coming Republic where religious freedom rather than sectarianism would prevail, this vision did leave "its mark on the body politic and is today reflected in the values of some right-wing Christians" (14).

The legacy is that certain contemporary views don't deviate much from America's historical past. Today, a good many people hold the view of the founding of the Republic and its meaning in a world historical context of that of John Winthrop's 1630 vision of America as a city on a hill. To them, the nation's destiny is as a New Israel from where the entire world could see the light of Christian truth. *America as God's witness* is just as much alive at the beginning of the 21st century as it was nearly four hundred years ago. Indeed, time has not diminished the sincerity and verve with which religious believers hold their nation's origin, fate and destiny.[1]

Complicating matters, however, in the era of the nation's founding religion was but an appendage of empire. Unfortunately, this is little understood, let alone factored-in, by those with the view of America as God's witness. The terminology of empire has been all but eradicated from the nation's lexicon.

The religions traveled, as it were, with the empires and their explorers, merchants and ambassadors; and so, rather obviously, French-settled areas of North America would be dominated by Roman Catholicism (Quebec and the deep south), English-settled areas would be Anglican/Episcopalianism, Spanish-settled areas would also be dominated by Roman Catholicism. The relationship between *empire* and *religion* effectively renders them indistinguishable in the exercising of power. The latter all too often, we will see, is a compliant, if not complicit, instrument of the former.

Much to its credit, the academic field of Religious Studies has been successful at a form of self-consciousness in describing its "subjects" and their "religions." Ever aware that scholars and researchers in their studies also reflect values, priorities and assumptions about the world, Religious Studies scholars have sought to factor these into their descriptions of the "other." Even more to the point has been the difficulty of singling-out and

---

1   With this history in America's background, the topics of chapters two, three and four become of theocratic-political importance. As the Biblical God's light in the world, the spirit of America could hardly be on the side of the evolutionist, atheist, and Palestinian. In regard to the last-named, the seventeenth-century terminology of America as a new Israel takes on new and ambiguous meaning in a post-1948 world where Israel's political meaning and potential are up for grabs in the wake of a newly created state in the Middle East.

defining "religious behavior" or "religion" cross-culturally and contemporarily, never mind cross-culturally and across the centuries. For example, on the question of the formation of the nation and its founding myths, these "narratives of origins can be a very effective means by which one group in society legitimizes its social and material privileges by appealing to authoritative narratives of origins that are either of their own creation or conducive to a particular political agenda" (McCutcheon, 46).

Richard Horsley additionally puts it well in his *Religion and Empire* when he states, "The most important task before us may be to consider how religious practices are related to the imperial power relations that have determined people's lives for centuries, but have gone unnoticed and unanalyzed" (4). "Although most Americans may not think of the United States as an imperial power, it picked up where the Spanish, French, and British left off almost as soon as it gained independence" (7). It is this mantle of empire that has shaped the forces of political dialogue and academic discourse, and to no small degree the historical content of Religious Studies, though its influence is mostly unseen.

A NEW WORLD for GOD'S OWN COUNTRY

Empires do not and cannot distribute power equally.

At the time of the founding of the Republic, people did not have equal access to freedom of religion. The descendants of any slave are keenly aware of this. In fact, sizeable portions of African Americans are cognizant of this historically unequal power distribution. Historically, the expression of their religious practices was curtailed by the vagaries of the master. What is American religious freedom supposed to mean in this context and to those on the receiving end of strict sanctions, or of any prohibitions at all, given the religious ideals of the founding documents?

By our day, the nation has had plenty of experience in dealing with these issues in practical ways. The history of the U.S. is replete with episodes of religious conscience locking horns with the laws and social conditions of the times to forge ever new and changing (sometimes expanding, sometimes contracting) definitions of, and with legal implications for, religious freedoms in the context of a democratic state. Think only of Prohibition, or the fundamentalist-modernist controversy centered upon evolution, or the ongoing battles over prayer in schools, or the mention of God in the pledge, or the right to an abortion, or gay marriage, even the Civil War can be understood as being motivated, at least in part, by the Emancipation movement which was of New England Christian conviction.

During a recent federal election cycle (2012), we saw the question of the separation of church and state re-examined and with a Roman Catholic challenger, this time in the form of a Republican Pennsylvania Senator named Rick Santorum. He does not accept the notions of religion as a private matter as John F. Kennedy famously stated. Santorum repudiates Thomas Jefferson's notion of a wall of separation between religion and state highlighting in his stump speeches to its mention not in official documents but in Jefferson's famously quoted personal letter. As Santorum recounts and repeats it; there is ample room in the public square for people of faith who, he insists, should not be sidelined or silenced in the policy debates. Fair enough. Agree or disagree with him, we know where he stands and can vote for him or not.

When a society is under stress, however, these worldviews play a heightened role in our understanding of our place in the world, and in some instances feed into an interpretation of the nature of the stress itself, especially if that stress is from a perceived external source.

On September 13, 2001, two days after the terrorist attack on New York City, Washington, D.C., and Shanksville, Pennsylvania, the Reverend Jerry Falwell (Southern Baptist) appeared on the *700 Club* television show hosted by Pat Robertson (also a Southern Baptist but with charismatic tendencies) and they both more-or-less agreed that the reason for the success of the attacks upon America was due to the fact that the country had abandoned its Christian ways and founding principles. Falwell said directly, America has become too secular, feminist, gay-friendly and liberal, so God spared his protection – something akin to the Babylonian destruction of Israel in the 6th century B.C./B.C.E. in which Hebrew righteous logic went thus: when the nation state is disobedient to God, then God owes not His protection to the people. This is a central theme in the covenant (contractual) religion between the Israelites and their God. To Falwell and Robertson and tens of millions of Americans, the logic is straight-forward enough and directly out of the Old Testament and applies right down to our times, modern Christian times.

This logic accepts on behalf of America (and all Americans vicariously) the covenant concept of religion that the ancient Israelite priests had developed and was centered in the Abrahamic legend of a promise made between man and God. Now, however, Babylon is not the enemy, Islam is. The imagery is socially explosive and for that matter, the geographic irony ought not to be lost – Babylon/Baghdad. In other times, and under other stressors, peoples of various backgrounds have become the "others" upon whom which the majority's fears were directed.

The Biblical observation found in Ecclesiastes stating "there is no new thing under the sun" finds pertinent application in the words of the American reverend. And he is hardly alone in the belief that the contemporary USA is out of step with the ways of heaven. Some estimates range as high as 100 million Americans are what are termed "evangelical Christians."[2] And while these folks cover a broad span of denominations, they share essentially the same core attributes: the belief in the Bible as a divine source of knowledge, guidance, and most importantly, authority; and the necessity of personal faith and a life of obedience to God's mores as interpreted from the Bible. These two core attributes constitute what could be called the basic "Christian conviction" of the modern American evangelical. These, together with a belief that God has a special place for the United States in His universal plan as He has had at other times for other nations, constitute and justify the very founding of the country and the freedoms we enjoy. In this sense, America is "God's own Country" and we would do wisely to remember this in our social and civic life.[3]

It is from this understanding of America and the opposition generated to it that our modern debate goes on, seemingly endlessly, and which, ultimately, precludes there ever being a single response to the question "what does religious freedom *mean* in contemporary USA?" This is not an unhealthy debate provided our ideals of pluralism and equal access to the safeguards provided by law are upheld and applied fairly. In fact, the debate should be liberating and facilitate the nation's pluralism thereby enhancing Americans' religious experiences of a cosmopolitan nature.

Americans have a keen awareness that it hasn't always been rosy implementing these lofty social ideals about religion into daily civic life. The early days of the Republic were no ecumenical picnic. "Eleven of the fourteen constitutions prohibited Jews and agnostics from holding office. Seven of fourteen prohibited Catholic officeholders. Nine of the fourteen limited civil rights to Protestants (five), Christians (three), or theists (one)" (Sehat, 29). To no small degree, the internecine Christian wars and rivalries of Europe, all built upon a Eurocentric understanding of the world, were transplanted to the new world. But, alas, these were the grow-

---

2   The term "fundamentalist" in reference to Christian denominations lost its popular use (and luster) in the mid-1990s as the socio-political rise of Islamic fundamentalism linked to international terrorism began to make its mark in Western societies. As recent as the late 1980s the term *Fundamentalist Journal* was used for the publication of Jerry Falwell's ministry.

3   Gregory Boyd's *The Myth of a Christian Nation* makes a case for an apolitical Christian church in the USA. As a minister he preached sermons explaining why their "church should not join the chorus of right wing political activity" during the 2004 election campaigning. He is also very aware that his views are controversial, and he lost twenty-percent, or one thousand members, of his congregation (9-10).

ing pangs of a young nation with lofty ideals. There were many sacrifices yet to be made for the ideals to take root in the new land.

"PARADISE, WE'VE got a PROBLEM"

The founding of grand things and great concepts, especially such things as a people's cultural, historic, or national beginnings, often seems to be accompanied by and shrouded with myths.[4] The Old Testament is a most familiar and poignant example, which also happens to have provided the model for many a theologically-minded American over the course of the young Republic's existence. It's as though the human imagination has some peculiar mania with "origins," that is, with the existential beginnings of things both human and non-human. The founding of a nation is no less, and perhaps much more, susceptible to the generation of myths and legends. John Corrigan and Lynn Seal put it descriptively:

> When we think of the "founding myth" of the United States, visions of pious Pilgrims fleeing religious persecution often come to mind. In the foreground of this imagined picture the "new" world of America represents liberty, as the tyranny symbolized by Europe fades in to the background. In the midst of this scene stands the brave and beleaguered Pilgrim, the iconic symbol of religious freedom attained. As the story continues, the defender of the American Republic – Washington, Jefferson, and Madison – inherited this Pilgrim legacy. They carried the banner of religious freedom to the battlefield and then to the documents framing our government, the Declaration of Independence and the Constitution. The First Amendment's protection of religious freedom, "Congress shall make no law respecting an establishment of religion or prohibiting the exercise thereof," was the light on the hill that made the United States unique and an example to the world. Ultimately, the story culminates in the twenty-first century with a United States that prides itself on being the most religiously diverse nation in the world (3).

No surprise then, those Christian settlers would narrate a Christian story rife with God's active participation and His hand generously and benev-

---

4   As to why this is the case, I defer to G.S. Kirk when he states, "Men have always been preoccupied with status: with their relations as individuals to families, as families to clans, as clans to tribes - more generally still with their own society's relation to the whole world outside. That world extends from its broadest cosmological aspects...to the immediate terrestrial environment...I would add that it is of a nature to seek oral expression, in the mythology of the people, even before seeking literary expression" (1970; 145-146). See also Robert Bellah's *The Broken Covenant* chapter one "America's Myth of Origin" for an overview of how mythology has figured into America's historical narratives.

olently guiding them in the dark, just as He did with the ancient Israelites. Today this view still captures the imagination of Christians of a certain persuasion, typically evangelical and of a Biblically-literalist point-of-view.

That there is a contradiction between, on the one hand, what religions', in this case mostly Protestant Christians', *ideals proclaim* is reality (mythology) and which is sometimes supported by officialdom, and on the other hand, what is *experienced* as reality (history) can be most easily illustrated by the chronological comparison of quotes preceding the Introduction to this book. Most notably, the first three which proclaim the *Christian (Puritanical) ideal*, the *philosophical foundation for the nation* as outlined in the Declaration of Independence, and finally, *the laws* as understood nearly one hundred years beyond the time of the writing of the Constitution. Each of these quotes stands nearly 100 years from the previous. Neither the earliest Christian ideal nor the later Enlightened-philosophical foundation provided the slave any meaningful protection. It took a full two hundred years for social change to catch-up in the form of the Thirteenth Amendment.

One modern commentator pointed out that both "evangelicals and secularists like to claim that our constitutional past and tradition support their approach" (Feldman, 9). In light of historical reality, perhaps neither should rush to claim credit. Religious freedom is an evolving set of rights that must constantly be guarded with vigilance, even in this day – perhaps especially in this day given the incidents in the following chapters.

Initially, however, colonial America remained a European-modeled class-based society, and since the laws reflected a particular class of people within that society, we are faced with the fact that the laws themselves expose the original myth of the founding of the nation as something little more than a social fantasy and hardly something a nation can be built upon, at least indefinitely, and especially a nation of the mixed people America would become. Laws reflecting only one myth, one culture's values, have not persisted in many of the Western nations. America would reckon with its pluralist population in no short-historical order, it would take centuries, especially considering Civil Rights for African Americans really only came about in the 1960s.

The nation has, nevertheless, made a particularly successful effort at its religious plurality, and has much to be emulated in that regard. In not every nation can a child exit the room during the singing of the nation's anthem as a Jehovah's Witness can and do in the US.

But getting to this point was not without eruptions of sometimes violent sectarianism.

Among the various and sundry Christian-transplanted groups, harmony did not always prevail. Far too often religious truth was the exclusive domain of a particular society. In Boston, Puritans and Quakers who were among the earliest to the New England colonies, "confrontation occurred between the Puritans who had left their homes in England to set up a pure Christian community and the Quakers who challenged their religious exclusiveness. When banishment failed to eliminate the Quakers, Governor Endicott ordered the death penalty. Three Quakers were hanged on Boston common (1660-61) because they chose to hold to their convictions rather than obey the authorities" (Dowley, 483).

Power indeed, is difficult to manage once in possession of it, even for the heavenly-minded. What this meant for the Puritans was that they, "who had been religious outsiders in England became the insiders in New England. They, in turn, were not willing to tolerate religious critics, or outsiders, within their ranks" (Stein, 17). "Toleration, however, was in short supply for those who questioned the Puritan Way … Massachusetts authorities … imposed fines on … dissenters, such as the Baptists" (Noll, 2002: 39). The inherent danger of a religious sect holding the reins of power in government was (and continues to be) a clear and present danger and the founding documents sought to deflect such an arrangement taking effect here in the new land's government and laws.

Perhaps serving as a harbinger of religion's "utility" in governing, New England had not progressed in over a hundred years such that by the 1770s a new-to-America religious order from England named the Shakers found themselves much distrusted in their new mission field. "In the minds of eighteenth-century New Englanders, Shakers dissent from orthodox beliefs and practices was so extreme as to be heretical: hence the prejudice, alarm, and violent opposition" (Andrews, 44). New England was simply not large enough for all the body of Christ and so the divisions of the old world were planted in the new.

Keep in mind it was the northern European Protestant Reformation itself that gave birth to the many Christian sects that found their way to the new world. But these sects were only the *offspring* of the Reformation. It was the southern European *mother* that had been torn asunder, in turn giving life to the rival northern sects. The Roman Catholic Church, in due time and new place, would find her own members confronting these same offspring's hostility in the new world.

As recent as 1960, it was fair and reasonable enough to critique the suitability of a Roman Catholic candidate for President in the person of

John F. Kennedy. He would be the first after all. A Roman Catholic's supposed allegiance to his church is not to be superseded by his allegiance to nation. But this remains a largely personal matter in the twenty-first century.[5] Not so in the past. Some among the early immigrant Protestants were "keen on limiting the rights of Catholics" (Corrigan and Seal, 50) recalling well the recent European Thirty Years' War of 1618-1638 in which violent Catholic opposition to and repression of the Protestant breakaway northern sects had cost many righteous their earthly lives.

When considering Roman Catholicism in the new world, we must again take into account the respective European powers and their empires. France and Spain were every bit as expansionary as their British cousins from across the channel. French and Spanish Catholicism had been particularly cruel in their European Wars – hence the fleeing from the northern regions early-on. New France (Quebec) and New Spain (US Southwest-Mexico-Latin America) would come to be dominated by a form of Catholicism that was an extension of colonial administrations. Maryland would be the only early colonial state with a significant Roman Catholic population, but these were made up of English Catholics and reflected the unique colonial history of that state (Noll, 1992: 26).

Spanish settlers had arrived and were active a generation before English permanent settlement. By 1607, the founding of Jamestown, "thousands of Indians had become at least nominal believers under Catholic missionaries in the New Mexico territories." And though "Colonial administration was heavy-handed and often displayed anything but the ideals of Jesus ... Spanish Catholicism had a notable history in the early days of European settlement" (Noll, 1992: 14). The San Xavier Church and mission estate near Tucson, Arizona built in 1692, remains standing to this day as an example of the historic significance of Spanish Catholic missions in New Spain.

In New England, French Roman Catholics had allied themselves with Native Americans in their effort to fight the English, a conflict which itself helped fuel one of the most notorious outbursts of religious fanaticism the country has experienced, in the form of the Salem Witch Trials of 1691-92, discussed below. The distinctly French character of Quebec was never matched south

---

5   Recently in 2012, evangelical Protestants voted for the Latter-Day Saint (Mormon) presidential candidate Mitt Romney in statistically similar numbers to previous Republican candidates, even more than others. Some evangelical Christians chose to stay away from the polls rather than vote for a member of what they deem a religious cult, but apparently this was only anecdotal. The issue of Romney's religion became more a matter of election-year expediency than a reflection of people's beliefs, highlighted by the fact that one of Romney's election contenders, Texas Governor Rick Perry, called him a member of a cult, https://billygraham.org/decision-magazine/october-2012/can-an-evangelical-christian-vote-for-a-mormon/ (accessed January 2019).

of the border, even though some cultural spill-over exists in New England. French Catholics simply lived as a minority in the English colonies. In the deep south of New Orleans, founded by the French who had been there since the 1680s, Roman Catholicism found a niche in which it was able to coexist with white Protestant landowners and their African slaves.

Mark Noll notes that by the time "the first century of British colonization was over, the diversity that would later flower into American religious pluralism had gained a secure foothold in North America. What had not yet been established in the British colonies, however, was a Christian presence among Native American or black slaves" (1992, 73).

Thoughtful and empathetic consideration of the treatment of Native Americans and African slaves could help balance today's Americans' understanding of the Republic's religious past. But for much of the Republic's history, it was white British Protestants telling the history of the country, and so their narrative prevailed. That narrative found its way into the nation's historical consciousness through churches and the national education system – both instruments of officialdom.

The very existence of these disparate Christian groups, of which only a few have been mentioned here, leaves the question of a singularly Christian definition of American religious freedom null and void of any meaningful social, never mind legal, content. The challenge has been for these same groups to coexist. In spite of a contentious, sectarian, bloodied and anything but charitable history of Christian brotherhood, churches across the land have propped-up a somewhat kumbya understanding of America's Christian history. But we would expect them to do so. Nowhere, however, are these myths better inculcated in children than throughout the public schools. The combine of *religions* and *public education* has created some of America's deepest delusions.

MANAGING the HEATHENS

> *Historically, American Indians have been the most lied-about subset of our population.*
> – James Loewen in his 1995 book *Lies My Teacher Told Me: Everything Your American History Textbook Got Wrong*[6]

James Loewen surveyed a dozen American History high school textbooks for historical accuracy versus mythmaking. He found plenty

---

6   2007 edition, page 93.

of the latter. Some of these myths included religion when discussing the motives for the arrival of Europeans (89), or the nature of indigenous American religions (114), or perpetuating the mythic, if self-serving, construct of American Exceptionalism (258). Even worse is the slavish acceptance these textbooks presume upon readers of statements about and by the federal government in its treatment of citizens. The peculiar fact is, the federal government is treated as something of a ghostly-entity in these textbooks – a faceless and nameless bureaucracy that acts out a mind of its own within a narrative that is mostly complimentary. Loewen uses the example of the Civil Rights Movement. He notes, "Not only do textbooks fail to blame the federal government (FBI) for its opposition to the civil rights movement, many actually credit the government, almost single-handedly, for the *advances* made during the period" (italics mine, 233). This is a painful distortion to those who suffered at the hands of the FBI – e.g., the family of Dr. Martin Luther King would be an example.

The distortions are multi-faceted and include religion as *only one* among several mythic constructs.

As for the treatment of Native Americans, the early explorers and settlers were less than benevolent. In fact, some viewed Native Americans as "not human at all, but rather an advanced kind of ape" (Harrison, 1990: 127). It was a challenge for early settlers to understand the Native Americans in a Biblical context (Corrigan and Neal, 20). Common theological interpretations centered on the "lost tribes" of Israel concept or theory which postulated the Native Americans as the descendants of Israelites. To settlers who found themselves in conflict with the Native Americans, they were akin to the Amalekites. The implications are foreboding indeed.

The nation's founding Christians' thoughts about the natives are quite at odds with a resolution passed in 1990 by the National Council of Churches of the United States on the "Christian mission" of Christopher Columbus giving him "significant responsibility for the "genocide, slavery, 'ecocide', and the exploitation of the wealth of the land" (Noll, 1992: 13).

Oh, the fibs our teachers told us!

While it is tempting, to make a point, to list the atrocities committed by the early European settlers, whether motivated by religion, survival, or a combination of both, the more instructive lesson sought here is that even among the Christian settlers, there was no unanimous view of the Native Americans resulting in their very uneven treatment. Some felt they needed conversion and European civilization in order to lift them out of their savagery. To these Christians the focus was upon evangelization and

47

the missionizing of the Native Americans. Others felt they were incapable of conversion and forever lost to the forces of heathenism. These were more prone for conflict with locals with intent, explicit or otherwise, of exterminating local populations and paving the way for complete Europeanization and Christianization of the new world. Since there was no unanimous Biblical-theological interpretation of the role and status of Native Americans in God's dispensations (plan for the world), the settlers could interpret the indigenes in any manner they saw fit.

As noted, the French would form alliances with Natives to attack English settlements. Some few missionaries devoted their preaching to the Natives in the hope of converting them and in fact had been quite successful in New Spain/New Mexico with tens of thousands of Native converts (Noll: 1992, 14).

Overall, Native Americans were ill-treated by their European American "brothers" and it is impossible to reconcile the history of their treatment into any image of a divinely-birthed nation. After three centuries of its traditional observation, the national holiday of Thanksgiving has lost some of its luster. But America's story isn't over yet. To a young nation facing many unknown perils, the spiritual dangers were not least among them. And the Native American's brother-in-mistreatment, the African slave, can take solace only in knowing he was not alone.

Regarding the general treatment of African-Americans in the US, Mark Noll has put it thus: "From a religious viewpoint, the great scandal of American history is the support that white believers found in Scripture and Christian traditions for slavery and even longer-lasting convictions about black racial inferiority" (1992: 542). "Contacts between European Christians and African slaves were, if anything, even more skewed than those between Europeans and Native Americans" (77).

Just as some settlers were not only eager to stamp out the native religions of the "savages" or to convert them, all forms of superstitions were to be avoided and put down as satanic incursions. These measures were not restricted only to the beliefs of Native Americans but against heathen, pagan or any "outsider" or non-Christian religion, which at the time could include Roman Catholic Church. The complication arises in that the "world of magic was not remote from daily life in the colonies ... [where the] ... colonists regularly consulted almanacs for astrological information ... related to the best days for planting crops and gardens, conducting business, taking a trip, or engaging in a host of other activities" (Stein, 24, 28). This ambiguity toward the occult and alternative sources of information is what allowed the young girls to be possessed in the first place. *Spectral evidence*[7] will be their stock-in-trade, presumably a Christian manifestation.

In addition, and as might should be expected given that it is found in most all religions, physical healing is a frequently sought miracle and was no less sought after in colonial America. Fervent and emotional prayers would not have been uncommon at the bedsides of the infirm. New England Puritanism, being infused as it was with Biblical Literalism and the paramount stature of the Bible as God's Word, meant that the spiritual possibilities were endless, as were the hazards. Foremost among the hazards was the wiling Satan, ever seeking to disrupt God's earthly plans. And disrupt he would in the harsh winter of 1691-1692.

One of America's most popular colloquialism's, to go on a "witch-hunt," takes its origin from an entirely religious-inspired event, of which at the heart were an irrational fear of voodoo, witches and the devil himself. The infamous Salem Witch Trials case which began in the winter of 1691-92, demonstrates that a convergence of events built upon hardened religious views, social and environmental stresses, an ambiguous attitude toward, and understanding of, the occult (in this case spectral evidence), coupled with the politico-religious exploitation of easily-manipulated young girls combined to cause social mayhem, the physical deaths of twenty people and the utter disgracing of a religious group, the Puritans.

The Massachusetts Bay Colony, as it was called at the time, was little more than sixty years on when this most notorious outburst of religious irrationality occurred, and to the horror of many an onlooker. A recently published (and there were many) and bestselling book by Cotton Mather titled *Memorable Providences, Relating to Witchcrafts and Possessions* on the dangers of witchcraft and how to combat it,[8] fueled the participants' imaginations of the fears at hand.

7   Spectral evidence was admitted by the court until, "Encouraged by their successes, the afflicted people [the young girls who were being used as "witnesses" to route-out witches and affirm accusations against towns people by wailing and squealing, going into trances, gyrating on the floor and other emotional outbursts in the courtroom] began to accuse some of the more important people in the colony" (Bonfanti, no page number).

8   As we know from our own time's experiences, publications of books, cartoons, movies and the like have a way of inflaming populations and causing protests or worse. This is especially true when political tensions exist between parties of different religions. Think only of the 1988 Salman Rushdie affair after the publication of his *The Satanic Verses*, or the 2006 Danish Muhammed cartoon incident, and perhaps even the tragic deaths in 2012 of US Embassy workers in Libya egged-on by a documentary exposé critical of Islam. Admittedly, tensions between American and Western interests in the Middle East fuel these instances, but the dynamic of social change and upheaval remain basically the same. Starkey reminds us that "for all its apparent remoteness, [Salem village] was not 'an island unto itself,' but a throbbing part of the great world. Its flare-up of irrationality was to some extent a product of the ideological intensities which rent its age no less than they do ours" (15).

The incident was triggered when several "girls, who, inflamed by the horrors of Calvinism,[9] as their immature minds understood it, depressed by the lack of any legitimate outlet for their natural high spirits, found relief for their tensions in an emotional orgy which eventually engulfed not only their village but the Massachusetts Bay Colony" (Starkey, 14).

We must also be willing to consider that, as anthropologist I.M. Lewis noted in his classic *Ecstatic Religion*, sometimes outbursts of extreme possession are "thinly disguised protest movements against the dominant sex" (26). The helplessness felt by the colonials was real enough. For the women, perhaps it was compounded by their low status in society and this "spectral" gift was a certainty for garnering the attention of the town's elites. In addition, it was a female majority who received the brunt of the accusations and punishments.

Caught in the center was Tituba, one of two household slaves of the Reverend Samuel Parris, minister of Salem Village. His owning slaves were "relics of his Barbados venture" (Starkey, 29). Tituba's race has been reported to be "half Carib and half negro," while other accounts state she was an American Indian of West Indian derivation (Stein, 26). Black slaves were very few in the earliest colonies, but they were present. In any case, Tituba served as family cook and housekeeper for the esteemed minister and his "self-effacing and merciful wife." The slaves' labors enabled the Parris family the privileges that come from wealth and status and possessing domestic help. Mrs. Parris was known for charitable acts and their children as living like little princes.

By Starkey's account many blamed Samuel for beating a confession out of Tituba that she had performed witchcraft. She had done mystical-storytelling with the minister's young daughters and friends. Her exotic past in Barbados and her family history included witchcraft, spiritual exercises such as palm-reading, hypnosis, divining the future, and communing with

---

9   John Calvin's widely-known though not universally agreed-upon reformulation of the doctrine of predestination involves a mystery or paradox in which God's grace predetermines that some human beings are born destined for heaven and some destined for damnation. Sometimes this is called "double-predestination." It was controversial since its formulation early in church history (first with Augustine in the fourth-century and again later in the sixteenth-century Protestant Reformation with Calvin) for its moral ambiguity. Since there is no external way to determine between the saved and the lost among the Christians, and therefore a certain angst was present in the theology of the many and proliferate Christian sects swayed by Calvinism. There is an unresolvable cognitive tension in knowing the possibility that one may not be among the chosen. Such were the "horrors" (as Starkey refers to them) of salvation's uncertainty. Under such conditions, reassurances of one's salvation are at times sought through public displays of piety, and obviously quite excessive displays. This is hardly the first, nor will it be the last time an eruption of over-zealous religion caused or will cause social upheaval. It is always society's response to it that is the measure of the soundness of that society.

the Devil and evil spirits (Bonfanti, no page numbers). No doubt stories of spirit possession, so common a trait among African-based religions prevalent in the Caribbean, captured these Christian girls' imaginations and so they duplicated the behaviors Tituba had described.

From descriptive accounts of their possessions and wailings before the courtroom, coupled with their trance-like staring off into space, what we would have seen with them is little different than what can be witnessed in a super-charged Pentecostal service of today, or what, "a rousing religious revival will bring out" (Starkey, 46). Heightened and exaggerated emotions coupled with verbal utterances of a garbled, i.e., unintelligible, mystical nature are the hallmarks of ecstatic, charismatic or spiritualistic religion. Hence the term *holy-roller* religion emerged as one common modern euphemism for the Pentecostal experience.

These young girls however, found their spirits possessed a full two centuries prior to the modern American Pentecostal experience. The bursting forth of uncontrolled or even contrived, emotional states is not confined to any particular century or millennia, or for that matter any particular group. Emotional release can be found widespread in religious activities. Therefore, the scandalous and shameful elements of the Salem Witch Trials are better attributed to where chronicler Marion Starkey finds them – in the community at large for tolerating such a circumstance; she states that what was most remarkable about the entire incident, and the lesson best learned from it, was "less the antics of the girls than the way the community received them" (Starkey, 46).

What followed was an orgy of accusations lasting several months against various townspeople across several Massachusetts and New Hampshire towns – some 400 unfortunate individuals (mainly women of relatively low social status, some divorced) were accused of being witches, though most would later be pardoned. Nineteen people, however, were hanged and one old man pressed to death for refusing to testify. The court and the girls' hysterics ended only when accusations against prominent members of several towns provoked people to begin to speak-up against the court that accepted *spectral evidence* as sufficient to determine guilt.

The absurdity of what took place seems obvious to us now and did so to many at the time. The fact is, it was *not only society's failure* to push back and speak-out against the hysteria, *but political opportunism*, in the form of a newly-appointed governor of the Bay State, Sir William Phips, stirred by Puritan minister Increase Mather and his son Cotton Mather, mentioned above as having become something of an authority on the matter and who further inflamed the situation by writing a passionate defense of the trials which were little more than kangaroo courts, that all came down to bear upon the raw emotional phenomenon.

Tituba had been thoroughly thrashed by her Puritan master, whipped into confessing that she practiced witchcraft and that she had taught the minister's daughter and friends what she knew from her occult past in Barbados (Starkey, 58). She would accept Christ as her savior, tell the courts what they wanted to hear, and later move to Virginia. Her treatment constitutes another example of treatment of slaves by their Christian masters and how it was not always so flattering a reflection upon their religion. Curiously, perhaps ironically, Samuel Sewall, "member of the council under the new charter, 1692-1725, a judge in the special court at Salem which tried and executed the supposed witches, was of so heroic a mold that five years later he could make public acknowledgment of his error ... wrote and published a small pamphlet, *The Selling of Joseph, 1700*, the first antislavery tract in America" (Miller-Johnson, 276). History, perhaps people, can be full of surprises.

But it would be an entire century-and-a-half from the time of the Salem Witch Trials of the late seventeenth-century until well into the nineteenth-century when the Church of England allowed Africans to be baptized. Until then, the Anglo attitude toward indigenous people of all sorts was as Peter Harrison described in the quote above as "blacks were not sufficiently human to be baptized" (Finke and Starke, 31).

In that one hundred-fifty years Black slaves endured the vagaries of the masters' attitudes toward his religion. If he let his slaves practice their own version of religion, then so much the better and a religious syncretism developed that was practiced by many slaves. Generally, however, "the Christianization of slaves was opposed by their masters on the grounds that the promises of liberation contained in the New Testament might be taken too literally in a political sense (Williams, 39). The political implications of religion were clearly recognized by these Christian land/slave owners and they were not to be underestimated.

But all was not lost for the reputation of Christian charity for in that early American Christian consciousness there was no unanimity in the view of slavery or the African and Native American. Ultimately, it would be this same Christian consciousness that would provide the impetus for emancipation of the African from his white master-owner. Quakers protested and had always been against slavery (Noll, 1992: 77) and "several British colonies imposed heavy fines on Quakers for doing so" (Finke and Starke, 31). From Northampton, Massachusetts and the spiritual revival of the Second Great Awakening of the early 1800s would come the fuel for the abolitionist movement.

The very existence of the third quote preceding the Introduction to this book (Amendment XIII) is intended to remind us of a situation that had persisted up until then, 1865.

A situation when ideals did not include the entirety of society or the population. I would ask the reader to review in sequence those three quotes spanning the first two hundred years of the new world's settlement. To today's African-American, what is to be made of the statement in the U.S. Declaration of Independence that "all men are created equal by their Creator"? Clearly, it didn't include *their* ancestors and it would take yet another hundred years for anything even approaching a social movement toward equality to begin. There was certainly no freedom for these slaves, religious or otherwise, as this brief recounting of history has illustrated.

Having sampled in a very narrow way the diversity of America's early religions and Christianities, it should be clearer that no single religious (Christian) view prevailed. This has not always been valued and appreciated, never mind extolled in published histories of the country, as James Loewen's book *Lies My Teacher Told Me* reminds us. Fortunately for religious freedoms, it was not from among only one or another of the religious groups that the lawmakers would emerge. They would come from among several of the mostly Protestant Christian sects, but, more importantly, it was not from Christianity that their inspiration would be drawn. In the course of *dissolving the political bands which had connected them* ... and ... *in order to form a more perfect union,* the Enlightenment would provide the pathway to good governance.

The FOUNDERS' VIEWS:
BENIGN MONOTHEISM with a FREEMASONIC TWIST

The competition for ideas in an emerging modern Europe meant that Christianity alone would not call all the shots. The influence of the European Enlightenment of the 1700s and its emphasis upon natural law and reason governing our understanding of the universe would make its mark upon the ones we know as the Founding Fathers. Their notions of the divine must be factored-in if we are to comprehend the form of government they strove to create and religion's role in it. To their minds, the Creator of the Declaration of Independence was in no way, shape, or form the orthodox Christian god, or the Triune One. Quite the contrary, they leaned toward what is today called the *higher criticism* of religious texts.

53

This simply means that Bibles, Qurans and holy books in general must be subjected to the same critiques and forms of analysis as other historical writings. They must be cross-referenced against other historical texts and the archaeological record as they are conventionally understood. This is the exact opposite of the idea described above about the Puritans and their Protestant Reformation Biblical Literalism in which the Bible is above and beyond all criticism.

When Benjamin Franklin states in the quote below that he "apprehend[s] it has received various corrupting changes," he is referring to the New Testament documents specifically, and the Bible generally. By his day scriptural analysis had developed to the point that the ideas of *revealed religion* or *revelation through scripture* were not serious approaches to understanding historical texts. The previous century had seen Biblical studies and interpretation develop in its earliest modern form with rationalist philosopher and historian Baruch (Benedict) Spinoza. Cutting right to the chase, he "deserves credit for the fact that there is today wide agreement that scripture has no authoritative role in the making of public law and that the same historical and critical methods apply to scripture as to other ancient documents" (Preus, 17).

The God of the Bible was not the same god of the founders but for only in skeletal outline. Theirs was a god of creativity and unity who was, for the most part, neutered. He wielded no hegemony in the world of mankind but sought influence only through the light of reason and conscience. His influence and presence were to be seen and measured, if you will, in the natural laws that govern the cosmos. These laws could be seen as emanating from a deity, their enlightened minds could accede. In fact, it is because these laws come from god that they are inviolable. The laws themselves are absolute and not to be added-to or taken-away from. The possibility of miracles, which are by their very definition a violation of natural laws, is virtually none. There is no possibility of miraculous intervention; it is a ruse and a fantasy of religious irrationality that ought to be rejected. There is no place in the enlightened mind for superstitions and the miraculous, and so their god was thoroughly naturalized. Theirs was the god of Deism

That the founding fathers were Christians by birth and family association is plain and obvious enough. Most were children of the Church of England and its worldwide Anglican Communion.[10] Some founders came from

---

10   In the United States the English church would take the term Episcopal or Protestant Episcopal Church after the American Revolution and independence. Until then, colonists who supported England went to its church, the Church of England and belonged to the worldwide Anglican Communion, the motherland's church scattered throughout her empire.

among the dissenters' camps – Baptists and Unitarians being two common English-based reformist-minded denominations. That is not to say the same thing as they were orthodox Christian believers. They certainly were not. Deism was a popular "gentleman's religion," and some or other version of it resonated with George Washington through at least the first half-dozen presidents. In effect, Deism afforded one the respectability of tradition that came with religious, if not affiliation, ideation, without becoming mired in the creedal orthodoxy that had ravaged Europe through the previous two centuries – hence, a form of benign monotheism.

Deism was and remains far more intellectually palatable to those who would be persuaded by science and the existence of nature's laws, since the rejection of supernaturalism (superstitions) is the hallmark of Deism. Yet, an acknowledgment of the mysteries in life and the many questions to which there may be no way of knowing the answer, leaves one an opportunity to be open to the postulations of religions. And while Deism would see no need to fixate on such questions, their existence leads the prudent philosopher to temper his speculations on them in the full understanding that *speculations* are all humans have. Basically, Deism understands the limits of human knowledge without thoroughly repudiating theological speculations – provided those speculations conformed to reason and human dignity. Such an enlightened mind is too wise to be an atheist. It reasoned thus: why should anyone commit to a position (atheism) when there is no definitive confirmation of it? In the *absence of any* existential or physical evidence for a god, atheism presumes the *absolute absence of any* sort of god, and there is no need for that. Deism was and remains the perfect intellectually-palatable and socially-respectable compromise.

Perhaps the clearest articulation of this position comes from a letter Benjamin Franklin wrote to a fellow philosopher whom he addressed as 'reverend' and whom had inquired into the former's views on religion:

> You desire to know something of my Religion. It is the first time I have been questioned upon it. But I cannot take your curiosity amiss, and shall endeavor in a few words to gratify it. Here is my creed. I believe in one God, Creator of the universe. That he governs it by his Providence. That he ought to be worshipped. That the most acceptable service we render to him is doing good to his other children. That the soul of man is immortal, and will be treated with justice in another life respecting its conduct in this. These I take to be the fundamental principles of all sound religion, and I regard them as you do in whatever sect I meet with them.

As to Jesus of Nazareth, my opinion of whom you particularly desire, I think his system of morals and his religion, as he left them to us, the best the world ever saw or is likely to see; but I apprehend it has received various corrupting changes, and I have, with most of the present dissenters in England, some doubts as to his divinity; tho' it is a question I do not dogmatize upon, having never studied it, and think it needless to busy myself with I now, when I expect soon an opportunity of knowing the truth with less trouble. I see no harm, however, in its being believed, if that belief has the good consequence, as probably it has, of making his doctrines more respected and better observed; especially as I do not perceive that the Supreme takes it amiss, by distinguishing the unbelievers in his government of the world with any peculiar marks of his displeasure (Kramnick, 166-167).

Franklin is unwavering in his devotion to the precepts of science and his view is tempered with the awareness that the very account of Jesus' life (the written gospels of the New Testament) ought not to be taken literally. By his day, the science of historiography had developed sufficiently such that no historically-conscious scholar, linguist or otherwise, viewed religious texts in the manner of the Protestant reform churches, as noted earlier. The principles of scientific observation and categorization had replaced Biblical Literalism as the chief method of understanding the cosmos. And even if the Protestant emphasis on literalism in scripture had itself contributed to this shift in emphasis, in leaving the allegorical behind,[11] there could still be no compelling reason to minds the likes of Franklin's to refer to Jesus of Nazareth as a god or God.

His ecumenical view of religions and God's providence put him squarely at odds with most any creed that would have identified as orthodox Christian. His reference to "one God" is in direct contradiction to the doctrine of the *Trinity*.[12] There is no ambiguity in Franklin's position: men are

---

11   Peter Harrison charts a very interesting historical progression in European thought from the Protestant Reformation to what we recognize today as modern science. While he does not claim to offer a "monocausal thesis for the rise of modern science," he does demonstrate that the "demise of allegory due largely to the efforts of the Protestant reformers" meant that "the study of the natural world was liberated from the specifically religious concern of biblical interpretation, and the sphere of nature was opened to new ordering principles" (1998, 4-8).
12   The doctrine of the Trinity has its roots in fourth-century Christianity. It defines the nature of God in a Father-Son-Holy Spirit configuration that was intended to preclude certain beliefs of the time considered "heresies." In essence, the Trinity teaches that God became a man in the form of Jesus. The emphasis of God being in-the-flesh (incarnate) poses certain theological problems (apparently), and hence, a history of doctrinal Christian infighting has plagued the church for centuries. To this day, certain Christian-based historical groups are considered non-traditional or unorthodox based principally upon this doctrine, Jehovah's Witnesses, Latter-Day Saints (Mormons), and of course, Unitarian (in contradistinction to Trinitarian) Universalists fit this bill.

not god/s, therefore Jesus was a man – only. This fourth-century orthodox Christian doctrine had survived the Protestant Reformation to be transplanted among most, though not all, of the Christians settling the new world. But in no way was this doctrine to be reflected in the laws of the land in the minds of the men who would write those same laws. The insert below is a window into the religious views that prevailed in government. This is a document signed in support of trade with the Ottoman Muslim state of North Africa. It was ratified by Congress in June 1797 and was designed to clear the way for commerce in the Mediterranean where both great nations, the American and the Ottoman, had significant interests.

> *ARTICLE 11 of the Barbary Treaties: Treaty of Peace and Friendship*
>
> As the government of the United States of America is not in any sense founded on the Christian Religion, as it has in itself no character of enmity against the laws, religion or tranquility of Musselmen [Muslims], and as the said States never have entered into any war or act of hostility against any Mehomitan nation, it is declared by the parties that no pretext arising from religious opinions shall ever produce an interruption of the harmony existing between the two countries.
>
> – Signed November 4, 1796 Tripoli

So, what *did* the founding fathers believe regarding religion generally, Christianity specifically, and the various religions that were part of their world and how to govern in a manner reflective of the religious aspirations of the colonists and soon-to-be nation? This is not unlike answering the question of the founding of the nation itself; there is no single answer, though there are more consensuses in this group since they came from the same class within society. George Washington, Thomas Jefferson, James Madison (Presidents 1, 3, and 4) were Episcopalian (US) or Anglican (England) by their family's affiliation. After U.S. independence the Anglican Church took on the name Episcopal in an effort to steer away from the concepts of royalty and hierarchy, which were being expressly rejected at the time and the preferred reference to the bishops (*episcopal*, as in governed by bishops) rather than a single person of authority as with the King or Queen being head of the Anglican Church, aka, Church of England. This new religious construct of cooperating bishops better reflected the ideals of the budding democratic republic.

Washington was more than willing to couch his religious terminology in conventional terms (Hutson, 110). This was not unexpected. Much the same way a current-day president addresses crowds and uses the term "God Bless America," we do not make much of the president's theology in his use of these terms and nor should we of the first president. He was a child of the empire and its Anglican religion. His appeals to providence were few but present, though little elaborated upon. He never abandoned his family's church even though Deism was a factor in his theological views, which were, again, not so much discussed by him.

The second president John Adams was a Unitarian – and this fact alone is worthy of study for today's religiously-curious American. It's enough to say that the very existence of the Unitarian Church, which had its origins in England in the eighteenth-century, reveals the theological disagreement that existed between orthodox Christianity which is solidly Trinitarian and the surrounding intellectual culture. The very term 'Unitarian' is meant to distinguish its beliefs from the historically-dominant and orthodox doctrines of the Church of England (Anglican), and for that matter other orthodox churches who were all Trinitarian.

Jefferson and Madison shared a similar religious background in that they originated from Anglican-Episcopalian families but were more persuaded by Deism. Jefferson "at most was a nondoctrinal Christian, both nonsectarian and non-practicing" (Church, 47). His attendance at religious services was a matter of good social protocol. It appears from Jefferson's writings that he is of the mind that god is beyond comprehension and we should look for his handiwork around us in nature. He sees no reason to repudiate the idea of god, in fact, the orderliness of nature seems to intimate it. But that's as far as science and the human mind can go (Hutson, 108-109).

Though most remained affiliated to one degree or the other with his family's church, they were persuaded more with the intellectual life of the Enlightenment and science and the rules governing good social conduct. From Franklin's quote above, we can gather that he does not favor a particular religion's privilege in government since he finds good conduct in "whatever sect" he may find it. The documents the Founding Fathers left behind stipulate there will be no official religion in the new republic. Religious freedom for all was the ideal, even if the full implementation at the time was lacking.

God would ultimately *not* make an appearance in the Constitution as it was finally drafted and ratified. There is no mention of divinity, only religious freedom. "Nature's God," as the founders put it, is to be found in the Declaration of Independence where the rationale for founding a new government and writing a new set of laws were stipulated. The essence of their rationale was that it was the whole purpose of government whatsoever, its *raison d'être*, "to assume among the Powers of the Earth, the separate and equal Station of one People to which the Laws of Nature and of *Nature's God* entitle them" … and to protect the "Life, Liberty and the Pursuit of Happiness" of its equal citizens.

The idea of God in government is a chimera. The idea of divinity to the early fathers of the nation is that of an *unknowable transcendent reference point* from which no other entity on this earth, human or state, has the authority to override. He is not a co-participant in a board meeting with whom you negotiate. And since nothing less than Nature's own God has endowed man with these rights, they are unassailable. The early fathers, however, were unable to sufficiently extend these rights to any and all beyond their station and class in society, as their eighteenth-century minds had been thus conditioned. Therefore, it has been left to us the effort to continue to extend and apply the Constitution's fullness. Their work is not complete. The Constitution should not become the government's equivalent of a Protestant Reformation Bible and read with a similar form of literalism to that of Biblical Literalism and that does not allow for expanding rights and ever-perfecting the union. *Creating* "a more perfect union" implies an effort that does not cease.

Contemporary evangelical Christians have had an academically difficult time with this. And though they are not known for their intellectual prowess, preferring zeal over intellect, they have gone to great lengths to "Christianize" the founders in accordance with their understanding of religious freedom (Mark Noll, 1994). But this moral zeal does not sufficiently mask the historical distortions required to turn the intents of the nation's founders into modern day evangelical intents. One recent casualty read thus, "Zondervan Pulls Jefferson Book over Inaccuracies." In the battle to claim the founding fathers as their own, evangelicals have overreached (Stump).

For the Fathers, religion in general and Christianity specifically held enormous potential to civilize and develop the fledgling republic. But by no means were they limited in their outlook and so they saw fit to draw from any number of sources for intellectual inspiration. Beyond the European philosophical and historical traditions, enlightened thinkers generally sought as broad a view from which to base their knowledge. The moral and intellectual traditions of the Bible writers were hardly unique in world historic literature, and these traditions could be most helpful in governing a civil society. In this sense, the founders spoke approvingly of religion's role in public life, and they saw nothing to be gained in repudiating history and tradition and a people's religion. The greater task was to balance the various interests while maximizing individual freedoms.

The intellectual motive for Thomas Jefferson's assembling *The Jefferson Bible: The Life and Morals of Jesus of Nazareth* was to draw-out from the gospels and highlight that most excellent example of ethical and civil life as exemplified in the person of Jesus. What Jefferson does to the New Testament would horrify a contemporary Bible-believer of the literalistic or fundamentalist sort. Jefferson takes a pair of scissors and cuts away all the superstitious stuff. No virgin conceptions, no healing miracles, no raisings from the dead, of anyone, Lazarus or Jesus. Jesus the magician no longer exists in Jefferson's Bible and he is certainly not the God-man of Greco-Roman-based orthodox Christianity. In the hands of the Jews, Jesus was a despised rabbi. In the hands of the newly-emerging catholic-orthodox church of 100-400 AD/CE, he was the divine-man, one member of a heavenly ensemble who will come to be known as the Trinity (Father-Son-Holy Spirit). To the Enlightened founding fathers, men are not gods. To the Church of England, the Roman Catholic Church, and to many of the Protestant Reformation churches who populated the New World settlements, the question of Jesus' divinity was not raised. It was a given. Only among select of the dissenter groups was Jesus' godhood a theological problem. Hence, the importance in the new republic for religious freedom and the abolishment of anything resembling a religious requirement for participation in civic life.

But, in a far more practical manner, and in a manner better suited for the building of a society both physically and ideologically, the influence of Freemasonic thought and philosophy would bear a more striking mark on the actual formation of the nation than religion. This is not to say that occult practices (if they deserve being called such and I'm not certain that they do) were the principal concern of the early fathers' participation in Freemasonry. In a very practical way, the Freemasonic Lodge and its social organization is most logical in a hierarchical society. Fraternities and private parties constitute venues where the elite can exchange their interests. In much the same way *Skull and Bones* at Yale University, or the fabled *Illuminati* whose origin dates back to 1776, or *Bohemian Grove* in northern California, or the *Bilderberg* group who meets annually in the summer at various resorts around the globe, the Freemasons is a gathering of like-minded individuals who share common social and monetary interests. It's no surprise that relationships formed or cultivated in these venues would carry over into political life.

Paul M. Bessel has compiled the statistics of Freemasonry among the founding fathers. By his count 16% of the signers of the Declaration of Independence, 33% of the signers of the Constitution, and a full 46% of Generals in the Continental Army were members of the Freemasonic lodge (Bessel, 2014). These numbers do not seem remarkable in any significant way.

George Washington was a Freemason and "three of Washington's first Cabinet of four were Freemasons: Thomas Jefferson, head of the Department of Foreign Affairs, Edmund Randolph, Attorney General, and Henry Knox, Secretary of War ... [and we] ... have already seen that of the 56 signers of the Declaration of Independence, 53 may have been Master Masons and that the model for the constitution was based on Anderson's Constitutions, so the design of the new State was literally Freemasonic" (Haggar, 163).

Many Americans may be familiar with diagrams of the physical layout of Washington, D.C. and the "eerie" (again, if it deserves being called such and I'm not certain that it does) formation of the streets in accordance with Masonic symbolism (see diagram in Haggar, plate 33; and can be easily looked up on the Internet). This layout was drawn by George Washington himself during 1790-92. The five-pointed star surrounding the pentagonal center is a most evil symbol from the Christian worldview – yet it constitutes the very design of the capital city!

We would be remiss to interpret such a view of history as a conspiratorial one. The founders themselves were conscious that conspiracies to undermine the colony would be afoot, and so they separated the powers accordingly. The division of powers reflected the founders' beliefs that "political power [was] a corrupting influence that makes political conspiracies against the people's interests and liberties almost inevitable" (Introduction; deHaven-Smith, 7). The safeguards they built in to the republican form of government, when operating with the freedom of the press to serve as a fourth pillar, ought to be sufficient to resist any form of tyranny that seek to combine and consolidate. Religion, like Freemasonry, would not be given ultimate authority and citizens need not be required to be members of the latter nor baptized by the former to hold public office.

Ultimately, current applications of the laws of the land hang in the balance with our understanding of how the writers of the Constitution interpreted the role of religion in the republic. It is their philosophical predispositions that informed the documents that guided their lawmaking and, in the end, the laws themselves. The writers of those documents were keenly aware of the havoc religions had played back in the old countries of Europe. Had the Puritans won the day and prevailed in having their views of government become the law of the land, by George, we'd all be Christians by decree. There was no way the founders were going to let that be duplicated here, and so the American tradition of "separation of church and state" became established. There would be no Church of America as there was a Church of England. The American ideal would be *freedom of religion for all.*

REFERENCES
Books/Essays:

Andrews, Edward Deming (1953). *The People Called Shakers: A Search for the Perfect Society*. New York: Dover Publications, 1963.

Bellah, Robert N. (1992). *The Broken Covenant: American Civil Religion in a Time of Trial*. 2nd Edition. Chicago: University of Chicago Press. First edition 1975.

Bessel, Paul M. (2014). *Freemasons Among the U.S. Founding Fathers*. http://bessel.org/foundmas.htm (accessed January 2019).

Bonfanti, Leo (n.d.). "A Summary of the Witchcraft Hysteria of 1692." *New England Historical Series*. Wakefield, Massachusetts: Pride Publications, Inc.

Boyd, Gregory A. (2005). *The Myth of the Christian Nation: How the Quest for Political Power is Destroying the Church*. Grand Rapids, Michigan: Zondervan.

Church, Forrest, ed. (2004). *The Separation of Church and State: Writings on a Fundamental Freedom by America's Founders*. Boston: Beacon Press.

Corrigan, John and Lynn S. Neal, eds. (2010). *Religious Intolerance in America: A Documentary History*. Chapel Hill, North Carolina: University of North Carolina Press.

Dowley, Tim, ed. (1977). *Eerdmans Handbook to the History of Christianity*. Grand Rapids, Michigan: W.B. Eerdmans. 1987.

Falwell, Jerry (1980). *Listen, America!* New York: Bantam, 1981.

Feldman, Noah (2005). *Divided By God: America's Church-State Problem – And What We Should Do About It*. New York: Farrar, Straus, Giroux.

Finke, Roger and Rodney Stark (2005). *The Churching of America 1776-2005: Winners and Losers in Our Religious Economy*. New Brunswick, New Jersey: Rutgers University Press, 2006.

Guyatt, Nicholas (2007). *Providence and the Invention of the United States, 1607-1876*. Cambridge: Cambridge University Press.

Hagger, Nicholas (2009). *The Secret Founding of America: The Real Story of Freemasons, Puritans and the Battle for the New World*. London: Watkins Publishing.

Harrison, Peter (1998). *The Bible, Protestantism, and the Rise of Science*. Cambridge: Cambridge University Press.

Harrison, Peter (1990). *"Religion" and the religions in the English Enlightenment*. Cambridge: Cambridge University Press.

Horsley, Richard A. (2003). *Religion and Empire: People, Power, and the Life of the Spirit.* Minneapolis: Fortress Press.

Hutson, James H., ed. (2005). *The Founders on Religion: A Book of Quotations.* Princeton, New Jersey: Princeton University Press.

Jefferson, Thomas (1989). *The Jefferson Bible: The Life and Morals of Jesus of Nazareth.* Boston: Beacon Press.

Kirk, G.S. (1970). *Myth: Its Meaning and Functions in Ancient and Other Cultures.* Berkeley: University of California Press.

Kramnick, Isaac, ed. (1995). *The Portable Enlightenment Reader.* New York: Penguin.

Lewis, I.M. (1971). *Ecstatic Religion: A Study of Shamanism and Spirit Possession.* 2nd Ed. London: Routledge, 1989.

Loewen, James. W. (2007). *Lies My Teacher Told Me: Everything Your American History Textbook Got Wrong.* New York: Simon & Schuster. (1st ed. 1995).

McCutcheon, Russell T. (1997). *Manufacturing Religion: The Discourse on Sui Generis Religion and the Politics of Nostalgia.* New York: Oxford University Press.

Miller, Perry and Thomas H. Johnson, eds. (1938). *The Puritans: A Sourcebook of Their Writings.* Vol. 1. New York: Harper Torchbooks, 1963.

Morgenstern, Madeleine (2011). Franklin Graham Answers: Can an Evangelical Christian Vote for a Mormon? *Christian Broadcasting Network.* Dec. 17.

Noll, Mark A. (1992). *A History of Christianity in the United States and Canada.* Grand Rapids, Michigan: Eerdmans, 2003.

Noll, Mark A. (1994). *The Scandal of the Evangelical Mind.* Grand Rapids, Michigan: Eerdmans.

Noll, Mark A. (2002). *The Old Religion in a New World: The History of North American Christianity.* Grand Rapids, Michigan: Wm. B. Eerdmans.

Preus, J. Samuel (2001). *Spinoza and the Irrelevance of Biblical Authority.* Cambridge: Cambridge University Press. 2008.

Sehat, David (2011). *The Myth of American Religious Freedom.* New York: Oxford University Press.

Starkey, Marion L. (1949). *The Devil in Massachusetts: A Modern Inquiry in the Salem Witch Trial.* New York: Vintage Books, 1969.

Stein, Stephen J. (2000). *Communities of Dissent: A History of Alternative Religions in America.* New York: Oxford University Press.

Stump, Scott (2012). Publisher Pulls Jefferson Book Over Inaccuracies. NBC News, Today. Aug. 10. https://www.npr.org/sections/thetwo-way/2012/08/09/158510648/publisher-pulls-controversial-thomas-jefferson-book-citing-loss-of-confidence (accessed January 2019).

Taylor, Mark Lewis (2005). *Religion, Politics, and the Christian Right: Post-9/11 Powers and American Empire.* Minneapolis, Minnesota: Fortress Press.

Williams, Peter W. (1980). *Popular Religion in America: Symbolic Change and the Modernization Process in Historical Perspective.* Urbana: University of Illinois Press, 1989.

Government Documents

The Declaration of Independence and the Constitution of the United States (1776). New York: Bantam Books. 1998.

The Barbary Treaties 1786-1816. The Treaty of Peace and Friendship, Signed at Tripoli November 4, 1796. The Avalon Project at Yale Law School. http://avalon.law.yale.edu/18th_century/bar1796t.asp#art11 (accessed January 2019).

2

EVOLUTION VS CREATION, THE BATTLE FOR THE COUNTRY'S BODY AND SOUL

The delusion: *A great stand-off between science and religion took place in 1925 in Dayton, Tennessee in the form of the Scopes "Monkey" Trial, when an intellectually-rebellious science teacher taught Darwin's theory of evolution in contradiction to the laws of the State. Ever since, science and religion have been in heated battle over how best to describe human origins and the origins of life and the universe in general. The "model" of creationism is equally valid as the scientific model of evolution.*

The correction: *The ideological background to the Scopes case was rooted in concerns more directly related to Social Darwinism than biological evolution and this is often lost in the theatrical narrative of Science vs. the Bible, which was the angle the media promoted at the time. But the mundane and very worldly-oriented motives for the trial itself make it a matter of <u>local economics</u> more than politics coupled with national media sensationalism – in the form of the newly-available-to-the-masses technology of radio. Coinciding with the introduction of this technology the Scopes Trial was positioned to be staged, as it were, as the first-ever legal case of any kind to be aired to the public. This, naturally, captured the attention of many Americans. Together, they combined to propel the topic into the population's consciousness rendering the scientific basis for the entire event all but irrelevant, if non-existent.[1]*

---

1   Though several sources are listed in the References for this chapter, the documentary program by the once-defunct and recently-resurrected CourtTV is alone sufficient to make this correction clear. Though that program does not delve into the role of Social Darwinism beyond mentioning it, the genesis of the legal battle is well-contextualized. This is the first chapter to intimate my method of using a single and concise documentary source to counter a delusion. However, this chapter has a full References page.

Quotes

In Flanders fields the poppies blow
Between the crosses, row on row,
That mark our place; and in the sky
The larks, still bravely singing, fly
Scarce heard amid the guns below.
We are the dead. Short days ago
We lived, felt dawn, saw sunset glow,
Loved, and were loved, and now we lie
In Flanders fields.

Take up our quarrel with the foe:
To you from failing hands we throw
The torch; be yours to hold it high.
If ye break faith with us who die
We shall not sleep, though poppies grow
In Flanders fields.

– WWI war poem by Canadian Army Major John McCrae, surgeon attached to the 1ˢᵗ Field Artillery Brigade, 1915; written two weeks after the first use of poison mustard gas in warfare

Those who believed in eugenics, a fashionable view at the time even in Britain and the United States, became enthusiastic about the programme. Nazism was seen as Darwinism in action. However, many people were put to death just because they were seen to be economically unproductive. The Nazis referred to them as 'useless eaters.'
– on Hitler's T-4 Euthanasia Program, *The Story of the SS*, pg. 279

Whatever the course of social philosophy in the future, however, a few conclusions are now accepted by most humanists: that such biological ideas as the "survival of the fittest," whatever their doubtful value in natural science, are utterly useless in attempting to understand society.
– Richard Hofstadter, 1944 in *Social Darwinism in American Thought*, pg. 204

DARWINISM or SOCIAL DARWINISM? THAT is the QUESTION

The appearance in England of Charles Darwin's *Origin of Species By Means of Natural Selection, or the Preservation of Favored Races in the Struggle for Life* in 1859 opened-up new possibilities for biological research and scientific theorizing in any number of sub-disciplines, most notably social and cultural anthropology. However, in addition to the scientific promises Darwin's theory also caused social-political waves that continue to ripple to this day. You could say it was a twofold impact: one impact was on the biological and life sciences themselves, the other on the *meaning* of biological evolution and the implications for human dignity and for cultural worth. Darwin recognized himself that "A grand almost untrodden field of inquiry will be opened, on the causes and laws of variation, on correlation, on the effects of use and disuse, on the direct action of external conditions, and so forth" (Darwin, 372).

At the heart of the rift is the *nature vs nurture* debate, or put another way, biology vs. culture. A society's opinions of which of the two is deemed most influential in the development of species and individuals can have social and cultural implications for the overall study and understanding of humankind and what is emphasized (and more importantly what is funded).[2] If humankind's potential is entirely dependent or determinant upon biological endowments, then certain judgments can be made about individuals' contributions to the overall fitness of his race. If, on the other hand, no judgments can be made solely upon one's biological endowments, but instead it requires a lifetime of interactions with other human beings coupled with a nurturing education to bring-out the abilities and aptitudes of the individual, then each and every individual intrinsically deserves that lifetime in which to reach his or her maximum potential.

Navigating between the two, nature or nurture, is Darwin's theory of *natural selection*. Does nature select biologically only, or does nature select using culture too? That was the question being posed at the time, and one that is still of relevance to decision-makers today.

If natural selection uses culture to determine the success of species, then humans must govern and regulate in accordance with this and implement policies that reflect the successful traits – those characteristics nature has "selected" and which foster human success. Successful cultures are, by deduction, fit cultures and deserving of perseverance while weaker cultures are fated to extinction. This is nature's way, it could be assumed.

The problem arises in the manner "Steven M. Stanley, a leading paleontologist, concludes, 'I tend to agree with those who have viewed natural selections as a tautology [a circular and invalid argument] rather than a true theory.... The doctrine of natural selections states that the fittest succeed, but we define the fittest as those that succeed'" (Rolston, 96). The result was that the

---

2   Such questions inevitably have ethical and political answers much in the same way as, perhaps, today's surveillance technology or cloning capabilities raise similar concerns. The potential for policy outcomes could go in any number of directions, some not so pleasant and are discussed below.

victors in war and conquest would determine who and what is fit and worthy. Similarly, within a society, and among the victors, the temptation is so very great to deem oneself and class as the epitome of one's own civilization. This ambiguity over fitness opened the door for Social Darwinism.

The challenges of Darwin's observations, encapsulated in an over-ly-simplified term *survival of the fittest,* seemed to be most contradicted by a religious worldview in which each individual has been granted a measure of human dignity by virtue of the fact that he or she is a product of God's creation. Remove the Creator, and there is no assurance of rights. *If Nature alone has granted humans rights, then anything deemed by the State or by science contrary to the good of Nature is fit to destroy. In other words, if only Nature grants it, the State can seize it. Individuals are subsumed by the State, but not if there is a Creator, who subsumes the State.* Without a transcendent reference point from which the rights of mankind originate, then those same rights may fairly be contested by the powerful.

Ultimately, human life and nature's selection processes are more complex (and more valued and valuable) than their simply being *fit* or *unfit.* But this wasn't and isn't always understood and appreciated. A "might makes right" doctrine would be the war cry of nations and was fueled by a sense of cultural and racial superiority. British, American, German and other European elites all fell prey to the self-aggrandizing worldview that they were a master race destined to become the conquering rulers. Renowned historian Barbara Tuchman attributes these attitudes directly to the impact of evolutionary thought.

> Such sentiments were among the indirect results of the most fateful voyage since Columbus – Charles Darwin's aboard the *Beagle.* Darwin's findings in *The Origin of Species,* when applied to human society, supplied the philosophical basis for the theory that war was both inherent in nature and ennobling. War was a conflict in which the stronger and superior race survived, thus advancing civilization. Germany's thinkers, historians, political and military scientists, working upon the theory with the industry of moles and the tenacity of bulldogs, raised it to a national dogma (290).

The question then arises: does evolution imply that human life has only a materialistic origin? What does it mean that mankind evolved? *Mean* is the operative word in the question. And does humanity owe it to itself to begin applying the survival of the fittest principles to societal life, cultural institutions, and in the case of conflict, to those vanquished in battle? For the first several decades of the development of these ideas it was wide-open as to where the theorizing would lead, especially in the social policy realm.

The theoretical bifurcation of nature vs nurture is very similar philosophically to that of the rift between science and religion. The two apparently opposing views need not be understood as opposing but can be complementary. The rift is more ascribable, in my opinion, to what C.P. Snow called in his book (coincidentally published 100 years to the year after Darwin's) *The Two Cultures*: that of the "humanities and arts" on the one hand, and on the other the "sciences." Rather than being a contest between two absolutist worldviews, science vs. religion, the two paths parallel each other rather than cross. And while this may be an oversimplification and not fully intellectually satisfying (see David Ray Griffin for an in-depth "resolution" to the conflict), the divide as Snow sees it, is a sufficient-enough understanding and description of the problem faced here.

Mary Midgley frames it as the "interconnectedness of facts and values" – facts synonymous with science, values equating to religion – though she aptly recognizes that "Neither facts nor values can be properly conceived in this drastic isolation from each other and from the central conceptual area which connects them" (17). Nevertheless, the contest continues between science and religion and is suggested by the sampling of books included in the Preface to this book. Those listed are representative of recent volumes that challenge religious faith and are examples that this divide continues in American cultural thought. Snow had stated that he found "Between the two a gulf of mutual incomprehension – sometimes (particularly among the young) hostility and dislike, but most of all lack of understanding" (4).

The issue with the books I listed is that they address *only one* element of human life, that of the measurable – the facts and science. We humans measure ourselves by so much more than the material and tangible. And while it may not be necessary to resort to the gods for explanations and psychological justifications and comforts, neither is there a need to resort to any number of "escapist" behaviors that could be considered nihilistic – void of meaning. The humanities and the arts are ways in which the human race creatively deals with life and meaning and "escapes" the confines of nature and the reality it presents us to (or imprisons us in). It seems to me that poetry is no more/less un/necessary or meaningless/ful than the gods. So isn't a good song. None is essential, but all possibly therapeutic, and potentially beautiful. But these evaluations are not conducive to scientific-style scrutiny. In the end, and fear not, science will proceed with all the characteristically-human input (itself value-laden) recognized by scientific theorists like Thomas Kuhn and Paul Feyerabend,[3] coupled with the constraining guidance of the scientific method.

This branching or divergence in biological science took place early with Darwin's original ideas, but would not stop there. Nature/nurture; science/humanities; science/religion; biology/environment; these dual emphases within the progression of knowledge are better seen as corresponding elements that impress upon the individual organism with the result being a unique and valuable human being. For better rather than worse, Darwinian evolutionary thought's influence evolved and extended its range far beyond areas not at first obvious, such as cultural evolution, and the applications of Darwin's ideas are still being theorized (see Aunger and Blackmore).

What would emerge from biological Darwinism in a relatively short time to become Social Darwinism seemed a logical outcome of the former. This is what William Jennings Bryan, the "Great Commoner" and defender of John Scopes and Biblical creationism, sought to push back against, at least in part. As a populist, he was aware of the potentially abusive effects of such policies and who they might be skewed to benefit. He didn't have far to look to see the effects of such policies as they were being implemented all around him; he could go to the movies and see advocacy for infant euthanasia, or he could refer to any number of states' laws permitting, if not requiring, racial and mental hygiene. The weaker elements of life may in fact be destined to die-off, but, as Bryan's reasoning goes, that does not mean that there is no value in the potential achievements that the weak may reach. In life there is value, it is no mere commodity.

This debasing of human life had to have a cause. Yes, in part it was the cruelty of the corrupt corporate industrialists, of the bankers and their trusts (bundled investment certificates, roughly the 1920's equivalent of today's derivatives and seen then by Bryan and those distrusting of Wall Street as the source of monetary corruption by bankers exacerbating unemployment and inflicting human misery – sound familiar?), of imperialism and particularly of the science of evolution with its evil concomitant, Social Darwinism. The application of Social Darwinism had earned a nasty reputation for fostering cruel attitudes toward inferiority and fostering racial superiority over the lower working classes while espousing a veneer of scientific credibility. It was the new science of the time – a science that could improve humanity itself.

3   Both of these writers have challenged the notion that science and the progression of knowledge develop along rigid methodological lines. Kuhn's 1962 *The Structure of Scientific Revolutions* and Feyerabend's 1975 *Against Method*, are, in the words of the latter, "different approach[es] to applying the same term to a similar (not an identical) situation. His approach was historical while mine was abstract … and thus having been made aware of the great complexity of Kuhn's thought I am not at all sure that our differences are as great as I often thought they were" (230).

The new science was termed *eugenics*. Very generally conceived, there were positive and negative eugenics. *Positive eugenics* encouraged healthy lifestyles with proper select breeding built up to the ideal of racial fitness. *Negative eugenics* sought to purge the race of undesirable qualities such as disease, mental deficiency, criminality and laziness. Within culturally specific groups this may be possible, to a point. But in a geographically large area of mixed ethnicities and races, these philosophies had potentially racist and tribal overtones. The potential of this "new science" coupling itself to an ideology was far too great a risk in the minds of many. Echoes of this already existed in German nationalism and the ideals of Aryan superiority in northern Europe in the first two decades of the 1900. By the 1920s eugenics was introduced as part and parcel of Swedish social policy in the welfare state. The practice of racial hygiene is fully implemented in order to "protect the Swedish stock" (see the documentary film *Homo Sapiens 1900* for a riveting account of this history).

Evaluating class superiority and its connection to biological fitness goes back to Malthus' 1798 *Essay on Population* and its influence on Herbert Spencer who died in 1903 and in-turn had significant influence in American intellectual circles. "With only the most casual acquaintance with biology he promoted his notion of the 'survival of the fittest' as a social ideal. This had enormous effect, above all in the United States, where he outsold every other philosopher in his day" (Midgley, 118). *Class privilege* does not die easily and seeks opportunities to reinforce its status and so the threat is ever present. This is what eugenics represented to many people at the time, including the populist Bryan.

A Pulitzer Prize winning book on the infamous Scopes Monkey Trial titled *Summer for the Gods* makes mention that

> Everywhere the public debate over eugenics colored people's thinking about evolution. Popular evangelist Billy Sunday, for example, repeatedly linked eugenics with teaching evolution during his 1925 Memphis crusade, which coincided with legislative consideration of the Tennessee antievolution bill (Larson, 28).

In addition to Billy Sunday, the author makes no mention of that "everywhere" in which eugenics was coloring people's views of evolution. This gives the impression that only, or mostly, religious folks were concerned about eugenics. This was certainly not the case.

Both before and after the 1925 Scopes Trial, Franz Boas an American anthropologist who is still much admired today for his writings and ideas about human life and culture, cautioned the white race for its overly prideful attitude for his accomplishments (1911: 2-29). He presciently warned that "achievements of race do not warrant us in assuming that one race is more highly gifted than another." This was in 1911. In a few years he counseled again that:

> the wish for the elimination of suffering is divided by a narrow margin from the wish for the elimination of all suffering. The possibility of raising the standards of human physique and mentality by judicious means has been preached for years by the apostles of eugenics, and has taken hold of the public mind to such an extent that eugenic measures have found a place on the statute books of a number of States, and that the public conscience disapproves of marriages that are thought bound to produce unhealthy offspring.... While, humanely speaking, this may be a beautiful ideal, it is unattainable (1928: 120, 107).

Franz Boas is raising the same concern that Bryan was by his participation in the Monkey Trial. In the late 1920s German anthropology is dominated by eugenics and by this time the rhetoric coming from the Nazi party clearly echoed the worst potentialities of negative eugenics. The problem becomes, at what point do conscious efforts at assisting humankind's evolution, and presumably his optimal fitness, *tread on the rights of individuals*? Furthermore, who decides who's fittest? The victors? The strongest among the victorious group? The elites? It sure looked as though some of these decisions were being made in Germany in the form of Aryanism, and to horrifying ends.

Even earlier, in the American century (1900s), it was recognized how this philosophy of Social Darwinism could serve class purposes, of the *higher* classes of course.

> [A]t an American Sociological Society meeting in 1906 during a discussion of 'Social Darwinism', [a] previous speaker had presented a social–Darwinist thesis advocating careful elimination of the unfit and dependent, chiefly by eugenic methods, In reply [Lester] Ward branded the doctrine presented as 'the most complete example of the oligocentric world-view which is coming to prevail in the higher classes of society and would center the entire attention of the whole world upon an almost infinitesimal fraction of the human race and ignore the rest' (Hofstadter, 82).

This would be more-or-less what happened to the great masses of humanity as capitalist and socialist industrialism overcame the western nations. As the power of concentrated wealth consolidated, it posed threats that invariably accompany such "commanding heights" and the results were wars, cyclical economic recessions and depressions based in the manipulation of currencies, and the sponsorship of a science that validated their position in those oligarchical positions, and for which the full consequences may as yet to be determined, even in our time.

In more recent decades, and since Snow's argument on the two separate cultures within society, the bridging of the biological sciences within evolutionary thought with that of the cultural life of humankind encompassing the humanities has been mostly successfully accomplished in the form of the new science called Evolutionary Psychology. This still-new science constitutes a further development of Sociobiology and constitutes a newer branch of anthropological thought that combines *evolutionary biology* and *cognitive psychology* and seeks to explain a host of human behaviors in light of humankind's biological, and of course psychological, evolution.[4] This allows the theories of evolution to be extended to all areas

4   See Robert Wright's 1994 *The Moral Animal: The New Science of Evolutionary Psychology* for a popular account and for a denser volume that digs deeper into the theories themselves see the 1992 *The Adapted Mind: Evolutionary Psychology and the Generation of Culture* by Jerome Barkow, Leda Cosmides and John Tooby. Carrying this research over to Religious Studies has been a productive area of research. To understand that religion must also be part of the culturally adaptive capabilities of human evolution resolves for some researchers once for all any questions as to its efficacy for the fitness of

of life without reducing humanity to mere biology. There are dynamics of psychology at work that are cross-cultural and span the global ethnic spectrum that ought to be better understood rather than be simply judged unfit, or unsuccessful. By integrating the cognitive[5] into its understanding of biological evolution, human behavior and cultural traits can be understood for the much more complex set of interactions that they constitute.

Take an example we can all understand in our modern and apparently fast-paced life: divorce. The practice of divorce, so often in history viewed as a *moral weakness* and something reflecting the degeneracy of an individual since he/she is violating a natural inclination (monogamy – presumably on behalf of child-rearing) and therefore often deserving of some sort of sanction or punitive measure, now, with Evolutionary Psychology, divorce is seen as a *choice of strategy* initiated by both men and women for the furtherance of individual progress (Wright, 133-135). This change in understanding and attitude has social, cultural and legal implications. Most importantly, it removes the dehumanizing element of social judgment and punishment out of consideration when confronting the hard choices that life (nature) presents us with.

This further "evolution" of scientific thought in the form of Evolutionary Psychology should hopefully interject a healthy dose of humaneness into our modern day biological, psychological and social sciences. The recognition that nature is not one-dimensional and has any number of tools in her toolkit by which to fashion and perfect her handiwork, can only aid in humanity's continued evolution.

One British novelist writing at the turn of the century put it perfectly in his, as it states on the cover, "classic autobiographical study of the clash of temperaments in post-Darwinian England: My father's religious teaching to me was almost exclusively doctrinal. He did not observe the value of negative education, that is to say, of leaving Nature alone to fill the gaps which it is her design to deal with at a later and riper date" (Gosse, 74).

Another hundred years on and the table has even been turned such that now religion itself can be better understood using this new science. Hopefully, the abuses of earlier times can be avoided, and that *empathy*

---

human life. See Bowker, Boyer, Burkert, Hinde, Laughlin and d'Aquili, and d'Aquili and Newberg for a sampling of this type of research. Again, it was really Edward Wilson's *Sociobiology: The New Synthesis* of 1975 that would set in motion, or at least propel, this research.

5   By cognitive psychology is meant the recent notion that the brain/mind of humans works according to its own internal logic, principles and interactions. Very basically, "evolutionary psychologists stress the importance of understanding how genetic and environmental factors interact and point out that genes often build different minds in response to different environments" (Evans and Zarate, 159).

will pervade all elements of science. Perhaps, the inhumanity that gripped and horrified the turn of the centuries from the 1800s to the 1900s tempered the transition from 1900s to the 2000s – though our world is still rather bloodied. Yet, we can only hope the humanizing trend continues. Beyond hoping for such, stripping ourselves of past scientific and religious delusions will serve to clear the path for that very trend.

A CRUEL WORLD at the TURN of the PREVIOUS CENTURY

As an undergraduate in the late 1980s one course I found myself in as part of my history roster was titled *World War I: The Real War, its Causes and Effects.* That war was called the "Great War," or the "War to End all Wars," and lasted from 1914 through to 1918. The reasons it had these titles was due to its previously-unconceived barbarity and the numbers dead in battle were greater than ever seen before. The grisly nature and number of the deaths were beyond all comprehension. Only the hordes of Genghis Khan in the thirteenth-century rivaled the numbers! The professor who taught my class was an emotional man and would break-down into tears while lecturing. He gave vivid descriptions of how that this being the first war since the industrial revolution and the mechanization of large-scale industry and manufacturing, the ability to kill men in battle and utterly destroy civilians in cities was unprecedented. Men suffered and died in the trenches of Europe amidst rats, muck and barbed wire, facing rapid machine gun fire and poison gas all while enduring ungodly bombardment from massive artillery shells. It was no place for man or reptile. For the first time in battle soldiers faced flamethrowers, hand grenades, tanks, shells when exploded releasing poison gas, and as the war progressed even airplanes were used to strafe the trenches with machine gun fire. And of course, there were diseases in these deplorable conditions.

The stories of the Battle of the Somme alone in which over one million humans were killed or wounded still boggle the mind. Imagine, a million people in one battle lasting over four months! Only the Battle of Stalingrad and Siege of Leningrad during WWII would rival these numbers – and these lasted years.

The professor had us read Paul Fussell's *The Great War and Modern Memory.* It effectively portrays how utterly fragile and seemingly valueless life had become in the face of modern warfare and the mass killing it produced and how this expressed itself in British literary works and culture. He writes, "The German use of gas – soon to be imitated by the British – was thought an atrocity by the ignorant, who did not know that … gas is the 'least inhumane of the modern weapons'" (11). This was the British experience of the war – devastating in its effects and all-encompassing in its reach. Fussell goes on, "The five last months of 1914, starting August 4, when the British declared war on the Central Powers, began with free maneuver in Belgium and Northern France and ended with both sides locked into the infamous trench system" (9). And to think the war was just getting going and would not cease for another four years.

The war left a lasting impression on the participants and unforgiving sacrifices of all sorts were made by the British population. Fussell writes:

> Even cuisine commemorates the war. Eggs and chips became pop-
> ular during the war because both bacon and steak were scarce and
> costly.... After the war women dramatically outnumbered men,
> and a common sight in the thirties – to be seen, for some reason,
> especially on railway trains – was the standard middle-aged Lesbi-
> an couple in tweeds, who had come together as girls after each had
> lost a fiancé, lover, or husband (342).

All Quiet on the Western Front portrays the conflict from the German infantry man's point of view and is a classic novel of the effects of war for the soldier on the ground. Being Canadian-born, I grew-up with great affection for the poem In Flanders Fields by Major John McCrae who had "spent seventeen days treating injured men – Canadians, British, Indians, French, and Germans – in the Ypres salient" ... McCrae would recount, "I wish I could embody on paper some of the varied sensations of that seventeen days.... Seventeen days of Hades! At the end of the first day if anyone had told us we had to spend seventeen days there, we would have folded our hands and said it could not have been done" (Dancocks, 344).

A description of the trenches of WWI conveys the horror:

> Shell fire was one of the worst experiences a soldier could have. The
> mind-numbing, near-deafening noise and bone-rattling vibrations
> from even distant explosions were bad enough, but the wounds
> were worse – much worse. 'At its worst [a busting shell] could dis-
> integrate a human being, so that nothing recognizable – sometimes
> apparently nothing at all – remained of him' writes noted historian
> John Keegan. 'Such projectiles ... often travelled in clusters, which
> would inflict several large or many small wounds on the same per-
> son ... shell blasts could create over-pressures or vacuums in the
> body's organs, rupturing the lungs and producing hemorrhages in
> the brain and spinal cord' (Dancocks, 203).

Alas, the poppies blow in Flanders Fields.

No war is without bloodshed, but in the case of WWI, the scale was unimagined. From the machines in use that maximized the carnage to the poison gas wafting through the air terrorizing all biological life, man's power over life and death seemed godlike. By war's end in 1918 the total numbers of deaths in battle was topping sixteen million; seven million of these were civilians. An additional twenty million people were injured.

Against this backdrop of the mass carnage of WWI, which seemed to threaten to engulf the world, life was being assaulted as it was entering that same world in the form of eugenics policies finding popularity in governments across the Western hemisphere.

During that same war and at a time when the U.S. was teetering on entering the conflict, Americans were viewing a different sort of nihilism that was expressing itself. In the 1916 movie *The Black Stork*, Dr. Harry J. Haiselden a eugenicist advocate, takes the cold-hearted decision to allow a newborn baby with a birth deformation to die of exposure on the cold hospital gurney. The caption beneath the scene reads *"There are times when saving a life is a greater crime than taking one."* The nurse at his side is clearly distressed and conflicted about what to do. In the end she follows her orders and exits the room knowing full well the baby's fate is certain death, alone on that table.

The doctor in the film was an advocate of "racial hygiene," an effort within the eugenics community to purge the race of defective qualities, deformations and disabilities. Racial hygiene meant the enactment of laws of negative eugenics.

"The National Conference on Race Betterment in 1914 showed how thoroughly the eugenic ideal had made its way into the medical profession, the colleges, social work, and charitable organizations. The ideas of the movement began to receive practical application in 1907, when Indian became the first state to adopt a sterilization law; by 1915 twelve states had passed similar measures" (Hofstadter, 162). Some of these laws would persist into the 1960s, believe it or not. It seems unimaginable to a contemporary American that German and later Nazi eugenicists actually took their cue from American eugenicists and admired the latters' success at forced sterilization: "The importance of the United States for German eugenicists was revealed by the allusions in nearly every German medical dissertation about sterilization in the United States as the first country to enforce comprehensive eugenic legislation.... In particular, the American Immigration Restriction Act of 1924 was applauded by German racial hygienists (Kühl, 25-26).

Mass sterilizations were not uncommon. Laws would be written in "over 30 states that led to more than 60,000 sterilizations of disabled individuals. Many of these individuals were sterilized because of a disability: they were mentally disabled or ill, or belonged to socially disadvantaged groups living on the margins of society" (Kaelber). While these laws were being activated in the United States, German anthropology was dominated by eugenics at the turn of the century also. In fact, they much-admired in Germany the American way of implementing eugenic policies. From our vantage point in the early twenty-first century, it does not require a crystal ball to see where these laws took Germany when in the hands of fanatics. The warning is clear what the near future in any age of any country *could* hold should these policies be coupled with an ideology of superiority.

As much as I hate to indulge in what feels like hyperbole, it is simply unavoidable at this juncture. Lutz Kaelber goes on with his presentation: "American eugenic laws and practices implemented in the first decades of the twentieth century influenced the much larger National Socialist compulsory sterilization program, which between 1934 and 1945 led to approximately 350,000 compulsory sterilizations and was a stepping stone to the Holocaust." He demonstrates the way the two nations' programs intersected.

William Jennings Bryan, "the great commoner" as he was called, was a populist. He understood the language of the people he sought to represent and fought on their behalf using their images. By 1925 he had made three unsuccessful attempts for the presidency and so was a seasoned campaigner. He knew from where the threats to the working class and the poor came, from the power-hungry industrialists and financers who sought to justify their crushing exploitation of the working classes.[6]

Upton Sinclair caught the mood in his *The Flivver King, A Story of Ford-America*, a novel of great historical worth. In its own way the novel describes the fight between the forces of capital and its elite owners against the working classes:

> So Abner Shutt became a cog in a machine which had been con-
> ceived in the brain of Henry Ford, and was now in process of in-

---

6   Interestingly, the author of *The Great War and Modern Memory* also wrote a book about the American system of social stratification titled *Class: A Guide Through the American Status System*. Rather than attribute to nature the system of privilege that is without doubt in place in modern America, he instead ascribes it to *inherited wealth*: "old money" in the vulgar phrase – is the indispensable principle defining the top three classes and it's best if the money's been in the family for three or four generations (29). He defines these as the "top-out-of-sight class: Rockefellers, Pews, DuPonts, Mellons, Fords, and Vanderbilts." These are who we would call today in the post-Occupy Wall Street world, the 1%, or perhaps better, the .1%.

cubation. Alone in his shop, Mr. Ford had been free to do what he pleased; but whenever he had gone out among other men and become a part of their organizations, he had been obliged to do what they told him, Now, for the first time in his life, he was going to have an organization of his own; other men were going to obey him, and be shaped according to his ideas (15).

Industrial capital had been built on the backs of the masses. The health and welfare of the masses, in turn, depended upon the success of capital. Henry Ford's own attitudes toward his workers and race are chronicled in his *Dearborn Independent*, "a series of articles on The International Jew.... All the world's troubles, wars, strikes, insurrections, revolutions, crime, drunkenness, epidemics, and disaster were the work of organized malignant, corrupting Jews ... and of the theory of evolution, all were parts of the Jewish plot against the Gentile world" (56). Should the reader be shocked, then, to learn of the master capitalist's support for fascist Germany? Perhaps not, if left unchecked and uncoupled to an ideology, eugenics can justify anything.

But the reader ought to be aware that this is the first chapter topically, though only the second numerically, to have an overlay with the darkest element of the religious delusions covered in the rest of the book. That dark element is the fascist worldview. The reader may think that we are too early in a discussion of the Scoped Monkey Trial for the influence of Nazi-like ideas, but keep in mind that the applications of Social Darwinism took many forms.[7]

NECESSITY and the MOTHERS of INVENTION

Out of the economic hardship preceding and precipitating the Great Depression of 1929-30, local economies were being gutted. Dayton, Tennessee in 1925 had seen its coal and iron mines close and unemployment rise precipitously. The town went into bankruptcy. The lawyer handling the bankruptcy, George Rappleyea, got the idea that it could

---

[7]   To my movie-going generation, the Academy Award winning *Cabaret* (1972) highlights the essence of this nihilism in pre-Nazi Germany. The movie is set in 1923 Germany, between the two world wars and right around the time of the Scopes Monkey Trial in the USA. With the German economy in shambles and still reeling from the Treatise of Versailles' economic reparations, the average German was reduced to groveling out a meager existence. The theatrical nature of life is the theme of the movie that pivots the characters around a desperate and hopeless existence. A personal favorite, mostly due to the fact that as a young teenager I didn't really understand what I was seeing which only intensified the fear, is an even darker version of the times in Ingmar Bergman's 1977 *The Serpent's Egg* which captures the macabre future to where Germany's nihilism was headed and alludes to the gruesome experiments by Nazi doctors such as Joseph Mengele. These Nazi eugenicists had free political rein to do as they pleased without ethical restrictions. They could implement their full vision of a eugenically-perfected Aryan who has the inherent right granted to him to rule the world. The SS represented (to their minds) the best of the Aryan best.

be good for the town if he took–up the ACLU (American Civil Liberties Union – in existence since early-on after WWI)[8] on its offer to defend anyone who challenged the recently-passed Tennessee's anti-evolution law, the Butler Act.

The town's businessmen congregated at the local Robinson's Drugstore to scheme their stunt. They were referred to literally as the "Drugstore Conspirators" (and even posed for a photo afterwards; see *The Monkey Trial* documentary at 11:18 or Larson, 90) and were the town's own mothers of invention who collectively represented a best hope to spark economic boom. If their plan was successful, Dayton's cash registers would ring, and outsiders and investors would be drawn there to make a buck. So, these men plotted to challenge the law.

F. E. Robinson, in addition to being the owner of the town's drugstore, was also president of the school board and knew who he would choose to play the rebellious intellectual and brave school teacher: John Thomas Scopes. Though not initially in on the plan, Scopes does deserve, however, the good reputation for his defense of science and free speech. As a teacher, he understood the value of the freedom of the mind, thought and speech. He *did* see that the law's outcome was not a good one for open scientific or even religious free speech and debate. So he agreed to be arrested. Rappleyea calls the sheriff, and Scopes is charged and released on his own recognizance back to his tennis game, which he had interrupted to appear in court.

The textbook Scopes used was *Civic Biology,* and it did include references to eugenics applications that already existed at that time in the USA and in Europe as noted above. This would certainly bolster the cause for Bryan's mind as he "had targeted eugenic thinking as one of the evil consequences of teaching evolution" in the past (Larson, 115).

The drama was heightened by the fact that both the prosecution's and defense's attorneys were well-known in their respective worlds, Bryan the political, Darrow the legal. They both fought for the common man against the oppressive oligarchs. Darrow had even supported Bryan in his first presidential run in 1896. Religion had caused the two men to part ways and since both were public figures, this only heightened the drama yet further.

---

8   Taken from the current website of the ACLU: One of the ACLU's earliest battles was the Scopes Trial of 1925. When the state of Tennessee passed a law banning the teaching of evolution, the ACLU recruited biology teacher John T. Scopes to challenge the law by teaching the banned subject in his class. When Scopes was eventually prosecuted, the ACLU partnered with celebrated attorney Clarence Darrow to defend him. Although Scopes was found guilty (the verdict was later overturned because of a sentencing error), the trial made national headlines and helped persuade the public on the importance of academic freedom. https://www.aclu.org/aclu-history (accessed January 2019).

The town's only decent-sized hotel was filled as the town had been overrun by reporters from not only the USA but Europe and Asia. It truly was a global event – radio would see to that.

The world was about to hear the "Monkey Trial" complete with carnival-like atmosphere generously provided by the local Chamber of Commerce.

We must remember that the trial is taking place at a moment in American history when religious growth and social change initiated by religious causes were quite widespread. To no small degree was Prohibition supported and advocated as a political cause by the wives of men drenched in the hopelessness and joblessness of the time. What's not to support, the populist mind could be forgiven for thinking, in prohibiting access to the devil's brew? Such measures are not unthinkable even in our own day, what with the prohibition on certain classes of drugs, even those which are purely natural.

In any case, in the 1920s this religious growth and advocacy had a name: *fundamentalism*. It was the resurgent branch of Anglo and mainland European Protestantism, which by the 1920s had as one of its chief characteristics a rigid form of Biblical Literalism. Reading the Bible in this way meant that there was no wiggle room for any alteration of the creation story and God's role in it. This mindset was most despised and ridiculed by secular popular commentators of which the celebrated H.L. Mencken epitomizes. Sent out to Tennessee by the *Baltimore Sun* to cover the story, Mencken's sole intention was that of highlighting the buffoonery, as he saw it, of the fundamentalist cause and crusade against science. He would write in 1930 on the "imbecility" of the fundamentalists:

> The rise of biology, the great event of the Nineteenth Century, is responsible for that change [in attitudes toward science and away from superstitions], and especially the appearance and acceptance of the Darwinian hypothesis of organic evolution. Darwin, to be sure, did not answer any of the basic riddles of existence, but he at least show that the theological answers were rubbish, and he thereby completed the revolutionary work of Galileo, Newton, Leibniz, Harvey and Leeuwenhoek. Today no really civilized man or woman believes in the cosmogony of Genesis, nor in the reality of Hell, nor in any of the other ancient imbecilities that still entertain the mob (252).

Whatever such scoffers may say, the stark reality of tough economic times in which people were experiencing existential hardships coupled with a god-forsaken philosophy of eugenics which reflected crudely Darwin's ideas in a "presentation of evolution as the survival of the fittest, intermingled with the social

Darwinist baggage, commonplace in the period, applying the same *eliminationist* message to people races and ideas" (Italics mine; chapter one; Feldman, 140). It's hard not to get the feeling that the individual was under assault.

As is so often the case in historical-material reality, religion is only one very tangential part of a greater event moving the actors forward. From the points of view of the characters in the courtroom, if religion's validity is reduced to simply about scientific facts and what should prevail in the classroom as science, then the verdict is victory for science. Darrow and Scopes prevailed over Bryan and fundamentalism in the narrative of the myth of the fight between evolution and creation. Though ironically, they lost the case, the Butler Act was upheld, and Scopes fined, it was really a victory over Bryan and the fundamentalists who simply could not make scriptures provide a material understanding of the universe. What does a "day" mean when there is no sun in the sky? How do Adam and Eve's children have children? These Sunday school-level technical issues that the book of Genesis raises for the laws of nature are not amenable to scientific debate and discussion. Bryan was left looking foolish by being roped into a line of thoroughly tortuous reasoning that no one could extrapolate himself from in the hands of a crafty lawyer, such as Darrow was.

A simple acknowledgment of Snow's two cultures would go very long way to resolving this needless and repetitive debate. But such were the times.

Science has and should win the battle in the science classroom. But when science period is over, and we shuffle down the hall to the history or civics class, then we may in cultural and historical context discuss the ideas of creationism. Even if one sees the science of evolution as encouraging policy-makers practicing Social Darwinism and racial hygiene (or eliminationist, and ultimately extermination) then one may be inclined to seek an authority (God) to override such a policy and which can be found in the Constitution as previously noted.

But seeking this God-based legal protection is no excuse for creationism in the science class, or its recent incarnation Intelligent Design, discussed below. The science classroom is not the battleground for that fight. This is better undertaken in the public policy world of national politics, which will forever remain in the second of Snow's two cultures, the humanities and arts. The political domain represents the value-creating arena of citizen participation and where Social Darwinism is to be battled, not in the science classroom.

Unfortunately, *the delusion of the contest between science and religion* has hurt most those who perpetuate it: the fundamentalist, evangelical, conservative, or in descriptive parlance, those *unfortunate Christians snared by Biblical Literalism*. That is a key problem that ought to be addressed by public education in a very concerted and respectful way.

Sadly, Christians have been subjected to arguments such as the following apologist who has framed the debate as being between two differing theories of knowledge.

> The primary debate between creationists and evolutionists was not over fossils, biological classification, or geological evidence, though these were involved. The major debate that Darwin surfaced was between two competing epistemes... [which are]... a set of assumptions about the nature and limits of knowledge. It is roughly synonymous with a paradigm in Kuhn's sense of a world view that includes a picture of what counts as good science. An episteme involved the idea of science itself: what counts as good science, how science should be practiced, the limits of science, and so on (Moreland, 215).

For him there is no line separating faith and knowledge, the two are intertwined by an all-encompassing theology. In reality, *faith can say little to nothing about what is good science*. This ambiguity and confusion have been exploited in formal religious apologetics and is at the heart of the religious delusion regarding evolution and creation. Creation requires faith that no description of material evidence can confirm. Even the Big Bang Theory requires a certain amount of faith, even if of a slightly different nature and more theoretically-grounded. Evolutionary biology requires no faith and simply explains elements of development in the material world, nothing more.

Moreover, the type of religion that requires an evidentiary base and is not a religion of pure faith, puts intellectual demands on their believers that cannot be fulfilled. Faith accepts a certain amount of mystery and tolerates the possibility of doubt. Science strives to overcome the mysteries of nature, which are not mysteries at all but rather opportunities for exploration, by solving misunderstandings and filling-in gaps in knowledge and replacing theories with new knowledge as it develops.

Science is the how not the why; religion is the why not the how. Astronomer Galileo put it poetically: "The Bible tell us how to go to heaven, not how the heavens go."

Theories by their very nature are meant to be temporary and limited, until the explanation can be more fully understood. There is no real opportunity for knowledge dispelling a faith inclusive of mystery. Faith endures and is its own separate type of understanding (not separate type of knowledge) of the world. Faith is never knowledge, and to demand a form of intellectual credence for one's faith only seems to demonstrate the lack of it. Faith and science are mutually exclusive in scientific discourse, but thoroughly compatible in the discourse of the humanities and arts. It must be left at that.

One of the effects of the "politico-religious capital" that was garnered by fundamentalists and later evangelicals by the Scopes Monkey Trial was that succeeding generations of conservative religious believers have turned their attention to demonstrating the compatibility of the Bible and science with ever such renewed vigor. Rather than take the opportunity to create a theology compatible with modern science by not overstating what the Bible can possibly achieve, they instead sought a science compatible with their pre-existing, indeed orthodox, theology. They were simply unable to decouple knowledge from faith.

Mark Noll, chronicler of American Christianity, notes that even before the Scopes Monkey Trial fundamentalist Christianity struggled with the precepts of modernization:

> Against this combination of new money, social Darwinism, naturalistic science, and accommodating Protestantism, the old synthesis of evangelical convictions, American ideals, and a common-sense Baconian science faded rapidly away. The collapse of that synthesis signaled the collapse of the effort by conservative evangelicals to construct a Christian mind in America. From the point of view of the new university, the effort to view knowledge whole was increasingly abandoned under the assumption that discrete parts of truth, discovered through empirical science, could stand on their own. The effort to integrate religious faith with learning was either given up entirely, under the assumption that the pursuit of science carried with it no antecedent commitments to a worldview (chapter one; Noll, 1994: 113-114).

The attempt to re-synthesize the two cultures has not been successful. Out of the tortured logic required to make religious faith believable, Christian scholars have resorted to any number of interpretive acrobatics to fit the Bible with modern geology, anthropology, archaeology, etc. There is absolutely no reason for religious faith, but motivated by its own intellectual anxieties, to produce a volume along the lines of *The Genesis Flood*.[9] It is an intellectually disgraceful and strained piece of writing mak-

9   This 1961 book is, or was, something on the order of a canonical text for teaching modern creationism. It has sold over a quarter of a million copies and was reprinted for 2011 in a 50th

ing statements that stretch even a Sunday school teacher's religious faith, for example, "the Scriptures seem to imply that written records were made and kept by at least a portion of the human race during the entire period from Adam to Abraham" (Whitcomb/Morris, 40). And it is difficult not to read with a certain puzzlement the authors' elaborate calculations for getting the animals into Noah's ark, even to the point of citing *Types and Market Classes of Live Stock* (69) as supportive evidence.

Unfortunately, the result is not only an untenable science but a perverse form of religion that undermines the value of personal faith by insisting upon everyone, including those in science, acknowledging its claims as objective reality and similar to other types of knowledge. This is due to religions' too often absolutist attitude toward knowledge and literalism in the reading of the Bible. This viewpoint can be traced back to the Protestant Reformation discussed in the previous chapter as being at the heart of Puritan Biblical Literalism, witch-hunting and the use of spectral evidence in the courtroom.

The belief that the Bible is an inspired text is a common trait in conservative forms of Christianity. Until the Bible is viewed as an historical text that is equal with other texts, then it will hold this special status that opens the door for beliefs to be held in a literalistic-absolutist manner. The attack against the Bible's authority was a direct blow to the Christian foundation of the nation itself, the fundamentalist mind perceived. Mark Noll describes this version in his *A History of Christianity in the United States and Canada* when he says, "[William Jennings] Bryan's campaign against evolution, which in 1925 culminated in his celebrated clash with Clarence Darrow at the Scopes Trial in Dayton, Tennessee, was not so much a fight against new ideas itself as it was a fight against what he and other fundamentalists felt the new ideas were doing to destroy the nation's Christian heritage" (chapter one; 1992: 383). As I've noted, this is true, but only partially.

The end of the previous century saw a revamping of standard creationism. Since the 1990s, and contemporaneously with the development of Evolutionary Psychology mentioned earlier, Intelligent Design (ID) has emerged as a reformulation of traditional creationism. ID attempts to be more inductive based, or observation based, in an attempt to interpret the material world as possessing a set of drafting plans, or "watch-maker" concept. To say that "God made it" is not a theory, it is a statement of religious faith. It cannot be checked, verified or even inferred from the evidence as ID attempts. It can only be postulated.

A scientific theory must always come from the bottom up, not the top down. Scientists do not have faith in their theories. The theories must be discarded when a better explanation for observations surfaces. No religious theorizing has ever entertained the possibility of discarding god. Of course, there was the Death of God movement of the 1950-60s but that has largely passed and/or morphed into a largely benign and silent (intimidated?) liberalism – it was never intended as a purely atheistic philosophy.

There is absolutely no reason to expect that ID will be any more successful at persuading those participating in scientific debates, but its presence may still be welcomed if tempered with the compromise expected in American constitutional democracy.

The POWER of COINCIDING EVENTS

Some Americans reading this may have a visual memory of O. J. Simpson's white Ford Bronco barreling down the California highway with a convoy of police cars in hot pursuit. The June 1994 drama was intense. You knew as you were watching it that you were witnessing something of bigger significance than simply a police chase. Hundreds, perhaps thousands, congregated on roadsides and overpasses as the "Juice" fled. When all was said and done, some sixteen months later when he was acquitted, the initial onlooker's hunch was right. It *was* far bigger than the guilt or innocence of one man; police-race relations in Los Angeles, and vicariously all America, were put on trial. Can one honestly say that the 2014 "Black Lives Matter" movement was unforeseen? It seems a stretch given recent American history.

In the case of O.J Simpson, the reaction to the verdict was culturally telling, if not a little chilling: Whites almost universally were horrified by the acquittal, while most Blacks were relieved. What was to account for the disparity? It all depended upon one's own upbringing and, overwhelmingly if a bit coincidentally given our topic, one's race. And just like the Scopes Trial, when all was said and done, one side won a legal victory, but there was no such clear-cut verdict on where this victory would lead society.

Yes, Simpson was acquitted, and though it was a momentary victory for one side, it did not put to rest the sense of racial injustice Black Americans feel subjected to in society – and it was only a peek at the topic for most White Americans. Any broader message seemed lost in the did-he-or-didn't-he-do-it fixation. Simpson's trial must also be seen in the context of the timeline of the Rodney King beating four years earlier and the Los Angeles Police's acquittal three years prior. That acquittal sparked the infamous 1992 Los Angeles Riots.

Historical events do not take place in a vacuum.

Even if Simpson were in fact guilty of the crime, the greater historical issue[10] of the decades and longer of racial injustice African Americans have endured was inextricably mixed into the overall justice of the case. This is the only way to understand the differing responses of the two races. For Whites, connecting O.J.'s guilt to the broader issues was simply not done. That would require a conscious effort (education) and an acknowledgment of issues still of some matter of social, cultural and political sensitivity.[11]

Where do we go from here? This was the question in the mid-1990s for everyone across country who watched the initial Bronco chase or who had tuned-into the trial over the course of eight months. One could not live in America during the year 1995 without hearing about the Simpson trial. The media made it a ubiquitous event no matter what time of the day one tuned-in. After the verdict was read, we were left with a sense of "what next?" For African Americans, the question was, how will justice for our community come next? The Simpson case *only drew attention to the problem*, that of relations between city police and the African American minority community. For White Americans it appeared as aborted justice – the more immediate issue of Simpson's guilt/innocence was the crux of the matter. Other groups will have their own reflections on the significance of it.

Much the same in 1925; though lasting only eight days, in the Scopes Trial there was an immediate verdict of relevance to John Scopes, a one hundred dollar fine which was later tossed-out on a technicality. Scopes didn't stick around town long after the affair. He was a temporary substitute teacher only filling-in at the time. Yes, the Butler Act was upheld, but the teaching of evolution was left ambiguous and a matter of individual schools' educational policies more than politics, law or proper science. There was no immediate sense of victory for either side. But as we've seen in the battle of ideas when the sides are hardened-into their positions, forces unrelated to the issues at hand can come to bear down on historical reality. The dawning of our own age's technological advancement had taken a giant leap forward around the time of the Scopes Trial and sharply analogizes the two trials' historical relevance.

---

10   This statement is made with the sincerest awareness that there is no "greater historical issue" when loved ones are involved. I beg the reader's forbearance in order to make a point of generational societal significance.

11   The "Blue Lives Matter" phenomenon in reaction to the 2014 "Black Lives Matter" movement, reveals to this author that certain sectors of the population still respond as in the days of O.J. Simpson's acquittal. One has to wonder to what degree is *social engineering* at work in civil society on the part of state actors, indeed, perhaps even foreign state actors; as of 2019 this has become a commonly understood phenomenon in the form of "Russian meddling" in American elections via social media.

The far more important comparison between the Scopes and Simpson trials is that these two events become emblematic of deeper cause with a more widespread social impact. That impact coupled with the application of mass technology propels isolated events into the public's imagination in a revolutionary way and with political capital.

In 1925, the coincidence of the recent development of radio and the Scopes Trial being the first-ever broadcast had a powerful cultural effect. The principal effect was to convince millions of Americans to accept the very notion that there is some legitimate scientific debate on this matter at all. WGN of Chicago broadcast the trial every day into Americans' homes, but the new technology was global in its reach. "Some two hundred journalists came from as far away as Hong Kong to chronicle the trial" (*Landmark American Trials*, 10:50).

The power and reach of this new medium were revolutionary and global at that time and helped direct public opinion on this topic up to the present day. It stands as a matter of historical record. Without the role of radio in this event, chances are very great there would be no evolution vs creation debate, at least in the public's imagination. Science and religion would have found other ways to mediate their contradictions if so compelled.

The documentary *The Goebbels Experiment* profiles the state of German technology in 1933 at the launch of the Third Reich. At 39:00 Goebbels is shown speaking after having tested some new radio technology at the Broadcasting Fair, from Goebbels' diary the narrator reads,

> Saw the exhibition, television is only months away. I made a call to the far-east, to the captain of the Bremen at sea, I could clearly be heard; people are stunned by the technological advances. The strength of good radio programming lies in creating the right mix of entertainment, enjoyment, instruction, education and politics.

As if speaking prophetically, Goebbels' words foretold just how influential the media would become in our world today, and we are barely two generations from the time when he spoke.

Only five years after that speech in 1938, in an incident that came to be re-popularized later in the 1975 made-for-TV movie *The Night that Panicked America*, radio would be used to stunning and dramatic effect to fool people into mobilization. At the time, Orson Welles' radio broadcast of H.G. Wells' *War of the Worlds* was sufficiently believable and realistic to send unbeknownst listeners fleeing for the countryside in the fear that planet earth was under siege by Martians. While the intent was to make as realistic a rendition of the original novel, the ability of media to convince people of the nature of events ought to be the take-away warning. By 1938 radio had been a part of American life for over fifteen years, yet people were nevertheless capable of being unduly influenced and misled by it.

In the hands of the right technicians and artists, media is a force in itself (see Conclusion; McLuhan). Today's technicians, operating it seems in a value-vacuum, face the same questions today about their sciences and their applications as the characters in the Scopes Monkey Trial.

Value is not sought by biological evolution, only survival. Beauty is not appreciated for its own sake by biological evolution, only cultural evolution places value upon beauty. While society ought properly to separate science from religion in culture, may society not discard god to its own humanistic peril. This is no mere revision of Pascal's Wager – the hedging of a bet one can't lose, even if is only self-interested. Rather, it is a safeguard within the world of man for those rights which ought never be taken away. If from a temporal source our rights stem, with the giver of those rights being state (law) or person (dictator), then our rights are also most temporal and transient. If God, on the other hand, be the granter of our rights, then no state or human acting in the name of a state can rescind those same rights. One could think of "God" in society and politics as a legal loophole in the shape of humankind through which citizens may avoid all forms of state tyranny and political barriers to find freedom on the other side. The founding fathers were enlightened enough to look beyond the strictly scientific and to imbibe their political philosophy with a non-sectarian and benign monotheism.

In the end, the epic battle was for human dignity. The founders knew full well what they were doing when they grounded the rights of human beings in the Creator. Far from being a capitulation to orthodox religions or to include god into state law and mandate religious participation, reference to the Creator was included *only* to preserve for the individual certain inalienable rights that no man, local, state, or federal government can take away.

The WARNING FROM the PAST

Closing his oft-cited book on the topic of Social Darwinism, Richard Hofstadter gives a nod to the insight of William Jennings Bryan and his intuitive perceptions into the potential abuses of evolution. He writes,

> For many years Bryan had been troubled about the possible social implications of Darwinism. In 1905 E.A. Ross, then teaching at Nebraska University, had found Bryan reading *The Descent of Man*, and Bryan had told him that such teachings would 'weaken the cause of democracy and strengthen class pride and the power of wealth.' Here, as in other matters, Bryan had sound intuitions that his intellect had not the power to discipline (200).

One man's populist vision of a better future, poorly articulated and executed to be sure, captured the attention of a nation and helped sell it a story that would bring hope to many at a time when life seemed so little-valued and reasons for despair were manifold. From the efforts of one man's very humane vision, a myth was made. Alas, and from time immemorial, this is how myths have been made.

Again, with the help of Hollywood, the myth is given life in mass cultural form.

Having already once in this chapter referred to Hollywood films and their ability to capture (or set) the mood of an historical event, I will take the liberty of doing so again. In this instance, a movie was most successful at evoking very emotive-laden scenes and in capturing the intellectual implications. The 1960 movie *Inherit the Wind* was the first in-board feature presentation on a commercial flight. A comforting message in 1960 to those flying-high in the latest Boeing jetliners while America was burning 35,000 feet below in African Americans' struggle for Civil Rights. The social stratifications of society are frequently drawn-out from the background to become central when the fight for political control of society is at stake, only to then be swiftly swept-under the carpet in public opinion.

Nowhere in this film is the concept of Social Darwinism either mentioned by name or cited as a background issue or potential social danger in the hands of the ruling class. Only to God's eyes is Darwinism offensive, not to a humane and socially-democratic understanding of man, the film would have us believe anyway.

Consider this exchange between the fictional Drummond who is Darrow and Brady standing in for Bryan; the former is defending the progress of science and advancement, and the latter is the populist politician and lawyer seeking to defend religious fundamentalism's values over and against science's evil:

> **Drummond:** Now I suppose you can quote me chapter and verse right straight through the King James Version?

> **Brady**: There are many portions of the Holy Bible that I have committed to memory.
>
> **Drummond**: I don't suppose there are many portions of this book you've committed to memory, *The Origin of Species*.
>
> **Brady**: I'm not the least interested in the pagan hypotheses of that book. I've never read it and I never will.

But this is false if the observation of E.A. Ross is accurate. The film is perpetuating not simply an omission, but a distortion, misinformation, or disinformation. This is not simply a matter of "bad intelligence," but of deception. "*Inherit the Wind* dramatically illustrates why so many Americans continue to believe in the mythical war between science and religion,' Ronald Numbers later wrote. 'But in doing so, it sacrifices the far more complex historical reality,'" wrote Edward Larson in his Pulitzer Prize winner *Summer for the Gods* (242). And while the film may in its own way be more a response to McCarthyism as Larson notes, this hardly facilitates dispelling the delusions Americans persist in holding about religion and science.

What's worse is that in the film the threat as understood by Bryan at that time is reversed such that it is not the oppressive racially-cleansing philosophies of eugenics that are the threat to human dignity and freedom, but religion's oppression to the freedom of mind. And, granted, a certain secular freedom may have to from time-to-time stand its ground in the face of the strong-arm religion, the threat of powerful elites and oligarchs armed with eugenics philosophies is a far greater "clear and present danger" to the weakest in society than the battle for free speech, important as that may be.

In another exchange only moments after the one above, Drummond/Darrow and Brady/Bryan go at it:

> **Brady**: …Is it possible that something is holy to the celebrated agnostic?
>
> **Drummond**: Yes, the individual human mind … an idea is a greater monument than a cathedral. And the advance of man's knowledge is a greater miracle than all the sticks turned to snakes or parting of the waters. But now, are we to forego all this progress because Mr. Brady now frightens us with a fable?

The preceding scenes contain arguments in which Brady/Bryan is made to look like a buffoon by forcing a literal interpretation upon the reading of Genesis. He is taunted by Drummond/Darrow using Bible passages in the most ludicrous of explanations such as what a "day" meant prior to the fourth day when god created the sun. At the end of the courtroom drama Brady/Bryan is preaching to an inattentive courtroom waving the scriptures above his head until finally he collapses onto the floor, his wife haplessly looking on teary-eyed as her husband unravels.

The point is not to overstate eugenics' role in Bryan's efforts, but it seems logical that a populist politician would take the effort to understand the basic threats to those he was politically courting. He spoke their language, the language of fundamentalism, but he fused it with his own understanding of evolution's potential abuse in the form of eugenics which he could see around him in the laws of the nations.

The lesson of the Scopes Monkey Trial is that the Founding Fathers' concepts of God and of the tempered integration of religion into civic life are sufficient to carry the democratic ideal into the future. There is no need to modify it in the face of scientific advancement. If the two are properly separated, there is no conflict ... the two cultures complement.

The First Amendment is today still strong enough to fight back against censorship of all kinds whether sponsored by religion or not (I would argue that politically-intimidated speech is more sinister in the open society than speech challenged openly by religious voices which may then be defended for/against in the public square), but if the government closes down the square, chokes-off the message and limits the people's access to information and its free-flow in the square, the threats will be far greater.

And so, the epic duel between the forces of Satan, evil and human oppression in the form of biological evolution and its evil twin eugenics, confronting the forces of God, good and human freedom in the form of the Book of Genesis was fought to a stalemate in the annals of American cultural and legal history. Central to this myth was the fight for human dignity rooted in religion, and it has given America nearly one hundred years of ammunition in that fight.

But myths can be hijacked and redirected, and Bryan's cautionary warnings need still be heeded.

In this day, we need to be ever wary of those social engineers who have access to a sophisticated repertoire of technologies by which to engineer. As we proceed through the topics of this book, keep in mind that the human condition (human nature) in its essence has not fundamentally changed, and that, despite an exponential increase in knowledge. The temptation of those in power to control societies' destinies has not diminished. Warnings from current cultural observers, and they are plenty, ought to be duly noted. When we read that U.S. federal government administration (meaning the President's) officials advocate for the *cognitive infiltration* of dissent groups who oppose government policies and who protest or become citizen activists, we need be alarmed.[12] Consider the ruminations of Edward O. Wilson, the father of Sociobiology:

> It is the dream that acquired general currency at the Earth Summit, the historic United Nations Conference on Environment and Development held in June 1992 in Rio de Janeiro. The representatives of 172 nations, including 106 heads of government, met to establish guidelines by which a sustainable world order might be reached. They signed binding conventions on climate change and the protection of biological diversity. They agreed to the forty nonbinding chapters of **Agenda 21**, offering procedures by which virtually all of the general problems of the environment can be addressed, if not solved. Most of the initiatives were blunted by political squabbles arising from national self-interest, and global cooperation afterward was principally limited to rhetorical exercise on state occasions. The $600 billion additional expenditure recommended to put Agenda 21 into effect, with $125 billion donated to developing countries by industrialized countries, has not been forthcoming. Still, the principle of sustainable development has been generally accepted, an idea previously little more than the dream of an environmentalist elite. By 1996 no fewer than 117 governments had appointed commissions to develop Agenda 21 strategies (*italics* and **bold** mine, Wilson, 1998: 317).

Efforts like the Earth Summit, Agenda 21 and "living sustainably" all sound like noble projects with humanitarian ends. But an outcome of a humanitarian nature is not a certainty. There is no historical reason why the knowledge and policy implications of these efforts cannot fall into the hands of those with much narrower interests than the Common Good. And what about the risk of tyrants? With the technological capabilities that are available in certain quarters, coupled with highly subjective evaluations and applications of the above statements, the outcome could be disastrous for large swaths of the earth's populations.

---

12   The academic field of Religious Studies deserves some noteworthy attention at this point. Russell T. McCutcheon perceptively noted early-on the tendency of "members of luxurious groups" (political elites) to identify "some dissent [as] just plain old nonsense and some new ideas are utterly unreasonable. The free flow of ideas is apparently not as free as one might think" (see Introduction; 2005; 64-65). David Ray Griffin elaborates upon this in detail in his 2011 book *Cognitive Infiltration: An Obama Appointee's Plan to Undermine the 9/11 Conspiracy Theory* where McCutcheon's concerns have presciently come to pass.

At the hands of industrialists, corporate bankers, and the political elites, humanity from time to time must protect itself from a thrashing of the cruelest proportions. Keep in mind just what Agenda 21 is advocating. In the BBC documentary *Planet Earth*, the author of the above statement, Edward Wilson, states that world population should be ideally kept at 500 million to 1 billion. This is apparently optimal for all life forms. What if at some future time the technological capabilities for accomplishing such a scenario (rapid depopulation) were to fall into the hands of eugenicists of the enthusiasm and determination of the Nazis? As of this writing in 2019 the planet's population is just upwards of seven-and-a-half billion human souls and rapidly approaching eight.

That's a lot of souls that need to go!

But I believe there has been improvement in the overall understanding of biology's role in human social life. In the 1990s a book titled *The Bell Curve* stirred controversy that Social Darwinism still had its apologists. Some saw alarm in the thesis, others a realistic assessment of human inheritable capabilities. Still others saw it as simply bad science. At least, however, the authors included, and duly emphasized (italics theirs) *"Measures of intelligence have reliable statistical relationships with important social phenomena, but they are a limited tool for deciding what to make of any given individual"* (21). If this is true, then why bother devoting over 800 pages to the issue? It seems that the attempt at a deflection away from the implications of their theories suggests the limited, arbitrary, and socially-divisive nature of their work. Paradigmatically-positive scientific theories do not have deleterious social consequences, only negative political and social theories do.

The implications of the book's thesis were strident enough to stir the now-late Stephen Jay Gould, one of America's evolutionist luminaries, to respond in the *New Yorker* in 1994.

> We must fight the doctrine of *The Bell Curve* both because it is wrong and because it will, if activated, cut off all possibility of proper nurturance for everyone's intelligence.... It is a manifesto of conservative ideology; the book's inadequate and biased treatment of data displays it primary purpose – advocacy.

If Gould is correct, and I suspect he is, the modern efforts to define who is fit to survive not only predates Darwin's own biological evolutionary theories, but, more ominously, survives to this day rearing its head seeking to convince the ruling masters that theirs is a rule by privilege and due to their innate perfection. Perhaps it is imbedded in the ideology of empire that such delusions of racial and cultural superiority must prevail. So much the better should religion facilitate the empire's myths. And better still to have the population focused upon a mythical battle that never saw the theatre of war but for the theatre of a courtroom and all the hyped drama therein.

Yes, so much the better for them (the social and political elites) that the masses focus upon a battle of good vs evil than have that same population catch wind of the plans in store for them. From their stationed positions in life, those *considering themselves* wise and honored make the weightiest of decisions for all of humanity. But can we be assured they will set the Common Good as their goal? Ever watchful and wary we must be.

REFERENCES

Books/Essays

Aunger, Robert (2000). *Darwinizing Culture: The Status of Memetics as a Science.* Oxford: Oxford University Press.

Barkow, Jerome H., Leda Cosmides, and John Tooby (1992). *The Adapted Mind: Evolutionary Psychology and the Generation of Culture.* New York: Oxford University Press.

Blackmore, Susan (1999). *The Meme Machine.* Oxford: Oxford University Press.

Boas, Franz (1911). *The Mind of Primitive Man.* New York: Macmillan.

Boas, Franz (1928). *Anthropology and Modern Life.* New York: Dover, 1986.

Bowker, John (1995). *Is God a Virus?* London: The Society for Promoting Christian Knowledge, (SPCK).

Boyer, Pascal (1994). *The Naturalness of Religious Ideas: A Cognitive Theory of Religion.* Berkeley: University of California Press.

Boyer, Pascal (2001). *Religion Explained: The Evolutionary Origins of Religious Thought.* New York: Basic Books.

Burkert, Walter (1996). *Creation of the Sacred: Tracks of Biology in Early Religions.* Cambridge, Massachusetts: Harvard University Press.

Cawthorne, Nigel (2012). *The Story of the SS: Hitler's Infamous Legions of Death.* London: Arcturus Publishing, 2014.

Dancocks, Daniel G. (1988). *Welcome to Flanders Field: The First Canadian Battle of the Great War: Ypres, 1915.* Toronto: McClelland & Stewart.

D'Aquili, Eugene and Andrew B. Newberg (1999). *The Mystical Mind: Probing the Biology of Religious Experience.* Minneapolis, Minnesota: Fortress Press.

Darwin, Charles (1859/1871). *The Origin of Species by Means of Natural Selection and The Descent of Man.* New York: Modern Library, no date.

Evans, Dylan and Oscar Zarate (1999). *Introducing Evolutionary Psychology*. New York: Totem Books.

Fussell, Paul (1975). *The Great War and Modern Memory*. New York: Oxford University Press, 2013.

Fussell, Paul (1983). *Class: A Guide Through the American Status System*. New York: Dorset, 1990.

Gosse, Edmund (1907). *Father and Son*. New York: W.W. Norton. 1963.

Gould, Stephen Jay (1994). "Curveball." *The New Yorker*. November 28. Book review; pgs. 139-149.

Griffin, David Ray (2000). *Religion and Scientific Naturalism: Overcoming the Conflicts*. Albany: State University of New York Press.

Herrnstein, Richard J. and Charles Murray (1994). *The Bell Curve: Intelligence and Class Structure in American Life*. New York: The Free Press.

Hinde, Robert A. (1999). *Why Gods Persist: A Scientific Approach to Religion*. London: Routledge.

Hofstadter, Richard (1944). *Social Darwinism in American Thought*. Boston: Beacon Press, 1992.

Johnson, Phillip K. (1991). *Darwin on Trial*. Downers Grove, Illinois: InterVarsity Press.

Kaelber, Lutz (2012). Eugenics: Compulsory Sterilization in 50 American States. Presentation about "eugenic sterilizations" in comparative perspective at the 2012 Social Science History Association. http://www.uvm.edu/~lkaelber/eugenics/ (accessed January 2019).

Kühl, Stefan (1994). *The Nazi Connection: Eugenics, American Racism, and German National Socialism*. New York: Oxford University Press.

Larson, Edward J. (1997). *Summer for the Gods: The Scopes Trial and America's Continuing Debate over Science and Religion*. New York: Basic Books, 2006.

Laughlin Jr., Charles D. and Eugene G. d'Aquili (1974). *Biogenetic Structuralism*. New York: Columbia University Press.

• Not strictly about religion and somewhat pre-Evolutionary Psychology, but it is an early example of the study of human social behavior and cultural studies benefiting from the knowledge of what biological evolution tells us about the brain and its functions. D'Aquili and Newberg carry the work forward – see their entry above.

Mencken, H.L. (1946). *Treatise on the Gods*. 2nd Ed. Baltimore: Johns Hopkins University Press. 1997. 1st edition 1930.

Midgley, Mary (1985). *Evolution as a Religion: Strange Hopes and Stranger Fears*. London/New York: Methuen.

Moreland, J.P. (1989). *Christianity and the Nature of Science: A Philosophical Investigation*. Grand Rapids, Michigan: Baker Book House.

Noll, Mark A. (2003). *A History of Christianity in the United States and Canada.* 1992. Grand Rapids, Michigan: Eerdmans.

Rolston, III, Holmes (1987). *Science and Religion: A Critical Survey.* Philadelphia: Temple University Press.

Sinclair, Upton (1937). *The Flivver King: A Story of Ford-America.* Chicago: Charles H. Kerr Publishing, 1984.

Snow, C.P. (1959). *The Two Cultures.* Cambridge: Cambridge University Press, 1993.

Stern, Alexandra Minna (2005). Sterilized in the Name of Public Health: Race, Immigration, and Reproductive Control in Modern California. *American Journal of Public Health.* July Volume 95, No. 7: pgs. 1128-1138. http://www. ncbi.nlm.nih.gov/pmc/articles/PMC1449330/ (accessed January 2019).

Tuchman, Barbara W. (1966). *The Proud Tower: A Portrait of the World Before the War: 1890-1914.* New York: Bantam Books, 1967.

Whitcomb, John C. and Henry M. Morris (1961). *The Genesis Flood: The Biblical Record and its Scientific Implications.* Grand Rapids, Michigan: Baker Book House, 1987.

Wilson, Edward O. (1978). *On Human Nature.* Cambridge, Massachusetts: Harvard University Press.

Wilson, Edward O. (1998). *Consilience: The Unity of Knowledge.* New York: Vintage Books, 1999.

Wright, Robert (1994). *The Moral Animal: The New Science of Evolutionary Psychology.* New York: Vintage Books, 1995.

Films/Documentaries

Bussler, Mark (2006). *World War I: American Legacy.* Narrated by David Carradine. http://topdocumentaryfilms.com/world-war-one-american-legacy/ (accessed January 2019). Also check YouTube. This is a very informative documentary with coverage of the themes discussed here, especially the new methods of war that so shocked the participants' psyches.

Cohen, Peter (1998). *Homo Sapiens 1900.* Directed by Peter Cohen. Arte Factum. Sweden.

Hachmeister, Lutz and Michael Kloft (2004). *The Goebbels Experiment: The Man Behind Hitler.* First Run Features, HMR Produktion Spiegel TV in association with BBC and History Television Canada. This film contains excerpts from Joseph Goebbels' diary beginning in 1924 and throughout his career with the Nazis.

Ober, Eric, producer (1998). *The Scopes "Monkey Trial"* – 1925 Landmark American Trials and CourtTV. (52 minutes) Narrated by James Naughton. (Not located on Internet). A similar documentary containing many of the same interviewees as this one and posted at YouTube is titled Scopes Monkey Trial. https://www.youtube.com/watch?v=xOgI0b-tEAg (accessed January 2019).

Young, Nedrick and Harold Jacob Smith (1960). *Inherit the Wind.* Produced and

Madalyn Murray O'Hair

3

THE COLD WAR RHETORIC OF ATHEISM

The delusion: *Marxist-Leninist Soviet-style atheism is at the heart of communism, socialism, and by extension, the social democracies of Europe. This atheism, most symbolized by Karl Marx's infamous statement that religion is the "opium of the people" and his desired outcome of the destruction of organized religions and religious freedom as conceived in the US, is at the heart of the organization of communist society. This creeping atheistic-communism has inspired political movements around the world and may even threaten religious freedom here within the U.S. as the nation and its interests become encircled by countries yielding to Soviet influence (e.g., Central and Latin America, Middle East) This atheism as a political ideology is intent upon infiltrating the USA and destroying all religion. Today, in a post-Soviet era, the threat lives-on in the form of liberal and humanistic ideologies which result in the denial of God's existence and all too often socialistic governments.*

The correction: *Atheism was a genuine but scapegoated and exaggerated ideology used by the US-intelligence services, political opportunists, mass-media, and of course American religious interests for their own reasons, to help propagandize Americans against the Soviet Union in order to justify billions of dollars of defense spending and, to no small degree, reinforce traditional religious and social values here at home and using neo-colonialism to spread those same values abroad. Intelligence documents reveal that the CIA (Central Intelligence Agency) systematically misrepresented the Soviet threat in its reports about Soviet nuclear missile capabilities to justify huge military and intelligence budgets. The exaggeration of an atheistic ideology as a threat is but one part of a much wider disinformation campaign waged against the American people in the interest of capitalistic Cold War politics (on behalf of American business interests) and fueling the growth of, what one president warned as a potential danger, the "military industrial complex."*

Quotes

The Creation is therefore an idea very difficult to dislodge from popular consciousness.

– Karl Marx, Economic and Philosophic Manuscripts of 1844, in Tucker, *The Marx-Engels Reader*, pg. 91

Our work, as I understand it, is based on a single assumption that the West is never going to be the aggressor. Thus, we do disagreeable things, but we are defensive. Our policies are peaceful, but our methods can't afford to be less ruthless than those of the opposition. Can they? No, I'd say, since the war, our methods, our techniques that is, and those of the communists, have become very much the same. Yes, I mean, occasionally, we have to do wicked things, very wicked things indeed, but you can't be less wicked than your enemy simply because your government's policies are benevolent…

– *The Spy Who Came in From the Cold* (1965)

After blowing-up a Kaos agent:
99: *Oh, Max. How terrible.*
86: *He deserved it 99, he was a Kaos killer.*
99: *Sometimes I wonder if we're any better, Max.*
86: *What are you talking about 99? We have to shoot and kill and destroy. We represent everything that's wholesome and good in the world.*

– *Get Smart* (Season 2, 1966: Island of the Darned)

We will never abandon our belief in God. [Long Applause] And we will never stop searching for a genuine peace, but we can assure none of these things America stands for through the so-called nuclear freeze solutions proposed by some.

– 40th U.S. President Ronald Reagan 1983 Speech to the National Assoc. of Evangelicals

In a certain sense, Habermas demands intrinsically a political proof of God. Only if religion would be able once more to unite personal and collective identity, could the charge of the obsolescence of religion be dropped. For such political proof of God Habermas does not so far see any indication in the late capitalistic or socialistic action systems.

– Rudolf Siebert, 1985 in *The Critical Theory of Religion*, pg. 83

NO RELIGION (and RELIGION)
As CULTURAL MEANS of COERCION[1]

> *Religious distress is at the same time the expression of real distress and the protest against real distress. Religion is the sigh of the oppressed creature, the heart of a heartless world, just as it is the spirit of a spiritless situation. It is the opium of the people*
> (Italics original, Marx and Engels, 42).

I f the Scopes Monkey Trial was, as argued in the previous chapter, at its core something in addition to a symbolic and ideological battle between science and religion or simply about the merits of human evolution vs creation, *but rather* it was one battle in a much bigger war for human dignity and a measure of equality and protection under the law in the face of a cruel Social Darwinism, *then perhaps* the trial can be understood as an example of the real and existential distress of the sort to which Marx and Engels allude.

To be sure, the Scopes Trial represents *religion's attempt* to push back against social injustices. Religion must use the tools at its disposal in the same way atheistic Marxism sought to bring about social and political reform with the regulation of private property and the economy. The language of religion with its appeal to a God (Transcendent Common Good) is its very essence and strength, and so must be regarded as part and parcel of its message. Grounding the individual rights of mankind in the notion of a God/Creator, simply yet most importantly, means those same rights cannot be vetoed by man, nature, or state.[2] This has social a political implications ... big ones ... especially in the age of unrestrained eugenics!

First and foremost, this linking of individual rights to an external Creator is a powerful legal protection for each human being and should in no-way be weakened or conceded in a democratic-republic form of government. This is what the founders established in the Declaration of Independence – all men created equal – and what is taken for granted in the Constitution – freedom of religion (see Quotes over the Centuries

---

1   The term "cultural means of coercion" is adopted from Stark and Bainbridge's 1987 work *A Theory of Religion* (ATOR Def. 40: 80/327) which creates and implements a theoretical and practical model of human religious activities that I am persuaded helps explain some of the religious-social-cultural realities American society has been and currently is experiencing. Hereafter, references to A Theory of Religion will appear as above: ATOR with the Axiom, Definition, and/or Proposition's corresponding pages numbers – see References for explanation of ATOR page citations.

2   In the views of the Constitution and its Bill of Rights, though at the time not extended to all Americans in a manner acceptable today, this was the principal intent: to limit the referencing of a precise deity in the first place. The rights of an individual are sacred, in this sense, and not limited to those of a particular sect or religion

preceding the Introduction). In this Constitutional understanding of Creator/religion, it is a protective set of rights untouchable by the temporal powers of nature, man, and state.

As for the anesthetizing effects of religion, is it to be questioned that to the truly oppressed person relief may come in any form and be welcomed indeed? How could one deny the relief, intangible as it may be, that religion affords? This is not to deny, underestimate, or undermine the spiritual power and efficacy of good deeds in the alleviation of suffering. It is simply to acknowledge that pain takes many forms, and so potentially may the remedies be commensurately numerous and polymorphous.

In a relatively affluent or comfortable society, the anesthetizing effects of religion originate from one's own mind – nothing more. Religion is opium *only to the particular individual* for whom such dulling measures and remedies innately appeal – e.g., someone looking for an excuse to do nothing will find it, and so a certain religious fatalism may charm him. Only starting with a negative view of religion would one be eager and willing to highlight such degrading examples. In contrast, no self-motivated and gregarious individual would be lulled into complacency and inertia by beliefs alone, of any sort, religious or otherwise. The observer must dig deeper to find the sources of religious beliefs and behavior.

In a practical and psychological sense, a fatalistic outlook of religion *does* have its usefulness in that spiritless situation – a situation in which one's own efforts will amount to nothing. Under such circumstances (e.g., the death of a loved one) fatalism is not fatalism at all, but realism. The impulse, for example, to pray pleading for rescue during the final moments of a doomed airliner can hardly be considered an outburst of irrationality!

Call it hope. Faith is a synonym, but with a bit more hopefulness. Hope and faith are required to achieve goals of many kinds, or, as in the analysis here, to achieve a vision of social arrangement that is yet to exist but can now (potentially) be realized. In this way, hope and faith are similar to the creative, aesthetic and artistic side of humanity. This, I maintain, is part of the humanities and literary arts that C.P. Snow discussed in *The Two Cultures* and to which I referred in the previous chapter.

Similarly, Religious Studies social theorists and historians Rodney Stark and William Bainbridge aptly note that "Human action would be impossible without a measure of faith and optimism, without the willingness to act despite uncertainty" (180).

How and why it is that *certain people act* while *others remain inert* in the face of these uncertainties is not something that can be effectively predicted by laws of nature. This is what gives humanity one of its great features of uniqueness: *it possesses a hope rooted in religion and doing so while in a desperate and hopeless world.* This non-rational feature of life ought not to be disparaged or viewed merely as irrational. And although it could be regarded as a last unproven source, bastion, and refuge of meaning in an otherwise meaningless world and existence, it also need not, consequently, be understood as the opium for which Marx criticizes it. This non-rational feature of life does, however, give the human species a certain degree of unpredictability.

Religion is far more often a motivator than a stifler of active behavior, and for behavior that is generally more positive than negative in its social outcome, i.e., do-goodism.[3] If religion is understood more precisely in its theoretical aspects rather than described metaphorically and typically too generally (Stark and Bainbridge, 11), then religion as a socially-expressed behavior can be better assessed in its logical forms and constituent elements. In addition, then, we can better understand how religion might facilitate social-political engineering (e.g., using the psychology of fear in religious manipulation) and the commandeering of society by political elites.[4]

There is every reason to suspect that these same elites themselves have set it among their priorities to understand religion in all its complexities in order to benefit from its utility in the organization and management of society. *A Theory of Religion* calls this *religious engineering* which is sometimes undertaken in order to deceive (*ATOR* Def. 78:173/329; P164: 173/339).

It is this subversive use of religion by political elites that is of particular concern to this book's arguments and only a theoretical understanding of religion will reveal its misuse by deception (resulting in delusions) by those same political elites. Communist Marxism's coercive use of *no religion* in society was upfront and a matter of policy. Whether the people approved or not, it was to be reckoned with at its face value, though it was implemented by means of a *repressive state* (*ATOR* Def. 43: 80/327). Not so, however, with American religious delusions. They are perpetuated far more covertly and violate, or at least render unintelligible, the laws of social theory because of the surreptitious nature in which they are implemented. This is a matter for social scientists to sort out and to which I make this attempt to instigate interest. In this way, American religious delusions are much more devious.

---

3   See also by Rodney Stark *America's Blessings: How Religion Benefits Everyone, Including Atheists* for some sociological research along these very lines.
4   More is written below on this topic of combining social scientific theory in *Religious Studies with Evolutionary Psychology.*

The public, however, has a far greater existential concern in understanding these actions of the political elites who use religion to subvert or destabilize the public's will through falsification of events and the manipulation of public opinion. Those same elites, being positioned as the governors of society, should, in fact *must*, be kept in check-and-balance per the nation's founding documents, i.e., the Constitution and Bill of Rights. Without exaggeration lives depend upon it, both foreign and domestic as the political elites will (religiously) engineer society to their advantage – here no less than the former Soviet state did so using atheism. The difference in the U.S. is the absence of the repressive state for use by the elites, at least in its overt form.[5] The net result is the same, however. In each respective society, those who can (the political elite) will "monopolize the use of coercion" (*ATOR* Def. 42: 80/327).

As for state sponsorship of atheism at the heart of the Russian-Soviet government, it was doomed to failure from the outset. Given that religion is a part of culture which accrues over centuries of generations, it cannot simply be legislated into non-existence. *ATOR* defines Culture as "the total complex of explanations exchanged by humans" (*ATOR* Def. 30: 63/327). Considering that culture accumulates through time and that religion is part of culture (*ATOR* P35 and P36: 63/332 and 64/333), it was sheer folly on the part of the political elites of Russia to think they could assemble the state without its people's religion.

In Marx's quote cited at the beginning of the chapter, he begins by acknowledging that the religious expression of distress is the same "real distress" that he is attempting to address with his socialistic vision. In his estimation, real and actual distress is brought about by the exploitation and alienation of the worker from his labor. While Marx's philosophic-political solutions are rooted in a materialistic understanding of humankind, they too serve as something of a drug to politically domesticate the population for the implementation of socio-economic policies. The ideology of the abolishment of private property as a means for egalitarianism, only serves to sever people from their families' pasts and traditions in the form of inheritance. Materialistic solutions – meaning the exclusive emphasis upon private property and labor[6] – ultimately prove illusory in the face

---

5   It is tempting to argue that P330 – a state consisting of a political monopoly is a repressive state—may also apply to the USA and that citizens ought not be fooled by the two-party political system (ATOR P330: 297/349). Given the scope of power (political and cultural) necessary to cover-up some of activities contributing to the religious delusions detailed in this book, P331 would also come into play – a state consisting of a political monopoly will seek to repress religion; (ATOR P331: 299/349).

6   Marx and Engels put it thus: "the theory of the Communists may be summed up in the single phrase: Abolition of private property" (1964: 82).

of cultural tradition and its powerful affiliate, nostalgia. These sentiments fall under the domain of the humanities and cannot so easily, if ever, be extinguished, but only externally suppressed – and seldom successfully short of complete cultural annihilation.

The Bolshevik Revolution of 1917 which brought the Marxist-Leninist communists to power in Russia and inaugurated the Soviet Union took place *only eight years before* the Scopes Trial and *during* WWI. Prior to and during WWII, Russia/Soviet Union was the U.S.'s ally against the Germans in both World Wars. Only subsequent to WWII and in the years beginning in 1946 and since did the two nations, the U.S. and U.S.S.R., part ways and embark upon the arms build-up, which was presented to their respective publics as ostensibly for the protection of the one from the other. The fact remains, America found it in its best interest to ally itself in those early years of the twentieth-century with the very same nation, its atheism notwithstanding, that one president would later call an "evil empire."

During moments of the Soviet era, the official status of the centuries-old Russian Orthodox Church was that of persecution and restriction. Initially repressed by the Bolsheviks, the Russian church would by the 1940s find some relaxation for its practices. Since political expediency typically wins the day in these matters, when the Politburo was threatened with Nazi fascism in 1942, the atheist government would solicit the church's support (Curtis). So much for the opiating and hypnotic effect of religion; when it is expedient, religion is sought for its assistance by the state. This should come as no surprise to the reader by now.

Nevertheless, the official state policy toward religions in the Russian-Soviet government was hostile. This put groups on the margins of political life; groups like the Jehovah's Witnesses,[7] Jews, and any other minority or fringe religious group was *de facto* in doubtful social standing. Typically, when repressive measures are exercised, socially conspicuous dissenting groups are the first to be scrutinized. Most of the rest go underground as did the Jehovah's Witnesses (whose refusal to pledge allegiance to any earthly national authority garnered suspicion as it had with the Nazis) and various evangelical-missionary groups who likewise risked reprisals. The state policy of atheism and *no religion,* enforced by a repressive state, served as a means of coercion and intimidation of religious groups

---

7   Jehovah's Witnesses are generally Christian by belief but with some modification to orthodoxy and the doctrine of the Trinity. More importantly, they are conspicuously apolitical and will pledge no allegiances to nations' governments, they sing no national anthems nor recite oaths or loyalties beyond their specific religion. They do not participate in the political life of any nation where they reside and consequently run afoul of regimes that demand a loyalty oath or test of allegiance to nationalism or patriotism.

and a test of loyalty by citizens to the state. In the west, we were reminded constantly in the media of the oppressive nature of atheist-Soviet communism. For example, testimonies of Jews who could not emigrate from the USSR to the newly founded state of Israel in 1948 and afterwards, would come to resonate in American churches during the Soviet period. Not all testimonies were groundless or exaggerated either, regardless of how they served the narrative of conservative American religious and political positions.

Whether thought ironic or not, here in America atheism was persecuted in the early days of this land of religious freedoms. For example, it wasn't uncommon according to the folk logic of the time of the early colonies that atheism merely on its own would have presumed guilt for an accused party in a criminal act; it was a moral given that a non-believer would have no restraining factors absent belief in eternal judgment. And while intolerance of atheism may have been more permissive in the early colonies (see chapter one; Corrigan, 36) intolerance of atheism *after* WWII, however, was not popular in the broader free-speech context, and religion came to be seen as something of a bully in many of its attempts to push-back against non-belief. American atheists before and during the Cold War faced stigmas, some harsher than others depending upon the times and circumstances.

Clearly, for the post WWII-era the threats and evils of German fascism and its vicious intolerances were the potential consequence inherent in any form of opposition to the expression of non-belief or dissident freedom of thought in general; take as examples the threats culminating in the 1950s Red Scare when high-profile people were shamelessly accused of being "commie" or "red" (and not so infrequently "homosexual") and their careers destroyed by the mere accusation.

In the context of the high stakes Cold War, and with the participation of actors from various federal government agencies, e.g., executive – FBI, CIA, military, legislative – Congressional oversight, hearings, and commissions, and the involvement of filmmakers in Hollywood, there was a great deal of *religious engineering* underway (*ATOR* Def. 78) on the part of the political elites. This means they consciously design elements of culture for use in what I refer to (in the Conclusion) as "American politics as national civic cult." Something of a culture war would ensue with Hollywood and a liberal, presumably atheist, left at the center of a storm of an eternal-moral tug-of-war. Religion came to be seen by Hollywood as a suppressor of free thought and speech, and ultimately artistic expression.

Recall the issues raised in the previous chapter about the 1960 film *Inherit the Wind* and its relationship to *actual* events. It is noteworthy to understand the movie-makers' motivation for slanting the storyline in the manner they did as that protesting the stifling of free speech by religion rather than religion pushing back against perceived social injustice. The reason being the film had far more to do with the Red Scare of the 1950s[8] and the prohibition of teaching evolution as a matter of freedom of thought and speech, which, if recalled, played a remarkably small role in the existential historical account of the story. *The film, then, was principally about religious fundamentalism stifling the free speech of science.* Watching the movie in 1960 it would have been very clear what the plotline was alluding to about the recent past: Senator Joe McCarthy's irrational fears of communism sending chills through society with fears of persecution for those who are deemed communist sympathizers. The implications for free speech and the stifling of intellectual creativity knew potentially no bounds with the likes of Senator McCarthy at the microphone.

Whether stemming from religious fundamentalism or irrational political fears, a witch-hunt is a witch-hunt.

And so, *no religion* and *religion* fought it out, much as they do today, in the social-cultural realm dominated by popular culture. And as these things go, there were victims along the way, and those harboring divine doubts were among them.

Though counter to the ideals of free thought and speech, the unpopularity and stigmatization of atheism as an adjunct to communism during the Cold War lead to an exaggeration of perceived threats that come from *within* America in addition to the external Soviet military threat. This idea was most-especially promoted in conservative churches. Atheism and atheists found themselves on the harsh end of a rhetorical smear campaign.[9] Very often liberal left or secular humanistic philosophies were to blame for the infusion of atheism in popular culture, or so the traditionalist/conservative religious communities would have Americans believe. A natural starting point for their critique of the humanistic/atheistic philosophy of communism was the science that justified such godless philosophies in the first placed, and which made god's role in creation unnecessary: namely, Darwinian evolution.

8   There were two Red Scares in American history: the first in the 1920s as a reaction-response to the Bolshevik Revolution and new Russian government in the form of the Soviets; and then the 1950s persecution of communists by Senator Joseph McCarthy.

9   The atheist/communist vs religious/capitalist ideological split also served to neatly divide the electorate in the mold of the two-party system, which itself is key to consolidation of political power in the hands of the political elites.

Evolution leads to atheism which leads to communism; its natural progression was a theme resonating with a newly-growing religious movement, or at least a renewed interest in religion on the part of increasing numbers of Americans during the 1950-60s and ultimately leading to the formation and growth of the Moral Majority and Christian Evangelical phenomenon of the 1970-1980s.[10]

History records: "In 1961, a bill to repeal Tennessee's monkey laws, still in force thirty years after the Scopes trial, met prompt and passionate rejection by people who argue that evolution theory "drives God out of universe" and "leads to communism" (Nelkin, 34). The next year saw the Supreme Court ban school prayer. To fundamentalists it must have seemed as though America had gone off the rails. And in a way, it had.

> In reality, the 1962 Supreme Court decision meant the beginning of the end of Christian cultural hegemony in America. Banning official school prayers was a blow to civil religion, to the Puritan-inspired image of America as a Christian commonwealth, a nation whose institutions operate with divine sanction. During the 1960s, the antiwar movement, the civil rights movement, the sexual revolution, and the women's movement began to challenge the assumption that as long as God was in His heaven, all was right with America (Flake, 37).

This was no longer the America of the Pilgrims. Even the forefathers' liberal definitions of god and religion were unrecognizable in an atheistic America seemingly infested with internal apostasy. Compounding this internal threat was the ever-growing and menacing military of the USSR. The nature of atheist-communism and the governments it produced were imagined and projected as being imposed here – with atheism paving the way. A generation of school children would rehearse "duck and cover" in the classroom to bring home the nearness of the looming communist threat. As one might imagine, this made no small impression upon the minds of generations of young Americans.

Atheists have long pushed-back against the notion of the atheism-communism connection. "This irrational and grossly unfair practice of linking atheism with communism is losing popularity and is rarely encountered any longer except among political conservatives" (Smith, 22). This was the judgment of an author whose book on atheism has served, accord-

---

10   This period also saw the rise in the popularity of New Religious Movements (NRMs), perhaps as a way to express religious sentiments without resorting to the Protestant Christian political power of the establishment or being classified as atheist-communist.

ing to the publisher, as "the world's most popular book on unbelief." Be that as it may, the atheists' remains an uphill climb for widespread cultural sympathy (and even more so political sympathy – no President of the United States to this day dare fail to say "God Bless America" at the close of a public address).

Why is this so? And should it remain so? This is for society to decide as it surely will. The challenge is to do so in the most humane and Constitutional way achievable. The terminology of the Declaration of Independence wherein "all Men are created equal, that they are endowed by their Creator with certain unalienable Rights" most certainly encompasses the atheist and serves as her protective legal layer that is not be compromised. For Karl Marx, religion would be the last vestige of irrationality and therefore held no positive or uniquely protective human rights significance. But this overlooks the political potential of religion in society in which religion functions as a legal concept imparting certain rights. This is overlooked or jettisoned to the peril of individual rights.

For their part, atheists might as well pack-it-up and go home if their goal is a world free of religious beliefs – a godless world is a fantasy and dream of people such as Karl Marx and Sigmund Freud who find religion an obstacle to progress and the development of a modern civil society. Furthermore, as if to mock and not just contradict these atheist wishful-thinkers, one additional legacy of this Cold War history is a strong streak of Biblical Literalism in the American people's thinking. Even today, nearly one third of Americans believe that the "Bible is the actual word of God and is to be taken literally, word for word" (Blow). This is quite remarkable in an age dominated by technology and a rampant materialism. This tells us that side-by-side in the mind of modern mankind there exists room for the two cultures, the scientific (rational) and the religious-artistic-humanities (non-rational).

In the political world, the two cultures have been theatrically, if disingenuously due to religious engineering, positioned in the stance of a duel – similarly as creation-evolution and science-religion. Social understanding and progress have been made in spite of, and sometimes as a result of (as in chapter two), that very same duel. But in the end the duel is illusory. Science has not the power to explain away religion, nor should it be (mis)credited as having such power. In the Cold War era, science/evolution and its bastard child atheism were a matter of pure politics and super power expediency in the service of *religious engineering and the manipulation of public opinion.*

Take for example Stark and Bainbridge's assertion that "it was the religious revival of the period immediately after World War II and the continuing encounter with stubborn religious effects on such diverse matters as voting and fertility that led to resurrection of active research on religion" (1987; 12). The *stubborn religious effects* to which they refer are not only the result of the socio-religious analyses of the type their theory addresses (rational exchanges within society's religions), but in addition it must be considered, or at least factored-in, the *disinformation* intentionally spread within society that distorts normal "exchange rates." I suspect this is why even a sophisticated and highly-developed theory as that produced by Stark and Bainbridge can fall short and why the latter author laments (in a separate book) the ineffectiveness in predicting certain types of religious behavior (Bainbridge, 359).

This disinformation rippling within academic research may in part stem from the very financial sponsorship of that same research by U.S. federal government agencies (McCutcheon, 2004; this is also addressed in the Conclusion to this book). And although other Religious Studies researchers determine there was "no evidence that any direct support, whether from government agency or private foundation ... [that] research agendas were influenced to any great degree by specific Cold War values, despite the assertions of Jacob Neusner and Russell McCutcheon" (Wiebe, 280), given what the subsequent decades have revealed in religious American history, especially as detailed in the chapters of this book, I'm suspecting that Wiebe is underestimating "what happens behind closed doors: his [C.P. Snow's] assumed model of how the 'two cultures' thesis bore upon policy-making consisted of a small group of politicians and their advisers" (Collini, lxx). By 1959, when C.P. Snow delivered his original lecture that would result in *The Two Cultures*, he was attuned to the shadowy nature of power – we would do wisely to also be so attuned.

As for Religious Studies as an academic field developing under these conditions, it's difficult not to wince reading the following passage by a noted anthropologist who was most influential in today's field of Religious Studies as it emerged from earlier established disciplines:

> In these theories [anthropological theories of the nineteenth and early twentieth centuries] it was assumed, taken for granted, that we were at one end of the scale of human progress and the so-called savages were at the other end, and that, because primitive men were on a rather low technological level, their thought and custom must in all respects be the antithesis of ours. We are rational, primitive

peoples prelogical, living in a world of dreams and make-believe, of mystery and awe; *we are capitalists, they communists*; we are monogamous, they promiscuous; we are monotheists, they fetishists, animists, pre-animists or what have you, and so on (italics mine; Evans-Pritchard, 105).

Communists? Primitives as communists? This was the judgment of British[11] anthropologists during the Cold War. A rather curious conclusion indeed. Indigenous people were viewed as communists by the mid-twentieth century, and this was yet one more dimension and characteristic of their savagery. Applying the term "communist" to the social organizations of indigenous peoples reflects the political orientation of the anthropological writers themselves. Evans-Pritchard's comments are made in 1965, well into the second of the two Red Scares (see footnote 55). Anthropologists attaching the communist label to research subjects would have been a natural epistemological reflex if working with the assumption that capitalism is politically superior and more advanced than communism.

In hindsight, the best way to comprehend this dynamic is not one of mal-intentions on the part of scholars, but more so that of "he who pays the piper calls the tune" and the subtle influence of the agenda having been set ahead of time by the sponsor. Even Wiebe argues that there's no way for "scientists and academics as much as … independent intellectuals in society at large" to fully escape the influences of the overarching political reality of the Cold War (269). Academic research was viewed as a frontline in combating communism and "facts about communism" (most especially the arms race and military spending as evidence of their hunger for world domination) would be casting a long shadow over all sorts of social-scientific researches.

Consider also as part of the "religious revival" referred to by the sociologists above that the insertion of God into the Pledge of Allegiance in 1954 was *done in an act of Congress* and constitutes a not-so-subtle form of psychological coercion upon a society in which there was to be no state-sponsorship religion. Fortunately for those who would be approving of the change, the word "God" is, at least, in keeping with the tradition of the founders and the notion of "benign monotheism" as the underpinning and guarantor of individuals' rights. The word has remained in the pledge without successful challenge for sixty-years and does not appear to be facing any contest soon.

---

11   Keep in mind, Donald Wiebe was referring to North American scholars and E.E. Evans Pritchard is British. The overarching threat of Soviet communism was, however, directed at both and the West generally felt under the same existential threats.

For those not approving of the change, protest was and remains unpopular and it represented something of a bullying on the part of religion. People felt *coerced* into religion, or at the very least, verbalizing homage to religious concepts they may in fact reject. Nevertheless, the mid-1950s was the peak of the Red Scare and Americans of all stripes were willing to wear their religion on their breast in the form of the pledge of allegiance if need be, to fight the dreaded atheist commie. Catholics, Jews and Protestants united under the banner of monotheism during the Cold War as a form of national faith (Prothero, 260).

Once the Red Scare quieted down, the 1960s became dominated by other issues such as the rise of the counterculture, beginnings of Vietnam War, Blacks' and Women's Liberation together with a general liberalization and pluralistic trend in culture. By the late 1970s religious activism began again. Broadcast television brought a few Christian programs into the home, but they were scant. As the 1970s ended, the nation was on the verge of installing a new technology into Americans' living rooms: cable television. It will serve the interests of a proliferating electronic church movement that will come to be termed *televangelism* and will have a parallel effect as that of radio during the Scopes Trial. This will signal the beginnings of the Religious Right and one of its major political activists The Moral Majority which couples the legacy in America of using religion as a cultural means of coercion, or in this case influence, but now returns its attention to an external enemy, the communist "evil empire" and its by now *absolute* existential threat to all of us in the age of nuclear annihilation.

SELLING an EXPENSIVE THREAT to the AMERICAN PEOPLE

With the world's biggest and most destructive weapons in the hands of godless men, then just about any apocalyptic scenario is potential and could more-or-less easily be sold to the American people as their political/existential reality. It is only logical that everything within the powers of the rulers must be engaged to fight such a threat – secrecy not excluded. The biggest and most destructive weapons of mankind were created in complete secret from the American people and cloaked in disinformation. For example, "America's work on the atomic bomb during World War II was shrouded in secrecy. Newspapers were asked not to print, in any context, phrases such as 'atomic energy,' and they did not" (Zuckermann, 16).

In such cases, silence is much more than golden, it is the life-essence of the project at hand, and the management of public becomes an end unto itself. The media's complicity in covering-up the nature of military activities is key to their success. One of the earliest of the deceptions lead-ing into the Cold War would be the surreptitious importation of Nazis into the U.S. under Operation Paperclip.[12] After WWII, "For the military, especially the air force, it was an ideal moment to fuel hysteria in order to win blanket authorization for the indiscriminate issue of visas to Ger-mans, despite the infamy or notoriety of their crimes" (Bower, 233).

The end of WWII in 1945 brought the end of Nazi fascism in Germany and pretty much *immediately* the new threat of Russian Soviet commu-nism became the focus of America's political energy. These were the con-glomeration of states swallowed-up by Soviet Russia in their advance to Berlin, which became the actual dividing lines between east and west; the eastern nations falling behind an "iron curtain."[13]

And so would commence the four-and-half-decades-long Cold War from 1945-1989 in which the U.S. and U.S.S.R. spent billions of dollars arming and preparing themselves for mutually assured destruction – MAD – with nuclear weapons. Both nations possessed long-range intercontinen-tal ballistic missiles (ICBMs) and the big fear was that scores if not hun-dreds (maybe even thousands, at the peak of the arms race each nation had assembled in excess of 50,000 ICBMs) of missiles may reign down on the nation. American school children dove under their desks in preparation.

Unexpectedly perhaps, *popular religion* and the *threat of no religion* together come to aid and abet the armaments build-ups. Religion sells fear, fear sells weapons. The January 1961 Eisenhower "military industrial complex" speech in the context of the Cold War warns the nation what is going and conservative religious-propagandizing in America was very helpful in selling the threat and manufacturing the defense. With nation-al security a priority and secrecy as a *modus operandi*, the books would be cooked to no small degree. In over-selling the amount the evil empire was spending on military expenditures, the Central Intelligence Agency (CIA) routinely exaggerated the threat to the homeland, as we now call it. One report sums it this way:

> It is disturbing that for the past 25 years the CIA has systematically tended to overstate Soviet ME [military expenditures] relative to U.S. ME; that the DIA estimates of ME and ME/GNP are taken se-riously in light of the flawed nature of DIA estimating techniques; and that under these circumstances, the DIA, whose figures for So-

---

12   Operation Paperclip is discussed in more depth in chapter five.
13   The metaphor of the iron curtain itself implied a political world of secrecy and danger to which Americans and Westerners generally could only imagine and fear.

viet ME, growth of ME, and ME/GNP usually exceed those of the CIA, appears to be "persuading" the CIA to adopt its estimates of ME/GNP, as well as an expansive definition of Soviet ME that is not comparable with U.S. ME (Holzman, 131).[14]

As if to underscore the importance that the role of a single individual may possess in cultivating these political narratives "One man, Paul Nitze, was behind the three most important reports that promoted the perception of a Soviet threat against the United States after World War II... NSC68 [1950], the Gaither report of 1957," and most important to the historical perspective cultivated in the thesis of this book:

> Nitze was also the founder of the Committee on the Present Danger (CPD). This was a political action group that brought about the remilitarization of the U.S. in the 1950s by promoting the ideas in NSC68. CPD was resurrected in 1975 and 1976 by Cold War hawks, including Donald Rumsfeld, who wanted to eliminate the policy of détente and Soviet containment in favor of another military build-up. The group was resurrected yet again in 2004 to promote a more aggressive War on Terror (see References to the Conclusion; Ryan, 179-180).

Cold War threats provide opportunity for something else: the extension of American empire in the form of neo-colonialism. This was part and parcel of the growth of the CIA as it spread across the world acting on behalf American interests and the containment of the Soviet Union. Created in 1947. Also populated by Operation Paperclip émigrés, the CIA spanned-out across the globe in their quest to gather intelligence on communist infiltrations in third-party countries, which it was commonly told to Americans was part of the Soviets own encirclement strategy of the USA. Cuba being a most memorable example.

Neo-colonialism was justified though unspoken under the banner of the Cold War. "For the methods of the neo-colonialists are subtle and varied.

---

14   Curiously, in the C-SPAN program listed in the References on "CIA Estimates of Soviet Military Expenditures," the panelists represent a think-tank named the American Enterprise Institute. One panelist, Richard Perle, was an insider in the second Bush administration under whose watch the 9/11 attacks occurred. The AEI which sponsors the C-SPAN discussion is a conservative and neo-conservative association. They, by the way, argue that our intelligence services underestimated what the Soviets were spending, a contradiction to Holzman. Apparently, the CIA "worshiped the model" it was using to estimate/calculate spending which led it into any number of errors, according to these panelists. In addition, many of the members of AEI were to be associated with the Project for the New American Century or PNAC, which provided the statement "New Pearl Harbor" and which came to inform the parlance of 9/11Truth discourse (see Conclusion insert; "Bibliography of David Ray Griffin on 9/11Truth," 2004/2008).

THE COLD WAR RHETORIC OF ATHEISM

They operate not only in the economic field, but also in the political, religious, ideological and cultural spheres" (Nkrumah, 239). Kwame Nkrumah, having served as Ghana's President from 1961-1966, saw firsthand the actions of the western powers, increasingly that of the US's influence, and the foreign economic control over his own nation and the African continent.

Nkrumah observed that "Foremost among the neo-colonialists is the United States, which has long exercised its power in Latin American..." He continues:

> Fumblingly at first she turned toward Europe, and then with more certainty after world war two when most countries of that continent were indebted to her. Since then with methodical thoroughness and touching attention to detail, the Pentagon set about consolidating its ascendancy, evidence of which can be seen all around the world. Who really rules such places as Great Britain, West Germany, Japan, Spain, Portugal or Italy? If General de Gaulle is "defecting" from U.S. monopoly control, what interpretation can be placed on his 'experiments' in the Sahara desert, his paratroopers in Gabon, or his trips to Cambodia and Latin America?
>
> Lurking behind such questions are the extended tentacles of the Wall Street octopus. And its suction cups and muscular strength are provided by a phenomenon dubbed "The Invisible Government," arising from Wall Street's connection with the Pentagon and various intelligence services (239-240).

The notion of an "invisible government"[15] is something that may not be familiar to all, but it is nevertheless a viable construct that can be detected with historical research by way of its actors and their actions. In its own way, the thesis of this book overlaps with that of an invisible group of actors (political elites) interjecting their influence in the nation's events (religious engineering) with very little public detection let alone scrutiny. Not that it/they cannot be detected, but for the political structures currently in place hinder its/their detection. Independent research, however, makes it abundantly clear that its influence is present.

The global spread of godless communism and its encirclement of America would become a big theme in the fiery sermons of Jimmy Swag-

---

15   We are cycling at this moment back through the topic of "conspiracies" touched-on in the Introduction. With this topic comes a vocabulary of descriptive, if colorful, terminology such as *secret government, shadow government, secret team,* and numerous other terms out of intelligence-espionage studies. Nkrumah goes on to quote at length from The Invisible Government by David Wise and Thomas B. Ross an adjunct topic to that here and well worth pursuing separately. If one has any doubts about the existence of a largely unseen government surveillance apparatus then I refer to the PBS documentary *Top Secret America: The Hidden Legacy of 9/11.*

gart in the 1980s on the threats of communism creeping up through Central America to the point where Americans will fall directly under the hammer and sickle themselves because "it will be El Paso next, or Tucson next...," you get the idea. These sermons were one manifestation I witnessed personally attending Pentecostal services in the early 1980s. The result was a form of neo-colonialism thoroughly justified by conservative Christianity and its fear of communist atheism.

In Central America, Liberation Theology (LT) was a favorite target of the Christian Right during the 1970s-80s. LT was used as an example of surreptitious communist infiltration into the church itself and thereby used an ideological weapon with conservative religious believers. In a way, Christianity was pitted against itself. LT was viewed as a theologizing of Marxist communism so therefore ultimately it abandons the orthodox notions of conservative Christianity (Nash, 6-7).

Liberation Theology was far more a threat to capitalism than it was a threat to the Christian message. Only in the highly politically-charged discourse of American right-wing religion can the activities of nuns and priests on behalf of displaced peasant farmers to defend them against multi-national conglomerates be considered an act of sabotage. Religion and empire in an age of neo-imperialism can be a dangerous mix as many clergy found out.

American right-wing conservative-style religion as we know it today was conceived during this time, though was only in its embryonic stages as a political force. Through the 1950s and 1960s liberalism became synonymous with communism and remains so to this day in some media spheres – FOX News would be a prime example. One observer notes, "Much of the intellectual anticommunism that existed had been heavily subsidized by the CIA (as described [in 1999] in fascinating detail by Frances Stonor Saunders in *The Cultural Cold War*). The resulting climate meant that the number of people working from a liberal viewpoint on American political issues, particularly on foreign policy, was severely limited (Schiffrin, 39).

The 1970s and 1980s saw the development and maturation of this right-wing Christianity as an American political forces as it crystallized its media savvy in the newly emerging phenomenon of *televangelism*. The installation of cable television into millions of residences brought audiences the very messages the political elites desired using religion through channel ownership by corporations. It opened-up venues to attract audiences by the millions, which it did.

Early in the cable years (1983) the airing of a CBS television program titled *The Day After*, in which the U.S. and Soviets launch hundreds of nuclear missiles at each other, had an audience of 100 million and demonstrated the best Hollywood could do at the time to vividly and frighteningly portray the dangers and devastation – MAD-ness. The world's atomic scientists put the minute-hand at "three minutes to midnight" on the Doomsday Clock not long after that program aired. One wonders, who is guiding whom?

Televangelists declared the potentially devastating horrors of the nuclear-armed commies too, and loudly. According to Hadden and Swann:

> To fundamentalists, the world is one giant battleground for the struggle between good and evil, which rages in all realms: moral, religious, social, spiritual, and political. There is no room in fundamentalism for differing social perspectives or political systems. Compromise is sin. This outlook informs their view of U.S. national defense and foreign policy. Many of them fully expect a final apocalyptic war between the United States and the Soviet Union – and they support this expectation with what they regard as specific prophecies in the Bible (94).

By 1988, Pat Robertson launched a Presidential campaign on his program the *700 Club*, which first began on radio in the late 1970s and then grew into broadcast then cable television and doing so along with any number of other evangelists on the small screen during the 1980s. Some few are still on today in this second decade of the twenty-first century – aged as they are. Sociologists noted at the time of Robertson's presidential run, "Perhaps Robertson alone will stand firmly with Reagan in insisting that American must stand up against communism in Central America. Should that happen, it could be a critical advantage" (Hadden and Shupe, 277). As it turned-out, it was not enough of an advantage to secure Robertson the nomination, but his message was certainly not lost on the American people as he did survive the first round of the primaries.

Jerry Falwell warned on the front page in his 1980 manifesto for Christian evangelical renewal in America titled *Listen, America!*:

> Everyone agrees that it is extremely important to rebuild the free enterprise system in America. If capitalism and free enterprise fail in America, everything else will be moot. Again, Americans everywhere are saying, 'I hope it isn't too late. I hope we can catch up with the Soviet Union.' But the real battle for America's survival lies in her ability to re-arm morally. Liberal forces such as the abortionists, the homosexuals, the pornographers, secular humanists, and Marxists have made significant inroads in the giant's house and have carried off much of our goods" (from the Bantam Books paperback edition of 1981, see References chapter one).

117

From his religious understanding of America's history and divine pur-pose in the world, we can better understand the words of the same author in the wake of the September 11, 2001 attacks (see the final quote be-fore Introduction). In Falwell's estimation, due to our failure to "morally re-arm," God was not obligated to protect the nation from its enemies. In the politically and militarily-tense atmosphere of the Cold War, this portrayal of atheism was used against Americans to demonize all sorts of movements. The rise of AIDs in the gay and drug-addict populations in the early 1980s were met with a certain apathy and lack of compassion by the conservative religious community in general and the Reagan adminis-tration was roundly criticized for providing no leadership during the early stages of the crisis. But with the evil empire on the march, there were oth-er more pressing, and more profitable, crises to manage.

Atheism, communism, evolution, along with the occasional rumbling of Islam's growing "power,"[16] terrorism, and weapons of mass destruction were packaged and peddled to the American public just as today's chief threats (radical Islam and sleeper cells) justifying huge military and other security expenditures. The political elites are able to effectively control the message and tone of public opinion, and this includes public opinion *about* religion, as there are many eager voices willing to participate in and benefit from the demagoguery. If the political elites are intent upon using religion to their advantage, then it serves citizens' best interests to have as clear an understanding of religions' roles in society, and some sense of the civic conduct that would emerge from these legitimate roles. I take for granted that any legitimate implementation of religion would foster civic pluralism, civil harmony, the Transcendent Common Good, the common good for the secularists and non-religious persons, and all outcomes striv-ing for the humanitarian approach to governance. These tendencies have *not* been what we've seen produced by the social-cultural-political system in the name of religion – alas, quite the contrary.

SEEKING a BETTER UNDERSTANDING of RELIGION for the SAKE of CIVIL SOCIETY: the *CRITICAL THEORY of RELIGION*

In addition to using Stark and Bainbridge's *A Theory of Religion*, I sup-plement my analysis of religion in these American historical delusions with the *Critical Theory of Religion* for its particular insights, which I deem highly relevant to the research in this book. Resulting from its own histor-ical genesis (in Germany during the ascension of Nazism), and its stated

---

16   See book photo caption in Postscript to chapter eight.

epistemological[17] intentions, Critical Theory seeks to reconcile *philosophy* and *real life* (Gary M. Simpson, 4; Siebert, 1985: 2).

But it is more than this; *Critical Theory* remains acutely self-aware of and focused upon *the source of human suffering*. Concern for human suffering is *the* hallmark concern of genuine religion, it must also, then, be part of the measurement by most any theory of religion. And, if that theory is to have any explanatory vigor, it must be *honest* about the source of that human suffering, even when that source emerges from the state and its officials from which/whom retaliatory measure may be a risk (see last sentence of next footnote).

This is the "critical" element about critical theory, as distinct from "conventional" theories about religion, e.g., sociological, anthropological, and psychological, etc., which all too often operate in something of a theoretical bubble with little or no awareness of the political forces coming to bear upon either their subjects or their theories.[18] Worse still, these conventional theories of religion are all too often solicited in the service of political ideologies and the empires they create, as with the reference to anthropologist Evans-Pritchard earlier in this section and his equating primitives to communists!

The understanding of religion provided by *Critical Theory* ought to aid the citizen in identifying *proper vs illegitimate* religion in society. The degree to which religion serves as an antidote to exploitation is the measure

---

17   Very generally, epistemology consists of those commonly-held ideas about knowledge, the limits of knowledge, and what is valid knowledge? Or consider the question, *how do we know about reality?* Immediately, the difference is apparent between *religion* and *science*, or similarly, and referring C.P. Snow's *The Two Cultures*, *science* and the *humanities/arts*. One important example as it relates to topics in this book, Biblical Literalism (a relevant issue later in this chapter and in chapter four), has certain epistemological assumptions about the Bible that pit it against a pluralistic national creed with civil rights as currently conceived. I would argue that there is no need for Biblical Literalism to take the political positions it does (e.g., anti-abortion or anti-gay rights) except for religious engineering and the goals of religious leaders. Their leaders could always, if they chose to do so, provide, create, or religiously innovate an alternate interpretation without abandoning the entire belief system (ATOR P223: 220/343). This is what I see as one of the main imperatives for current evangelical thought if it is to remain relevant in the modern world.

18   Some quarters of Religious Studies in recent decades have been better self-aware of the political nature of its work. Two books, Arnal and McCutcheon (2013) and Chidester (2014), orient the reader to this type of analysis. In the end, however, these fall far short of the *Critical Theory of Religion* in that they provide more the *philosophical* analyses but tend to deemphasize the *real life* of current political history as it implicates the activities of the contemporary nation-state and its crimes. Chidester's other, prior work (updated 2003) on Jonestown echoes the rhetoric of "conspiracy theory" equally so as the politico-media and academic establishments and their discourses. In Chidester's case, conspiracy theories are "strategies of political distancing" (36) designed to serve various political and psychological interests, and the involvements of government asserted in this book in chapter six are never entertained as serious alternatives. Then again, and as a chilling reminder of who is boss, critical theorist of religion Rudolf Siebert did receive FBI visits to his home in the 1960s and 1970s and a "large political police file" was kept on him during his teaching career in Michigan (Siebert, 2012: 80, 130).

of that same religion's worth. Thus, all religions, when operating at their epistemological best, understand reality and human action in relation to suffering or the potential for human suffering. The topics of most of the chapters of this book should be sufficient evidence that civilian populations are vulnerable to the vagaries of the political elites and their mostly-hidden interests and agendas. The remedy is really quite simple: to restore honesty (*ATOR* Def. 80: 174/329) to politics and bring to an end the deceptions (*ATOR* Def. 79: 173/329) that have been created by those with power (*ATOR* Def. 15: 33/326) to extort high exchanges rates from the less powerful and thereby create suffering.

A *Critical Theory of Religion*, if satisfactorily developed and applied to religion's actual (real life) roles in society, should point-the-way for religion's proper use in that same society with the guaranteed outcomes of civic pluralism and a healthy civil society with strong and transparent institutions. This is an imperative in a multi-cultural society such as the United States, or any nation that hosts immigrants, or allows any level of cultural globalization (the international freedom of exchange of information and physical movement) for its citizens.

> Religion (ri·lij´in) n. *refers to the collection of all human behaviors that refer to the supernatural, a God or gods, and/or to a life beyond this one or any other type of description of the universe beyond the realm of the senses as we commonly understand those to be, the so-called "five senses"*
> – author's definition
>
> A *Theory of Religion* defines religion as *"systems of general compensators [the promise of rewards] based on supernatural assumptions"*
> – Def. 22: 39/326

Ultimately, the fatal weakness of Marx and Engels' thought on religion is that it simply fails to recognize the multi-faceted motivational dimensions of religion, and that these are deeply culturally-ingrained within us. Human beings are compelled to action guided and directed not solely by religions' teachings and worldviews, but by host of dynamic human factors. These are better explained by the philosophical-social-psychology-biological sciences than a purely psycho-economic history and understanding of human action, as Marx did. For the Russian people and those who fell under Soviet domain, sadly, the implementation of a public policy regarding religion based in this narrow understanding of religion did not promote civic pluralism. And it was certainly unable to cultivate the religious freedoms taken for granted in American Constitutional government.

A combination of the sociological theories of *ATOR* (science) supplemented by the *Critical Theory of Religion* (humanities) and implemented courageously by scholars, journalists, politicians, activists, and humanitarians in society, ought to aid in producing the civic pluralism required in the twenty-first century. This will better serve our understanding of history, and how the future should look. Religious beliefs and behavior are and will be part of that history and must be studied and judged empirically as any other human phenomenon and integrated into the other human sciences. Since humans must navigate religions' traditions in their historical contexts, better understanding the principles of how humans do so is more revealing of not only religion's efficacy as a social phenomenon, but how it is that human beings organize their lives in the context of the survival mechanisms available to them.

The net effect of this new science and a better understanding of religion, will *not* result in a falling away from or abandonment of religion and traditional beliefs and values, as has been prognosticated at other times with other sciences. Instead, there will be a fuller understanding of the human being and his evolutionary interaction with nature, including other human beings – inter-subjectivity, the cognitively complex nature of these interactions, and the realization that one's biology plays only a partially-determinant role in the individual's life.

Stark and Bainbridge conclude *A Theory of Religion* with the calculation, "nowhere on the horizon of human progress do we see any prospect that the secular exchange of rewards, on which society is based, can ever eliminate the existential basics which sustain religion" (1987: 318). This research, admirable as it is, is itself vulnerable to the effect of the *manipulation of the historical record*. In the development of most social scientific theories, common epistemological assumptions about information and its credibility are rarely questioned. The sources of information are taken at face value with little to no awareness or acknowledgment of the potential for manipulation of facts.

I consider this an egregious and inexcusable failure, and a reversible one, on the part of the academic field of Religious Studies. If it is not those scholars within the field to clarify and correct this historical record, then who will it be? The important point is that the historical record is subject to manipulation and must be corrected accordingly if social scientific theorizing is to have any predictive value as a science. Let not the awareness of this failure throw into doubt *altogether* the utility of the theories developed in Religious Studies. I believe that, in fact, the opposite is true. The proper refinement of the existing theories in conjunction with Critical Theory will even help reveal the presence of contamination in the historical record and be able to highlight it.

In addition, this fuller understanding of religion need not be limited only to those academics interested in these types of questions and answers. Civil society in general is better prepared for pluralism when it possesses an adequate understanding of religion. To most of civil society, from whom the data of religious life in the world arises, religious beliefs and practices will continue on as before. Religion will operate within the confines of cultures, at times embracing and extolling it, at other times well as rebuffing and remolding it. But scientific knowledge generally, and a better understanding of religion by society can and will never banish religious beliefs and behavior. And there should be no expectation of such. Better that citizens should understand religion as it is in real life, coupling this with a sensitivity for the potential of human suffering, including that inflicted by the state's actions. This knowledge of the complexity of religion and an awareness of the attendance of *unpredictability* in human behaviors along with humanity's aspirations of hope, will of necessity produce a healthy civil society, civic pluralism, the common good/Transcendent Common Good.

Marx justified his ideas about religion based on his observations that the religious establishment in cahoots with the state in England had been oppressive and not liberating for the lower classes. He certainly was not wrong – religion in England created suffering. Consider his observations in London during the middle of the nineteenth-century:

> The first measure of religious coercion was the Beer Bill, which shut down all places of public entertainment on Sundays, except between 6 and 10 p.m. This bill was smuggled through the House at the end of a sparsely attended sitting, after the pietists had bought the support of the big public-house owners of London…Then came the Sunday Trading Bill…This new coercive measure too was ensured the vote of big capital, because only small shopkeepers keep open on Sunday and the proprietors of the big shops are quite willing to do away with the Sunday competition of the small fry by parliamentary means. In both cases there is a conspiracy of the Church with monopoly capital, but in the both cases there are religious penal laws against the lower classes to set the consciences of the privileged classes at rest (Marx and Engels, 128).

Hard-times they were. Marx is not abstracting about economic theory and/or religion. He can see quite clearly the collusion between the state and big business using religious measures against smaller entities in order to enrich themselves. They were most willing to use sneaky political means to achieve their goals. We've all heard about the bills passed in Congress that no one had a chance to read because it wasn't printed until the middle of the night. Sometimes these bills run thousands of pages long. The 2001 Patriot Act created in the aftermath of the 9/11 attacks fits the bill. In the research developed in this book, this is a clear example of religion (Islam) used as fodder for the military-industrial-complex and its desired hegemony in the Middle East (similarly chapter four is an example of Christianity being used by the American political establishment for Middle Eastern hegemony via Israel).

To the degree that religion blinds its followers to the true nature of reality, then indeed it is a drug with anesthetizing potential. When religion is complicit in the oppression of society or sections of it (classes), then it is the negative that Marx makes it out to be.

Who could disagree with such impeccable logic?

Similarly, one traditional interpretation of religion, or theoretical understanding of religious behavior, comes from the French sociologist Emile Durkheim. Widely regarded as a founding father of modern Sociology and Anthropology, Durkheim grounds the religious dimensions of human life in our societal constitution. The very way in which we construct our societies and distribute power relationships are reflective of the way the gods do likewise.

I've found very effective demonstrating for students the comparative examples of the national anthem, the flag and the U.S. Constitution (very often posted on the wall up at the front of the classroom), our pledging allegiance to these symbols, and the relationship of the group/clan/community to its totem as described by Durkheim in *The Elementary Forms of the Religious Life*:

> Now the totem is the flag of the clan. It is therefore natural that the impressions aroused by the clan in individual minds – should fix themselves to the idea of the totem rather than that of the clan: for the clan is too complex a reality to be represented clearly in all its complex unity by such rudimentary intelligences. More than that, the primitive does not even see that these impressions come to him from the group.
>
> Since religious force is nothing other than the collective and anonymous force of the clan, and since this can be represented in the mind only in the form of the totem, the totemic emblem is liked the visible body of the god. Therefore, it is from it that those kindly and dreadful actions seem to emanate, which the cult seeks to provoke or prevent; consequently, it is to it that the cult is ad-

dressed. This is the explanation of why it holds the first place in the series of sacred things (252-253).

Imagine burning an American flag at a Veteran's Day parade! What type of reaction would it spark? This is the very condition (impressions, collective forces, sentiments) Durkheim is describing. The flag as symbolism transcends its own image to integrate the individuals of the society and conceive of them as a unit, e.g., a nation of communities, or a community of worshippers. An assault on a church, a mosque, or a temple is done so with just this is mind. An attack on a religion's conspicuous symbol is an attack on the entire community. For Durkheim,

> A religion so closely connected to a social system surpassing all others in simplicity may well be regarded as the most elementary religion we can possibly know. If we succeed in discovering the origins of the beliefs which we have analysed, we shall very probably discover at the same time the causes leading to the rise of the religious *sentiment* in humanity (italics mine, 195).

For God and Country, so the motto goes.

If the two are so intimately related, why then is religion's relationship to the political world so poorly understood in American history? It ought to be the focus of attention when religion can loom as large in the headlines as it currently does in American life and global politics. I suspect the *absence of the Critical Theory of religion* is rendering the sociological theories of religion rather neutralized of its explanatory potency.

To help get to the answer, I have been using terminology that comes from the social-scientific study of religion, most directly from *A Theory of Religion*. In this far-too-little-utilized yet extremely helpful and insightful book, the authors argue that what they mean by the term "'*cultural means of coercion*' refers to knowledge, capacities, and technologies that can inflict unbearable costs on the human organism" (*ATOR* Def. 32, 67/327). These become highly relevant when, as this book argues, the control of these mechanisms falls into the hands of a tiny group of people, i.e., the *political elite* (*ATOR* Def. 42 and Def. 43, 80/327). This opens the door for the marriage of the *Critical Theory* with the sociological theory. The need for such could not be more obvious when one considers the lament of William Bainbridge a decade after *A Theory of Religion* was published,

> Scholars of new religious movements have not had very great success developing a scientific model to predict which religious

movements might turn to violence. But when the government has chosen to move cautiously against a millenarian religious movement, and not storm in with guns drawn, the result has almost invariably been peaceful. Thus it would distort reality to base a policy concerning new religious movements on the desire to prevent future catastrophes like the Peoples Temple (Bainbridge, 359).

This muddying-of-the-waters will forever be the case until the *Critical Theory* is strategically-applied in conjunction with the other conventional theories of religion. As subsequent chapters in this book report, the historical record is not accurate. Jonestown, the Branch Davidians and the 9/11 terror attacks are not what they are commonly perceived to be, including by members of the field of Religious Studies. Perhaps most negatively for society, when members of the field of Religious Studies fail to comprehend and address what is happening in the real world of their religious research, then the narratives they create become fodder for political opportunists with a mind for religious engineering. The field of Religious Studies would not want to give ammunition to the political elites and their ill-conceived objectives as history will judge it accordingly.

In the Introduction to this book, in footnote seven, I agreed with authors Stark and Bainbridge in their other earlier book *The Future of Religion* and their assertion that a religion without any supernatural assumptions is not really a religion in the purest sense of that term. This suggests that the kind of religion that is *most motivating* is the one with a strongest belief in the supernatural, of which Biblical Literalism is one primary and powerful aspect for fundamentalist-style American Christians. This condition comes with the risk that the political elites are keenly aware of this tendency and so will seek to exploit it.

For his or her own political and social interests' sake, it is incumbent upon informed citizens to marginalize any political attempt to use religion and its holy books in a manner that fosters exclusivism in society or is exploitive of the individual. Both of these tendencies erode civil society and civic pluralism. The traditions and symbolism of public rituals need to be oriented to these inclusive ends. All public policies can be evaluated according to such a rubric of inclusion and civic pluralism and their capacities to reduce suffering in its real manifestations. In the end, this may be *the only* test of true and beneficial religion in society on this earth; and provide the only effective way to evaluate it.

NAVIGATING the BIPOLAR WORLD of RELIGION and NO RELIGION in a MOSTLY-FREE COUNTRY, WHAT *is* the CITIZEN to do?

In a country founded upon religious freedom and the citizen's right to follow her conscience, family tradition, or to fail to practice such by choice is fundamental to the law. This freedom of conscience is enshrined in cultural traditions which are inherited in ways not always controlled by the state. Culture is at work in the human being, and religion/culture is complex in the ways in which it molds us (*ATOR* P35 and P36).

So, what guidelines can a reasonable citizen expect from proper religious behavior in culture and society?

In the history of conservative Christian America, especially since the time of the Scopes Trial of 1925 and the broad cultural issue of evolution's role in American education, the combination of Biblical Literalism and Pentecostalism have been useful instruments in the hands of certain religious leaders and the political elites with whom they ideologically collude. Together Biblical Literalism and Pentecostalism fuse and allow for the expressions of both *reason* and *emotion* within the individual, making it a potent socio-political force in the hands of religious engineers.

For those who are persuaded, Biblical Literalism provides answers to life's questions. Most, if not all, of humans' cosmic puzzles find explanations in the Bible, and these explanations suffice to meet the requirements of reason. Coupled with the bond found in the communal worship of charismatic-ecstatic-emotional Pentecostal religion and embodied in the "speaking in tongues" experience, which provides both emotional catharsis *and* community, they together provide a persuasive foundation that meets the *total needs of the individual human being in his or her society*. This is a powerful socio-psychological force in religion. In fact, they are so persuasive as to have overtaken all other forms of Christianity in its global spread (Anderson, 1).

Together however, Biblical Literalism and Pentecostalism can also serve the purpose of keeping a population in political-check by managing intellectual needs and channeling emotional expressions in accordance with the wishes of social and religious engineers. Take as an example, the ideology of atheism and that it continues to intimidate certain individuals, even though it is losing its societal, political, and legal grip in the face of expanding knowledge and multi-culturalism. But there is a natural limit to atheism. The emotional side of humanity will never be placated by a godless and soulless universe and nation-states that legislate non-belief are not successful without use of repressive measures as history records. And even these are not successful in the long run.

So, there is nothing to be gained by politically constructing a godless-religion-free society. Much better for society to harness religious belief for the good of citizens and humankind, as the founding fathers sought to do, than see it wielded for sectarian and repressive purposes. After all, and metaphorically, Jesus (freedom of religion) belongs to everyone, and everyone belongs to Jesus (possesses free conscience and the right to follow the religion of one's choice).

Inclusiveness is *the* test of sensible religious beliefs and behavior in American democracy. So too with sensible atheism, as there is much to learn from and admire about Jesus' life and example.

But as can happen with stubborn atheism, Biblical Literalism severely restricts access to Jesus as only those with a *certain Christian persuasion* are included in the narrow path. This is the very trait of exclusivist religion, and the opposite outcome of what is desired by civil society and civic pluralism.

In addition, Biblical Literalism is an obstacle to progress in political unity in that it is a hardened position incapable of compromise or any hermeneutics (plural interpretations) which reflect the modern world and its current state of knowledge. Biblical Literalism must be mediated in the form of "empathetic" Biblical criticism in which the facts of the text are demythologized and recontextualized for a modern audience. The tools of modern history (historiography) can be judiciously applied to public education *about* religion and religions' histories and citizens would do right to demand such in public education. Education policy could and should reflect this humanitarian interpretation of religious texts and the meanings that can best be found in them.

These meanings must be measured against and consistent with civic pluralism and the Transcendent Common Good and not implemented for partisan gain. This takes the conscious crafting of public education policies regarding religion in history. Religions' histories must not be narrated to the contemporary population with current political expediency or narrow theological agendas in mind. These simply cannot work in a multi-cultural society such as the United States and the public educational system should reflect this awareness.

For example, within Biblical studies it has been noted that "a preference for the predicate 'Old Testament/Jewish' often goes with a more 'conservative' approach to religion and a preference for all that is 'Hellenistic' goes with a more 'liberal' or 'critical' attitude has not helped to produce an objective discussion" (Hengel, 2). Scholarship itself may, and too often does, have political leanings and these are where empathy is diminished, and civic pluralism undermined. In the American religious experience, this partisan alignment has been explicitly exaggerated and exploited – conservative and liberal versions of religions all too often politically align with the Republican and Democratic Parties respectively.

As will be covered in the next chapter, these competing interpretations of Jesus' nature and the nature of religion generally, will have even more direct domestic political and foreign-policy consequences as they pertain to the Middle East and Israel more narrowly. Much of the theological division in contemporary Christian churches is related to the doctrine of Biblical Literalism, or the notion that the Bible is the "Word of God." The very notion of a divinely-revealed and God-authorized text is one that must be straightforwardly and emphatically reckoned-with for the health of modern civil society and in the interest of civic pluralism.

The social and political interests of non-Christian Americans in a pluralistic nation and interconnected world are very much tied-to the health of civil society and the success of civic pluralism. A healthy civil society and robust civic pluralism together promote the empathetic element of religion so necessary for religions in general to exist, co-exist, and flourish within society and to not feel threatened by difference. In this way, toleration and integration into the mainstream of society of alternative spiritualties, non-majority religions and religious pluralism in general *enhance the majority religion's sacred role*, and even its status as a leader among religions, by demonstrating its own commitment to the Transcendent Common Good by peacefully accepting the existence and thriving of other religions.

This is called *cosmopolitanism* and is an essential element in religious pluralism (*ATOR* Def. 36: 77/327 and P42: 68/333).

Conversely, with the quest for political domination and exclusive authority on the part of the majority religion, there will arise conflicts between religions in a free and pluralistic society and so the *enforcement stance* of religion can *never* meet the needs of a free society. The majority religion of a country must not position itself in opposition to *the other*. This is a telling-sign of the political ambitions of a religion and a certain social degradation is bound to occur. I consider the case of Madalyn O'Hair an example.

It was an odd drama to emerge in the battle between *religion* and *no religion* during the Cold War – the colorful and contentious life, then mysterious disappearance and death, of the infamous American atheist Madalyn Murray O'Hair. Though her disappearance in 1995 was in the post-Soviet era, people hated her for decades because of her attacks on public religious rituals. In the life of one woman, she magnified and personified the vilification of atheists and atheism in American public life by conservative Christianity during the darkest of Cold War hours. She routinely got death threats and other forms of harassments. Consider that O'Hair's court battle victory removing prayers from the schools (1963) was within one decade from when the phrase "Under God" had been inserted into the Pledge of Allegiance (1954), and that to all so much popular fanfare and great political enthusiasm. This new-found legal openness toward atheism in the 1960s was not much appreciated even into the 1990s by traditionalist religious circles. O'Hair's troubles and ultimate disappearance were met at times with the most lukewarm of responses by authorities in Texas (Bryce).

The website BeliefNet.com, a Christian-sourced database of information on world religions and religious news which holds a very sympathetic view toward religions generally, carries the following statement about Madalyn O'Hair: "Whether or not O'Hair's cases had a marked effect on future legal battles, her unabashed atheism in a period marked by religious zeal during the Cold War made nonbelievers feel more at home in the U.S." (Beliefnet.com).

The idea that non-believers pose anything of a threat to civil society comes from restrictions of the Israelite religion of nearly 3,000 years ago. To the ancient Israelites the neighbor tribes posed something of an identity crisis for the fledgling tribe. The threat of being dominated and eradicated by a larger cultural force (the Egyptians or Babylonians) posed one type of threat. But the fear of creeping assimilation posed by smaller, neighboring cultures who were far weaker military forces such as Amalekites or Canaanites was still deemed dangerous.

Of urgent concern today is the purging of Biblical Literalism from American religion. It has had and continues to have a deleterious effect on politics and is intellectually and socially contrary to civic pluralism. It is a misapplication of ancient historical customs into the current era and reaps a fatally-flawed approach to civil society. As the nation becomes ever more ethnically and racially diverse, the need for civic pluralism is tantamount. All religious efforts can be judged by their ability to develop civic and religious pluralism.

American religion would be best expressed by not taking the enforcement stance and repudiating the strategy of engaging the laws of the state to conform to their religious opinions. Upon such righteous decrees do free people fall into slavery and oppression of all sorts and the principal reason for the founders "non-establishment" clause in the Constitution. Marrying the two grants far too much religious authority to the state in matters of personal liberties and individual freedoms. The political elites will seize that authority and manipulate it unto their own ends.

This posture of hostility toward atheism on the part of the Christian (or any other) religious community is a naturally logical outgrowth of the doctrine of Biblical Literalism (or divine revelation) and regrettably provides the rationalization and justification for degrading and devaluing citizens who disagree – the other. This "cultural populism" will inevitably be exploited by religious leaders. Exclusivism needs to be avoided and repudiated, while inclusivism and pluralism are cultivated and nurtured by religion. In addition, religion can be a potent guarantor of freedom for all, including the atheist, from oppression via Constitutional mandates. When it comes to our individual liberties, in the Creator we do wisely to trust.

American Christian theologian and writer (late) Robert E. Webber pointed to people's sense of *mystery in the liturgical churches* as an antidote to fundamentalism and the "rational approach to religion." His spiritual-prescription is more in keeping with the "two cultures" approach to knowledge and is beneficial to synthesizing the two. Americans would do themselves a good deed to develop an understanding of religion that balances the framework of the two cultures of science and the humanities recognizing that both must be reconciled in the human mind (*ATOR* Def. 7: 29/325). The emphasis upon mystery (not possessing all the cosmic answers), coupled with a community sharing the hope of a better future and an as yet intangible reward, can serve the deepest of humans needs. This alone goes a long way to fending-off radicalism and religious extremes and serves the interests and health of civil society.

By knowing what *to expect* and what *not to expect* from religion in society and possessing a correct understanding of both (the rational and the emotional), the citizen will be aided in navigating the demagoguery of political elites and their cultural means of coercion both inside and outside political, media and religious establishments.

For this very reason one influential Middle Eastern scholar said "the religiosity of rulers is always suspect. That's my rule" (see insert below).

It was my good fortune to make acquaintance with Syrian-born professor Sadik al-Azm (1934-2016) in the last decade prior to his passing. After having read that he had written a book about religion in Arabic that had landed him in jail in Beirut, Lebanon in December 1969-January 1970, and that his book had never been translated into English, I made some inquiries. Discovering al-Azm was lecturing in Europe, I contacted him about a translation project. Long-story-short, we sat down for an interview in May 2006 for a brief introduction and discussion:

Excerpt from author's 2006 Interview with Sadik al-Azm

> **BG**: *This is where I see striking parallels between your critique and our religious leaders. Now, our religious leaders and our politicians,* [G.W.] *Bush falls into this category, and the manipulation of conservatives in this country, the right-wing religious evangelicals and fundamentalists who are a huge voting block and they are connected with a network of about 200,000 conservative churches, some with satellite link-ups and in the 2004 election politicians addressed these congregations. I personally hold evangelical and fundamentalist leaders responsible for reinstalling Bush. Even after it was revealed about the President's manipulation of 9-11, the wars in Afghanistan and Iraq, could the right wing here put Bush back into office but by sidetracking them with issues like abortion, stem cell research, creationism, and gay rights? Our regime is manipulating the religious population in order to preserve their own power.*
>
> **SA**: *That's right, that's what they do and that's why I wrote what I did. Otherwise you could quite simply understand it* [the religious visions of Fatima referred to in previous writings] *as a spontaneous phenomenon by a population under stress. This happens everywhere. But then it was being manipulated by regimes and various forces. That's why I wrote the book. The religiosity of rulers is always suspect. That's my rule. And I know it because I come from a ruling class family. Religion is at the service of rulers.*
>
> —see chapter four; Sadik al-Azm, 2006

UNITED THEY (*elites*) STAND, DIVIDED WE (*civil society* and *culture*) FALL[19]

> *"... this Establishment is no longer a regional faction in any sense, [it] has absorbed all competing regional groupings of any importance, and represents the united front of the finance oligarchs of the entire country."*
> —Webster Tarpley, *Surviving the Cataclysm: Your Guide Through the Greatest Financial Crisis in Human History*[20]

Just as there was a warning from the turn of the previous century about the cruelty of eugenics that threatened to overtake humanity's basic sense of decency, so does the Cold War rhetoric of atheism come with

---

19   The terms *elite, political elite, society*, and *culture* all have precise definitions from ATOR; see in References Def. 51, Def. 42, Def. 29, and Def. 30 respectively.
20   3rd Edition. Page 650.

its own cautionary tale. Exaggerated threats both physical and spiritual, rigid two-party politics, coupled with the ideological bifurcation (red or dead) of the electorate combine to produce the result of that same electorate's domination by a very small number of political elites. Religion is a remarkably pliable tool in the hands of the social engineers and this tool must be seized back by the People. Only through a re-education of religion's role in history and in current life can these problems be addressed.

My calculation is the anti-thesis of Freud's proclamation of almost one hundred years ago, namely that there would be a turning-away from religion in the face of scientific progress. I suggest that there will be a continued and more-or-less steady need/demand for religion, including the more exclusive, literalistic, and emotive-based religions, but that these will give way to more moderate versions of religion rooted in community cohesion and values, rather than seeking to control. Humans must meet their own personal and social needs and will find ways to do so within the bounds of community without the requirement for cultural control, unless religious engineering for purposes of deception, usually fear-based, are foisted-upon the population. And this will always be a risk and so the awareness admonished by the Critical Theory of religion will always be desirable.

But religious history in the USA would take another turn.

In American Cold War history Jesus was only partially depaganized of his European roots (Greco-Roman Catholicism) even though he had also been reimagined as a thoroughly "Judeo-Christian Jesus." And though this was aided by the de-Nazification process which Christian scholarship underwent post-WWII, what emerged was something of a uniquely American messiah. This messiah is the savior of what has evolved into a national civic cult. This cult is in the full service of American empire and requires religious delusions maintain its course.

This American interpretation and adoption of Jesus as Israel's son rather than the son of Hellenized or Greco-Roman culture with implied pluralistic tendencies, further helped rally public opinion at home and cement allies in the Middle East in the larger battle for global dominance and the containment of Soviet communistic atheism and in the establishment of a *pax-Americana*. This Jewish-emphasized Jesus served Zionism's goals, just as the capitalization of Jesus served American Cold War interests and American-led globalization and neo-colonialism.

From the Cold War's emphasis upon US-Soviet antagonisms to the post-Cold War's emphasis upon "international terrorism," which would soon transform into Islamic terrorism, would come the new invention of an enemy for the military-industrial complex's needs, indeed, including the American economy's needs. Religion was used by the elites to engineer public opinion and the interests of imperial hegemony and global economic supremacy with its foothold in the oil-rich Middle East.

George Kennan noted, "Were the Soviet Union to sink tomorrow under the waters of the ocean, the American military-industrial complex would have to go on, substantially unchanged, until some other adversary could be invented. Anything else would be an unacceptable shock to the American economy" (Cousins, 11-12).

This is precisely what happened, as if on cue.

Even before the collapse of communism, the next enemy was selected, and the American people were primed for the new adversary who would threaten our very way of life, this time in the form of a conquering Middle Eastern prophet named Muhammed. In a 1979 Jerusalem Conference on International Terrorism, Benjamin Netanyahu exploited Islamic extremism in the form of Israel's foe, the Palestinians. This would have the effect of achieving two separate political goals, both serving America's long-term military and economic stability (Ahmed, 3). America's ally Israel would be bolstered as a result of the policy, and the Arab Middle East countries would further be dependent upon the USA (some on the USSR and later Russia) as they hardened their status as client-states dependent upon America for their existential survival. The 1990-1991 Gulf War would make this clear enough when Saudi Arabia pleaded to the United States to protect it from Saddam Hussain of Iraq, who the US, in turn, had supported and armed in Iraq's separate previous war with Iran (1980-1988).

Now, in the post-Soviet communist new millennium[21] and most especially after 9/11, Islamic extremism would be the "new adversary" that the military-industrial complex *created* and with whom we have been at war since the end of the Cold War – this has been identified as a state of "perpetual war for perpetual peace" (Vidal).

As a result, there is another deep warning coming from this historical thread in our past, and it is this: by and large, wars are falsely created to sustain large sectors of domestic economies. Empires depend upon this *modus operandi* even more so than nation-states which rest content within their borders. Not so with empires, ever-seeking to expand their hegemony over what they deem their "spheres of influence."

21   China is emerging as the new communist threat while Russia poses its own strategic challenges in the new millennium.

The challenge for American Christian religion today in what appears to be a world returning to a multi-polar political dynamic is re-theologizing the American Jesus (and by extension *all American religion* generally) to domestic concerns and working within the limits of global realities. Jesus/religion must be de-capitalized (detached from materialism), de-globalized (removed as head of the American-Christian empire) and remade into a local, or at most an unofficial national hero/belief system with a return to his/its humanitarian emphases and a sense of caring for the well-being of the greater society.

To accomplish this would necessitate a turn away from empire, a step the nation should take before long, and most certainly before it is *forced* to by circumstances out of its control. Civil populations within a democracy need not allow the political elite to use that same population's religions against them for goals they have no say in. Indeed, the political elites may want *us* to keep singing to the gods while *they* consolidate their rule at whatever cost to the nation and civilian population (*ATOR* Def.43: 80/327). These become the hallmarks of the fascist-oriented state and a drift away from democratic tendencies.

Religion, regrettably, plays efficiently into these tendencies. Much like Durkheim's nationalism/patriotism and other forms/definitions of social groupings, the exchange ratios and social capital religions bring to a population possess the force and authority of tradition and history and all of the metaphysical hope contained therein which is of incalculable value to the religious and social engineers. Conveniently for these engineers, religions come with their own built-in authority and so when melded with political power the two are a potent national force. Thus, the political elites will articulate and employ religion to their advantage when given opportunity.

The elites will encourage us to sing along with their patriotic songs. They might even, and likely will attempt to, *trick us* into singing. But all the while they will be consolidating their power if citizens aren't watching closely with a free and forceful media. The elites' greatest fear is uncontrolled protest, a universal solidarity that has the ability to bring the political system to a stand-still for the sake of civil society.

Here, *Critical Theory* suggests citizens do both – sing (express their personal autonomy) and protest (act in universal solidarity). *Critical Theory* can also embolden the scholar to articulate *honest* rather than *deceptive* grievances. For citizens living in the modern state, to sing and fight the good fight of faith must become a way of life. Sing together and push back against deceptive and oppressive rulers. The people that sing together will fight together – and in doing so may thwart the political elites' deceptive and ill-intentions. We may fall while singing, but *must* we fall? In the last analysis, it appears we do not fall at all, but for being pushed, manipulated, and cajoled into a political position by a political elite intent on using its cultural means of coercion, including religion, against we, the people.

A *Critical Theory of Religion* ought to give scholars the framework (and nerve) to begin to identify and call-out the political elites and their creations and disseminations of religious delusions via religious engineering. The sociological tools of *A Theory of Religion* will assist in that identification by providing a systematic and more-or-less comprehensive theoretical framework from which to understand and contextualize religious understanding as it is happening to the citizenry.

The erosion of the Constitutional powers is a harbinger of this deception and the dystopian use of religion in society. The Jonestown-Branch Davidian-9/11 deceptions all represent symptoms of the advanced decay of civil institutions. If the voting system does not allow for the people's expression of their very real pain, the kind that Marx alluded to in the beginning, then social and political instability are risks.

Recall Rudolph Bultmann's admonition in the Quotes preceding the Introduction that "we should...guard ourselves against falsifications of the faith by national religiosity, as against a falsification of national piety by Christian trimmings." And he stated this after witnessing the rise of fascism asserting its false religious pretenses of cultural and racial superiority.

The political elites would do themselves a favor to be informed by such an analysis and also to be reminded of Proposition 215: [that] "the victim in a coercive exchange relationship will seek means to remove the coercion" (*ATOR* P215: 208/342). The hold on power could turn out to be, in the end, quite tenuous indeed as earlier fascist regimes learned. The key is not to let the elites conquer us with their deceptions and thereby degrade civil society, civic pluralism, and culture in the process. In a prognosis for the future, I recommend the decapitalization of Jesus of Nazareth who can then serve American national interests by bringing the humane and ethical Jesus (whether Jew or Greek) back into circulation and fostering the health of civil society and the Transcendent Common Good.

REFERENCES
Books/Essays

Ahmed, Nafeez Mosaddeq (2005). *The War on Truth: 9/11, Disinformation, and the Anatomy of Terrorism*. Northampton, Massachusetts: Olive Branch Press.

Anderson, Allan (2004). *An Introduction to Pentecostalism: Global Charismatic Christianity*. Cambridge: Cambridge University Press.

Arnal, William E. and Russell T. McCutcheon (2013). *The Sacred is the Profane: The Political Nature of "Religion."* New York: Oxford University Press.

Bainbridge, William Sims (1997). *The Sociology of Religious Movements*. New York: Routledge.

Beliefnet.com (no author, no date). http://www.beliefnet.com/Faiths/Secular-Philosophies/Who-Was-Madalyn-Murray-Ohair.aspx?p=1 (accessed January 2019).

Blow, Charles M. (2014). Religious Constriction. *New York Times*. June 8.

Bower, Tom (1987). *The Paperclip Conspiracy: The Hunt for the Nazi Scientists*. Boston: Little, Brown and Company.

Bryce, Robert (1999). Preying on Atheists, The Oldest Motive: Revenge. The Austin Chronicle. 4 June. https://www.austinchronicle.com/news/1999-06-04/522124/ (accessed January 2019).

Bultmann, Rudolph (1956). *Primitive Christianity in its Contemporary Setting*. German Edition 1949. Trans. Reginald H. Fuller. Philadelphia: Fortress Press, 1988.

Central Intelligence Agency official website. https://www.cia.gov/about-cia (accessed January 2019). Posted December 19, 2006; Updated November 1, 2016.

Chidester, David (1988). *Salvation and Suicide: Jim Jones, The Peoples Temple, and Jonestown*. Revised edition. Bloomington: Indiana University Press, 2003.

Chidester, David (2014). *Empire of Religion: Imperialism and Comparative Religion*. Chicago: University of Chicago Press.

Collini, Stefan (1993). Introduction. In C. P. Snow's *The Two Cultures*. Canto edition. Cambridge: Cambridge University Press.

Cousins, Norman (1987). *The Pathology of Power*. New York: W.W. Norton.

Curtis, Glenn E., ed. (1996). The Russian Orthodox Church. Russia: A Country Study. Washington: GPO for the Library of Congress. http://countrystudies.us/russia/38.htm (accessed January 2019).

Doležalová, Iva, Luther H. Martin & Dalibor Papoušek, eds. (2001). *The Academic Study of Religion During the Cold War: East and West*. Toronto Studies in Religion, Vol. 27. New York: Peter Lang.

Durkheim, Emile (1915). *The Elementary Forms of the Religious Life*. Trans. Joseph Ward Swain. New York: Free Press, 1965.

Evans-Pritchard, E. E. (1965). *Theories of Primitive Religion*. Oxford: Oxford University Press, 1987.

Evica, George Michael (2011). *A Certain Arrogance: The Sacrificing of Lee Harvey Oswald and the Cold War Manipulation of Religious Groups by US Intelligence*. 2nd Ed. Walterville, Oregon: Trine Day.

Flake, Carol (1984). *Redemptorama: Culture, Politics, and the New Evangelicalism.* New York: Penguin Books, 1985.

Freud, Sigmund (1927). *The Future of an Illusion.* Translated from German by James Strachey. New York: W.W. Norton, 1961.

Gadsby, Blair A. (2006). Teaching *Religion(s)* in the Community College: Students Can Handle Theory Early. *Bulletin of the Council of Societies for the Study of Religion.* November. 35: 4. 92-95.

Gatto, John Taylor (1992). *Dumbing us Down: The Hidden Curriculum of Compulsory Education.* [2005] Gabriola Island, British Columbia: New Society Press. 2008.

Gutierrez, Gustavo (1973). *A Theology of Liberation: History, Politics, and Salvation.* Maryknoll, New York: Orbis Books, 1988.

Hadden, Jeffrey K. and Anson Shupe (1988). *Televangelism: Power and Politics on God's Frontier.* New York: Henry Holt.

Hadden, Jeffrey K. and Charles E. Swann (1981). *Prime Time Preachers: The Rising Power of Televangelism.* Reading, Massachusetts: Addison-Wesley Publishing.

Hench, John B. (2010). *Books as Weapons: Propaganda, Publishing, and the Battle for Global Markets in the Era of World War II.* Ithaca, New York: Cornell University Press.

Hengel, Martin (1989). *The 'Hellenization' of Judaea in the First Century after Christ.* London and Philadelphia: SCM Press and Trinity Press.

Holzman, Franklyn D. (1989). Politics and Guesswork: CIA and DIA Estimates of Soviet Military Spending. *International Security.* Vol. 14, No. 2. Fall. Pgs. 101-131. Published by MIT Press. (CIA is the Central Intelligence Agency, and the DIA is the Defense Intelligence Agency – research arm of the Department of Defense)

Leab, Daniel J. (2007). *Orwell Subverted: The CIA and the Filming of Animal Farm.* University Park, Pennsylvania: Pennsylvania State University Press.

Marx, Karl and Friedrich Engels (1957). *On Religion.* New York: Schocken Books.

Marx, Karl and Friedrich Engels (1964). *The Communist Manifesto.* Trans. Samuel Moore. Ed. Joseph Katz. New York: Washington Square Press-Pocket Books. [Original English edition 1888]

McCutcheon, Russell T. (2004). 'Just Follow the Money': The Cold War, The Humanistic Study of Religion, and the Fallacy of Insufficient Cynicism. *Culture and Religion.* Vol. 5, No. 1: 41-69.

Nash, Ronald H., ed. (1984). *Liberation Theology.* Milford, Michigan: Mott Media.

Nelkin, Dorothy (1982). *The Creation Controversy: Science or Scripture in the Schools.* Boston: Beacon Press.

Nkrumah, Kwame (1965). *Neo-Colonialism: The Last Stage of Imperialism.* New York: International Press, 1966.

Postman, Neil and Steve Powers (2008). *How To Watch TV News*. Rev. Ed. [1992] New York: Penguin.

Prothero, Stephen (2003). *American Jesus: How the Son of God Became a National Icon*. New York: Farrar, Straus, Geroux.

Reagan, Ronald (1983). Address to the National Association of Evangelicals. March 8. Text can be found at any number of websites.

Runions, Erin (2014). *The Babylon Complex: Theopolitical Fantasies of War, Sex, and Sovereignty*. New York: Fordham University Press.

Schiffrin, André (2001). *The Business of Books: How International Conglomerates Took Over Publishing and Changed the Way We Read*. New York: Verso Books.

Siebert, Rudolf J. (1985). *The Critical Theory of Religion: The Frankfurt School*. Lanham, Maryland: Scarecrow Press, 2001.

Siebert, Rudolf J. (2012). *From Critical Theory to Critical Political Theology: Personal Autonomy and Universal Solidarity*. Revised edition. New York: Peter Lang. Original edition 1994.

Simpson, Christopher, ed. (1998). *Universities and Empire: Money and Politics in the Social Sciences During the Cold War*. New York: The New Press.

Simpson, Gary M. (2002). *Critical Social Theory: Prophetic Reason, Civil Society, and Christian Imagination*. Minneapolis, Minnesota: Fortress Press.

Smith, George H. (1989). *Atheism: The Case Against God*. Buffalo, New York: Prometheus Books.

Stark, Rodney (2004). SSSR Presidential Address, 2004: Putting an End to Ancestor Worship. *Journal for the Scientific Study of Religion*. Vol. 43:4, 465-475.

Stark, Rodney (2012). *America's Blessings: How Religion Benefits Everyone, Including Atheists*. West Conshohocken, Pennsylvania: Templeton Press, 2013.

Stark, Rodney and William Sims Bainbridge (1987). *A Theory of Religion*. New Brunswick, New Jersey: Rutgers University Press, 1996. (*ATOR*)

- Throughout the chapter, references to *ATOR* include dual page numbers where the Axiom/Definition/Proposition first appears in *ATOR*'s main text and then in its Appendix, where "[f]or the easy reference of the reader, we have listed the axioms, definitions and propositions, in the order in which they were derived in the text" (325-350). Below they are listed in the order they appear in this chapter.

Def. 40 *Cultural means of coercion* refers to knowledge, capacities, and technologies that can inflict unbearable costs on the human organism.

Def. 78: *Religious engineering* is the conscious design of compensator packages and other elements of culture for use in cults.

P164 Religious engineering may be undertaken either in order to practice deception or in the belief that the product constitutes a real value.

Def. 43 A *repressive state* exists when the political elite use their monopoly on the cultural means of coercion to impose below market exchange ratios on non-elite members of the society.

Def. 42 Those who monopolize the use of coercion are the *political elite*.

Def. 30 *Culture* is the total complex of explanations exchanged by humans.

P35 Human culture occurs through the accumulation and transmission of explanations over time.

P36 The explanations of religion are a cultural system.

Def. 80 *Honesty* is the interaction strategy of offering only those explanations to others which one personally accepts.

Def. 79 *Deception* is any interaction strategy that intentionally leads other people to accept explanations which one privately rejects.

Def. 15 *Power* is the degree of control over one's exchange ratio.

P330 A state consisting of a political monopoly is a repressive state.

P331 A state consisting of a political monopoly will seek to repress religion.

Def. 22 *Religion* refers to systems of general compensators based on supernatural assumption.

Def. 32 *Complexity* of culture refers to the number, scope and detail of explanations, and the amount of technology.

Def. 36 *Cosmopolitan* refers to the existence of plural cultures within a society.

P42 As a society grows and endures, it will come to have a progressively more complex culture.

Def. 7 The *mind* is the set of human functions that directs the actions of a person.

Def. 51 An *elite* is a group with great control over its exchange ratio.

Def. 29 A *society* is a closed structure of social relations.

P215 The victim in a coercive exchange relationship will seek means to remove the coercion.

Tarpley, Webster G. (2011). *Surviving the Cataclysm: Your Guide Through the Greatest Financial Crisis in Human History*. 3rd Ed. Joshua Tree, California: Progressive Press.

Tucker, Robert C., ed. (1978). *The Marx-Engels Reader.* 2nd Ed. New York: W.W. Norton.

Vahanian, Gabriel (1957). *The Death of God: The Culture of Our Post-Christian Era.* New York: George Braziller, 1966.

Vidal, Gore (2002). *Perpetual War for Perpetual Peace: How We Got to be So Hated.* New York: Thunder's Mouth Press/Nation Books.

Vidal, Gore (2002). *Dreaming War: Blood for Oil and the Cheney-Bush Junta.* New York: Thunder's Mouth Press/Nation Books.

Webber, Robert E. (1985). *Evangelicals on the Canterbury Trail: Why Evangelicals are Attracted to the Liturgical Church.* Waco, Texas: Word Books.

Wiebe, Donald (2001). Religious Studies in North America During the Cold War. In Doležalová, Iva, Luther H. Martin & Dalibor Papoušek, Eds. (2001). *The Academic Study of Religion During the Cold War: East and West.* Toronto Studies in Religion, Vol. 27. New York: Peter Lang.

Wise, David and Thomas B. Ross (1964). *The Invisible Government.* New York: Bantam Books, 1965. Mass-market paperback.

Zuckerman, Edward (1979). *The Day After World War III: The Shocking True Account of the U.S. Government's Plans for Helping us "Survive" Nuclear War.* New York: Avon.

Films, Documentaries, Internet Discussions

C-SPAN (1995). CIA Estimates of Soviet Military Expenditures. May 30. http://www.c-span.org/video/?65442-1/cia-estimates-soviet-military-expenditures (accessed January 2019).

Kirk, Michael and Mike Wiser (2011). *Top Secret America: The Hidden Legacy of 9/11.* A Frontline Production with Kirk Documentary Group, Ltd. Producers Michael Kirk, Jim Gilmore and Mike Wiser. Based upon the reporting of Dana Priest of *The Washington Post.* Aired April 30, 2013. https://www.pbs.org/wgbh/frontline/film/topsecretamerica/ (accessed February 2019).

Kuran, Peter (1995). *Trinity and Beyond: The Atomic Bomb Movie.* Produced by Peter Kuran and Alan Munro. Documentary Film Works Production.

4

JESUS AND THE PALESTINIANS:
CHRISTIAN ZIONISM[1]

The delusion: *Since ancient times and continuing through to the 1947-1948 political creation of modern Israel, God has chosen the Hebrew-Jewish people and their nation to be unique among nations as they are to serve as His "light unto the world." This is established by the fact that they were chosen to be the authors of the Biblical text, which is "God's revealed Word" to humankind. Part of understanding the Bible is deciphering the prophetic meaning of passages written centuries ago. Since God acts through and uses nations is a common Biblical theme, America can also be interpreted within this schema. A nation that supports Israel is a nation that is supporting God's cause in the world. Therefore, in a current political context, U.S. foreign policy toward Israel is decisive to the very well-being of the U.S. itself because God is un-questioningly on the side of Israel over and above the Palestinians who are Arab-Muslims and/or Christians living in territory designated by God for Jewish settlement. Therefore, justice for the Palestinian cause is second in priority to Israel's interests and the Jewish people's continued survival and success as a nation, even if the oppressive status-quo regarding the Palestinians must be maintained, and politically regressive (or worse) measures must be used against them.*

The correction: *This is a topic of pure political theology, or theological politics, either way, it is grounded in a particular view of the Biblical text and is an outgrowth of Biblical Literalism. Christian Zionism is the idea that the United States as a Christian nation ought to support the Jewish state of Israel, for good or for ill, and that America's very survival depends upon it. This is promoted in mostly conservative, evangelical, or other fundamentalist "Bible-believing" churches across America. As an influential political theology, it is having the consequence of dislodging the Palestinians from their land through the narrative of Israel's*

---

1   Zionism is the "international, political, and ideological movement dedicated to restoring Erez (the land of) Israel to the Jewish people" *(Oxford Concise Dictionary of World Religions,* John Bowker, ed.). It began in 1897 as a political idea and culminated in 1948 with the State of Israel declaring its independence.

God-given right-of-possession of all or most of Judea and Samaria. Is-raeli politicians have consistently sought to court this American audi-ence to aid and abet, and to finance via pilgrimage-tourism, domestic Israeli political concerns. Geopolitically, this has been a marriage of convenience for both nations as it facilitates American geostrategic in-terests in the Middle East by providing a solid proxy in a region rich in petroleum resources but whose Arab-Muslim governments cannot always be counted upon for political support of American interests in the region.

Quotes

And take heed, lest you lift your eyes to heaven, and when you see the sun, the moon, and the stars, all the host of heaven, you feel driven to worship and serve them, which the Lord your God has given to all the peoples under the whole heaven as a heritage.

– Deuteronomy 4: 19 (New King James Version)

But if you [prophets, magicians, soothsayers, diviners, astrologers] will not make known the dream to me, there is only one decree for you! For you have agreed to speak lying and corrupt words before me till the time has changed [thus avoiding execution]. Therefore tell me the dream, and I shall know that you can give me its interpretation.

– Daniel 2:9

With the Jewish nation reborn in the land of Palestine, ancient Jeru-salem once again under total Jewish control for the first time in 2600 years, and talk of rebuilding the great Temple, the most important pro-phetic sign of Jesus Christ's soon coming is before us. This has now set the stage for the other predicted signs to develop in history. It is like the key piece of a jigsaw puzzle being found and then having the many ad-jacent pieces rapidly fall into place.

– Hal Lindsey, 1970 in *The Late Great Planet Earth*, pg. 47

When childish beliefs are held by adults, no political good results.

-author

The 1988 COUNTDOWN

In a Massachusetts Bible study on Friday May 13, 1988, the eve of the fortieth anniversary of Israel's existence as a modern nation-state, we four participants watched as the clock approached – then passed – midnight. The next day of Saturday May 14 (the Sabbath, no less) had all the prophetic possibilities of being the last day of human history – for some of us, at least. Those of us among the true believers would be whisked-off by Jesus before the real troubles began. *Then* the world would be plunged into something of a hell-on-earth.

We could only wait with hopeful yet uneasy anticipation.

The thinking went like this: 1988 being the fortieth year of the "rebirth" of Israel was interpreted to be the historical moment Jesus was referring to when He said in Matthew 24:34 "Verily, I say unto you, *this generation* shall not pass, until all these things be fulfilled" (italics mine). *This generation* was the generation of people who saw the re-establishment of the nation of Israel in 1948 and the Jews return there from a nearly two thousand year-long diaspora, or scattering, away from their ancestral and Biblical homeland.

We were this generation.

Add to this, forty is a number with curious symbolic significance in Hebrew mythology and literature. For example, when God is inclined to signal to humanity that He is creating a new beginning and ending something that has been unpleasing to Him, often forty is the symbolic-numerical "end of one and start of another." Hence, we read in the Hebrew Bible about forty days of rain to wipe-out a rebellious and sinful humanity, or forty years of wandering in the wilderness for the people of Israel to purge a generation of memories of the polluting gods of Egypt. Christians are not unfamiliar with their own messiah spending a grueling forty days and forty nights in the desert being tempted by none other than Satan himself. This was the test-of-all-tests for God's own Son, Christians understand, after which he had proved himself as worthy to be the sacrifice for all humankind. Therefore, the imagery of forty is doubly portentous in this end-of-the-world segment of the drama.

To those of us in the Bible study, the geopolitics of the number forty and the implications of our current generation being *the* generation to see the fulfillment of Jesus' prophecies were straightforward enough. Upon these events the history of the planet hinged our cosmology told us.

Or so we had been taught.

In retrospect and self-reflection, I now conclude that numerological speculation coupled with a selection of relevant current events[2] were all

---

2   Some events, perhaps most, are selected for utmost dramatic effect and are strained-to-fit a preconceived scenario. See Lindsey-Carlson page 150 on nuclear exchange. One could argue the entire futuristic prophetic enterprise is built in just this same way.

that was required to activate and engage the religious imagination of our small group, and as it turns out, no small number of modern believers. Since ancient times, numbers have had a mystical quality about them, especially about the true nature of their existence and how they interact with our mind and the world. Personally, all I have to do is look at any one of the equations (especially the big confusing ones) mathematicians use to make sense of the universe and from which they derive twenty-first century cosmology – think Stephen Hawking or *The Big Bang Theory*! – to be struck by the mysticism of numbers. How these mathematical symbols relate to reality will always be a *mystery* to me and my mind.

Beyond numerology, the mystical way of thinking is not the type of thinking that is easily dislodged from the human imagination – much the same way that Karl Marx had noted (quoted in the beginning of the previous chapter) that creationism is no easy concept to jettison at the mere suggestion of an alternate scientific view. Whether imbibed with a logic of its own or not, *the mystical[3] (as with creation) is intertwined with the meaningful* and the two are not subject to normal rational scrutiny.[4] Humans are both rational and emotional and are informed by both science and religion (humanities).

The meaningfulness of life is rooted in the connections we have to other people, and to our collective history *as* a people (e.g., family, village, town, city and nation). Religion is a source from which we derive a broader context to our meaningfulness and locate ourselves and society within the universe. This meaning becomes part of culture. And even if this universe is understood from a mostly-scientific position, this *will never* and *can never* preclude the meaningful: the question of *how* we got here does not overlap with the question *why* we are here. Scientific answers do not of necessity conflict with the elements of the mystical. Bible prophecy constitutes *but one* feature or element of the non-rational or emotional side of religion and is in its own way *mystical as distinct from the literal.*

Yet it must be pointed out that history provides a series of examples[5] in which the mystical has been fused with the meaningful in such a way to

---

3   The mystical in religion is defined by Funk and Wagnalls dictionary as "a truth that can be known only through divine revelation and cannot be fully understood by men." This meaning applies to the numerological prophecy regarding Israel's existence in the modern world and the timing surrounding its creation. Perhaps one could also implicate or compare the "mysterious nature of coincidences" as part of the appeal this type of meaning holds for people.

4   Recall chapter one, footnote 4 [page 42] and G.S. Kirk on myth's ability to orient meaning for society and its relationship to the outside world.

5   The episodes in this book serve to highlight how religion's (including the mystical's) efficacy in constructing a meaningful social narrative can go awry when deceptively exploited for subversive ends or is subject to religious engineering.

produce social outcomes of human suffering, or at the very least, economic and political exploitation. In these instances, I would offer the explanation that the mystical has been exchanged for (perhaps better, usurped by) the superstitious. Alas, the superstitious is far more fear-based than general mysticism, and as a result is less empathetic, and from where any number of troubles begin. Superstition in the service of witch-burning during the Catholic-Protestant Inquisitions of old Europe, not unlike the Salem Witch Trials here in America complete with spectral evidence, serves as a reminder of the dangers of allowing the mystical mind to drift too far away from the empathy necessary of human actions for civic pluralism to thrive.

Human societies' literatures and arts have historically, and likely always will, find outlets for mystical interpretations. However, these outlets must be restrained in the social and political realms to those outcomes with *positive and humane benefits*. A narrative that overlooks the blatant injustices toward an entire group of people needs to be rejected, and uncompromisingly so. For the Palestinian people, this has been their collective social and political outcome of American Christian Zionism. American conservative Christians have been too often sheltered from this existential consequence of the Israeli-Palestinian conflict which has dragged-on for decades and resulted in an acutely inhumane set of circumstances for Palestinians. This, in turn, has fomented yet more inhumanity in the form of reactionary political terrorism.

Maintaining the emphasis upon humane (the health of civil society) and socially beneficial (civic pluralism) outcomes of all manner of religious thought is doubly imperative in the highly globalized and technologically-holistic world in which Americans live and work. And even if many Americans do not frequently come into *direct contact* with members of other religions, they sure do *hear from politicians and in the media* about the (mostly) notorious exploits of those *other* religious members when the purpose serves the requisite vested interests (goals of the political elites). This gulf in knowledge between the American people's *ignorance of* vs *the actuality of* the plight of the Palestinians on the one hand, coupled with the demagoguery of Islamic terrorism by political elites and their cultural means of coercion (mass mainstream media) on the other hand, provide fertile ground for the planting of the seeds of the manipulation of public opinion, i.e., religious engineering, on the topic of Israel-Palestine relations.

Here again, Biblical Literalism provides a convenient and authoritative tool in the hands of religious engineers to shape public opinion. It has done so effectively for the past *one hundred years* in the imagination of many an evangelical, fundamentalist, and Pentecostal and very success-fully so for the past *sixty years* on behalf of the state of Israel in the form of Bible prophecy.

As in the previous chapter addressing religion's cultural battle with atheism, *humaneness* in religious behaviors must be sought and is the stan-dard by which society can measure the validity of religious actions, in-cluding the interpretation of texts for today's world. Since the Palestinians have not been dealt with in a just and humane manner in today's world, the issue of American Christian Zionism's Biblical interpretation must be held suspect and subject to scrutiny as it is a driving force in American politics as regards Israel (Gavshon).

In today's ideological-political defenses of the two nations' origins (Israel and Palestine), conservative Christian religion fueled by Biblical Literalism provides enormous assistance in the mediation, and mostly exacerbation, of the public's image of the other – in this case the Palestinian – whom will be on the receiving end of national policies based in perceived national in-terests and threats. Religious narratives must be used with extreme caution combined with empathy to ensure that public opinion remains oriented to-ward an inclusive, pluralistic and democratic outcome.

Due to their historical origins in the world of *real-life* religious texts, in contrast to being idealized as divinely-inspired or divinely-revealed, are laden with the competition and conflict of the times in which they were written. However, in traditionalist (ancient) forms of religion and their texts, the pluralistic values sought today were not the desired outcome of conflict. Typically, narratives of competition and conquest were the mythic forms such conflicts stimulated.[6]

These texts must be reinterpreted if positive meaning is to be extracted from them for the current times. This effort is called *hermeneutics* and is a mat-ter of some controversy among theological opinions. The topic of this chap-ter, Bible prophecy understood as literal futuristic fortune-telling, is only one

---

6　　The terms *hagiography* and *historiography* are useful here. The former applies to and in-cludes Biblical Literalism as it is any narrative that is considered a religious creation and often used for some morally, ethically, socially or even politically instructive goal or end. Hagiography means literally "writings about the saints" and includes any and all stories that defy known scientific laws, e.g., resurrections, miracles, and the like. So, for example, *God giving the land of Palestine-Israel solely to the Jewish people* is a hagiographic narrative. In contrast, historiography refers to the "hard core approach" to history, if you will. This is the narrating of history and sticking as close to the facts as they can best be known absent divine inferences. So, the Jewish people's historical sojourn in the land and subsequent expulsion from it with all of the competition and conflicts they encountered, minus the hand of God's intervention, constitute a historiographic account of the life of the Jewish people. The two are as far-removed as the *divine-parting* of the Red Sea so the Jewish people can escape the Egyptians is from the *divine-abandonment* of Jewish people to the Nazis. Only the cre-ativity of the human imagination could reconcile the two.

example. The narrative use of these passages must be stripped of its ability to have a deleterious effect on civil society and civic pluralism. And though the individual can and ought-to always cherish his or her traditions and articles of faith and beliefs, such an appreciation cannot be done at the expense of disrupting society or undermining religious pluralism, and of course may never violate the common good or Transcendent Common Good.

The invoking of religion in the quest of policy, both domestic and foreign, ought to be rare at the worst of times and absent in the best of times. Very little guidance comes from soliciting strictly-defined categories (essentialism) extrapolated from ancient religious texts when forging policy for a common democratic good within a modern pluralistic society. Such texts are rooted in particular traditional cultural and historical identities and only very generally, if at all, transpose into modern society.

Only in the most desperate of times would soliciting a non-specific and vaguely-defined Transcendent Common Good be appropriate – much as the Declaration of Independence echoes when declaring *WE hold these Truths to be self-evident, that all Men are created equal, that they are endowed by their Creator with certain unalienable Rights*. Only when this value has been firmly established in public declaration and is commonly understood by all, then and only then, should matters of an overtly religious nature be invoked. Otherwise, "the religiosity of rulers is always suspect."

Exclusionism in public declarations of religion are constitutionally unacceptable. Recent history has shown that a pattern of soliciting religious motifs, values, laws, and even prejudices has plagued American society, politics and foreign policy to ill-effect. Christian Zionism has played just such a role of oppressor in recent American religious history to the detriment of the Palestinians. The hagiography of Biblical Literalism and prophetic fortune-telling is a contributing perpetrator of the Palestinians' subjugation by Israel.

This is a pattern that can and *must* be broken for the greater benefit of society and for which Religious Studies is well-positioned to address, and it should actively do so even if only for its own credibility as it runs the risk of echoing a complicity with the motives of government public foreign policy (hence the need for a *Critical Theory of Religion* in American cultural, social, political, and academic life). In the Conclusion I will return to this subject of the inherent perils of Religious Studies serving as a flack for government policies.

As it pertains to U.S. foreign policy toward Israel, the Palestinians, the Middle East, and then extending out to the greater war on terror, the pattern can be broken by first addressing the ideological underpinning of current policies that enables a *religious claim* to the land on the part of only

147

one side, Israel, and how this enables so much human misery as a direct outcome.[7] Within the U.S. there is little-to-no challenge to, and very few voices raised against, the Zionist message and effort. And the Palestinians' plight gets little-to-no sympathetic media coverage.

The Jewish people's, and all contemporary Israelis' (both religious and secular), claim to the land cannot preclude granting rights for Palestinians as full citizens. Power-sharing is nothing new in the human political landscape and can be achieved if there is cooperative determination and economic fair play. But too often competition and rivalry prevail in the political power play, leaving us living in a world where one side is doomed to suffer loss. And religion, rather than fostering reconciliation, breeds division. This need not be inevitable, but it will require a re-visioning of certain sectors of American Christianity away from the literal and politico-competitive and toward the symbolic and politico-cooperative. The failure of the 1988 prophecy with its much-hoped-for grand climactic conclusion to all human history, proved that much more work still needs to be done *this* side of eternity.

A WORLD of WINNERS and LOSERS: ISRAEL/U.S. WINNERS, PALESTINIANS, WELL...

Whether out of survival-necessity, the innate potential for human barbarity, or the sheer force of individual personality, many mythologies and theologies across the world (and in the monotheistic-anthropomorphic theologies particularly) possess literary content that is replete with imageries of a battle for power, both eternal and temporal. The gods battle among themselves or are battling the forces of evil. In so many ways, religions harness the language of conflict and the associated consequences and with mythological outcomes that can be remarkably inhumane and bloodily so, if not torturously so.

In the telling of these violent stories is the nexus of where hagiography and historiography converge in the making of human meaning and the creation of culture.

Examples range from the ancient Indian-Hindu justification in the *Vedas* for social stratification called the *caste system* and from which miseries have been generated over millennia, to the Hebrew-Biblical commands (see Samuel 15: 1-11) to slaughter the enemies of the Israelites in ancient times (a story which is accepted quite literally by so many Americans to this day), or even within the tribe of Israel the story of the inheritor-winner Jacob over

7   There have, in fact, been any number of American Christian ministries who recognized the injustice of the Israeli-Palestinian conflict and address it directly. A brief search of the Internet will reveal this. Sadly, they are far too few and with very little public influence.

his rival brother the disinherited-loser Esau bring the message of competing winners-and-losers into sharp family focus, to finally and more recently, the British-Anglican theological-rationalization that Africans were not fit for Christian conversion thereby justifying their enslavement, and which is echoed in the earliest decades of the American republic (see Quotations over the Centuries 1776 and 1865 preceding the Introduction).

Basically enough, these are the hard-competitive realities of life (tribe, nation and empire) and must be accepted and endured, if unavoidably and regrettably perpetuated – after all, there is only so much wealth to spread or land to occupy. Or so our myths teach us and our political leaders warn us (and even threaten us with exaggerated fears, usually of scarcity caused by those *others*). In these same myths, God is rarely neutral over matters of national survival and issues of historical significance. Not surprisingly, the events of any given age must work in the political favor of the narrators of the story whose status and often survival are dependent upon the outcome of God's wishes, which are then reflected in the popular historical understanding of those same events to be retold in culture via religious texts.

In human battle certainly, and at times out of survival necessity, a degree of *indifference* to the needs and sufferings of individuals caught in the rivalry is simply part of the reality and not to be overly concerned with. Too frequently in theological narratives divine indifference to those same individuals' sufferings is part of the victory of the storytellers and without it there can often be no joyous victory.

These ancient and *real life competitions become religious memes* transcending time and place and also providing a divine rationale for unspeakable cruelty. The "winner-take-all/zero-sum game" policy in national political consciousness need today be viewed very suspiciously and as a relic of the mythical-historical past, not a present-day guide for diplomacy. Citizens of modern democratic societies ought to better understand this relationship/dynamic (between the political and religious) or opportunists and demagogues will exploit the population to very narrowly-interested ends.

This is precisely what has taken place in conservative Christian American politics regarding the state of Israel. American historical and political backing for the state of Israel has had several sources of support and *not all* are illegitimate. The first four listed below are well-within keeping of the American democratic ideals of nationhood, citizenship, human rights and foreign affairs in the modern world and constitute *legitimate* bases for political activism and policy creation:

1. The horror of the 1938-1945 Nazi Holocaust against the Jewish people has garnered political sympathy for the needs and issues of the modern nation-state created as a safe haven for them. Much of that support came from Jews who have been living in America since the early days of the republic; this results in the outcome of the second concern. For many non-Jewish Americans likewise, the Nazi atrocities fueled support for a Jewish homeland (compassion).

2. American Jewish political support for the state of Israel among U.S. policy-makers. Jewish people have been in America long enough to have important political influence regarding Israeli matters of national security in the halls of Congress. And this is a good thing. An imbalance, however, comes into play given there is no commensurate representation for the Palestinian-Arabs and their claims to the land, which are equally valid. It is worthy to note that not all Jewish Americans agree about these same issues (domestic political competition).

3. Diplomacy and international credibility require that the U.S. honor its commitment to allies, and Israel is and has always been from its inception in 1948 a stalwart American ally. During the Cold War Israel was a supporter of U.S. interests when at the same time Arab nations were aligning themselves with communist Russia. Israel was and continues to be fully reciprocated for its allegiance to America during periods of international crises (foreign relations).

4. Israel's strategic position in the Levant/eastern Mediterranean is important in a region of the world with significant petroleum resources. Though not oil-rich itself, Israel sits in a neighborhood where there is plenty of (relatively cheap-to-extract) petroleum. This cannot be overlooked for it is far too pragmatic to a nation the size of the United States which requires vast amounts of petroleum to function, and for whose international oil companies do business with nations around the world (strategic interests).

These reasons are not in themselves objectionable nor disqualified as legitimate political concerns to American politicians. If a particular issue or set of issues are of concern to American citizens, then it is by virtue of the democratic process that these same concerns be addressed by their elected officials. These matters pertaining to Israel, like any other "special interest," deserve their fair hearing and opportunity to make an appeal to the electorate and their representatives. To articulate and argue that it is in the United States' best interest to support Israel and its welfare is fair enough, regardless from whom the argument comes. But this argument must conform to the requirement of a common democratic good in a pluralistic society and from which, because it is a *theological* claim, a Transcendent Common Good can be ensured for all parties involved or affected in the outcome.

But this is *not* what has happened.

For several generations there has been *no* common good to come about for the Palestinians in the narrative of Zionist conservative American Christianity, and this urgently stands in need of correction.

The religious issue of concern for the past one hundred and fifty years, and which constitutes an *illegitimate* fifth source of support for Israel, and one that is *much less in keeping* with these same American ideals required to produce a Transcendent Common Good. Furthermore, it is here where the religious delusion of this chapter comes to the fore distorting historical analysis and imposing the contrivance of *Biblical prophecy-as-fortune-telling* upon current Middle Eastern events, and these events' relationship to American interests. This circumstance can be summarized as follows:

> 1. Christian conservatives who view Zionism from the Biblical Literalism interpretation of God's support for the nation of Israel constitute a substantial voting bloc rivaling in sheer political force most any other single entity within the current two-party system. There is no competing philosophical viewpoint that could effectively counterbalance the political influence of this apocalyptic cosmology[8] which is shared by this sizeable constituency for Republican Party politicians. This support for Israel, the Jewish people, and Zionism has as an unfortunate side-effect in the collective willingness to ignore, overlook, tolerate and thereby negate those same political and human rights to the non-Jewish Palestinian population.

American Christians who interpret the Bible prophecy in the manner of Biblical Literalism far too readily perpetuate these memes. Conservative Christianity has held political views towards Israel-Zionism and the Palestinians that have resulted in *anything but* a positive and socially-beneficial political outcome for the latter.[9] The list of grievances that the Pales-

8   This view should properly be referred to as *"eschatological religion"* as it puts an emphasis upon the literal culmination of history, the *end times*, in some form of dramatic even cataclysmic ending, e.g., an apocalypse, Armageddon, or other divinely-directed cosmic battle fought down here on earth.

9   See quote by Jerry Falwell before the Introduction for his thoroughly mythical interpretation of September 11, 2001 wherein he revives the Old Testament understanding of God's protection of the nation being contingent upon the people's adequate religious performance. America's tolerance of those secularizing forces Falwell refers to is to him equally imperiling to the nation just as would be forsaking Israel and the Zionist effort, Palestinians notwithstanding.

tinians have accumulated over the course of the past seventy years is well documented, if insufficiently underscored, in American news and political discourse. The failure to underscore this situation was, and continues to be, partly responsible for helping obscure the motives of the accused terrorists who violently visited the U.S. in September of 2001.

The misery of the Palestinians is in its own way intimately implicated in the *actual motivations* of any number of terrorist attacks carried out by political *jihadi* Muslims. For all of their relatively young lives, these Muslims (we witness today) have observed Israel as the principal cause of suffering for the Palestinian people. Recall the Introduction where this was the third of three reasons Osama bin Laden used to justify to his followers the killing of Americans (see page 8). The American political and military establishments have supported Israel since its inception in 1948 and continue to do so. Israel obtains much military and financial assistance from the United States and this fact is not lost on the broader Islamic world. To the American news-viewing public, the narrative of the Israeli-Palestinian conflict is uniformly that of Israeli victims of Palestinian terrorism. It requires only a minor adjustment in the narrative to produce Jewish victims of Muslim terror and thereby implicate religions in the cause of the fighting.

To the mindset of our 1988 Bible study, had there been any way we could have understood that a future event we now call 9/11 would be an outcome of the *very same* political circumstances we were promoting in our religious viewpoints, this would have been chalked-up to the price of establishing divine will on earth and something unavoidable, if regrettable. It wasn't *our* will, this was *God's will*. This is a common, and apparently indispensable, intellectual posture in human self-justification and rationalization of other people's suffering by our hands.

Moreover, God had already taken sides.

Bible prophecy[10] centering on Israel's sovereignty when reconfigured into political ideology segues with U.S. conservative Christian political support for Israel and helps explain a sizeable sector of the U.S. population's rational for unwavering, and *always uncritical*, support for the modern state of Israel. "The theme of restoration has figured as well in

---

10   In its entirety in an extreme application, Israel and the Jewish people should have *absolute control* of the entire region of the Levant or eastern shores of the Mediterranean. There is simply no place or real estate for the Palestinians who ought to yield to this Hebrew-Biblical vision of Israelites/Jews solely inhabiting the land. See McTernan for a recent (2006 revised in 2012) overview of these ideas in their extreme. The back cover reads, "[T]here is a direct correlation between the alarming numbers of massive disasters striking America and her leaders pressuring Israel to surrender her land for 'peace.'" I don't believe the concept could be stated any more forthrightly and suggestively, if not more ahistorically and superstitiously.

Christian eschatology, which held that a Jewish return to Palestine was a precondition of the second coming of Jesus. In both synagogue and church those motifs have lasted to the present" (Cohen, 2-3).

This blend of prophecy and contemporary Middle Eastern events has proven politically significant and influential when marketed to congregants of this religious persuasion of Biblical Literalism. Theirs is not a truly political analysis but a matter of the message from the pulpit. Correlating the two (prophetic literature and current events) becomes an exercise in creatively connecting them in a persuasive argument that will bolster political capital for *only one* of the parties – the party God has chosen. This process is not grounded in a fair assessment of historical events. Rather, it is an extension of an ancient mythological-political way of thinking and it possesses a threat to stability in a democratic and humane world.

This is demonstrated by the outcomes seen thus far: untold misery and hardship for the Palestinian population singly. The Israelis are the stronger player in this conflict and therefore has more choices to negotiate the terms of a peaceful settlement. The weaker side has not the same the degree of political or military options, i.e., power; or in the parlance of *A Theory of Religion*, the same degree of control over its exchange ratios (see chapter three; Stark and Bainbridge, Def. 15: 33/326).

The Palestinians have consistently gotten a bad deal.

To get a sense of the numbers of Christian Americans who identify with this Biblical understanding of the Israeli-Palestinian issue, the beliefs of our 1988 Bible study group were the direct result of *one writer's* interpretation that made a mass-market sensation and became the *best-selling non-fiction paperback for the <u>entire</u> decade of the 1970s!* That book was Hal Lindsey's *The Late Great Planet Earth*[11] published in 1970 – first by a Christian press then by the mass-market publisher Bantam Books.[12] Today it ranks 46,000[th] at Amazon.com which includes tens of millions of books in the ranking. Not too shabby at all. The political weight of the support Israel garners from this segment of the American electorate is incalculable and ongoing.

The Late Great Planet Earth would later be made into a rather slick, for the mid-1970s anyway, film version melding visuals of current events, mostly disaster film footage of nuclear blasts, which seemed to correlate with the images of Bible prophecy and were narrated by the burly and familiarly-authoritative Orson Welles. This initial book was only the begin-

11   See Gorenberg, pages 120-123.
12   Bantam Books will figure relatively far-reaching in influence among the topics discussed in this book. See photo in Endnote to chapter five for examples of Bantam's activities.

ning for Hal Lindsey. He went on to author several books, all variations on the themes of Biblical Literalism, fundamentalist/evangelical theology and his unique brand of Bible prophecy coupled with pro-Israel Zionism and current events. Even today Hal Lindsey takes his television viewers on pilgrimages to the Holy Land and keeps them current on the Internet with *The Hal Lindsey Report*.

For the cause of Zionism, Lindsey's two later books on Bible prophecy, *The 1980's: Countdown to Armageddon* (1981) and *The Rapture: Truth or Consequences* (1983), were the most directly influential upon the 1988 deadline set for the culmination of world events. These were the books widely influential in evangelical churches in the lead-up to that critical year and were blueprints of future history for those of us participating in the Bible Study. Though lost on us, these books served a potent political special interest (Israel-Jewish) that came at great cost to an entire ethnic-religious (Palestinian/Arab-Muslim/Christian) community.

Honestly, the political concerns of the Palestinians were never considered an issue in our Bible study's conversations surrounding Biblical prophecy, other than how they thwarted or enhanced the potential for our Biblical vision's fulfillment. Our sympathies were with the Jewish side of the story and not the *other's*. This makes it a political theology whether or not such is intended by individual believers. American conservative Christian evangelists are most aware of the political nature of the texts, as one historian noted, "What was unusual about Israelite prophecy ... prophets expect to influence the political structure of society" (Seltzer, 79).

The origin of this modern political theology has its roots in England in the writings of John Nelson Darby (1800-1882) and was further developed and incorporated into the *Scofield Reference Bible* first published in 1909 in both England and the USA. This Biblically-literalist political theology took as its focus and cause the newly emerging (at the time) nationalist movement of Zionism. This fit hand-in-glove with the final "dispensations"[13] these Christians interpreted from the Bible. Though the history of futuristic prognosticating efforts is colorful if not tragic and sometimes comical, it has been a compelling set of ideas for sizeable segments of the Bible-reading population.

Cyrus Scofield and others, as originators of dispensationalism, were literarily active more-or-less contemporaneously with the rise of Zionism in Europe. In some ways, it was a "match made in heaven." Picked-up by evan-

---

13   Dispensations are periods of time which God utilizes to unfold a grand historical plan, like the chapters of a book successively reveal the plot elements of a story. Perhaps you've heard the childish quip best-suited for Sunday school, "history is His Story."

gelical and fundamentalist Americans in the 1920s during the fundamentalist battles discussed earlier in chapter two, apocalyptic symbolism would appeal well-beyond orthodox Christian groups. In fact, some of the most vibrant and fast-growing groups in the late-eighteenth and early-twentieth centuries were not from the mainstream of orthodox Christianity. Nevertheless, they were forged from the same American cultural milieu to which apocalyptic themes resonated both as *religious beliefs* and as *real-life experience* through economic collapse and social despair and threats of war. Apocalyptic notions were heightened as the country progressed through the wake of the Civil War (Millerites-Seventh-Day Adventists) then WWI (Jehovah's Witnesses) then post-WWII (evangelical).

A reflection on this eschatological[14] religious history is instructive. Also, it is a critical reflection worthwhile for all citizens as some of these same patterns persist today and will likely continue to persist in some manner or other in the context of American Christian beliefs for the foreseeable future. It is important to keep in mind that Christians who accept these general ideas about prophetic events are organized and united on issues and ideas that go far beyond that of interpreting the current events of any given decade (Melton, 147). This allows a group to persist beyond the date of any give failed prophecy.

The net effect of these ideas, however, and especially when organized through a network of churches, is that collectively they come to bear enormous weight upon political leaders who are dependent upon special interests for financing their campaigns and who directly benefit from these religious congregations. In contrast, the Palestinians have little to offer these same politicians and constitute the losers in the fight for representation in the American political process. Couple these with the American two-party system that is mostly evenly-bifurcated on the Israeli-Palestinian issue, which itself contributes to the stalemate by hamstringing any significant pressure from U.S. Congressional leaders coming to bear upon Israel's leaders, in whose hands the solutions ultimately lie.

In fact, one important facet of evangelical belief has been its universal condemnation and uniform, if overly simplistic, understanding of Islam, the prophet Muhammed, and, to be expected due to current world geopolitics, *jihad* in the context of Islamic and modern history. Biblically literalistic Christians will often deliberately stand in direct opposition to

---

14   Eschatology in religion are those ideas focused upon the end of history, whether one's own in death (in the more liberal versions of Christianity) or in world history and future events (as with the conservative fundamentalist, evangelical, and Pentecostal churches). Some associated terms are last days, end times, Armageddon, apocalyptic, millennialism, to name several. In the case of the Biblical Literalists this imagery is no imagery at all but a coded description of future events.

those who profess allegiance to the Qur'an and will too frequently deny to it the same status of "revealed scripture" that they grant to their own Bible. Ironically, Islam is sometimes interpreted by Muslims themselves as part of the Biblical prophecies and it (Islam) has a role in bringing about the end of the world scenario with the Middle East as its backdrop.

In Christianity, the eschatological worldview is a rich and imaginative panoply of scenarios conjured from the Good Book, most especially the books of Daniel and Revelation. These have also provided Hollywood with material for end-of-the-world dramas replete with the latest computer-graphics technology, which by now has become visual overload. Compare, for example, the two *Left Behind* films: released in the years 2000 and 2014. These two films showcase the dramatically-increased use and sophistication of computerized graphics in apocalyptic scenarios with the Bible providing the plot elements. Today's movies are the perfect medium for conveying these imaginative scenarios and planting into viewers' minds the seeds of a "Biblical" apocalyptic future.

The media *is* the message.

In the end, Hal Lindsey captained his readers on an imaginative voyage that others had charted before. It is a voyage steeped in a utopian vision of everlasting peace, but only after a trial-by-fire of unimaginable proportions. The point is to tame the imagination's use of these apocalyptic images and mold them into something spiritually-nourishing rather than temporally-destructive. The hope of a better future is not to be repudiated, but rather it is something worth working toward. However, it must be done in a manner that demands the common good be the standard and ultimate goal for all of humanity, in this case not only for Israelis but also for Palestinians. The key is not to repeat the errors of the past, and instead to infuse eschatological religion with the Transcendent Common Good and to develop within it a vision of the future expressed by civic pluralism.

REGARDING SIGNS of THINGS to COME (a):
WE'VE BEEN HERE BEFORE

American religious history is no stranger to, or stranger *because of*, the eschatological-apocalyptic elements that have weaved through it. Apocalyptism has its place in the religious imagination and cosmology of any number of religions, ancient and modern, and so is hardly anomalous in American Christianity. Religions offer to human beings a vision of ultimate goals and an as-yet-unrealized future filled with possibilities. For the believer, these possibilities are what may be focused-upon so that the drudgery of day-to-day living can be more easily endured – recall Marx. Little wonder the human mind finds intrigue and no small degree of solace in the realms of the as-yet-unattained and the possibly-unattainable.

These are where *hope* and *faith* reside, after all.

To an assortment of contemporary conservative Christian denominations, these topics of eschatological religion are frequently, if not disproportionately, highlighted. In sermons, discussions and literature, the end of humanity and its ultimate fate can be of central and paramount importance to the Christian message itself, even giving a sense urgency to their overall mission here in this life. My best guess is the last time someone came-a-callin' at your door with a message of Jesus and salvation, it was very likely a pair of Jehovah's Witnesses, *Awake* and *Watchtower* in-hand. Theirs is a particularly time-sensitive theology which motivates members to go out to the community, and they do so very systematically and thoroughly at that, to spread the message of an imminent summation to history. Conversely to the evangelical-fundamentalist eschatologists, the Jehovah's Witnesses have remained thoroughly apolitical and have thrown-in their lots with neither Republican nor Democrat, commie nor capitalist. The entire world and its governments are all lost causes, say the JWs, so it's best not to mess with them while awaiting the arrival of God's Kingdom.

Evidently the understandings of how God's coming kingdom ought to look now in this life or how it will look upon its final implementation have many possibilities.

The creation of eschatology is entirely imaginative and open to creative interpretation, and just as Hal Lindsey had articulated the prophetic path for evangelical Christians during the last quarter of the past century, the young American republic early-on saw William Miller (1784-1849) and the *Millerites* (est. 1860) as the first of the uniquely-American apocalyptic traditions. The Millerites would be the forerunners of today's Seventh-Day Adventists (SDA) and later Jehovah's Witnesses (JW) who are by now mainstream American Christian groups. In addition, these denominations would provide the institutional foundation for the off-shoot schismatic Texas group that came to be known as the Branch Davidians. Theirs is the history that precedes those unfortunate persons involved in the fateful Waco disaster of 1993, which comprises the topic of chapter seven.

Not unlike the May 1988 unfulfilled prophecy of our Bible study, the predicted return of Jesus in 1843/1844 similarly did not materialize for the Millerites and SDAs. Their disappointment was crushing, especially given that so many of them had sold all their material wealth in order to wait-it-out in the New York countryside. So much so, that it is known to this day as the "Great Disappointment" and serves as a cautionary tale in going out-on-the-limb of prophetic literalism. To their great credit, and as a positive testament to religious innovation, out of that disappointment came a health-promoting lifestyle that in many ways is the envy of American healthcare.

Groups who have experienced the failure of a prophecy don't necessarily disband in the face of religious contradiction or disillusionment and the cognitive dissonance these can generate. Religion is hardly the only area of human existence or intellectual life that creates contradictions. I would suggest that nature itself poses any number of life's contradictions and religion is the response to rationalize them or sort them out into some meaningful arrangement.

The regrouping of Seventh Day Adventism around the issues of health as a principal concern of the religious life, demonstrates how religion can evolve into more beneficial and practical concerns – and this from a belief steeped in eschatological mysticism. Because eschatological imagery is subject-to and created-by the imaginative processes, it can thereby be reinterpreted in almost any reasonable direction that makes sense to the congregation. In the case of the SDA failed prophecies, it was the extraordinary ability of the human mind to readjust to its new reality of the failed prophecy that kept the group going during its darkest hours.

Here again this could be called religious innovation.

As *A Theory of Religion* reminds us, "if a single explanation in a cultural system fails, people tend to seek another to replace it, without disturbing the rest of the system" and "when explanations in a cultural system fail, people will seek the most modest revision of it that will apparently repair the damage" (*ATOR*, P222 and P223: 220/343). With the failed 1884 SDA prophecy only a minor adjustment needed to be made. By modify their understanding or definition of a *miracle* from something other than an external event that violates the laws of nature (e.g., the supernatural and in this case cosmically supernatural) to something more mundane and personal, then the prophecy, and the group, could be salvaged (Stark and Finke, 109).

Today the SDAs continue to hold the belief that the messiah *did* return as previously promised. Only now they understand that it is their *bodies* that are the location of the Lord's return and not the planet earth. Jesus' arrival in 1844 was a *spiritual* arrival, not a cosmic one. Therefore, it is their bodies that must be cared for as they are the 'temples of the

Lord." Hence, the prophecies reveal, we ought to take maximum care of our physical bodies in order to properly honor and glorify the Lord. The most direct way to do this is to eat properly.

All too often though, humans do not learn from their own mistakes let alone the mistakes of their forerunners. The allure of the cosmically-climactic and apocalyptically-spectacular is just far more appealing than eating an apple a day.

But perhaps Charles Taze Russell (1852-1916) could be forgiven his exaggerations of the end-of-the-world prophecy given that "wars and rumors of wars" loom large in activating the prophetic imagination. Having been a former Adventist, the founder of the Jehovah's Witnesses was impressed that the world would come to an end in 1914. And to the many who participated in the "war to end all wars" it surely did, and to a devastating degree thanks to mustard gas and heavy-mechanized artillery (recall chapter two).

When it was over, the war had *not* brought all life on mother earth to an end, nor had it ushered-in the new millennium. Instead, the prophecy was subsequently revised by Russell to be a "spiritual" second coming rather than an actual or physical arrival. More-or-less the same strategy used by his SDA forerunners – a lesson he was wise learn. No need to reinvent the wheel, so to speak. As most readers will be well-aware, the JWs may be witnessed to this day strolling through the streets two-by-two of many a modern city.

These apocalyptic groups nowadays mostly refrain from pinning precise dates upon events having learned their lesson. Though if the reader were to attend a contemporary Kingdom Hall gathering of the Jehovah's Witnesses, she or he would find sermons focused upon how current events shadow Biblical passages. Pick-up any copy of *AWAKE* magazine and that is its emphasis. On occasions of international turmoil these speculations are especially-stirred with Middle Eastern wars and Israel's political struggles with the Palestinians easily conjuring the Bible-prophecy imagination. Fortunately, most prophetic speculations are immediately identified by the common sense of the average citizen as foolish, and rightly so.

But only so much egg can be wiped-off the face of the Biblical fortune-teller before the reasoned mind demands another meaning of the prophetic literature. In the meantime, and regrettably, in the hands of religious engineers with political motives in mind, the Bible as prophetic crystal ball can have enormous partisan persuasion.

REGARDING SIGNS of THINGS to COME (b):
WE DON'T HAVE to GO THERE AGAIN

The point of critiquing eschatological religion (just as with Biblical Literalism generally) is to realign its worldview consistent with the knowledge of science as we understand it today and to promote the Transcendent Common Good, civic pluralism and a healthy civil society. For their own social relevance's sake, not to mention their intellectual credibility, today evangelicals ought to reject an absolutist (essentialist) supernaturalist-eschatology and embrace a form of mystery in their religion that does not require the abandonment of reason and science to superstition (see chapter three and the reference to Robert E. Webber).

In addition, and as a consequence of the absence of such a realignment, foreign policy and the human rights of Palestinians are being deleteriously affected by this view and by the activism of its political supporters.

Celebrated evangelical author and historian Mark Noll scolds his fellow believers for disregarding history and common sense by embracing Bible prophecy. This is part of the overall abandonment of the intellect to which evangelical Christians have succumbed (Noll, 3). As if they could not have learned from the experiences of those others in the American prophetic past, evangelicals again put their credibility on the line, and their gullibility on display, in the wake of the 1990-1991 Gulf War. "Within weeks of the outbreak of this conflict, evangelical publishers provided a spate of books featuring efforts to read this latest Middle East crisis as a direct fulfillment of biblical prophecy heralding the end of the world" (Noll, 1994: 13).

The plea here is for modern believers, and not only Christian, to be "historical believers" and to accept their faith as a faith that is rooted in history and not fantasy. This will require the critical-historical approach that has been viewed as hostile to "Bible-believing faith," but this is a misnomer and an unwarranted confusion.

For the past one hundred years Biblical Literalism has served as something of an intellectual and moral scourge upon Christianity in the United States and must today be repudiated and rebuked by Christian believers themselves. It's not enough for outsiders to polemically criticize (see Foreword) or to academically critique the Bible-in-and-of-itself. This will only come across as an unjustified criticism, if not a spiritual and/or satanic attack. Even to the non-Biblical Literalist, to criticize the Bible itself, is to miss the point. The Bible is an historical document giving us an exemplary window into the Ancient Near East.*[15]* *It is not in need of repudiation but rather humane interpretation in light of historical knowledge.*

I suggest citizens, including believers, view the Bible (and any other ancient text that has survived the centuries) in the same way an architect would view an ancient building that also has survived the pummels of history. The fact that the building has been preserved as a result of the structure being re-purposed from its original use into that of some other contemporaneous use, and thereby maintained as a "living structure," is the principal benefit of those subsequent uses.

Consider the survival of the Pantheon in Rome similarly to the persistence of the Bible as a religious text. Commissioned during the reign of Augustus (27 BCE-14 CE) and completed under Hadrian (117-138 CE) the Pantheon was dedicated to "all the gods" of Rome and is one of the most architecturally-advanced buildings for its time. It was consecrated as a Christian church in the early seventh-century when the old pagan gods were removed and replaced with the churches' martyrs and saints. In more recent centuries, it even serves as a tomb for some of Italy's notables among whom is the Renaissance master Raphael. For the architect, however, the building stands as an historic monument to Roman construction techniques that still prove worthwhile to appreciate. What an unlikely historical prize!

The same is true of the Bible.

The Bible as an *historical text* has been preserved because of the churches' use of it as a *living text*. It is beside the point what other later people interpreted it to mean. As an artifact of history, it has incalculable worth by providing insights into ancient times, both mythological and actual. The challenge is to draw from it the lessons applicable to modern society without becoming trapped by ancient laws that do not properly reflect current times, values, and culture. The modern tools of historiography help today's historians and scholars do just that.

Even a cursory reading of the Old Testament reveals an antipathy on God's part for his people the Israelites, and today by logical extension *all believers*, questioning or doubting Him, never mind disobeying Him. The people of Israel were to have faith in the power of their God to deliver them from their enemies. All they had to do was obey God's law and fruitfully multiply. Seems easy enough. Seeking any type of prosperity or wealth, physical or spiritual comfort, or the affections of the women of

---

15   Ancient Near East is an historical-archaeological term to designate the region we today refer to as the Middle East.

other cultures was strictly forbidden to the Hebrews/Israelites by their Yahweh – a distant and rather stern deity at that.

No less was consulting the oracles of other deities an affront to God that he could not tolerate.

But humans can be unrepentantly-inquisitive, even to the knowledge of their own destruction. Yahweh warns his people not to consult diviners, soothsayers, astrologers, or sorcerers and there are any number of injunctions against such. Deuteronomy 18:14 and Jeremiah 27:9 are examples. The entire enterprise of "prophecy" as a form of literature in the Hebrew-Old Testament was less about fortune-telling than it was about establishing a precedent for a people who were flirting with disobedience. The prophetic voice was a contemporaneous warning about straying from the law by using the historical experiences of the people to amplify the story. Similar to a parent saying to their child as its adolescence approaches, "don't be sexually promiscuous or you will catch a sexually-transmitted disease," or in the kindly advice to a friend, "you had better eat properly or you will develop heart disease or diabetes." In neither of these instances does the advisor *know for certain* that the listener will succumb to the risk, it's only that it has happened to others in the past. Much in the same way we all *know* the sun will rise in the morning, it is a knowledge based upon past events.

So too with God's warnings and admonishments.

Let me use the Book of Daniel as an example. Daniel is often cited as a prophetic book by contemporary Christians who see any number of warnings to today's believers embedded within it, and with allusions to current world events (e.g., Middle East conflicts especially, but sometimes implicating Russia). As the *New Bible Dictionary* puts it, "This important apocalyptic book proved the basic framework for Jewish and Gentile history from the time of Nebuchadrezzar to the second advent of Christ" (Douglas, et al., 264). The author of Daniel begins his book, *In the third year of the reign of Jehoiakim king of Judah, Nebuchadnezzar* [same king as Nebuchadrezzar] *king of Babylon came to Jerusalem and besieged it* (Amplified Bible). This gives the reader the impression that the author is living sometime between 605-562 B.C.E. The dates of kings are well-recorded and known and so that is when the author wants his reader to believe he is writing. Therefore, when he states later in his book that the Medes and the Persians will destroy Babylon and he mentions the kings Belshazzar, Darius and later Alexander the Great and Antiochus IV, these would all be future events to him.

But Daniel's prophetic crystal ball suddenly goes dark before Augustus and the Romans and sometime after Antiochus IV invaded and committed the sacrilege of the temple in 167 BCE. The desecration of the Jewish temple by Antiochus was an affront to the Israelites and their religion to be sure. It sparked the Maccabean Revolt of 167-164 B.C.E. Terrible as that desecration of Antiochus' was, it was nowhere near the devastating event of the Second Destruction of the Temple by the Roman Titus in 70 C.E. The obvious question is, why would Daniel stop short of prophesying the calamitous Second Destruction?

Quite simply, it had not yet happened at the time of the authoring of the Book of Daniel. "Critics claim that the book was compiled by an unknown author about 165 BC, because it contains prophecies of post-Babylonian kings and wars which supposedly become increasingly accurate as they approach that date" (Douglas, 263).

A comparable scenario would be if I were to write today: "I, Blair Alan Gadsby, living in the year of Our Lord 1792, being the third year of George Washington's presidency, do declare that the following President's will reign in the New World..." I proceed to list some Presidents by name, mention various events such as the Civil War, WWI, the Depression, WWII, some other wars, and refer accurately to Presidents only up to Obama and Trump. Someone reading my rendering one hundred years from now, not to mention one thousand years from now, should be able to accurately discern when my authorship took place.

There is a simple axiom at work here in human affairs: *The past can be known but not influenced and the future may be influenced but not known.* All human knowledge conforms to this law, no exceptions (*ATOR*, Def. 1 and Def. 2: 27/325). In the Book of Daniel those past events widely-known to the Israelites were used as cautionary warnings against disobeying God or consulting diviners, but also to encourage those who were rebelling during the Maccabean Revolt to keep-up the good fight as God was on their side. The prophet project then, is using knowledge of the past as future guide, much as in the parent-child STD conversation.

Today there can be no forbearance on the part of religious believers justifying ideas, prophetic or otherwise, that can be directly linked to the source of human suffering. The *Critical Theory of Religion* cultivated in my arguments cannot allow for it and therefore this explanation of Bible prophecy is in order. Religious Studies scholarship as a science has as one of its goals to challenge theological assumptions and prompt theological openness to reinterpretation that can thereby create a new understanding of the Bible and Israel that uplifts the Palestinian people to their rightful place in the land of *their* ancestors.[16]

---

16   On the topic of reading the Bible in light of modern understandings of history and

Just as the Israelite God was most merciless in the Hebrew Old Testament, Jesus would subsequently soften the image of God in the New Testament, but then the apostle Paul injects into his epistles, and thereby into Christianity generally, the exclusivist-style religion of Judaism of the centuries when the texts were being written. It is of some consequence that Paul is the author of much of the rest of the New Testament beyond the Gospels.

So, for example, one major stumbling-block for contemporary Christian is where Paul demands of his readers: "And if Christ be not raised from the dead, then our faith is in vain" (1 Corinthians 15:14). This is taken most literally. For many a Christian with a literalist Biblical view, these words compel them to believing in the historicity of Jesus' resurrection. But there is no requirement for such a belief. These words of the former Jewish Pharisee Saul now writing as the Christian Apostle Paul need not be taken literally. The Jewish religion of Paul's day was itself very dogmatic, literalistic, exclusivist, and highly legalized. Once Paul had been frightened by his vision of Jesus on the Road to Damascus (Acts 9: 1-31) he transposes his legalism into the newly-developing faith community (see Galatians 1: 6-9 for a sample of Paul's views about apostasy and maintaining a certain purity of faith).

His admonishments are simply not fit for a modern pluralistic society such as contemporary America's.

There will always be a tension between the two interpretations, the literal and the metaphorical. Recall Stark and Bainbridge's observation that there really is no religion without something of a literal reference point, beyond personal storytelling and metaphors. The modern world, far from repudiating such literal notions of the future, have embraced these age-old concepts with a new, even technologically-informed interpretation of these themes.

As noted, Hal Lindsey's *Late Great Planet Earth* mastered this synthesis which was responsible for its enormous success. In the documentary version, Orson Welles skillfully and convincingly tells us how 70% of the Bible's prophecies have come true, and with a video-backdrop of disaster footage on a global scale. The two interpretations of eschatological imagery fuse in the visual media so as to make the metaphorical literal – and frighteningly so. This put-the-fear-of-God-in-you-imagery was the intent all along of the prophetic voice, even in ancient times. Perhaps that's why it works so wonderfully with modern media imagery.

religious literature (scriptures), i.e., historiography, I recommend Borg, Noll (1991), and White.

True, in the early church, proofs of working wonders and miracles were the standard by which the ancients judged their messengers. Who *isn't* seduced by magic? Superstitions are nothing new. They simply must not be the basis upon which we apportion rights to individuals in a constitutional democracy. Therefore, detaching the ancient Judaic-Biblical notion of prophecy and the prophetic message from the current Christian divination-based theologies of futuristic fortune-telling, which are more akin to superstitions than religious faith, is a necessary step in orienting today's American theologies *away from the political obsession over the disputed land.*

Focusing upon the spirit is by-far preferable.

I would reemphasize the admonition of John Carroll that the return of Jesus need not be considered a literal return but can be seen better in the context of a *personal eschatology* – one's personal end-of-days. Rather than the "collective imminent eschatology of the earliest Christian generation," one can today interpret the second coming of Christ within the framework of the fact that,

> one does not know when one will die, and in any case we are given only a few years of life. (Perhaps social institutions like churches, not just individuals, might benefit from such a self-understanding.) The *parousia* of Jesus as cosmic judge and liberator is thus transformed into a personal coming of Jesus to the individual at the moment of death.... The central New Testament image of the triumphant return of Christ need not be interpreted literally, as if Jesus would actually ride the clouds back to earth in a show of glory and power visible to all. But this potent symbol of Christian hope must be taken seriously, for it points to the completion of God's work of life and salvation for this planet and all who call it home (Carroll, 197-198).

Religious maturity of this type can lead to true and lasting civic pluralism and a healthy civil society as citizens (human beings) exercise their faith in the light of their own mortality. In such a society where religious pluralism is understood and synthesized into the civic mind, the incidents cited in the following chapters would be far less apt to succeed as people would see more clearly through the *façade of religion as motivator of behavior*, and instead see the incidents for what they truly are, political opportunism of the most partisan sort.

By impeding this religious maturity in society via religious engineering, the political elites' agendas have come at a very deep civic cost and have produced a primitive form of political life within the United States. The nation is currently stuck in a two-party system that has pitted conservatives against liberals, straights against gays, pro-choice against pro-life, Black lives against Blue lives, and even long-past the Soviet collapse, socialism is frequently revived and burned-in-effigy as the current threat to democratic freedoms – "no socialized healthcare" the conservative's slogan goes all the while the U.S. ranks abysmally in infant and general mortality rates and overall access to healthcare for millions – not to mention the American healthcare system is by far the costliest system among advanced nations. This is well-known and understood by the population at large.

Primarily conservative evangelical religion continues to serve as a national civic cult in service to capitalism's excesses, in spite of the damage to human welfare – American and Palestinian.

On more than one level then, lessons could be learned from the Seventh-Day Adventists. Channeling their own prophetic energies (and disappointments) into a lifestyle of healthy living, they have developed a food-based philosophy and theology webbing together the scientific with the humanities to create a religion of sustainable living. In addition, their strong community bonds reinforce their theology of the priority of civic health (life longevity among SDAs is claimed to be five-to-ten years longer than the average American, in addition to certain other better-health indicators – Doblmeier). Religious pluralism is less of a focus with them as theirs is a socio-defined religious community, which by the way, just happens to be apolitical. Be that as it may, the existence of such a group is well within the reach of all those of good-will in building a healthy civil society and fostering civic pluralism.

But as we have seen already, political tensions and fears fuel religious imaginings.

It would be a contradictory and portentous time for America in the period after WWII and the nation needed some type of celestial confirmation of its soon-to-be-dominant role in earthly affairs thereby fulfilling the vision of John Winthrop that America be a "city on a hill" (see page 30). For it was only in the previous year before the Star of David flew over the newly-declared state of Israel that the sightings of the first flying saucers over the skies of America would signal the dawn of a new technological age and its Cold War atheist-leaning enemy complete with atomic horrors. Both of these events (the founding of Israel in 1948 and the coming of the saucers in 1947) were as though harbingers of America's pre-eminent role, indeed destiny, to lead the world into the future. Both the *re-*

turn of the Jews to their Biblical homeland and the *arrival of extraterrestrial visitors* seemed as confirmations of that role for America. Both narratives were imbibed with celestial implications: one alien the other Biblical. Little wonder one author would state *God Drives a Flying Saucer* (Dione) – it was only a matter of time, if of little originality.

But destiny was calling the Land of the Free to a higher mission.

For many a believer and non-believer alike, America seemed poised in the post-WWII era to carry forth the light of freedom to the world in the face of godless communism. For the believer, one-way America could shine that light was helping the Biblical children of God establish themselves in the land of their ancestors. To help make that happen, not only did the Jews need to find favor among American Christians, but the Palestinians would have to be positioned in the minds of *all* Americans as the villain. For the social and religious engineers, such a time was propitious for the meme of the lone gunman.

IN ALL THINGS RELIGIOUS, the PAST *is* NOW, and THERE *is* HERE

As illustrated initially in the Introduction with the Roman Nero's persecution of Christians in the first century, religion was and continues to be a potent tool in the hands of political leaders to orient public opinion and accomplish any number of personal, tribal or national ambitions. In this modern example of Christian Zionism, global political and international relations are set in motion and/or sustained, in part, with religious mythologies. Regrettably, the belief we held as "Bible-believing Christians" in 1988 that Israel's and indeed the world's history would radically change due to *eternal-supernatural* intervention, came at a horrible *temporal-humanitarian* cost to the Palestinian people. Conservative Christian denominations are far more likely to support American intervention on behalf of Israel and deny or downplay Israel's mishandling of Palestinian human rights. As an ongoing historical reality for the Palestinians, these policies have resulted in untold suffering for a civilian population for over half a century.

But there is an even darker and more menacing side to these long-laid plans.

In the effort to build sympathy and support for the Jewish-Zionist-Israeli cause, a certain amount of *pathos of distance*, and the employment of the *other*, had to be generated toward the Muslim-Arab-Middle East nations in the "hearts and minds" of the American people. In a research inquiry such as the one undertaken here, a person can only ponder under what conditions was this strategic connection constructed in the political psyche of Americans to link all things Palestinian and Arab to our enemies? Considering the long-practiced cinema-graphic demonization of Arabs in American films, there is little doubt that portraying Arab-Palestinians as terrorists (and soon enough *potentially all Muslims* due to radical Islamic teachings) was a very small adjustment for the American mind to be engineered to make.

But U.S. support for the modern state of Israel draws from well beyond religious sources to the broader cultural myths perpetuated within movies and news media. Support for Israel is one component of America's broader Middle East strategy and so must be seen in relationship to the military industrial complex and the conglomerate of power for which it operates since military interests and investment rank high in the region. America's mostly-undiscussed relationship to Zionism is only one component, even if important. Little wonder the very term "Zionism" is obscure to most Americans, therefore so are the root causes and potential solutions.

Part of the American pro-Zionist effort has been to tilt the ideological playing field against Arabs and their religion, principally Islam, in the minds of the American public. There has been a consistent and sustained effort on the part of Hollywood productions to portray Arabs and Muslims as villains, even when incidental to the story. These instances have been documented sufficiently in Jack Shaheen's *Reel Bad Arabs: How Hollywood Vilifies a People*. Without rhyme or reason the Arab is an innately bad human being to the American movie-goer. This caricature of the Arab as someone to be universally feared has impacted the American psyche and continues to have political capital in the ongoing war on terrorism. Middle East historian Rashid Khalidi describes it this way:

> In some sense the more recent mode of analysis [rarely emphasizing Western interference] is worse than the earlier one, for it has spawned a ubiquitous and influential school of "terrorism" studies,[17] invariably focusing on the Middle East. The distortion in reporting on the Middle East in the 1950s thus has a certain enduring relevance, as it forms the foundation for a structure of misunderstanding regarding the region which still prevails in some sectors of American government, the media, and public discourse (188).

17   This is what I referred to when I stated in the Introduction that by the President telling Americans that radicals Muslims *hated us because of our freedoms* and *not* because of anything that the United States has done in the Middle East by way of military actions, sponsoring and enabling repressive client states, and/or supporting Israel, that this opened the door for mass confusion, the "why do they hate us?" questions, and ultimately served as the pretext for a very ugly covert government operation; the subject of chapter eight.

This is called "conditioning": preparing a population's collective mind to respond in a predetermined way to external incitements – and fear can be counted upon as an effective incitement. Promoting Israel necessitated demonizing the Palestinians. We find ourselves today entangled politically with Israel and siding with our ally even when it behaves in a very questionable manner concerning the human rights of non-Israeli citizens of the region. This arrangement should be an unacceptable outcome for the contemporary Christian mind and conscience in order to satisfy the demands of a Bible prophecy, and a politically unacceptable outcome for the American citizen and politician in order to satisfy the demands of foreign policy commitments and national security concerns.

But the imagery is pushed upon the population with intent to control the thoughts and minds of viewers.

As has happened, and by design, "radical Islam" emerged from having been conjoined to the Arab-Palestinian cause in the context of broader Middle East conflict. Though radical Islam would ultimately become the principal delusion for Middle East entanglements, the Palestinian and accused Robert F. Kennedy assassin, Sirhan Sirhan's personal story and epic historic importance to American political-Middle Eastern lore are of crucial significance in getting the initial political orientation of the country and the narrative-story tilted in Israel's favor and against Palestinians-Arabs-Muslims.

A valuable 2007 documentary titled *RFK Must Die* reminds us that the assassination of Robert F. Kennedy was considered the "first Arab terrorist act" against the United States (O'Sullivan; 59:00; see also Issenberg). RFK had agreed to make a sale of U.S. military technology (missiles) to Israel and so his Sirhan's motives can be constructed quite easily. Since his fellow countrymen, the Palestinians and Arab nations generally, will be on the receiving end of these missiles, thus validating or justifying, at least logically, Sirhan's actions. He was never reported to have a violent personality or was much politically-ideological committed to causes.

RFK's assassination would take place, with the curious note of timing, one-year-to-the-day of the break-out of the Israeli-Arab 6-Day War from June 5-10, 1967 setting in motion an American political (mythological?) synergy with Israel over and against the Palestinians and the Arab-Muslim world. To the degree that Sirhan's ethnicity (Arab) and nationality (Palestinian) come to bear upon his motives, then it is one facet of the argument for American support for Israel and the consequences thereof – his Palestinian-*Christian* origins aside.

But alas, the myth of the lone gunman rears its head in a Manchurian Candidate manner.

Sirhan's involvement in the June 5, 1968 assassination is what many researchers consider a mind-control operation with the use of Sirhan as a patsy, conducted possibly by agents of the U.S. federal government, most especially the Central Intelligence Agency (CIA), other military intelligence offices, and/or paramilitary or even private intelligence firms. The combination of questions raised by the muzzle distance of the fatal shot (O'Sullivan, 33:42), the angle at which the fatal shot is itself fired (38:50), and unaccounted-for shots fired in the pantry where the murder took place (41:30), do not comport with the story of a single gunman firing from the front where Sirhan was known to be positioned. The very credible eyewitness accounts of armed security guards among the seventy-seven people in the pantry and in the vicinity of the murder (44:30), and three young people escaping out the back of the hotel declaring "we've shot him" – one being the infamous "girl in the polka-dot dress" (46:50, 53:30), the unjustifiably coercive interrogation of the eyewitness Sandra Serrano (52:20) all point to a more complex picture than the sole assassination.

Upon these facts the reader may pass his or her own judgments.

Nevertheless, circumstantially, the assassination is contemporaneous with a long-run CIA-military program known as "MK Ultra" and its cousins which are various attempts at direct mind control, both with *individuals* and as *public opinion persuasion campaigns in the media*. As an example of the former, indications that Sirhan may have been drugged (1:12:00) would suggest as much.

Also, much has been made of the fact that Sirhan claims to recall none of his actions and he to this day consistently psychologically responds and behaves as a person completely dissociated from the event. Curiously, found among Sirhan's possessions was a notebook containing cryptic writing of a political but repetitive nature that has all the hallmarks of hypnotic programing: "RFK must die RFK must die RFK must be assassinated Robert F Kennedy Robert F Kennedy Robert F Kennedy must be assassinated assassinated assassinated ..." (1:20:30).[18]

With the case of Sirhan Sirhan the introduction of *overt mind-control techniques* at the individual level are utilized in the manipulation of the

---

18   Colin Ross has studied the role of American psychiatrists in inducing multiple personalities. He refers to "Sirhan Sirhan was a self-created Manchurian Candidate at the dissociative disorder not otherwise specified (DDNOS) level." That is, "a self-created assassin, but not consciously so." Ross does not dismiss the possibility of external actors in Sirhan's mental conditioning, he simply avoids it to instead focus-upon and establish Sirhan's medical-psychiatric diagnosis, about which he confirms was in a dissociative state, regardless of its origin (See chapter six; Ross, 216-217).

public mind. And while this assertion may the strike the reader as absurd, it is far from it. Chapter six will delve into the topic of the mind control experiment known as the Peoples Temple/Jonestown community of the 1950s through to November 1978 which was itself *only one* effort in the much larger CIA-MK Ultra mind control program referred to above. About this there is much publicly available confirmation.

By this late stage today some fifty-years after the assassination, the assertion that Sirhan's status as the "first Arab terrorist" (Issenberg, 2008) comes with enormous historical and political implications. The benefit of hindsight, and the comments of FBI officials that Sirhan longed to avenge the Palestinian cause (1:02:00), make this observation even clearer as we can now see it as the beginning of a long narrative with Middle East policy implications lasting decades and implementing large military activations on behalf of US-ally Israel.

Another example of a disinformation campaign against the public on behalf of Israel's war efforts and security, if not hegemony, in the Middle East comes in the form of the tragic attack by Israel upon the American Naval research ship *USS Liberty*.

As always, the way high public officials handle international incidents is revealing of motives and agendas. In the case of the state of Israel, committed ally of the U.S., the *USS Liberty* incident may be yet another example of state power using deception to gain military advantage in the form of the justification for an attack, in this case against Egypt; or maybe to suppress information as the Liberty was an intelligence ship and not an attack ship and may have had intelligence Israel did not want America to possess, for example, an Israeli-planned attack against the Golan Heights in Syria, or the killing of Egyptian POWs in the Sinai. The precise motivations pale to the handling of the incident by officials *after the fact*.

U.S. officials up to the level of President Johnson go to bat on behalf of Israeli officials in order to help cover-up what actually happened. If there was a deeper motive on the part of Israel (military expediency suggests that an attack upon a U.S. ship in neutral waters off the coast of Egypt would/could be easily confused for an Egyptian attack and therefore Egypt would sustain the retaliatory effects directly aiding Israel's efforts in its war against Egypt) this would be a case of a false flag military attack, something the reader will encounter again later in these pages.

For the thesis of this book *it does not matter what the Israeli's motives were*, whether a case of mistaken identity (official story) or a deliberate act for some reason known only to Israeli commanders (conspiracy theories).

As always forensics must win the day in our explanations of events. And in the case of the *USS Liberty*, forensics indicates the mislabeled "conspiracy theories" possess the best factual basis (that is, *repeated* Israeli attacks on the helpless *Liberty* betray the assertion of mistaken identity).[19]

What is of interest, instead, to the thesis of this book is *the subsequent American political management of the incident*. The point highlighted here is U.S. officials' willingness to take political risks on behalf of the state of Israel and to foster smoothly working diplomatic relations with them. Less of a direct concern would be a motive to satisfy the politically-significant and wealthy sector the U.S. elite establishment that includes both American Christians as well as American Jews on behalf of the Zionist cause.

The Arab world was militarily and politically put back on its heels after the Israeli victory of 1967. To them, the miracle for the Jews was a disaster. Thereafter, as suggested above, a systematic pro-Israel, anti-Arab, and by implication, anti-Muslim worldview was promulgated in American culture.

The Middle East nations, like much of the rest of the globe, succumbed to the Cold War partitioning between supporters of the West and American-style democracy or the East and Soviet-style communism. As much of chapter three argued, the Cold War was a spending-bonanza for the military-industrial-complex as arms sales soared and client nation-states purchased arms from their respective patron, either the USA or USSSR.

With Israel solidly on the side of American democracy and the surrounding Arab nations aligning themselves with and purchasing the armaments of the Soviets, the stage was effectively set for Cold War tensions in the Middle East. Within the Arab world, the struggle for political self-determination from colonialism with its deep investments in oil, the history of ruling family regimes, the drive for self-definition with or without an Islamic influence all converge in the aftermaths of two World Wars, the realization of Zionism, and then the Six-Day War and the rise of Palestinian nationalism. And this brief overview does not begin to detail the complexity of the political arrangements forged *within* Middle East countries; think Lebanon and the fragile alliances that have resulted in internal factionalism only to be compounded by external Israeli pressure.

For my generation the mid-1970s Lebanese civil war inaugurated our education to the horrors of the Middle East, culminating with the bombing of the international peacekeeping force's barracks in 1983 in which three hundred people were killed among whom were 241 Americans. But

---

19   The reader might find the topic of the "USS Liberty Incident" a fascinating and relevant one in light of the research presented here. A YouTube search will yield plenty of uncontroversial material on the subject.

even the Lebanese war was complicated by Israel's military dominance in the region post-6 Day War.

Stepping into this volatile political milieu was Syrian philosopher and author Sadik al-Azm (mentioned in the previous chapter). Coming from an historically-influential family in the Syrian Ottoman Empire, and educated in Philosophy at Yale, he published two books in Arabic in the immediate aftermath of the Six-Day War, *Self-Criticism After the Defeat* (1968) and *Critique of Religious Thought* (1969) that were both controversial and the second landed him a short stint in a Lebanese prison on charges of fomenting sectarian tensions. The former book critiqued the Arab nations' cultural and political responses to Israel's decisive military victory and al-Azm found them wanting. All too often resorting to tribal superstitions for explanations regarding their existential situation. He quotes the

> Mufti of the Hashemite Kingdom of Jordan, in the course of explaining the Arab defeat and the meanings and moral to be drawn from it to the newspaper *Al-Dustur* (December 22, 1967) stated about the Jews: They lack the prowess, boldness, or courage to accomplish these deeds, and we know them better than most others do. However, God desired to impose this group upon us because of *our distance from our religion* (italics mine; 2011: 39-40).

The reasoning of the Mufti is identical to that of American preacher Jerry Falwell's assertion quoted preceding the Introduction to this book wherein he blames the 9/11 terrorist attack on "the pagans, abortionists, feminists, gays, lesbians … the ACLU, People for the American Way … all of them who tried to secularize America, I point the finger in their faces and say you helped this happen." At its heart, this is a superstitious understanding of the event – God let it happen on purpose, or God made it happen on purpose! Take your pick.

But it was in the second of his books, *Critique of Religious Thought*, that Sadik reserved his harshest criticisms of religious manipulation of the masses by Arab elites. In a chapter titled "On the Apparition of Mary" he blasts the religious, media, and political elites for endangering the masses by capitalizing-upon the religious expressions of the general population.

> It is truly regrettable that not a single intellectual … thinker … literary critic, writer, or journalist … has raised his or her voice to respond to these wild claims and to call those … who were struck by this madness to rationality, balance and refraining from manipulating the religious feelings of the masses (2015: 141).

> This happens everywhere [referring the apparition]. But then it was being manipulated by regimes and various forces. That's why I wrote the book. The religiosity of rulers is always suspect. That's my rule. And I know it because I come from a ruling class family. Religion is at the service of rulers (2006).

As discussed in the previous chapter, I had the opportunity to meet Sadik in the last decade of his life. He was a generous man who gave to me freely of his time as I sought to piece together the complex web of political relations within the Middle East and the interactions the U.S. had there prior to and in the wake of 9/11.[20] I had read about his book *Critique of Religious Thought* published in Beirut in 1969 in the wake of the *nakba*,[21] or the defeat of the Arab armies to Israel in the Six-Day War – a history we know far too little of in the USA is that of Middle East and Arab national politics. A tragedy given that we are so deeply involved in the region. Arab national politics were very tumultuous in the post-Nasserite period (1958-1961) and then again in the post-Six Day War (1967) decades as the Cold War overshadowed and infiltrated local relations in most every region of the world.

Religion's use by the American politico-media establishment is not dissimilar to the conditions of the Arab world as it was in the post-1967 political crisis milieu. Sadik observed back then,

> Even before the defeat of 1967, the Arab liberation movement knew that Arab reactionaries and their international allies were using religious thought as an ideological weapon, and yet no great importance was attached to this fact (Al-Azm, 2007: 93).

This observation would even be found on the back of the original 1969 Arabic edition of *Critique of Religious Thought*:

> Rarely does modern Arab thought attempt to openly challenge the intellectual structures and the dominant metaphysical ideology of our society, because penetrating this realm touches its most sensitive area, which is the religious question. But the contemporary Arab revolution cannot endlessly avoid addressing

20   Sadik al-Azm was a Sunni Arab Syrian intellectual of some repute both by family-name and personal intellectual force. A recent article published shortly after Sadik's passing pays something of a tribute to the man and his political views (Ze'evi).

21   Nakba" is the Arabic word for disaster, tragedy or calamity and is used politically as a reference to the June 1967 Six-Day War between Israel and the surrounding Arab states. In this sense, the tragedy for Arab politicians and states was the hard realization that Israel was an insurmountable military force to be reckoned with. The term is also used to refer to the original 1947 partition and subsequent creation of Israel in 1948. In both cases, the civilian Palestinian population paid the heaviest price for the creation of Israel and the annexation of land required to do so.

vital questions that are connected with metaphysical religious ideology and its relationship with the revolution itself – including all the problems that arise from reactionary Arab forces using religion as a major "theoretical" weapon to mislead the masses (Chalala-Teague).

Sadik had himself addressed "conspiracy theories" in Arabic culture back in the 1960s and was critical of his fellow Arabs for resorting to religious explanations and political conspiracy theories as explanations for their governments' inadequate, or worse inept, abilities in negotiating successful diplomacy with Israel. But his criticisms were primarily reserved for those in power and only secondarily aimed at the average Muslim "mind" and its anti-modern tendencies. In an essay he wrote in the latter years of his career he recognized that *even he had* been deceived by political narratives. Sadik writes:

> Let me recount a small story from memory. Shortly after the Ba'ath party and the military seized power in Syria, 8 March 1963, Damascus was buzz with rumors about a conspiracy hatched by the CIA, in collusion with right wing Syrian forces and elements, to overthrow the new progressive regime.[22] Then, I had just returned to Damascus after finishing my studies in the United States and quickly joined the "rational center" there in criticizing the reigning conspiratorial mentality and in denouncing the resulting hysterical rhetoric and "absurd" accusations of the new authorities against the United States and the West in general. Many many decades later, and while in Washington DC, I learned from freshly released classified documents of the State Department that the crazy Syrian conspiracy theorists of those days were right on target, while we the sober rational center were dead wrong (Graf, 19).

We would do well to follow Sadik's rule he told me in that Los Angeles interview and mentioned in the previous chapter: "the religiosity of rulers is always suspect." I would today rephrase it thus, "statements about religion by officials are always suspect. Especially statements about other people's religions." If this awareness were consistently held in the public's consciousness, it would be far less vulnerable to religious engineering and social-political manipulation.

---

22   That progressive regime, the secularist Ba'athist party, would have the participation of Hafez al-Assad, father of Bashar al-Assad who is currently under fire in the same manner?

FROM TRINITY to TRIUMVIRATE:
The AMERICAN WAY of RELIGION

In the quest for a conceptual, philosophical and morally-authoritative grounding for laws and an application of those laws to the general public, we need look no further back in history than the time of the nation's founding. The general religious liberties granted in the founding documents transcend individual religious boundaries and free the public to create social and political space that values and cultivates religious pluralism. This is the only attitude toward religions that ensures *everyone's* equal rights and frees from suspicion select *other* religious groups by embracing them into the political process.

In American democracy, there is *no religious other – E Pluribus Unum* – out of the many comes the one. This is the American way of religion.

The point at hand is to reorient American Christianity *away from Biblical Literalism* (which has stultified American Christians' intellectual activities and thwarted social unity) and *toward the American Triumvirate* of documents (Declaration of Independence, Constitution, Bill of Rights) and the founding fathers' understanding of religions' role(s) in the American form of government and social structure. This is done with intent to guide social religious propriety and convention to foster the health of civil society and promote civic pluralism. The goal is more sociological than religious, as it ought to be.

American Christians need not fear what one evangelical leader called "sham unity" in matters of democratic cohesion. American citizens (not only Christians) also need *not* insist upon the type of unity one would better expect from a smaller social unit such as that found within a local community or church-gathering, than in a modern democracy of over 300 million people of diverse cultures. To compare such small-scale unity to that conceived in *e pluribus Unum* is misguided. J.I. Packer, the evangelical leader referred to above, in his book *"Fundamentalism" and the Word of God*, shows no self-awareness about the arbitrariness of his own position and its apparent "authoritative" i.e., Biblical, stance (45). Hence his willingness to consider it a *sham* to make attempts at unity with those who believe differently and thinking that it somehow compromises the ideals of the faith required by the Bible. Packer's admonishments are directed at other Christian denominations no less, and he states, "The more one probes the differences between Roman [Catholicism] and Protestant, Liberal and Evangelical, the deeper they prove to be" (45). How inter-religious dialogue (pluralism) fits into this mindset is difficult to see.

These types of religious injunctions ought to be rejected by citizens as unwarranted theological speculations detrimental to the health of civic society and civic pluralism, indeed they are detrimental to the Transcendent Common Good itself and rightly should give the evangelical-fundamentalist an "uneasy conscience." The evangelicals' problem has been diagnosed, but not transcended. Their struggle for social and intellectual legitimacy is in the balance and Biblical Literalism is their chief stumbling-block.

The father of modern fundamentalism, Carl F. Henry (1913-2003), recognized the fundamentalist-evangelicals' dilemma in 1947 but provided a problematic solution with no hope of success in that it too was stuck on the flypaper of Biblical Literalism,

> The failure of the evangelical movement to react favorably on any widespread front to campaigns against social evils has led, finally, to a suspicion on the part of non-evangelicals that there is something in the very nature of Fundamentalism which makes a world ethical view impossible. This modern mind-set, insisting that evangelical supernaturalism [i.e., Biblical Literalism] has inherent within it an ideological fault which precludes any vital social thrust is one of the most disturbing dividing lines in contemporary thought (Henry, 11).

Henry is correct in his recognition but wrong in his solution. A healthy civil society and civic pluralism cannot be built upon such narrow visions of meaning and authority, and "evangelical supernaturalism" has no place in civic pluralism. No form of *religious essentialism* is compatible with civic pluralism beyond that which can be interpreted to include the generalized welfare of all citizens. Religious essentialism creates fixed categories of all sorts that divide one from the *other*, an effort the project of civic pluralism is intended to correct.

This absence of fixed religious categories in Biblical Literalism is exemplified in the contradiction between Jesus' historical message and orthodox Christian belief in that the two are not-much related in time and space, nor in kind. The first-century Jewish Rabbi *Yeshua bin Joseph* (his Hebrew name) with his ethical message of love and humanity surpassing the precepts of the law, is not the same character as the resurrected Greco-Roman God-man of the New Testament who transcends Jew and Gentile. Further, the historical Jesus resembles even less-so the *Trinitarian deity of the fourth-century church* produced by the Council of Nicea in 325 C.E. Modern evangelical Christians could benefit from understanding this historical and doctrinal transition of their founder.

This was the understanding of Jesus the founding fathers possessed in their deistic enunciations expressed in the nation's documents.

In addition, the analysis undertaken here is not so much a theological challenge to the doctrine of the Trinity, as such challenges prove unjustified, unnecessary and ultimately pointless. It is not the *theological conception* that is the desired topic of scrutiny, but rather their Biblical vision in the *social and political realms* where positive and humane benefits are the outcomes for all involved and where no humanitarian crises are created unnecessarily, as with the denial of human rights for the Palestinians by the state of Israel and using the Bible to justify the Israelis complete domination of the land.

American conservative Christians have revealed their beliefs to be fully crypto-political and ahistorical. Therefore, the two (Biblical Literalism and Constitutional literalism) for them are inseparable, the political and religious, because they have transformed the political *into* a religious creed. Here is where religion can play a socially harmful role as a "national civic cult" (see Conclusion, American Politics as National Civic Cult) as it erects exclusion zones where the "other" resides.

While the Bible serves as a guide for spirituality and social propriety for hundreds of millions of people across the globe and tens of millions of Americans, the *U.S. Constitution* with the *Bill of Rights* (now nearly a quarter millennium old) serve as preservers of religious freedoms and models of tolerance and human rights. These documents also provide the guide for international affairs. This is not so with a literal reading of the Bible haunted by Middle Eastern demographics, not to mention the superstitions, of 3,000 to 2,000 years ago.

A revitalized and healthy American Christianity could have faith in the Trinity and yet strive to put into practice the Triumvirate. It is of special note that it is *only in* the Declaration of Independence that *a Creator is referred to*. In the Constitution, *only the practice of religion* is discussed. There is no rationale or justification for the state to acknowledge a god, and certainly no specific god as some American officials claim, and beyond that which the Declaration professes and permits. What we are left with for a national "creed" is a generalized, non-specific view of a Creator and nothing more. Our moral orientation comes through the teachings of our principal religions, with Christianity being favored only to the degree that it is the individual's choice of religion. The government has nothing to say about anything other than the individual's right to freely exercise his or her religion within the constraints of civil society and civic pluralism.

There is reason to believe that this more liberal trend in American Christian and religious belief in general is taking hold. Mark Chaves notes that "as a set of ideas, religious liberalism steadily has gained ground in the United States, whatever the fate of the denominations most closely associated with them" (88). He attributes this to the fact that more liberal-leaning ideas lead to less-strict institutional affiliation, and that "Today, more people raised in a mainline church become religious unaffiliated than become evangelical" (95). People feel freer to not attend, at least regularly, religious services even though they maintain a belief in religious, or perhaps "spiritual," ideas.

This gives me great hope.

But this hopefulness must be balanced with the awareness that religion is being politically activated through religious engineering in certain quarters of civic life in such a way as to undermine civic pluralism. Only by identifying the deficiencies in, and providing an alternative interpretation to, deep culturally-ingrained traits can society hope to forge that civic pluralism and the common good (Transcendent Common Good) necessary for the health of civil society. These same values of civic society need also be infused into American foreign policy and when Christians of all sorts read and use the Bible as a source of that message of futuristic hope as it comes to bear on Israel-Palestine relations – *their Creator* demands no less.

REFERENCES
Books/Essays

Al-Azm, Sadik J. (1968/2011). *Self-Criticism After the Defeat.* Trans. George Stergios. London: Saqi Books. [Original 1968 Arabic ed., Beirut, Lebanon: Dar al-Tali'ah].

Al-Azm, Sadik J. (1969/2015). *Critique of Religious Thought.* First Authorized English Edition of *Naqd al-Fikr ad-Dini* with a New Foreword by the Author. Translated from the Arabic by George Stergios and Mansour Ajami. Berlin: Gerlach Press. [Original 1969 Arabic ed., Beirut, Lebanon: Dar al-Tali'ah].

Al-Azm, Sadik J. (2006). Interview with Sadik Jalal al-Azm. University of California, Los Angeles. May 11. Unpublished transcript notes.

Al-Azm, Sadik J. (2007). A Criticism of Religious Thought. In *Islam in Transition: Muslim Perspectives.* John J. Donahue and John L. Esposito, eds. 2nd ed. New York: Oxford University Press. Pgs. 93-99.

• excerpts of *Critique of Religious Thought* appeared in English prior to the translation of the full text in 2015.

Ammerman, Nancy Tatom (1987). *Bible Believers: Fundamentalists in the Modern World*. New Brunswick, New Jersey: Rutgers University Press, 2002.

Arnold, Bettina (1992). The Past as Propaganda: How Hitler's Archaeologists Distorted European Prehistory to Justify Racist and Territorial Goals. *Archaeology*. July/August. Vol. 45 No. 4 pgs. 30-37.

Basham, Cortney S. (2012). Hal Lindsey's *The Late Great Planet Earth and the Rise of Popular Premillennialism in the 1970s*. Masters Theses & Specialist Projects. Paper 1205. Western Kentucky University. http://digitalcommons.wku.edu/cgi/viewcontent.cgi?article=2207&context=theses (accessed January 2019)

Borg, Marcus J. (2001). *Reading the Bible Again for the First Time: Taking the Bible Seriously But Not Literally*. New York: HarperCollins.

Carroll, John T. (2000). Centuries of Waiting: The Persistence of Apocalyptic Hope. In *The Return of Jesus in Early Christianity*. Peabody, Massachusetts: Hendrickson Publishers.

Chalala, Elie and Michael Teague (2014). 40 Year-Old Classic Remains Influential: Sadiq Jalal al-Azm's 'The Critique of Religious Thought'. Al Jadid. A Review and Record of Arab Culture and Arts. https://www.aljadid.com/node/2039 (accessed February 2019).

Chaves, Mark (2017). *American Religion: Contemporary Trends*. 2nd Ed. Princeton: Princeton University Press.

Cohen, Naomi W. (2003). *The Americanization of Zionism, 1897-1948*. Lebanon, New Hampshire: Brandeis University Press/University Press of New England.

Dione, R. L. (1969). *God Drives a Flying Saucer*. New York: Bantam, 1973.

Douglas, J. D., et al. (1982). *New Bible Dictionary*. 2nd ed. Wheaton, Illinois: Tyndale House Publishers.

Gorenberg, Gershom (2002). *The End of Days: Fundamentalism and the Struggle for the Temple Mount*. 2000. New York: Oxford University Press.

Graf, Arndt, et al, eds. (2010). *Orientalism and Conspiracy: Politics and Conspiracy Theory in the Islamic World, Essays in Honour of Sadik J. Al-Azm*. Library of Middle East Studies, Vol. 92. London: I.B. Tauris.

Graham, Billy (1983). *Approaching Hoofbeats: The Four Horsemen of the Apocalypse*. Waco, Texas: Word Books.

Henry, Carl F. H. (1947). *The Uneasy Conscience of Modern Fundamentalism*. Grand Rapids, Michigan: Eerdmans, 2003.

Issenberg, Sasha (2008). Slaying Gave US First Taste of Mideast Terror. *Boston Globe*. June 5. http://archive.boston.com/news/nation/articles/2008/06/05/slaying_gave_us_a_first_taste_of_mideast_terror/ (accessed January 2019).

Khalidi, Rashid (2002). Perceptions and Reality: The Arab World and the West. In *A Revolutionary Year: The Middle East in 1958*. Edited by Wm. Roger Louis and Roger Owen. London: I.B. Taurus, pgs. 181-208.

Lindsey, Hal (1982). *The 1980s: Countdown to Armageddon.* New York, Bantam.

Lindsey, Hal (1983). *The Rapture: Truth or Consequences.* New York, Bantam.

Lindsey, Hal with C.C. Carlson (1970). *The Late Great Planet Earth.* New York: Bantam Books. Published by Zondervan Publishing House in the same year.

Louis, Wm. Roger and Roger Owen, eds. (2002). *A Revolutionary Year: The Middle East in 1958.* London: I.B. Taurus.

Marsden, George M. (1991). *Understanding Fundamentalism and Evangelicalism.* Grand Rapids, Michigan: Eerdmans Publishing.

McTernan, John P. (2006). *As America Has Done to Israel.* New Kensington, Pennsylvania: Whitaker House, 2012.

Melton, J. Gordon (2000). Spiritualization and Reaffirmation: What Really Happens When Prophecy Fails? In Jon R. Stone, Ed. *Expecting Armageddon: Essential Readings in Failed Prophecy.* New York: Routledge, pgs. 145-157.

Noll, Mark A. (1991). *Between Faith and Criticism: Evangelicals, Scholarship, and the Bible in America.* 2nd ed. Vancouver, British Columbia: Regents College Publishing, 2004.

Noll, Mark A. (1994). *The Scandal of the Evangelical Mind.* Grand Rapids, Michigan: Eerdmans.

Packer, J.I. (1958). *"Fundamentalism" and the Word of God: Some Evangelical Principles.* Grand Rapids, Michigan: W.B. Eerdmans.

Rossing, Barbara R. (2004). *The Rapture Exposed: The Message of Hope in the Book of Revelation.* New York: Basic Books.

Sand, Shlomo (2012). *The Invention of the Land of Israel: From Holy Land to Homeland.* New York: Verso.

Scofield, Rev. C.I., ed. (1909/1917). *The Scofield Study Bible.* New York: Oxford University Press, 1996.

Seltzer, Robert M. (1980). *Jewish People, Jewish Thought: The Jewish Experience in History.* Upper Saddle River, New Jersey: Prentice Hall.

Shaheen, Jack G. (2001). *Reel Bad Arabs: How Hollywood Vilifies a People.* Updated Edition. Northampton, Massachusetts: Olive Branch Press, 2009.

Stark, Rodney and William Sims Bainbridge (1987). *A Theory of Religion.* New Brunswick, New Jersey: Rutgers University Press, 1996. (*ATOR*)

- -In order of appearance in this chapter:

Def. 15 *Power* is the degree of control over one's exchange ratios.

P222 If a single explanation in a cultural system fails, people tend to seek another to replace it, without disturbing the rest of the system.

P223 When explanations in a cultural system fail, people will seek the most modest revision of it that will apparently repair the damage.

181

Def. 1 The *past* consists of the universe of conditions which can be known but not influenced.

Def. 2 The *future* consists of the universe of conditions which can be influenced but not known.

Stark, Rodney and Roger Finke (2000). *Acts of Faith: Explaining the Human Side of Religion*. Berkeley: University of California Press. (*AF*)

- This book also contains a series of Propositions and Definitions useful for a systematic and theoretical understanding of religious beliefs and behavior. The difference between this work and *ATOR* is that this one tackles more so the personal contributions to religion (the micro) in addition to the sociological dynamics emphasized in *ATOR*.

Def. 19 *Miracles* are desirable effects believed to be caused by the intervention of a god or gods in world matters.

Unger, Craig (2005). American Rapture. *Vanity Fair*. December. Pgs. 204-222.

Weber, Timothy P. (1998). How Evangelicals Became Israel's Best Friend. Christianity Today. October 5. http://www.christianitytoday.com/ct/1998/october5/8tb038.html (accessed January 2019).

White, Benton J. (1993). *Taking the Bible Seriously: Honest Differences About Biblical Interpretation*. Louisville: Westminster/John Knox Press.

Ze'evi, Dror (2016). Goodbye to the Syrian intellectual who sought to liberate his homeland. +972 Magazine. December 18. https://972mag.com/goodbye-to-the-syrian-intellectual-who-called-to-liberate-his-homeland/123778/ (accessed February 2019).

- *972 Magazine* is a blog-based web magazine that is jointly owned by a group of journalists, bloggers, and photographers whose goal is to provide fresh, original, on-the-ground reporting and analysis of events in Israel and Palestine. Our collective is committed to human rights and freedom of information, and we oppose the occupation [of Palestine by Israel]. However, +972 *Magazine* does not represent any organization, political party or specific agenda. (From their homepage).

Films/Documentaries

Belkin, Alan, Producer (1976). *The Late Great Planet Earth*. American Cinema Group Productions. (91 minutes). https://www.youtube.com/watch?time_continue=7&v=ZzkvXp4eihU accessed January 2019).

Doblmeier, Martin (2010). *The Adventists*. Produced by Dan Juday. Journey Films, Inc.

Gavshon, Michael H. and Solly Granatstein, producers (2002). *Zion's Christian*

Soldiers. 60 Minutes-CBS News. Aired October 6. https://www.cbsnews. com/videos/zions-christian-soldiers/ (accessed January 2018).

O'Sullivan, Shane, Producer-Director (2007). *RFK Must Die: The Assassination of Bobby Kennedy*. MPI Media Group. (138 minutes).

5

CHARIOTS OF THE GODS?
UFO RELIGIONS

The delusion: *Beginning in the USA in June 1947 with pilot Kenneth Arnold's sighting of what were widely-reported as "flying saucers," coupled with the crash at Roswell, New Mexico only two weeks later in July of another aircraft from which eyewitness reports alien bodies were recovered, extraterrestrial unidentified flying objects (UFOs) have been visiting earth. Also since about that time, UFO encounters have included abductions, experimentations on human beings and animals, and claims of inter-galactic travel. The U.S. federal government may or may not be involved in a "conspiracy" to cover-up the facts, much in an X-Files-type fashion, from the American people. In either case, whether the government knows much and is hiding it or knows little-to-nothing, extraterrestrial aircraft and beings have made and likely continue to make visits to earth.*

The correction: *Captured Nazi technology was imported, developed, and test-flown by the U.S. Army/Air Force over the open skies of the USA in the aftermath of WWII and sightings of these flights constitute the earliest American flying saucer reports. These sightings begin in earnest in 1947 and represent the efforts of American aviation scientists and their German counterparts, some of whom were known Nazis and/or war criminals, brought into the USA under Operation Paperclip, a program that was largely concealed to the American public due to its understandably politically-controversial nature. In an effort to distract public attention away from the true source of the technology, American military and intelligence policy and their operatives in media deliberately fostered a disinformation campaign in which the idea of captured alien or extraterrestrial technology was promoted as the source of eyewitness sightings by the public of these test flights.*

Quotes

The military manipulation of civilian opinion and the military invasion of the civilian mind are now important ways in which the power of the warlords is steadily exerted.

– C. Wright Mills, 1956 in *The Power Elite*, pgs. 221-222

Barney Hill: *The evil face ... on the ... he looks like a German Nazi ... Nazi.*
Interviewer: *He is a Nazi? Did he have on a uniform?*
BH: *Yes.*
Int.: *What kind of uniform?*
BH: *Black, he had a black scarf around his neck dangling over his left shoulder.*
Int.: *How could you see the figures so clearly at that distance?*
BH: *I was looking at them with binoculars.*

– *Barney Hill*, 1964 under hypnosis with Dr. Benjamin Simon
in Boston (Fuller, pgs. 115-116)

In trying to manipulate a British traitor visiting Stalag 13 with information for the Nazis, Lt. Carter disguised as German General von Schlomm:
Carter: *So, Sir Charles, still wishing to return to England?*
Chitterly: *At once von Schlomm. It's countries like this (Germany) that give fascism a bad name.*

– *Hogan's Heroes* (Season 6, 1970: Lady Chitterly's Lover;
aired October 11)

For every one of these people there must be thousands out there also touched by this implanted vision. It's just a coincidence, the major suggested. It is a sociological event, the Frenchman corrected him ...

– Steven Spielberg, 1977 in *Close Encounters of the Third Kind*,
pg. 199

Folklorists have a word for the process whereby folktales bleed into reality; They call it 'ostension'. But when these tales are given a kick start by the intelligence agencies, I think we can simply call it deception.

– Mark Pilkington, 2010 in *Mirage Men*, pg.71

CLOSE ENCOUNTERS of the RURAL KIND

A thirteen year-old boy is riding a bicycle along a country road in southern Ontario, Canada. It is the summer of 1976. As he peddles alongside rolling hills and corn fields, past barns and pastures of grazing cattle, he sees sitting on a hill in the distance a silvery domed object. It surprises and shocks him as immediately he believes he is seeing a UFO that has landed on a small rise in a cornfield. He continues to peddle along the road hoping to catch a better glimpse of the object once he gets beyond a barn that now blocks his view. He peddles hurriedly and frantically as a sense of excitement grips him.

Having previously read popular accounts of UFOs widely circulated as mass-market paperback books, stories and images of those accounts included that of alien abductions – one particular story was about a man named Antonio Villas-Boas in South America[1] whom the adolescent had recently read. These images fueled his excited mind as he pursued his glimpse of the silver object.

Once beyond the barn the object comes back into view, only this time it had risen-up in height over the cornfield. The dome was supported by a shaft that appears to be still touching the ground and spans the full diameter of the dome. The more he peddles, the higher the object rises above the level of the cornfield. After another two hundred feet of peddling, he stops in his tracks.

He is dumfounded!

What he is seeing is not a UFO at all, but the top of a grain silo that is in the distance beyond the cornfield, and as he peddles forward the cornfield in the foreground slopes down revealing behind it the shaft of the silo. It was not even an optical illusion, but simply the juxtaposition of the silo behind the hill and the coming into view of the full shaft of the silo.

Instantly, UFO became barnyard architecture.

That excited boy hoping to catch a glimpse of a flying saucer was me!

The point of recounting this personal incident is to highlight that so much of what we see is in our own eye and from a very distinct perspective. As a youngster, I had a fascination with all things unexplained, from the paranormal, ghosts, the Loch Ness Monster and Bigfoot, to UFOs. I read many popular books about UFOs in the mid-1970s and was thor-

---

1   The highly-celebrated Villas-Boas story from Brazil was an early example in 1957 of what would become very widely popularized during the 1970s-1980s as the alien abduction phenomenon. His encounter along with Betty and Barney Hill's incident in 1960 would provide the prototypes for subsequent abduction testimonials.

oughly captivated by the topic.[2] I have little doubt this fascination would ultimately lead me in adulthood to Religious Studies as an academic discipline and ultimate vocation. As a youngster, however, an unidentified domed shiny object on a hill could be explained by only one thing: a landed flying saucer.

And I could hardly be considered alone in my judgment, rash as it was. My misidentification could be excused given the increasing reports and widespread acceptance of UFOs underway at the time in North America. Philip J. Klass noted,

> It is hardly surprising that a Gallup Poll conducted in mid-1978 indicated that 57 percent of the adult American population believes that UFOs "are real," an increase of 24 percent over the figure obtained in a similar survey in 1966. Gallup reported that for adults with a college education, the "belief" figure was an even higher 66 percent. When *Industrial Research/Development* magazine surveyed its readers in 1979, it found that 61 percent of the respondents believe that UFOs "probably" or "definitely" exist (Klass, 3).

More recent surveys (one in 2008 by Scripps Howard News Service and another in 2012 by *National Geographic*) put the number of Americans who "believe UFOs are real" at roughly one third of the population. Evidently, the American people have vacillated over the years, or perhaps have become more nuanced in their understanding of what "real" means! The *National Geographic* survey also showed that "a whopping 79 percent of people think the government has kept information about UFOs a secret from the public, and more than half (55 percent) believe there are real-life *Men in Black*-style agents who threaten people that spot UFOs."[3] Clearly the influence of major motion pictures and the media have had something to do with these numbers given that this last scenario of Men in Black is based purely upon fictional sources rather than traditional eyewitness-based reports that comprise research-based ufology. Abduction testimonials do not include the level of technological advancement portrayed in these fictional scenarios, even when factoring in "close encounters of the third kind."[4]

---

2   The 1970s saw a noted increase in American publications and media on the topic. It was a saturation-style publishing event that reached virtually the entire media-consuming population. Perhaps the epitome of this was the very popular 1977 movie *Close Encounters of the Third Kind* directed by Steven Spielberg and produced with the consultation of J. Allen Hynek

3   One-Third of Americans Believe in UFOs, Survey Says. June 27, 2012. Staff article. http://www.lifeslittlemysteries.com/2611-american-ufo-belief.html (accessed February 2019).

4   The ufologist J. Allen Hynek coined these terms in his famous 1972 book *The UFO Experience: A Scientific Inquiry* in which he "proposes a means whereby a process of scientific verification can be established." The three kinds of encounters would categorize the evidence along the lines

Religions are themselves culturally accepted *memes* (patterns of be-havior that are observed and repeated) resting on no less a subjective base than the claims of ufology.[5] Both must be accepted by *faith*, at least in their claims to extraterrestrial (ufology) and spiritual (religion) entities and existences. With both ufology and religions, any evidences offered up as proofs of claims, similarly lack the finality of establishing cause and ef-fect, and both seem unable to produce the measurable verifications upon which scientific and empirical statements are based.

Hence, the phenomenon of *sightings of UFOs and the culture stemming from them* has been academically subsumed under Religious Studies, where-as, the scientific *search for extraterrestrial communications* resides in projects like the Search for Extra-Terrestrial Intelligence (commonly referred to as SETI) and other cosmic-astronomic listening and exploration efforts. These scientific efforts are not interested in abduction testimonies and the sort of data that has been utilized by Religious Studies.[6] I take this as a clear and inviolable demarcation of the hard sciences (astronomy and radio wave sig-nal monitoring) from the softer social sciences and humanities (including Religious Studies) from which this work originates.

The term *ufology* applies hereafter only to the social sciences and hu-manities and to the phenomena of UFO sightings of all types and the me-mes, religious and non-religious, these have produced in popular culture.

The UFO RELIGIONS

In the study of UFO/flying saucer "cults" or religions, research histor-ically focused upon the *spiritualist* and *esoteric traditions* and their re-lationship to the newly-emerging and technologically-based worldview stemming from the rapid development of aircraft technology post-WWII. The communication and contact methods seemed to be similar in the two traditions, and both placed much emphasis upon receiving messages from beings from other dimensions. Robert Ellwood also points out that the "close interaction between Spiritualism and UFO cults is not surpris-ing, for one finds there is much exchange of persons between them (131).

Similarly, Christopher Partridge sums up his Conclusion to an over-view of the history of UFO religions by separating the two intersecting

of sightings only, sightings with physical evidence left behind and sightings "in which the presence of animated creatures is reported" (158).

5   Ufology refers to the topic in the broadest manner with all its cultural expressions in-cluding everything from movies and popular books to research groups such as the Aerial Phenom-ena Research Organization (APRO) and the Mutual UFO Network (MUFON) and of which UFO New Religious Movements (UFO-NRMs) is only one aspect.

6   The same holds true for Sociology, Cultural Studies, Anthropology, Psychology and re-lated disciplines.

189

histories of earlier spiritualists emerging from the late-nineteenth century and the later post-1947 flying saucer religions: "UFO religion *per se* emerged within the tradition of theosophical esotericism, becoming firmly established as 'UFO religion' during the wave of public interesting following the 1947 Arnold sighting" (2003, 36).

This is where my study picks-up with those modern sightings of UFOs that have given birth to a small variety of religions that are commonly referred to as "UFO New Religious Movements" (UFO-NRMs). These religions have been decidedly influenced by the rise of technology as an over-arching factor, indeed a dominant force, in world power. It is no coincidence that in the USA, ufology rises in the post WWII-era when the weapons of mass destruction were in their infancy and held enormous imaginative potential for global human destruction (Ellwood, 131).

Little more than two years after the detonations over Hiroshima and Nagasaki the hope of extraterrestrial salvation from our own self-destruction came in the form of "flying saucers."

By all accounts the crucial year of 1947 launches the phenomenon when two now-famous incidents, and all to so much media fanfare, initiated a wave of sightings across the USA. On June 24 pilot Kenneth Arnold saw nine craft he described as skipping across the sky like a saucer (not saucer shaped) as he flew near Mt. Rainier in the northwest. Newspapers would report Arnold saw "flying saucers" and thus began the use of that term. Then, after barely two weeks had passed, on July 8 the Roswell Army Air Force base reported a flying disc had crash-landed in the desert west of the base. Oddly, the Air Force would then report it as a crashed weather balloon. The reports, then retraction of reports, fed into the notion of an official cover-up or conspiracy within governments of their knowledge of alien visitors, which also has been part of ufology since its beginning.

And so was born the modern UFO mythology in America.

Psychologists may interpret this phenomenon as a response to the rise of the United States to absolute or near-absolute dominance on the world's war-front and political stage, and the nation's people crying out for someone beyond themselves to arrive and tame the ascendant beast. For this perspective one can tap the likes of Carl Jung's 1959 *Flying Saucers: A Modern Myth of Things Seen in the Skies* for psychological interpretations of the flying saucer mythology.

But in this UFO delusion, the psychology of sightings is not the concern. Far more convincing from historical evidence is what Mark Pilkington refers to in the Quotes at the beginning of this chapter: intelligence agency deception.

In the history of American religions, the UFO-NRMs are rather insignificant, somewhat infamous, and almost always eccentric. Part of this is due to the nature of the pervasive perceptions of cults generally. In addition, there is a widespread popular acceptance of ufology and UFO sightings phenomena in the national culture in which television shows, movies, annual events, and the general openness of Americans to the idea that life from elsewhere could visit here. This allows the general population to dissociate themselves completely from UFO-NRMs yet indulge their beliefs in ufology, akin to being "spiritual but not religious."

Perhaps this widespread cultural acceptance is something of a *hybrid intellectual construct* fusing together the scientific potentialities of the modern world and then extrapolating that to the cosmos (*Star Wars*), coupled with the humanistic elements of ufology as a belief system (*Close Encounters of the Third Kind*). Partridge referred to this construct by the "term 'physicalist religion', rather than 'scientific religion'" (which is sometimes used to describe these types of hybrid beliefs), simply because [he is] not convinced that the beliefs of UFO religions can, strictly speaking, be described as 'science'" (2003, 22).

For Partridge, the UFO-NRMs more-or-less converted what were previously spiritual interpretations of religious texts and their characters – the gods, angels, and spirits who populate that world – into physical interpretations. Gods are now aliens. Chariots are now UFOs. Demon possession is now alien abduction. Spiritual communications are now implantations or messages from "Space Brothers."

One important consistency between the religious mythic-message and its worldviews brought to us through the world religions and which persists into the UFO-NRMs' worldviews, is the characteristic of the benevolence of the visitors and their care and concern for human beings on planet earth. At least most of the time.

The period of the beginning and proliferation of these sightings post-WWII is an exceptionally tense time in Cold War politics. Also, keep in mind this is the dawn of the nuclear age and the scientific potentialities of increasing technology included human annihilation. It may come as no surprise then that the earliest alien communications received by contactees included a message of warning to the human race.

One of the earliest of these post-WWII UFO witnesses and writers who would popularize the "alien contact" (though not abduction) phenomenon was George Adamski (1891-1965). He could be considered the prototypical contactee and he very successfully promoted his story of having been in communication with "Space Brothers." In 1953, along with British occultist Desmond Leslie, he publishes the book *The Flying Saucers Have Landed* followed in 1955 with *Inside the Flying Saucers*.

He claims to have had a saucer sighting even before the two 1947 reports of Kenneth Arnold and the Roswell crash. Adamski's sighting was in October of 1946, but then again in November 1952 he had a much more up-close-and-personal contact experience with small anthropomorphic (humanoid) entities traveling in a large cigar-shaped craft. This preceded the publication of his first book mentioned above. These Space Brothers, as he termed them, came with a message of warning regarding humans' war-like tendencies and of the dangers of nuclear proliferation. The aliens had learned to live in peace in their world, and so they felt that humans also could achieve this tranquility.

What's more, Adamski had "photographed" the saucer that the Space Brothers emerged from in 1952. His critics had fun with him charging his pictures were somewhere between a chicken feeder and a hubcap. Nevertheless, he traveled the world recounting his experience and the message of peace brought by the Space Brothers.

Curiously, or perhaps fortuitously, earlier that same year beginning on Saturday July 12 and then again on the two following consecutive weekends, numerous bright objects were seen and filmed over Washington, D.C. These sightings were not confined to a small number of eyewitnesses out in the barren desert. In this case many, many people saw the objects, radar at Andrews Air Force Base detected them, and even Air Force jets were scrambled to protect the nation's capital.

To be sure, in a Pentagon press conference given on the 29th it was revealed by General John A. Samford that since 1947 the military had investigated between 1,000 and 2,000 reports of sightings, most being satisfactorily explained (to the Pentagon's satisfaction anyway) as either natural phenomena or misidentifications.[7] The position of the "government" was, for now, to downplay the significance of the sightings, at least for the time being. More comment on government efforts and "responses" in the next section.

Hollywood was most willing to do its part too. It would take a team effort to persuade the American population *en masse* that visitors from other worlds was a possible explanation for what eyewitnesses were seeing across the fruited plains, indeed what people were seeing across the globe.

---

7   General Samford's UFO press conference Pentagon, July 29, 1952. http://www.youtube.com/watch?v=tcRtkA1Rmvw (accessed January 2019)..

The 1951 release of *The Day the Earth Stood Still* and in two years *The War of the Worlds* brought alien visitors to the big screen. The first film was decidedly benevolent in its portrayal of alien intentions and instead it was humanity who was the gun-toting, trigger-happy and dangerous species. Not so in the second film where the aliens were on the attack and quite capable over overcoming human military defenses. The films together reveal an interesting and suggestively-persuasive bicameral and gestalt message of love/hate, good/evil. These increase the mass appeal and no doubt did not go unnoticed by intelligence (agency) psychologists and perhaps even intended by those involved in spreading and reinforcing the mythology. Culturally, Americans were under alien assault from all sides and with the releases of these two movies, the message was conveyed that alien life is/was/or could be benevolent toward us, but we humans pose a threat and so must be destroyed.

This is a frightful message for a people who live in a time when, as Gore Vidal put it in his 1954 novel *Messiah*, "Not a day passed but that some omen or portent was remarked by an anxious race, suspecting war." The Soviets were testing and exploding their own nuclear weapons of mass destruction in the early 1950s, so the threat was more than merely an extra-terrestrial abstraction. Whether the aliens were off-planet or on-planet (in the form of human warlords), the destruction was equally annihilating and horrifying.

Working-out our relationship with the extra-terrestrials was tantamount to smoothing-out our relations with the communists. What else could be inferred from the 1952 Washington, D.C. flybys? A very potent combination indeed: UFO-mystery mixed with superpower intrigue. The psychology of it all proved overwhelming, if irresistible, and certainly marketable. The net psychological and sociological[8] result would be that Americans would embrace the aliens in their most benevolent portrayal. Ufology, and soon UFO-NRMs, would become more-or-less increasingly accepted, even if not fully-equated with religion, as valid (quasi) religious-like expressions by the general population, much the same way New Age religions of eastern origin have been accepted and integrated into American religious life over the past few generations.

A summation of the view that the UFO religions are securely defined within the framework of American religious history is found in the *Pocket Dictionary of New Religious Movements*:

---

8   In the 1977 blockbuster *Close Encounters of the Third Kind* the comment was made by the French researcher to the American military commander that the reason some citizens had been drawn to Devil's Tower, Wyoming, where the climactic encounter would take place, was a "sociological event." This character is meant to reference Jacques Vallee, a popular French writer on ufology from the 1960s. See quote at beginning of this chapter.

UFO religions: Religions based on contact with space aliens who visit earth in Unidentified Flying Objects (UFOs). Since the publication of George Adamski's *Flying Saucers have Landed* (1953), numerous new religions have developed, all of which claim to be based on contact, real or telepathic, between their founder or founders and the occupants of UFOs. These are usually said to be spacecraft of an advanced civilization. Two of the most successful of these are the Aetherius Society, founded by George King, and the Raëlian Movement found by Claude Real. Other more infamous UFO groups include the Heaven's Gate Community and the Solar Temple (Hexham, 113).

The dictionary is right to describe these latter-named religions as "infamous" since they were embroiled in criminal and undoubtedly murderous intrigue: these were Heaven's Gate and the Solar Temple.

The second of these two is better categorized by the spiritualist and esoteric traditions referenced by Ellwood and Partridge above. Chryssides notes the "Solar Temple's teachings were highly esoteric, and could only be fully revealed to members after two degrees of initiation after admission" (58). The group has more in common with historical Templarism than it does with post-WWII sightings of aircraft and is rather late in the game when it comes to the UFO-NRMs of interest here. The Solar Temple was founded in 1984 and the most extraterrestrial references made in their theology is to that of "ascended masters" who have more in common with reincarnated spirits than popularly conceived aliens.

Just the same, The Solar Temple was catapulted into public consciousness in a traumatic way and on three separate occasions between October 1994 and March 1997. Each time a mass-suicide/murder occurred with numbers ranging from 63 dead in the first instance, 16 in the second, and 5 in the last – all in the French-speaking world, i.e., Quebec and Switzerland. This violent element also connected them to other religious cults more generally and provided enough parallel to the Jonestown incident of 1978 as to raise the public's awareness of the social influence of such groups into the coming years.

Timing and coincidences can be crucial in thematically connecting in people's minds an idea or narrative (recall what the advent of radio did for the evolution-creation narrative in broadcasting the Scopes Trial). The Solar Temple's final atrocity took place on March 23, 1997 and only three days later we learned of the Heaven's Gate mass-suicide in San Diego of thirty-nine members under the most bizarre of circumstances and in conjunction with the passing of a comet.[9]

---

9   In an odd coincidence, the mind of Americans, certainly Arizonans, was already much-consumed with matters of things in the sky. On March 13, 1997 – little less than two weeks

Though the two groups were not connected directly as communities, they were connected in the minds of those monitoring such events as parallel examples of religious cults gone-wrong much in the same way as the 1978 Jonestown event was "mostly suicide" (Dawson, 182).

Heaven's Gate first came to widespread knowledge on March 26, 1997 when, as mentioned, thirty-nine members including the founder Marshall Applewhite (1931-1997) were found deceased in a San Diego suburban mansion each under a purple blanket and with a five-dollar bill and some change in his or her pocket. Heaven's Gate had a very distinct history rooted in its founders' psychological troubles. Its classification as a UFO-NRM is most certainly justified given the background interests of its leaders and their professed theology.[10]

Applewhite made references in his writings and sermons to many of the popular cultural works of ufology: Erich von Däniken's *Chariots of the Gods* and the films *Close Encounters of the Third Kind* and *E.T. The Extra-Terrestrial* were works he and his followers were more than familiar with. His theology was but a blend of Christianity and ufology (Chryssides, 70). But this is where any connection between the historical facts of the technology of the sort pursued in this research, namely that resulting from Operation Paperclip, and the development of "religious cult" ends.

Heaven's Gate evolved more as a community rooted in the psychological idiosyncrasies of the founder and his ability to convince others of his spiritual ideas. Applewhite and his followers simply harnessed popular culture to feed their personal idiosyncrasies and pathologies. There are no special features of religious belief or cultic traits required to assemble together a group of like-minded personalities. Applewhite's obsessive and tight control of the group and their individual comings and goings indicates something of the co-dependent nature upon which these relationships were based.

One example of the manifestation of this suppression of the normalcy of life is the fact that eight of the male members were castrated some time before the suicides. The sexual life of the members was completely

prior to the suicides – the "Phoenix Lights" occurred. Thoroughly documented and never officially explained, the Phoenix Lights have entered the lore of ufology

10   Sometime in 1995 I unknowingly met a representative of the Heaven's Gate. It was at a City of Scottsdale Chamber of Commerce meeting where I was networking for a new business I was involved with at the time. An overly dressed-down woman sat next to me on a bench in a gathering of attendees. She initiated the conversation and offered her message in a typically evangelistic manner inviting me to a meeting of their group.

Though the details of this conversation are hazy, I recall her specifically saying that her leader, whose one syllable name I thought odd at the time but did not recognize and only later connected to Do, would never die and that she along with his other followers would also never die. I pressed her if she meant that literally or symbolically. She meant it most literally, she assured me. I responded (if a little sarcastically) that they were going to be very disappointed when their leader actually did die. She denied it could happen and that basically ended our discussion.

195

suppressed and dysfunctional. This appears, again, to be a peculiarity of Applewhite's given his homosexual orientation in early life and its conflict with his traditional Christian upbringing. This was no secret in his history.

By all indications, this appears to be the roots and genesis of Heaven's Gate: the meeting in 1974 of Applewhite and Bonnie Nettles, co-founder of the group. Through a novel interpretation of themselves into the Bible, their "mission, they believed, had something to do with fulfilling biblical prophecies, and it involved 'an update in understanding'" (Chryssides, 68). The appeal of the group was very limited, and it remained until its demise an oddity and anomaly among NRMs.

In a case of curious timing and in the French-speaking world, Raëlians emerge that same year (1974) on the wings of an eccentric fellow and former race-car journalist Claude Vorilhon, later Claude Raël after Elohim would change his name. This name change signifies that the Raëlian Movement, similar to Heaven's Gate, emerges out of the idiosyncrasies of a single individual in conjunction with traditional theological concepts. Raël is now the prophet who has superseded Christ and whose message is to hail the advent of Elohim. In this way, the belief is not so dissimilar to evangelical-style apocalyptic notions.

This French component to the mythology of UFOs and a French UFO-NRM was artistically represented in the figure of Claude Lancombe in the movie *Close Encounters of the Third Kind*. Lancombe was modeled consciously by Steven Spielberg on Jacques Vallee, the prominent French ufologist of the late 1960s and 1970s whose books were mass-marketed as part of the general publishing-bonanza in flying saucers across Western nations. The Raëlians remain small in numbers and represent not much of a presence in American religious life, mostly due to its French orientation. Just the same, they reflect, or are the result of, the broader push by American military and intelligence officials and cultural elites to make the UFO mythology (and ufology generally) thoroughly mainstream to all NATO members.

FLYING SAUCERS:
A MATTER of MOVIES MORE than RELIGIONS

The insignificance in numbers and infamy of these few UFO-NRMs *within* the broader history of American religions generally and the Christian churches specifically, coupled with the mass appeal and saturation of ufology in popular culture, have led to an absence of interest on the part of religious leaders in the topic of ufology. A smug rejectionist attitude may best describe that of the orthodox Christian churches both conservative and liberal toward the potentiality of "alien" life.

Furthermore, and from the standpoint of the Protestant and Roman Catholic establishments, ufology and UFO-NRMs have mostly been suspect within their own theological worldviews (Denzler 10). For example, evangelicals don't easily embrace ufology as it poses theological challenges to the Biblical narrative, a narrative taken literally in many if not most evangelical interpretations. More fundamentalist-style evangelicals may even attribute UFOs to demonic deceptions, which has the effect, then, of reabsorbing ufology back into traditional religion by classifying them as an evil force. Typically, UFOs have simply been diminished by religious teachings as mere fiction and entertainment.

Sometimes the Bible and ufology can directly be compatible if the interpreter is willing to stretch the bounds of conventional theological thinking, and it is reasonable to expect that some would do just that, if for no other reason than commercial capitalization. This provides another route for, and enables, the tenets of ufology to be absorbed into the religious community via mainstream channels such as popular books and films that initially do not contradict the community's religious interpretations. In fact, claims of scientific legitimacy for one's religious views are a favorable condition – even if coming from ufology.

One such example is the 1974 book titled *The Spaceships of Ezekiel* by Josef F. Blumrich.[11] He is a NASA engineer and designer who saw in the book of Ezekiel in the Old Testament a description of landing gear … coincidentally, he had been charged by NASA to design the same piece for a lunar lander. In addition, he appears in the 1975 motion picture *The Outer Space Connection* being interviewed as the NASA scientist who "take[s] the book of Ezekiel seriously from an engineering point of view" (Landsburg Productions, 1975). The evangelical proclivity for scientific legitimacy is most certainly bolstered with such claims as Blumrich's as they appear to lend credibility to the synthesis of ufology and Biblical religion (see also chapter four Dione).

Nonetheless, these secular or mainstream publications on UFOs that more-or-less validated scriptural narratives may have had some influence among evangelical thinkers, but not significantly.[12] They were viewed

---

11   Blumrich's career overlaps with the issues raised in the next two sections of this chapter concerning Project Paperclip and the importation into the United States of German technology after WWII. Whether or not Blumrich personally qualifies for inclusion in this controversial history is not of concern here, and furthermore it would be beside the point. His book and personal stature as a scientist and their effect upon American culture's acceptance of ufology is what is of interest here

12   See Peter Harrison's discussion on the efforts of theologians during the pre- and early-Enlightenment Europe (1600-1700s) to reconcile "the discovery of the Americas, combined with

more as novelties and mostly compartmentalized. More recently since 2008, and beginning with the Pope's Astronomer, the Roman Catholic Church has made some rather blunt statements about the possibilities of alien life. This was something of a departure for the institution which had largely remained silent about or doctrinally dismissed the relevance of ufology.[13] Nevertheless, the Roman Catholic Church has come to acknowledge its willingness to embrace alien life forms, assuming they're not hostile, even to the point of baptizing them!

This institutional acceptance indicates the ever-increasing broad-based integration of ufology into the mainstream of American cultural life and thereby only secondarily spilling-into American religious life. Collectively, however, the UFO-NRMs (Heaven's Gate, Solar Temple, and Raëlians) have stood apart from the mainstream of religious life and culture. Ufology, on the other hand, made for a certain accommodation between mainstream Christianity/religion and flying saucers. Works such as those by the "father of modern ufology" (my term) Erick von Däniken frequently refer to Aztec religion, ancient Near Eastern images (North African and Mesopotamian), including Biblical and Vedic (Hindu) scriptural passages:

> A curiosity that leaves me no rest has always drawn me to the old Indian source books. What a mass of fascinating and mysterious information about flying machines and fantastic weapons in the remote past can be found in the translations of the Indian Vedas and epics. The Old Testament with its vigorous, vivid descriptions pales beside these Indian jewels (1972: 127).

Religious Studies and sociological scholars Rodney Stark and William Bainbridge noted in the mid-1980s that "Flying saucer cults had their peak during the 1950s and early 1960s but today make up only 4 percent of the total" (199). The total they refer to is the national number of those people who identify themselves with a list of varied religious "cults."[14]

---

the Copernican theory of the solar system, [and how these] led to theorising about the possibility of extraterrestrial life" (128).

13   Vatican says aliens could exist. BBC News. 2008/13/5. http://news.bbc.co.uk/2/hi/7399661.stm (accessed January 2019).

14   The chart contained the following list of thirteen "cults": Mormon; Cult Communes; New Thought; Theosophy and Spiritualism; Occult Orders; Flying Saucer; Psychedelic; Magick, Witches, Satanism; Pagans; Asian Faiths; Jesus People; Miscellaneous. Keep in mind, this is research from the mid-1980s and reflects the general social, cultural and religious transformations the USA had been through in the previous generation and the consequent socio-categorization of religions. It seems unimaginable today, in the second decade of the twenty-first century, to classify an Asian religion such as Buddhism (Asian faith) as a cult, even in pure sociological terms. By now, it is a mainstream and historical World Religion having new roots in the New World.

This is most curious timing as the peak period identified by Stark and Bainbridge more-or-less coincides with the CIA's Operation Mirage in which the agency, and no doubt with the help of Hollywood as noted earlier, "deliberately manufactured UFO incidents all over the world" (Pilkington, 111).[15] These government-agency efforts were directed at the general public more so than those within the traditional UFO-NRMs. Ufology by the mid-1970s was intended for everyone in popular culture, not only the eccentrics – even if the eyewitness encounters were themselves highly eccentric, e.g., intergalactic sexual relations!

The Villas-Boas (1957) abduction was one of these CIA-manufactured[16] stories and it specifically fueled my own adolescent rural experience recounted at the opening of the chapter. Villas-Boas was a farmer who, when alone out in the fields one night, had an aircraft descend upon him and into which he was taken involuntarily where he copulated with a mostly-anthropomorphic female alien. This became one of the earliest "close encounters of the third kind" prior to the creation of the term by J. Allen Hynek in 1972. As if to underscore the international effort at cinematic influence of these UFO myths, the theme of human-alien sexual relations would show-up in the extremely-cheesy, if barely-watchable, 1977 Canadian-produced movie *Starship Invasions* starring Robert Vaughn and Christopher Lee – both rather high-profile actors. Anticipating the successful commercial wave amassing around *Close Encounters of the Third Kind, Starship Invasions* was inflicted upon the Canadian viewing audience within one month of the former's premiere and with the hapless farmer Rudy taken aboard a spacecraft for an irresistible sexual encounter with a voluptuous alien woman – a meme most appealing to young boys and men! The gestalt is unmistakable.

1951 (benevolence)   1953 (aggression)

---

15   In addition, the formation and ascendancy of Scientology also occurs during the 1950s and 1960s. Scientology, too, incorporates a sizeable portion of its cosmology with references to extraterrestrial entities and existences.

16   The fact of the Villas-Boas incident occurring in Brazil suggests the international reach of the CIA and the post-WWII defection of Nazis from Germany in the so-called "rat line."

Two early films highlight the gestalt nature of the psychological conditioning. In the 1951 The Day the Earth Stood Still *the aliens come with a benevolent warning about our use of nuclear weapons, much as with George Adamski's message. In the 1953* The War of the Worlds *the aliens come to kick our butts!*

Similarly, with the two 1977 blockbusters Star Wars *and* Close Encounters of the Third Kind *wherein the view of alien life is bifurcated between a perspective from outer space and one from the earth. Between the two pair of releases, the 1969 imagery of man's landing upon the moon facilitated the notion of space travel generally in the minds of all earthlings.*

A view from space   A view toward space

1977

Americans' consciousness of the topic of UFOs eased its way into the psychological mainstream of popular culture in the 1950s and was thoroughly embedded by the 1970s fostered by widely-distributed books and movies coupled with the images of the moon-landing. The entire effort was then marketed to younger people and with the next generation in mind with the release of *E.T.: The Extra-Terrestrial* in 1982. Beyond these, Hollywood has birthed a multitude of alien movies ranging across the genres, e.g. from *Men in Black* (1997) to *Cowboys and Aliens* (2011).

Believing in UFOs was deemed anything but religious by the 1980s after the psycho-success of the cultural and Hollywood media-blitzkrieg on the topic during the previous decade. This cultural acclimation paved the way for something of an escalation in the UFO experience: the alien abduction or "close encounter of the third kind," a designation created by J. Allen Hynek in his popular 1972 book *The UFO Experience: A Scientific Inquiry* (see References under Hynek and photo of comparative book covers). The alien abduction phenomenon gave outlet for any number of personal and interpersonal psycho-dramas to be played-out, but this is more a subject for clinical psychology than Religious Studies.

I contend that ufology (manipulated and used as a cover story for classified military activity) subsumed religion (as in NRMs) and made it a minor, if marginal, genre of cultural production/expression of the ideas about extraterrestrial life in the universe. Science via the SETI approach validates the generalized belief in the possibility of life elsewhere for the public's more reasoned imaginations. This coupled with the massive popular acculturation to ufology meant there was no need for ufology to embed itself within, or compete with, traditional religions since it had its own audience across the social spectrum of popular culture, even if remaining mostly dismissed by traditional religious denominations.

However, the connection between ufology and religions in general can be much more mainstream as in the exceedingly popular work of the writer Erich von Däniken and his first book *Chariots of the Gods?* published in German in 1968 and in English in 1970. The by-now (2019) decade-old and still-in-production History Channel program *Ancient Aliens* is based upon von Däniken's theories and he regularly appears in the program. For a series to be in production a full-decade is an achievement, and by any standard at that. In this case, it is testament to the appetite in American culture for these techno-religious themes.

Erich von Däniken's theories incorporate an alien source or connection into his interpretation of any number of ancient landmarks and archaeological ruins from the Egyptian Pyramids at Giza to the structures at Machu Picchu in Peru. His were the theories that informed my own young mind during the mid-1970s when through popular films and mass-market paperback publications the military industrial complex was able to launch one of the most internationally successful public-opinion manipulation campaigns to date – a myth that literally "took over the world" (Pilkington, 2014).

It's hard to avoid the conclusion that it cannot be a coincidence that it is once again the History Channel (this time in conjunction with Arts & Entertainment Studios) that has produced a dramatic series titled *Project Blue Book* centering upon J. Allen Hynek's investigations into UFOs under one of the Air Force's several "projects." These projects were designed more as public relations campaigns and as efforts at public opinion manipulation of reported sightings by the general public than they were to get to the bottom of the sightings phenomenon itself. This current 2019 dramatization is an eclectic mix of all things *X-Files* both early and late in the history of American ufology. It even tosses-in crop circles which were a not-much-reported phenomenon back in the Project Blue Book days of the early 1950s through to the late 1960s. The psychosocial intentions are unambiguous: to connect the current generations to the historic UFO phenomenon. As the show claims to be based upon the investigations conducted by Hynek who worked on the subject between 1948 until the "late 1960s [when] he turned against the Air Force" (Pilkington, 124), today's viewers are counseled here to remind themselves that Hynek's own "turning against" the government's efforts and "denouncing it a sham" played skillfully into the drama of obfuscation about what the government was really up to. Hynek was now free to create his own hypotheses on ufology and consequently birthed the "close encounters" template we are all now familiar with.

By 1972, the year Hynek's influential book was published, the American mind had been painstakingly ploughed for sowing and ripened for harvesting at the same time thanks to the adept manipulations of the warlords and military planners and their allies in the intelligence services and in Hollywood. As the Lorenzens put it, "Within this frame of reference, then, Blue Book appears as a key agency in a long term "deception" maneuver – a standard intelligence tool" (241). Even so, there was still so much more work to do.

The NEXUS of DISINFORMATION, PSYCHOLOGICAL WARFARE, and UFOs

I would ask the reader to here recall my earlier reference to George Orwell's 1945 novel *Animal Farm* and how it was made into a movie in 1954 at the initiation of the CIA and funded by the CIA in order to Americanize, or better still, to Cold-War-ize the classic anti-totalitarian story. In the U.S. military and intelligence services "psychological warfare, or 'psywar,' was a buzzword of the time" (chapter three; Leab, 16).

This *modus operandi* of the US's intelligence services upon the American mind was quite successfully used in cultivating and promoting the ufology phenomenon, and possibly in select UFO-NRMs. This last assertion is far more difficult to establish, and caution must be used when assessing such influence. Nevertheless, ignoring it has serious consequences to the integrity and veracity of research and the conclusions drawn therein. The later chapters in this book are cautionary examples of over-looking or ignoring the input of government agencies into these events and what the *Critical Theory of Religion* was intended to remedy.

American policy-makers have all along understood the need for evaluating the psycho-social effects of technological advancement upon the general population. In the era of Cold War politics, that same technological advancement had to be "managed" at a public level while simultaneously kept away from the prying eyes of Soviet agents seeking to understand what the United States was developing. Long-time advisor to the federal government, the now-late Zbigniew Brzezinski, gives insight into the government's interests and requirements:

> Anticipation of the social effects of technological innovation offers a good example of the necessary forms of cross-institutional cooperation. One of the nation's most urgent needs is the creation of a variety of mechanisms that link national and local governments, academia, and the business community (there the example of NASA may be especially rewarding) in the talk of evaluating not only the operational effects of the new technologies but their cultural and psychological effects. A series of national and local councils – not restricted to scientists but made up of various social groups, including the clergy – would be in keeping with both the need and the emerging pattern of social response to change (263).

The argument that the American military and intelligence services have manipulated and used the ufology phenomena across the American cultural landscape is more a matter of historical record than is often admitted publicly in the news media. Certainly, it is not a popular notion among UFO enthusiasts (believers) themselves who stand to lose the most – through the cognitive dissonance of loss of faith in light of the evidence to the contrary. In this sense, ufology is, or can be, very much similar to religion as a psychological phenomenon.[17] The element of "belief" and "faith" are ever necessary for the sociological effects to be felt. In fact, upon closer examination, the entire UFO phenomenon is more akin to a planned and determined psycho/sociological experiment upon a nation (the world, perhaps? Pilkington, 113) to brainwash the wider population for its own secretive, i.e., classified, ends.

Operation Mirage set out do just that – create a mirage.

The CIA's fingerprints, in concert with Pentagon planners, have been all over ufology since the 1950s when the agency and the topic of ufology were still in their infancy. As already mentioned, one of the cases that the intelligence services participated in, along with their Brazilian counterparts, was the Villas-Boas incident. I referred to it at the beginning of this

17   Psychologist Carl Jung got his views circulating early in the game with his 1959 (1958 in German) *Flying Saucers: A Modern Myth of Things Seen in the Sky*. The irony of this element in the psychological drama (that academia could so easily be fooled by the deceptions of military shenanigans) will seem ever less-amusing or ironic than frightening as these types of incidents occur and with increasing audacity and ruthlessness for the public at large.

chapter as one that captured my own young imagination, and which had me psychologically transforming barn silos to landed saucers. From the standpoint of brainwashing: mission accomplished, I would say.

In 1953 when George Adamski wrote his *Inside the Flying* Saucers the intelligence services were in maximum overdrive in their quest to win the minds of Americans against communist infiltration. There were speculations at the time that Adamski himself was in the service of the US government and researchers speculated about "Allen Dulles' stagecraft behind Adamski's encounters" (Pilkington, 99-114).

Researchers had good reason for thinking this as in that same year the Robertson Panel was convened and was "made up of five prominent physical scientists who met in early 1953 to study the UFO problem [and] was CIA sponsored (Lorenzen, 240; Denzler, 13-14). In 1997 the CIA admitted to having participated in a disinformation campaign regarding UFOs and this is no longer a hidden fact (Haines; Jacobs, 78-80; Malone).

It must be assumed, if not taken for granted, that official sources of information were influenced with the intentions of satisfying national securing concerns. The control of information passed to the news media in the USA by the intelligence services would be highly redacted (manipulated) in this regard. Such is the case with Project Paperclip, a secret transfer of German technology and manpower into the United States in the immediate aftermath of WWII. Secrecy was the norm and so the manipulation of public opinion was a must when they (the general public) caught a glimpse, as most assuredly they would, of the test flights of these aircraft. These exotic aircraft that would be under development for the next generation were of alien origin, to be sure. The caveat is, however, they were alien only in *international* not *intergalactic* terms.

One compelling motive for the ultra-secrecy and disinformation around the UFO phenomenon was the nature of the source of that technology – Nazi Germany. Consider having had a son fight and die in the war only to find out after the fact that the American government imported Nazi war criminals into the USA and put them on the federal payroll. Hence, there was a great political expediency to keep the origins of the technology a secret from the public.

LITTLE GREEN NAZIS

The intent here is to provide an historical context of the development of ufology in the USA with allusion to the "alien" (i.e., German/ Nazi) technology that was imported post-WWII. It is no coincidence that the first American sightings occur in 1947, two years after end of the war and allowing for enough time for the importation of German technology under Project Paperclip.[18]

One historian put it this way,

> By March of 1946 "Project Paperclip" had replaced Project Overcast, providing a stronger legal basis for the long-term exploitation of former enemy scientists and engineers and new scope to bend President Harry Truman's rules regarding Nazi war criminals: namely, that they emphatically should not be allowed into the United States as bona fide immigrants (Cornwell, 422).[19]

In the aftermath of the war, and with the awareness that German technology was equally coveted by the Soviets, it was a *fait accompli* from the military establishment's point of view as to the need for the German scientists – *obtain them at all costs*. The politics of it would have to be handled and managed elsewhere. Hence the reference to "paperclip" in the operation's name: literally a fake identity papering over the criminal or potentially-criminal past of the scientist, engineer, doctor, intelligence agent, military man, whomever was captured and paper-clipping it to the front of his personnel file.

With this chapter, then, comes into focus the meaning of the reference to a Germany-connection in the quotes page before the Introduction to this book. The reference to a non-American writer and his ideas on religion was inserted intentionally and provides the physical and historical link from the most recent European fascist era to the United States and its military industrial complex – and from which ufology emerged. The warnings that were not heeded at that time ought to be considered in our own era. It would be instructive for Religious Studies scholars and theologians alike to revisit the cautionary warnings raised in our recent past.

Rudolph Bultmann was a German theologian at this very politically tumultuous time in his country's history: the period of Adolf Hitler's ascendancy through his seizure of power (1923-1933). As noted in the quote before my Introduction, Bultmann's caution not to falsify the Christian faith by twisting it to suit nationalistic needs came three months after the burning of the German Reichstag, the equivalent of Capitol Hill in Washington.

---

18   While Project Paperclip, sometimes referred to as Operation Paperclip, is of enormous importance to this story, it is well-documented elsewhere and at this stage serves as but one link in the historical development of ufology in America. This history appears to have direct implications for chapter six as well.

19   Cornwell references the U.K. edition of Tom Bower's 1987 book *The Paperclip Conspiracy: The Battle for the Spoils and Secrets of Nazi Germany* and published in the USA as *The Paperclip Conspiracy: The Hunt for the Nazi Scientists* also in 1987.

This is tantamount to asking Americans *not to distort* the religious beliefs of Islam three months after September 11, 2001 and as the nation is mobilizing for military action in Afghanistan against those who had just attacked us.[20] Such a message runs counter to our demands for justice. Political rhetoric and demagoguery run very high at such moments and reactionary public policy is more easily assented-to by populations in times of terror.

This was Bultmann's fear: a form of government destructive to the freedoms of individuals. "The defamation of a person who thinks differently from you is not a noble means for winning a struggle. And once again I may appeal to a statement of Hitler, that those who think differently should not be suppressed, but rather won over" (Introduction; Johnson, 276).

Such are dark times for writers, intellectuals, journalists, theologians, and clergy who find it perilous to voice their true thoughts. It is difficult to comport Bultmann's warning with his inclusion of a quote from the Führer himself.

Or is it?

The language of "liberation" can itself be an obfuscation and tool of oppression.

The principal concern of this chapter is to discern from public policy and popular culture if the political orientation of the American government was altered in any way along with the transfer of that same aviation technology via Operation Paperclip?[21] The reader may find clues to that answer in the chapters following this one wherein the heavy-hand of government costs many individual citizens not only their liberties but their lives.

> fas·cism *n. 1. A one-party system of government in which each class has its distinct place, function and representation in the government but the individual is subordinated to the state and control is maintained by military force, secret police, rigid censorship, and governmental regimentation of industry and finance.*
> – Funk and Wagnalls Standard College Dictionary

---

20   The irony is President George W. Bush did ask the nation publicly not to confuse the terrorists' beliefs with mainstream Islam. He visited a mosque to show his support only days after the attack: https://www.c-span.org/video/?166111-1/presidential-visit-islamic-center (accessed February 2019). But even a President's voice can be drowned-out by the rhetoric of a 24-hour "news"-cycle on cable television and a cottage-industry in book-publishing on "radical Islam."

21   The reader will be cautioned not to over-respond or prejudge the use of the terminology referencing fascism and applying it to US history. First, it merely refers to the historical occurrence that the technology under consideration was first developed by the Nazis in Germany prior to WWII. Subsequent to the war that same technology was transferred and secretly further-developed here in the USA. Only secondarily do I want the reader to view the reference as a tendency *within governmental-rule* that has [or may have] applications in an American context – although some examples of that tendency are coming forthwith.

As noted in chapter three, the Cold War fostered a need for extreme measures and extreme deceptions, especially as the nuclear destructive odds were raised to the level known as MAD – Mutually Assured Destruction. Stakes get no higher than this.

As a result "falsifications of faith," Christian and otherwise, would come into play and be useful tools in leading the American people along a politically-determined primrose path the war-planners set before them. This is a very dangerous trend and portends a fascist-leaning future.[22]

In this way, American religious deception was and remains indistinguishable from the use of religion under previous and oppressive regimes. Recall only the reference to Nero and his blaming the Christians for the fire in Rome cited in the Introduction. Modern fascist regimes, most notably the fascist Social Democrats of the 1920s and 1930s Germany under Adolf Hitler also found it expedient to exploit religion as an instrument of power. Hitler's willingness to utilize religious rituals to foster his party's ascendancy and status among Germans was most explicit. Dabbling into the occult was not unheard of by certain high-level members of the Nazi party. Joseph Goebbels was also so-inclined as one recent made-for-television documentary pointed out (Cinnabar). The very image of the swastika itself was taken from Indian-Hindu culture and it implied to the Nazis Aryan historical superiority.

The Nazi's attitude toward those they conquered and religion's usefulness to them is chillingly clear in their treatment of the Polish people (Shirer, 938). His disdain for them was expressed by his willingness to either enslave or exterminate them. He wanted no Polish intelligentsia left alive. No one was to think separately and independently from the supreme warlord and his state. His policies and attitude were shared by hundreds if not thousands of other Nazis. As for the scientists in their service who were spirited to America post-war under Paperclip, were they also tarred with the same political views or were they merely following orders?

These questions may never be fully answered.

Another reason to raise this concern of fascist infiltration is the fact that the subjects of the next three chapters all coalesce around the nexus of limited (as in compartmentalized and bureaucratized) government involvement that is best described as a *shadow element* that is suppressed in the official narratives of these events. These narratives are dominated

---

22   As if to underscore the reality of this taking hold in America, the next three historic delusions: Jonestown, the Branch Davidians and the September 11 attacks will all qualify for inclusion as moments that resulted from fascist-leaning state actors. The forensic evidence is overwhelming in all three cases and with religion providing an effective, if exemplary, cover for miscreant government operatives.

by religion, but the motives of shadow government involvement are anything but righteous. Forensic analysis of these events reveal religion as insufficient to explain them.

Project Paperclip satisfies this criterion and constitutes a form of, albeit limited to those in-the-know, government involvement that functions in the shadows of official history. So, for example, Werner von Braun and the Nazi scientists imported into the USA to work on the Saturn V rockets for NASA had their former Nazi affiliations concealed from the public (Cromwell, 422).

Does Project Paperclip have any bearing upon these following incidents: Jonestown, the Branch Davidians and the September 11, 2001 attack? Not directly, necessarily. But I submit that there is a historical consistency here that reveals a certain attitude on the part of elements within the state toward its people. This attitude is one of a disregard for human life as secondary to national security, a tendency toward eugenics and a certain latent racism, or at least a classism – whichever may be suitable or efficacious for the political elite at any particular time. Not all these elements are equally present in each of these three incidents, but as policy actions, they are visible and discernible. These are shocking possibilities to be sure, but in the visual images available for each of these three incidents, and the perceptible limited government involvement, cause for concern is sufficient to sound a warning bell that fascist tendencies in regard to the public manipulation of religions, religious groups, or religious individuals have crept into policy quarters.

So, what were people in fact seeing in these reported crashes? Kenneth Arnold's "flying saucer" was in all likelihood America's reworking of the Horten HO229 which was under development by the Germans at the end of the war and was brought over to the USA shortly thereafter. It was one of the "wonder weapons" that the Germans were developing, and about which rumor circulated among the Allies and striking great fear, much like the V1 and V2 rockets, which were far from rumor – just ask any one of London's child evacuees:

> At 11 o'clock on the night of 15 September 1944, a new flying weapon appeared on the scene. The V1 or 'doodlebug' as it was nicknamed, was small plane without a pilot. It carried a high charge of explosive and was catapulted from the Continent in the direction of London. The first time I saw a V1 was from the balcony. It was late at night and, my mother and sisters safe in the underground shelter, I had left my father asleep and wandered out into

the clear night air to watch any action. It was not long in coming. Suddenly there was a familiar swishing noise and, as I dashed for the stairs, an explosion and a fierce gust of wind that blew me right down them. The next morning we discovered that our local post office had received a direct hit. Within days the Government issued a statement to the effect that Hitler had begun a new form of warfare.... The first V2 landed with a shattering explosion in London on 8 September. So shaken was the British Government that it was not until November that the nation finally heard the terrifying news that London was now under attack by a weapon that gave no warning of its approach (Wicks, 192, 194).

Sounds much like the predicament Saddam Hussein found himself in upon commencement of America's Gulf War of 1990-1991 as it unleashed the F-117A stealth bomber[23] upon Baghdad. The war would be over in 100 hours! No too shabby considering Saddam's army was the fourth largest in the world at that time.

But the Horten HO 229 was not yet fully-functional under the Germans, and so it did not enter service during the war. Further development of this new aircraft design was left for those who captured the Nazi scientists, which was the mission of Project Paperclip. The Soviets were just as eager as the Americans to capture that same technology and they did so.

In keeping with the fascist view of "human rights," human experimentation may be the explanation for what witnesses saw as "alien bodies" being retrieved from the crashed saucers.

Given what is known about human experimentation by the U.S. government, the use of human subjects flying as test "dummies" must be considered a possibility. Human test subjects or human "unfortunates" were routinely used in medical and other experiments by both Nazi scientists and, in time, by medical researchers here in the USA and Canada (chapter six alludes to these types of experiments conducted by U.S. officials and examples are cited).

This is a macabre twist to the benevolent green large-eyed aliens rendered in costume and effigy celebrated at annual events. The thought that our fellow human beings were the aliens all along must not come as a shock so unthinkable. We must be willing to reconcile ourselves with the darkest elements of our past if we are to forge a more humane future, let alone one characterized by the common civic good and pluralism.

23   Both Lockheed-Martin and Northrup-Grumman would separately work on stealth technology for the Department of Defense.

AMERICA'S NEAR-GLOBAL AIR DOMINANCE (for now)

The second half of the twentieth-century saw the rise of the *national security state* (often dated at 1947 with its origins in the National Security Act[24] and the creation of the Central Intelligence Agency) coupled with an increase in technological advancement in aviation, medicine, warfare and cyber capabilities. The second half of that same period (1975-2000) also saw an international political world order develop out of the Cold War Soviet-USA stand-off and unfold much as described in the 1996 book *The Clash of Civilizations and the Remaking of Word Order*:

> And only the United States will have the air power capable of bombing virtually any place in the world. These are the central elements of the military position of the United States as a global power and of the West as the dominant civilization in the world. For the immediate future the balance of conventional military power between the West and the rest will overwhelmingly favor the West (Huntington, 186).

Popular authors on the topic Ralph and Judy Blum make a noteworthy observation about the UFOs eyewitness were seeing when they state, "the Phenomenon always seemed to stay a step ahead of our technology – from airships to planes to rockets – until, by the end of World War II, people would once again look up into the skies and see shapes like those recorded on cave walls 15,000 years ago" (Blum-Blum, 56). Cave paintings would likely *not* be the first thing to come to mind in the average saucer eyewitness unless the similarity or connection was pointed-out and the eyewitness steered in the direction of such artwork. Given that the general public were catching glimpses of aircraft unlike what they were familiar with from contemporaneous public information (winged airplanes), it is not a surprise they would be suggestable to explanations from popular culture – I had been.

Alas, the imagination is powerful, indeed, and ripe for exploitation. And so the "saucers" became "chariots," and the "wheels" of Ezekiel became "spaceships."

One would do wisely to heed von Däniken's own words on the topic. Being most aware (if not having been officially briefed?!) of the government's far-reaching need for resources and, by way of political necessity, secrecy:

> Think tanks are springing up all over the world; what they amount to are monasteries of scientists of today, who are thinking for to-

---

24   National Security Act of 1947. Archived at the Office of the Historian. https://history. state.gov/milestones/1945-1952/national-security-act (accessed January 2019).

morrow. There are 164 of these think tanks at work in America alone. They accept commissions from the government and heavy industry. The most celebrated think tank is the Rand Corporation at Santa Monica in California. The U.S. Air Force was responsible for its foundation in 1945. The reason? High-ranking officers wanted a research program of their own on intercontinental warfare. Some 850 selected scientific authorities now work in the two-story magnificently laid-out research center.... As early as 1946 Rand scientists evaluated the military usefulness of a spaceship (151).

Von Däniken sums up his galactically-popular book *Chariots of the Gods?* with the assessment that "Governments have to decide on their military plans far in advance; big businesses have to calculate their investments for decades ahead" (152).

Did the UFO mythology-religion assist the Pentagon's concealment of imported Nazi (alien) technology? It appears that the mythology has provided plausible deniability for over half a century, in addition to generating much profitable entertainment.

The logic is clear enough: much better from the Pentagon's perspective to have people believe the government is covering-up extraterrestrial aliens and their interstellar travels to planet earth than Nazi's and their international travels into the USA – in spite of the technological necessity of doing so, the general public simply would not understand. Imagine how the American people would have felt to know the full extent of Operation Paperclip – to know that the U.S. government was in the business of importing Nazi technicians to further develop the "wonder weapons" that Hitler himself had boasted about. Not a palatable reality after nearly 1.1 million Americans had perished or were wounded or missing at the hands of the evil fascists. There is little question that so recent after the war, the public would have been outraged and that it would have been political suicide for any public official to admit to such an action.

Secrecy and concealment become the paradigm.

When in 1988 the Pentagon unveiled both the F-117A and the B-2 Stealth Bombers, those black triangular-shaped winged aircraft which would soon be employed in Panama in 1989 and Iraq in 1990,[25] we were witness to the end-product of forty years' worth of development and testing

25   The timing speaks volumes. Would the Iraq War (the first Gulf War of 1990-1991) have taken place without the readiness and capabilities of the F-117A bomber – the aircraft principally used in the conflict? It seems unlikely. And if not, as my calculation has it, then this begs the question *what* or *who* is determining public and foreign policy and the need for offensive war? By all appearances the military-industrial-complex guides and directs and leads the political world, not the reverse.

and its awesome war-making and winning capabilities. That very aircraft and its subsequent derivatives have come to secure the United States' standing in the world as virtually unchallenged in the realm of air-war dominance, and its bigger sister, space warfare – for the time being anyway.

This is the reality of a modern democratic empire and distinct from totalitarian rule: *grandiose delusions must be fostered and nurtured for empire to be sustained.* It is costly in earthly resources, blood and treasure to maintain a global power, so the reader can only imagine what preparations and contingency plans have been concocted within the top-secret halls of our military planners and global warlords. The myths will no doubt be commensurate to their schemes if the past is any clue. Only time will tell.

REFERENCES
Books/Essays

Bainbridge, William Sims (1987). Science and Religion: The Case of Scientology. In *The Future of New Religious Movements.* Edited by David G. Bromley and Phillip E. Hammond. Macon, Georgia: Mercer University Press.

Blum, Ralph with Judy Blum (1974). *Beyond Earth: Man's Contact with UFOs.* New York: Ballantine Books.

Blumrich, Josef F. (1974). *The Spaceships of Ezekiel.* New York: Bantam Books.

Brzezinski, Zbigniew (1970). *Between Two Ages: America's Role in the Technetronic Era.* New York: Viking Press.

Chryssides, George D. (1999). *Exploring New Religions.* London: Cassell.

Cornwell, John (2003). *Hitler's Scientists: Science, War, and the Devil's Pact.* New York: Penguin Books.

Dawson, Lorne L., ed. (2003). *Cults and New Religious Movements: A Reader.* Malden, Massachusetts: Blackwell Publishing.

Denzler, Brenda (2001). *The Lure of the Edge: Scientific Passions, Religious Beliefs, and the Pursuit of UFOs.* Berkeley: University of California Press.

Ellwood, Robert S. Jr. (1973). The Descent of the Mighty Ones: Spiritualism and UFO Cults. In his *Religious and Spiritual Groups in Modern America.* Englewood Cliffs, New Jersey: Prentice-Hall. Pgs. 131-156.

Fuller, John G. (1966). *The Interrupted Journey: Two Lost Hours Aboard a Flying Saucer.* New York: Berkley Medallion. Also in audio edition read by Whitley Strieber. 1989. Dial Press. An imprint of Harper Audio.

Haines, Gerald K. (2007). CIA's Role in the Study of UFOs, 1947-90: A Die-Hard Issue. Historical document. Last updated June 27, 2008. https://www.cia.gov/library/center-for-the-study-of-intelligence/csi-publications/csi-studies/studies/97unclass/ufo.html (accessed January 2019).

Harrison, Peter (1990). *'Religion' and the religions in the English Enlightenment*. Cambridge: Cambridge University Press.

Hexham, Irving (2002). *Pocket Dictionary of New Religious Movements*. Downers Grove, Illinois: InterVarsity Press.

Huntington, Samuel P. (1996). *The Clash of Civilizations and the Remaking of World Order*. New York: Simon & Schuster.

Hynek, J. Allen (1972). *The UFO Experience: A Scientific Inquiry*. New York: [Henry Regnery] Ballantine Books.

Book covers of two mass-market editions of J. Allen Hynek's 1972 book, the May 1974 (left) and October 1977 versions. The 1977 edition was published within a month of the release of Steven Spielberg's blockbuster motion picture Close Encounters of the Third Kind. *Hynek would even make a brief on-camera appearance during the final and dramatic scenes of the film.*

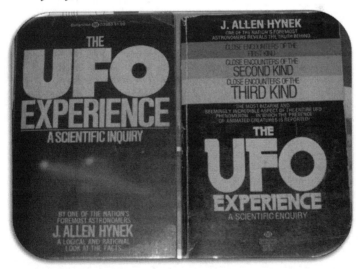

Jacobs, David Michael (1975). *The UFO Controversy in America*. New York: Signet/New American Library, 1976.

Jung, C.G. (1959). *Flying Saucers: A Modern Myth of Things Seen in the Skies*. New York: New American Library/Signet, 1969.

Keyhoe, Donald (1950). *The Flying Saucers Are Real*. New York: Fawcett Publications, Inc.

Klass, Philip J. (1983). *UFOs: The Public Deceived*. Amherst, New York: Prometheus Books

Kyle, Richard (1993). *The Religious Fringe: A History of Alternative Religions in America*. Downers Grove, Illinois: InterVarsity Press.

Landsburg, Alan and Sally (1975). *The Outer Space Connection*. New York: Bantam Books.

Lorenzen, Coral and Jim (1976). *Encounters with UFO Occupants*. New York: Berkley Medallion.

Partridge, Christopher, ed. (2003). *UFO Religions*. London: Routledge.

Partridge, Christopher, ed. (2004). *New Religions: A Guide, New Religious Movements, Sects and Alternative Spiritualities*. New York: Oxford University Press.

Pilkington, Mark (2010). *Mirage Men: An Adventure into Paranoia, Espionage, Psychological Warfare, and UFOs*. New York: Skyhorse Publishing. See also Pilkington below in Films/Documentaries.

Shirer, William L. (1960). *The Rise and Fall of the Third Reich: A History of Nazi Germany*. New York: Simon and Schuster, 2011.

Stark, Rodney and William Sims Bainbridge (1985). *The Future of Religion: Secularization, Revival, and Cult Formation*. Berkeley: University of California Press.

Spielberg, Steven (1977). *Close Encounters of the Third Kind*. New York: Dell Publishing.

Steiger, Brad, ed. (1976). *Project Blue Book: The Top Secret UFO Findings Revealed*. New York: Ballantine.

Von Däniken, Erich (1969). *Chariots of the Gods? Unsolved Mysteries of the Past*. German edition 1968. Trans. Michael Heron. New York: Bantam Books, 1971.

Von Däniken, Erich (1972). *Gods from Outer Space: Return to the Stars or Evidence for the Impossible*. German edition 1970. Trans. Michael Heron. New York: Bantam Books.

Wicks, Ben (1988). *No Time to Wave Goodbye*. Toronto: Stoddart.

Films/Documentaries

CBS Reports (1966). *UFO: Friend, Foe or Fantasy?* Written and produced by Joseph Wershba and Jack Beck. http://www.youtube.com/watch?v=VVpNqFz-h2c (accessed January 2019).

Cinnabar Pictures, Inc. for Discovery Channel (1998/2006). *Nazis: The Occult Conspiracy*. Produced and directed by Tracy Atkinson and Joan Baran. Aired on the Military Channel in 2011.

> • It is very difficult to justify the use of the term "conspiracy" in the title of this program. In what sense is a conspiracy at work? – most especially in its proper and legal definition of conspiring to commit a crime? As lamented in the Introduction, this term is used polemically, and it is most unnecessary and misleading to use in this manner. Throughout the program, they never elaborate or discuss in

what manner a conspiracy might be at work other than to insinuate that certain among the Nazis had more interest in the occult than others. For all of the atrocities of the Nazis, "conspiracy" is not an appropriate description of them, they were state crimes against humanity. The only motivation for using the term in this manner is to connect *conspiratorial behavior* in the audience's mind to that which is the most outlandish, eccentric, outrageous, bizarre, indeed, *unbelievable*. Insinuating that only Nazi-types could indulge in such government-conspiratorial activity is a simplistic take-away lesson revealing the motive for such a distortion in the presentation of history. How else could it be so easily and frequently repeated from Americans (principally white Americans as African-American history is conscious of the evils of power) that "no American could be so evil"? (See The Terms of Delusion later in this book)

Cook, Nick (2005). *UFOs: The Secret Evidence*. Produced by Susan Jones for Oxford Film and Television, Channel 4 in association with A&E Television Network. https://topdocumentaryfilms.com/ufos-the-secret-evidence/ (accessed January 2019).

Discovery Channel (2008). *Nazi UFO Conspiracy*. Produced by Flashback Television for the Discovery Channel and also aired on Military Channel. https://press.discovery.com/uk/dsc/programs/nazi-ufo-conspiracy/ (accessed January 2019).

• As with the above source *Nazis: The Occult Conspiracy*, one has to question the media's use of the term "conspiracy" in this consistently erroneous manner.

Knaap, George (1994). *UFOs Best Evidence: The Government Cover-Up*. Executive Producer Donald S. Williams. Produced and Directed by George Knaap and Bryan Gresh. Altamira Broadcasts. http://forbiddenknowledgetv.net/UFOs-Best-Evidence-The-Government-Cover-Up/ (accessed January 2019).

Landsburg, Alan, Productions (1975). *The Outer Space Connection*. Written and Directed by Fred Warshofsky. Narrated Rod Serling. Video Communications, Inc. (United Entertainment, 1987).

Pilkington, Mark (2014) *Mirage Men: How the U.S. Government Created a Myth That Took Over the World*. John Lundberg Director. Produced by Roland Denning, et al. Random Media-Perception Management.

Malone, Guy (2010). ROSWELL 1947: When The Mythology Is Stripped Away, What Facts Remain?: The Truth (?) Behind the Craft, the Bodies, and the Metal. Lecture originally presented July 2, 2010 at the Roswell Museum & Art Center, as part of the City of Roswell's 2010 Roswell 1947 UFO Symposium and again July 3, 2010 at the Roswell Public Library. 65 Minutes. www.roswellufocrash.com (accessed January 2019).

National Geographic Revealed (2005). *The Hunt for Hitler's Scientists*. Windfall Films. Written and produced by Mark Radice. (Archived at: http://www.windfall-films.com/show/1149/the-hunt-for-hitlers-scientists.aspx; January 2019).

United Artists (1956). *Unidentified Flying Objects: The True Story of Flying Saucers*. Clarence Greene and Russell Rouse Productions. (88 minutes).

> At the end of the movie the following summation is provided:
> THE MOTION PICTURE you have just seen is authentic.
> It is substantiated by documentation, eye-witness accounts supported by affidavits and official government reports.
> The evidence has been presented to you with integrity and objectivity to establish the fact that Unidentified Flying Objects, commonly known as "flying saucers," do exist.
> Some kind of flying objects have been photographed in the sky.
> If they cannot be identified as objects known to man.... What are they?
> If they are not man-made.... Who made them?
> If they are not from this planet.... Where are they from?

White, Chris (2012). *Ancient Aliens Debunked*. http://ancientaliensdebunked.com/ (accessed January 2019).

Endnote

If a picture's worth a thousand words…

Bantam's dual publishing ventures in 1970 (Psychic Discoveries) and 1974 (UFOs) of exposing secrets of the US's Cold War arch-enemy, the Soviet Union, and helping to lodge in the U.S. population's mind the global nature of the respective phenomena. Even the cover art betrays a certain continuity, if lack of creativity, in the selling of a message and of the common source of that message.

6

THE DANGEROUS RELIGIOUS CULT: JONESTOWN

The delusion: *900+ members of the Peoples Temple die in a mass-suicide-murder ritual at the hands of the deranged and mind-controlling "Reverend" Jim Jones in Guyana, South America in November 1978. This was a frightful, if extreme, example of religious manipulation and brainwashing at the hands of a charismatic "cult" leader and serves as a wake-up call to all people about the dangers of religious cults and those who promote them.*

The correction: *Excessive quantities of very potent psychotropic medications for a generalized group of adults and children; slow-to-develop body-count in the aftermath of the event; mishandling of cadavers – only seven autopsies done on over 900 bodies; military control of compound and a number of guns and ammunition associated with the group on-and-off site; scrubbing of site and no serious independent analysis of deceased members' personal effects; Jones' unusually high-profile and political connections; assassinations of former members/defectors* <u>subsequent</u> *to Jones' alleged death by gunshot, all serve to implicate agents far beyond the reach of a single person. Something more extensive (and perhaps ultimately unprovable due to tight control of site) than merely one man's religious followers obeying his commands was in operation in the Peoples Temple and at Jonestown. Ownership and handling of site indicate a government's (Guyanese) or governments' (British-American) roles in the administration and/or protection of the site and whatever was taking place there at the remote jungle compound before and after Jonestown.*

Quotes

Those who do not remember the past are condemned to repeat it.
– plaque hanging over Jim Jones' seat in main pavilion in
Jonestown, Guyana

The individual liberties of American citizens depend on government observance of the law. Under our form of Constitutional government, authority can be exercised only if it has been properly delegated to a particular department or agency by the Constitution or Congress.... Whenever the activities of a government agency exceed its authority, individual liberty may be impaired.
–Report to the President by the Commission on CIA Activities
Within the United States;1975, pg. 4

James Evans: You know something Junior, you might as well be in the CIA, because the more you talk the more you hang yourself.
–*Good Times* (season 2, 1975: Thelma's Scholarship;
aired March 11)

The CIA used the pastor of a church in a Third World country as a "principal agent" to carry out covert action projects, and as a spotter, assessor, asset developer, and recruiter. He collected information on po-litical developments and on personalities. He passed CIA propaganda to the local press. According to the CIA's description of the case, the pastor's analyses were based on his long-term friendships with the per-sonalities, and the agents under him were "well known to him in his professional life." At first the CIA provided only occasional gifts to the pastor in return for his services; later, for over ten years, the CIA paid him a salary that reached $11,414 annually.
– Final Report of the *Select Committee to Study Governmental Op-erations with Respect to Intelligence Activities*; 1976, pgs. 202-203

In the minds of many baby-boomers and older North Americans, Jim Jones and the Peoples Temple constitute Exhibit A for religion becoming evil.
– Charles Kimball, 2002 in *When Religion Becomes Evil*, pg. 85

The MOTHER of ALL CULTS

Who among us at one time or another has not been accused by a cynical friend or skeptic of something we said of "drinking the Kool-Aid"? This meme comes from the Jonestown "suicides." The applications of this meme are today unlimited and attest to the secretion into the broader culture of myths (and worse, outright deceptions fostering harmful and socially-damaging delusions) arising from very specific events and the cultural meaning that can become conjoined to those events. The tragic incident of Jonestown is single-handedly responsible for planting the fear into a generation and beyond of Americans' minds of the *menace of brainwashing-religious cults* (Moore, 2009: 119).

Jonestown was reported as more-or-less a mass-suicide by self-administered poisoning, with some few killings by gunshot (the alleged body of Jones was shot in the head), all motivated by religious abuse at the hands of a deranged and charismatic cult leader intent on destroying his flock. The historic implications have been incalculable. I would suggest it compares in the social, cultural, and most-especially the political spheres to an *event horizon* in the astronomical world.[1] Simply, it is an event so psychologically-traumatic or suggestive and/or historically-significant to the observers at a nationwide or even global level, that their psychological and political lives are influenced by the event for some time to follow. The World Wars are certainly in this category – time has been subsequently measured as either before or after the war. The 1925 Scopes Monkey Trial qualifies in America's religious history – the collective psychological impact was enormous. The assassinations of President John F. Kennedy (1963) and Dr. Martin Luther King, Jr. (1968) were so traumatic that many people remembered exactly where they were when they heard the news and the meme of the "flashbulb memory," especially in the case of JFK, was illustrated using his assassination as a case study (Rubin-McNeil, 10-11). For many, the fall of the Berlin Wall in 1989 is a moment to mark history. We still feel the effects of the September 11, 2001 event horizon.

In the case of the November 1978 Jonestown tragedy, the religious world was rocked by an apparent mass-suicide at the hands of a charis-

---

1   I use this term (here in a novel way) in parallel to its astronomical meaning in which a perimeter around a black hole demarcates an area from which nothing can escape. In my use, it refers to an event of such importance that subsequent similar (or perceived as similar) events cannot help but be seen in relation to it, and interpretations of events subsequent to the original are manufactured with the parts of the original. Similar to the meme (a social fact replicated through culture), an *event horizon* can be detected among social facts as all too frequently the efficacy of the event horizon to help shape public opinion is recognized by the political elites with their various means of cultural coercion. This was nakedly on display in the Branch Davidian siege with the frequent use of the rhetoric of Jonestown (see 2:13:07 in the Reference to chapter seven).

matic cult figure who had brainwashed his followers. In Jim Jones we saw something of an Elmer Gantry (a religious swindler)[2] turned controlling and violent proceed to commit mass-murder by his very command.

"Cult of death" was the headline across the two major national news magazines *TIME* and *Newsweek*. And barely more than a year later a feature-film *and* a CBS made-for-television movie were produced which together helped cement into viewers' minds the image of Jones as a raving, if drug-addled, lunatic obsessed with power and control.

While this is the case, by far and away, it is not the whole picture.

Certainly Jim Jones (1931-1978?) was a man who could legitimately be considered an abusive and evil-intentioned megalomaniac. But the over-emphasis placed upon *his* personality (i.e., the lone gunman myth, see The Terms of Delusion), and *his* adeptness at so-called *religious brainwashing* as the principal medium of abuse, explain *only part* of the forensic realities. There is much about what took place (both in the final event and in the span of Jones' career) that is simply beyond the reach of one man.

The very structure of the Peoples Temple was designed for control of the entire population. "Though 80% of the Temple membership was Black, nearly 100% of the Angels were Caucasian. Their numbers are not known, but by 1978, Jones referred to them as "The One Hundred"" (Meiers, 197).[3] It appears that Jones had a team of as many as one hundred loyalists he manipulated into doing his bidding. Among them were both willing participants but also those whom he forced into some kind of submission to his will. Any number of defectors and whistleblowers tell hair-raising tales of Jones' abuse of power over those who populated his Planning Commission (PC) which he had formed in 1972 and consisted of a sort of inner-circle alluded to above as the "The One Hundred."

As for the general congregation, he abused them with religious deceptions such as staged fake healings and had select members of the PC cooperate with the fakery. He financially deprived and alienated many elderly from their Social Security, Disability, or Welfare via his nursing home businesses in northern California. In Ukiah, Mendocino County north of San Francisco where Jones moved his Peoples Temple (PT) congregation in 1965 from Indiana, his organization was much-enmeshed with the local government

---

2   Sinclair Lewis' novel *Elmer Gantry* was published in 1927, two years after the Scopes Trial. This highly-successful novel helped orient the general population's awareness of the trial *away from the eugenics concerns* of William Jennings Bryan *and toward the excesses of religious fanaticism*, whether that be anti-science or religious hypocrisy. The image of the religious charlatan is perpetuated in the character of Elmer.

3   Other sources have the demography of Jonestown at 70% black and 64% women. https://jonestown.sdsu.edu/?page_id=70495 (accessed February 2019).

and he was assigned to the County's Grand Jury in 1967. Perhaps this is not surprising given the Assistant District Attorney (DA) for Mendocino County had joined the PT earlier the same summer. That DA, a character named Tim Stoen who would allow Jim Jones (JJ) to impregnate his wife Grace Stoen setting-up the conditions for a future custody battle and subsequent legal unraveling of Jones' efforts, would be instrumental in the downfall of Jonestown and a character who enabled Jones to wield much political influence in the California years of the PT (Meiers, 268-271).

This for me was always a curious element in researching Jim Jones-PT-Jonestown: and that was Jim Jones' high-profile political contacts at the city, state, national, and even international levels. Individually perhaps, these can be accounted for by rigorous networking and social outreach – but not to the extent he had cultivated, and certainly not for a missionary! Collectively, however, they comprise a list of contacts who were in positions to unwittingly or otherwise enable Jones to further his cause. More troubling is that these events in Jones' life are frequently omitted, or mentioned very selectively, from popular media narratives about JJ-PT-Jonestown and this establishes its own suspicions (see very last footnote to The Terms of Delusion on the interaction-relationship between a Hollywood drama and events surrounding the JFK assassination).

One post-massacre editorial summed-up longstanding frustrations by concerned citizens in California at getting the word out about the true nature of JJ-PT:

> If there is any morality in the committee which determines Pulitzer Prizes, there will be a special Pulitzer for Carolyn Pickering – and for Brenda Ganatos. Brenda is not a writer – but she was our best source in Ukiah, when Carolyn and I collaborated on the 1972 Jim Jones expose. Brenda still likes Ukiah – where Jones and his followers imposed an "atmosphere of terror," according to Ukiah Baptist minister Richard Taylor. Despite this, Brenda helped me obtain signed affidavits from witnesses whose names are now being reported nationally. She did this in a community where Jones' people had infiltrated the school system, the welfare department, law enforcement and the grand jury – of which Jones himself was appointed foreman (Kinsolving).

By date of association, Jones was in contact with the following officials, held government post, was provided government access or cover, or was given political legitimacy:

1950s – Jones meets Dan Mitrione (police officer, FBI agent, and later U.S. Government advisor for the CIA in Latin America) in Richmond, Indiana; Mitrione would work for the U.S. State Department's International Cooperation Administration in South America (Belo Horizonte, Brazil) from 1960-1967 teaching what we might call today "enhanced interrogation techniques"[4]

1961 – Jones is made Executive Director of the Indianapolis Human Rights Commission which "in his craving for publicity ... he exploited to feed both his career and his social goals, as well as to document the myths about his personal history" (Reiterman, 68)

1962-63 – Jones goes to Belo Horizonte, Brazil ostensibly as a missionary from his home church in Indiana; Dan Mitrione is there too. A local newspaper accuses Jones of being a CIA operative. His behavior is not that of a typical missionary (Thielmann, p. 26-27 he meets occasionally with Brazilian government officials; has a meeting with Fidel Castro en route to Brazil; p. 29 attends Brazilian spiritist/occult/voodoo meetings; p. 47 commits illicit sex for cash and openly discusses it; p. 50 he believes in reincarnation; and he lives "high-on-the-hog" (*San Jose Mercury*), though Thielmann, p. 23 states they were quite limited in income)

1967 – PT now relocated in Ukiah, California from Indianapolis (1965), Jones is appointed to the Mendocino County Grand Jury; Tim Stoen, DA for Mendocino County had previously joined the PT the same year

1973 – December 13 "Jones" arrested for homosexual activity in a Los Angeles movie theatre; charges were dropped and record sealed; fingerprints from this arrest were used to identify Jones' body post-massacre and Jones' known use of body doubles would raise questions about the veracity of post-massacre claims that Jones himself was dead

1973-74 – Scouts from PT arrive in Guyana seeking land for relocation; land owned by Guyanese government to be leased to PT with assistance of Phil Blakey (Meiers, 81-86; Conspiratus,

---

4   See the 1972 French-made film titled *Etat de Siege (State of Siege)* by Costa-Gavras which is based upon the activities of Dan Mitrione. From the IMDb website: "In Uruguay in the early 1970s, an official of the US Agency for International Development [USAID] (a group used as a front for training foreign police in counterinsurgency methods) is kidnapped by a group of urban guerillas. Using his interrogation as a backdrop, the film explores the often brutal consequences of the struggle between Uruguay's government and the leftist Tupamaro guerillas." Dan Mitrione was in real life killed in 1970 by the Tupamaro rebels in Uruguay. https://www.imdb.com/title/tt0070959/plotsummary?ref_=tt_ov_pl (accessed March 2019).

7:47:22-7:47:56);[5] February 1976 PT signs land-lease with Guyanese Government.

Advertisement for Jones' Appearance on a SF Television Show

OUTSTANDING HUMANITARIAN And HEALER

Pastor Jim Jones (Peoples Temple Christian Church), Who Was Recently Praised In The U.S. CONGRESSIONAL RECORD [June 1973] And Who Is Noted For His Sane SPIRITUAL HEALING And HUMAN SERVICE MINISTRY That Teaches Absolute Cooperation With Medical Science, Will Appear On THE JIM DUNBAR SHOW, Tues, July 24th At 7:00 A.M. On Channel 7. S.F.

1975 – PT helps Democrat George Moscone win the mayoral election of San Francisco and becomes high-profile activist in SF politics; PT supports Harvey Milk's run for the San Francisco Board of Supervisors;[6] PT was politically active across a range of issues and personalities in the mid-1970s, among them Black activist Angela Davis, The John Birch Society; the Lieutenant Governor of California; the Mayor, the District Attorney, Chief of Police; city supervisors (Conspiratus, 7:31:00); Native American activist Dennis Banks; Dick Gregory, Jane Fonda, Walter Mondale, Cesar Chavez all made appearances at PT or met with Jones

1976 – Jones appointed to San Francisco Housing Authority Commission by Mayor Moscone; Rosalynn Carter meets with Jim Jones during her husband's presidential campaign

1977 – Mass-migration of PT members to Guyana from California after critical article published "Why Jim Jones Should Be Investigated"; few suspicions raised

Finally and perhaps most disturbingly, post-massacre:

1978 – November 18 deaths begin approximately 5pm local time/4pm ET; presence of Richard Dwyer, State Department

---

5　　See documentary Frank Terpil: *Confessions of a Dangerous Man* at 51:08 where a visual reference to Jonestown insinuates that Terpil had knowledge of classified government operations relative to arming various nations' political rebel-guerillas; https://www.youtube.com/watch?v=iQygg-h7Ats8 (accessed March 2019). There is significant intrigue around the Guyanese/British ownership of land that Jonestown would ultimately reside upon, the arranging of the settlement of that land by Englishman Phil Blakey (the only foreign national employed by the Peoples Temple; Meiers, 78), and Deborah Layton Blakey, the first defector and agitator for the investigation led by Congressman Ryan.

6　　Both Moscone and Milk would be assassinated by Dan White two days after the Jonestown massacre. Curiously, White's defense centered upon his own mental state and he was described as "rigid, robot-like, programmed, controlled, automated and zombie-like" by the press. His "'diminished capacity" [was] due to political and economic pressures and a chemical imbalance in his body from his gluttonous consumption of junk food. It was dubbed "The Twinkie Defense"'" (Meiers, 304-331).

Embassy official and/or CIA agent/Station Chief accompanying Congressman Leo Ryan to Guyana at Jonestown *after* the murders (Rose, p. 221, see also *AJCPT*, Q042 Transcript, Jonestown Audiotape Primary Project: Transcripts prepared by Steve Rose, Tape Number: Q042, the so-called "Death Tape"; Smith, 130)

November 19, 3:30am – CIA radio message to NOIWON[7] received by National Military Command Center reporting 180-200 dead at Jonestown; the only known transmitter in the area belonged to the CIA and presumably Dwyer

November 19-25 – Guyanese military, U.S. State Department and U.S. military in control of site (see Chronology of military involvement provided by the Joint Chiefs of Staff "After Action Report" found in McCoy, 65-80); Guyanese officials impound all NBC recordings

1980 – February 26 Al and Jeannie Mills were shot along with their daughter Daphene in their San Francisco home; they founded and operated, first the Human Freedom Center beginning in 1975 and then Concerned Relatives beginning in Spring 1977; both groups assisted defectors and petitioned government officials to investigate PT and Jonestown; Jeannie published the book *Six Years With God* in May 1979.

This last event struck terror into the already-fearful PT former members that "hit squads" were in operation seeking-out defectors to silence them, intimidate them, or worse. The various abuses at the hands of Jones made this fear no exaggeration and a string of suspicious murders in the early-to-mid-1970s made hit squads seem like a plausible *modus operandi* of Jones and his Planning Commission (Meiers, 195-275). Chapter seven of *People's Temple, People's Tomb* is titled "Eight Mysterious Deaths" (Kerns/Wead, 135-149).

Obviously and boldly, the assassination by Larry Layton, who incidentally was acquitted in 1981, of Congressman Leo Ryan, whose investigation of and visit to Jonestown triggered the final event, was evidence enough that PT would go to any lengths to conceal the true nature of its purpose. The clear-and-present-danger and palpable menace to insiders of the PT was that there was plenty of dangerous and life-threatening activity going-on beyond the reach and control of the individual Jim Jones.

---

7   The National Operational Intelligence Watch Officer's Network (NOIWON) is a secure telephone conference-call system between major Washington national security watch centers, including the National Military Command Center, State Department Operations Center, CIA Operations Center, NSA Operations Center, The White House Situation Room, among other federal government centers. (Source Wikipedia)

Whether at his directive or some other external source, violent actions were being taken on behalf of Jones' cause.

One has to wonder in light of the revelation of the Church Report cited below (U.S. Government Printing Office, 1976) and its mention of "CIA activities in Chile" what the source of the films are Jeannie Mills is describing in her book:

> Movies graphically portraying the horrors of the Nazi concentration camps were shown to the church members. Several movies that had been smuggled out of Chile also made their way to our church services, horrifying us with pictures of tortures that had been used to try to force Chilean revolutionaries to give information to the fascist regime (Mills, 251).

No one was ever charged in the assassination of the Mills' family. Their oldest son, seventeen-year-old Edward, who was home at the time of the murders and claimed he heard nothing only muddied the waters. Neighbors heard nothing.[8] One neighbor saw a van leave the area around the time of the shooting. Police stated that a small, even microscopic, amount of gun powder residue was found on Edward's right hand, but they failed to press charges against him at the time. In 2005, twenty-five years after the murders, on a visit to the U.S. to see family, he was arrested based upon "new investigative methods and technology" by a zealous cold-case investigator but was again released for lack of evidence. Edward has lived in Japan with his family for decades.

It seems unlikely to me that the son, were he in fact the murderer, would leave the U.S. and raise his own family overseas, as Edward has done. That speaks to the actions of a scared but innocent person – especially in light of the tactics of intimidation used by Jones, et al. But I must leave it an open question. Nevertheless, it was not an isolated fear among PT members that hit squads operated to protect Jones' interests. As noted at the Alternative Considerations of Jonestown & Peoples Temple website:

> Finally, rumors circulated of Jonestown death squads, of avenging angels, and of people who had been allowed to survive in order to return to the States and kill the real and perceived enemies of Peoples Temple. As with the other rumors, the reports were exaggerated, born in a climate of fear and uncertainty, and – as it turned out – untrue (Was Jonestown an Armed Camp? Webpage at *ACJPT*).

---

8   Never suggested in most accounts of the murders is the possibility of the use of silencers on the firearms used to kill the Mills. This would account for the son's and possibly the neighbors' failure to hear shots. But this must remain unanswered.

The *ACJPT's* dismissal of the existence of hit squads notwithstanding, the Mills were not the only ones to hold these fears. The methods of fear and intimidation were used during routine temple operations and is frequently discussed by those who've written on the topic having participated in the meetings of the Planning Commission. For examples, Al Mills claims he witnessed his daughter being beaten no less than seventy-five times (White, documentary film); the Mills also describe how Jones openly and publicly talked about "physically punishing people, and we all sat in our seats, dumb-founded. "I want each of you to come forward now and get a whipping!" he shouted" (Mills, 208). The case of Peter Wotherspoon's beating before the Planning Commission instigated several defectors in the summer of 1976 (100 Events in History of Peoples Temple, Webpage at *ACJPT*; see also Guinn's very recent book for an account of Jones' treatment of Wother-spoon, Laurie Efrein and other PC members, 282-283).[9]

Jones' abuse of his congregation with cover and impunity must be better understood for an accurate understanding of Jonestown to emerge.

It is these connections, intrigues, and curious associations to characters who were themselves government officials or were affiliated with officials and offices that enabled Jones to accomplish his activities, and at the very least to maintain the appearance of social and political legitimacy. His meeting with Rosalynn Carter for example implies nothing more than that the political network and establishment around and supporting Jones validated his socio-political activities and status. These associations provide the circumstantial evidence that there was much more involved with Jim Jones, the PT and ultimately at Jonestown than religious brainwashing, manipulation through fear, and the egotistical malfeasance of a single person.

It is best to start with something of an introduction to this ignored (hidden-suppressed) history for a proper contextualizing of JJ-PT-Jonestown. Elements of the unfolding of the tragedy can best be understood and really only make sense when engaging and relating the facts of this history of government experimentation with and upon American

---

9   In deconstructing Guinn's book, it appears to be a "40th anniversary distraction" from any government complicity with or connection to JJ-PT-Jonestown; it portrays the government as an external actor and as Jones' antagonist (311), much as Jones himself proclaimed. Nowhere in Guinn's analysis is the question ever raised about the CIA's thoroughly-established mind control programs and any similar activities at PT. While giving the appearance of thoroughness (and there are plenty of well-researched elements of Guinn's narrative), this book fits that of an *establishment piece* that is too keen on spinning the story in a particular direction, namely *away from* covert government culpability. See Meiers comments about Reiterman's widely-heralded-as-authoritative book where he states, "the authors have gone suspiciously too far in trying to convince the reader Jones was an insane drug addict … and fail to report the obvious connections between Jim Jones and their former fields of expertise" (506). Reiterman's co-author John Jacobs had himself authored news pieces on CIA mind control (Jacobs, 1977).

citizens to the saga of Jonestown. To segue into this difficult topic, I quote Rebecca Moore, who is far from a conspiracy theorist:

> Enough credible references to the Central Intelligence Agency appeared early on to raise questions among the most skeptical people. For example, the *House Committee Report* on Ryan's assassination asserted that "no conclusive evidence is available to indicate that the CIA was acquiring information on Mr. Jones or People's Temple." But information released as a result of the FOIA lawsuit *McGehee v. CIA* indicated that the CIA was indeed "monitoring" Jonestown, and the earliest report of the deaths came from CIA intelligence (2009: 127).

U.S. CLANDESTINE ACTIVITIES

1975 through 1977 were bad years for the Central Intelligence Agency, and for that matter, for federal government law enforcement and intelligence agencies generally. The Congress had formed the U.S. House Select Committee on Assassinations in 1976. It was pursuing investigations into the dual murders of President John F. Kennedy in November 1963 and Dr. Martin Luther King, Jr. in April 1968. The committee would conclude that the Secret Service was incompetent or worse in the case of JFK, and both the Federal Bureau of Investigations (FBI) and the National Security Agency (NSA – military intelligence) were performing illegal activities against the Black civil rights leader. Here's a sketch of the committee's mandate:

> The Interim Report on Alleged Assassination Plots Involving Foreign Leaders, the report on CIA activities in Chile, the report on illegal NSA surveillances, and the disclosure of illegal activities on the part of FBI COINTELLPRO, the FBI's harassment of Dr. Martin Luther King, Jr., and other matters revealed in the Committee's public hearings, were all carefully considered by the Committee and the executive branch working together to determine what information could be declassified and revealed without damaging national security. In those reports and hearings, virtually all differences between the Committee and the Executive were resolved. The only significant exception concerned the release to the public of the Assassination Report, which the executive branch believed would harm national security. The Committee decided otherwise (14).[10]

---

10   The entire Congressional report can be read here (see also Reference entry under U.S. Government): https://www.senate.gov/artandhistory/history/common/investigations/Church-Committee.htm (accessed March 2019).

Beginning with the Bay of Pigs fiasco in 1962 through to the various high-profile political assassinations first in 1963 and 1968, the investigative leads and spotlight always seemed to come back to government agencies implicated in the crimes. The intelligence services and domestic law enforcement (and at the national level, e.g., FBI, CIA, Secret Service) fingerprints too often dot the scenes of the crimes. So much so that numerous Congressional inquiries had been opened-up to investigate, for example, *CIA Activities Within the United States,* to use the very explicit name of the Congressional document.

These issues have all been researched thoroughly as can be, and though the evidence is murky and always convoluted, it is unmistakable.

Since beginning this research, I have been repeatedly struck at the gap between *the degrees of importance a given bit of information or news event may innately hold vs the significance placed upon that same bit of information by the news media.* There isn't always a clearly understandable correlation between the two. I have become convinced that there are enormously important stories and information "out there" that are simply not brought into the public's sphere of understanding, and perhaps for obvious, if nefarious, reasons. Ultimately, it comes down to investigative journalism, which sadly is currently most weak in the United States within the mainstream and corporatized media that dominate the now digital airwaves, cable and satellite services, and most major print media.

Consider this example from a recent election cycle of this disparity between *importance* vs *coverage.* It was the 2008 Presidential campaign between the Democrat Barack Obama and Republican John McCain. At one point, the conservative and even the not-so-conservative media denounced Obama for his association with a Christian minister named Reverend Jeremiah Wright. The Chicago Reverend is an outspoken African-American who has done his research. He did not speak off the top of his head or from some sense of contempt for American and/or White culture when he said (back in 2001 and shortly after September 11) that the "chickens have come home to roost" in referring to the terrorism that was befalling the nation. In a 2003 speech he also said that America may be a nation that has been damned by God for its immoralities.

Again, the Reverend spoke no idle words of contempt for a White establishment, instead, he spoke history.[11]

---

11   His speech can be found at YouTube: Jeremiah Wright 'God Damn America," https://www.youtube.com/watch?v=TYqrXVNfYUI (accessed March 2019).

In the "God Damn America" speech, as it has come to be called, the Black Reverend lists the ways in which the government failed its own citizens. He makes reference to abuses of Black Americans and includes the use of human beings in experiments. When questioned about these experiments in the media he was vilified for suggesting the CIA or "the government" would experiment on unwitting Americans, in this case African-American citizens. But this is exactly what happened, and the Reverend recalled the Tuskegee Syphilis Study of 1932. This is not arcane historical information to Rev. Wright's generation, it affected their population directly. Nevertheless, Wright was maligned by certain Whites for bringing this up. It's as though it is utterly taboo to suggest the United States government has been involved in any wrong-doing.

Of course, no Black American of any significant age (50-60 or older) by now, ever accepted the murder of MLK for what the officials claimed it to be. The King family themselves all along were suspicious of the FBI's role in taking-out King (Conspiratus, 9:27:00-9:29:30).

This is a history that has been insufficiently emphasized such that most White Americans cannot fathom its implications easily or readily without a certain emotional shock and cognitive adjustment ("White," in this case, is more an expression of the majority population rather than race being the decisive factor, and certainly Native Americans, Asians or other non-White Americans may have reacted similarly to Whites). That same adjustment is not needed for generations of Black Americans, a victimized minority population. It should not come as a surprise to readers to learn of this monumental gulf in perceptions of any of a number of social events; think only, in addition to the MLK assassination and Blacks' perceptions of it, of the 1996 O.J. Simpson murder trial and acquittal. Whites were almost unanimously disappointed, and Blacks nearly universally were relieved. Two racial and, evidently, social-political-(economic?) groups with polar opposite views of American jurisprudence. Consider also how we now live in a "Black Lives Matter" political climate and what this tells us about American racial history.

I suggest to the reader that JJ-PT-Jonestown may be better understood as one of these experiments Reverend Wright is referring to. The research pointing in this direction is compelling and the timeline of Jones' government connections listed above makes this possibility more likely a probability.

Keep in mind these types of covert government experiments upon its citizens are not merely matters of the historical record and in some fashion or another continue, either in program or in the management of public perception, to these days. For example, the covering-up of past experiments is ongoing. As late as October 2010 (I write this in the winter-spring of 2019) the Secretary of State Hillary Clinton apologized to Guatemala for the fact that

> U.S. government medical researchers intentionally infected hundreds of people in Guatemala, including institutionalized mental patients, with gonorrhea and syphilis without their knowledge or permission more than 60 years ago.[12]

We cannot assume that there is nothing left to withhold from the public or even that some of these programs may not continue on in some form or other. We are only left to look for the patterns of activity that may insinuate a connection between the activities of JJ-PT-Jonestown and the known goals of these medical research programs, specifically programs that concerned themselves with so-called *mind control.*

The history of these activities can be found in accounts like that of John Marks' 1979 book *The Search for the Manchurian Candidate: The CIA and Mind Control* which have long-established the existence of these programs, and beyond any dispute. Congressional inquiries headed by Frank Church in 1975 would establish their existence and reveal that many of the documents associated with these programs had been destroyed (U.S. GPO 1976, 389). Reasoned judgment demands that such behavior is *always* a sign that something is being conducted without all the proper channels of authorization. In this way, they could be considered "rogue" activities under the umbrella of a larger institution's mandate.

In recent months the National Geographic Channel re-broadcast a very interesting documentary called "CIA Secret Experiments: Mind Control." What the committee was able to establish was that the CIA had embedded its covert activities in "44 colleges and institutions, 15 research foundations, 12 hospitals and clinics and 3 penal institutions; and that the CIA had demonstrated a "callous disregard for the value of human life" (Marks quoted in Thalman).

The purpose here, however, is not to expose the gruesome details of this kind of research as this has already been adequately accomplished elsewhere (Price). The goal here is to establish that there are sufficient evidences to suggest the pattern of activities taking place prior to, during the unfolding, and in the aftermath of the Jonestown event that are best explained when seen in the context of government (or perhaps even private sponsorship but with governmental cover or assistance) control of

---

12   Robert Bazell, U.S. Apologizes for Guatemala STD Experiments. NBC News, 10/1/2010.

operations and personnel. These known facts must not be dismissed in Religious Studies or any other accounts of JJ-PT-Jonestown. It is unfortunate that far too much research has ignored this element of America's history in general, and consequently it has been ignored how this same history overlaps with religious history – most notoriously, how religions have provided cover for some of the darkest covert activities.

It is enough to recognize the possibility that rogue factions within our own government can be responsible for actions against American citizens which can include their deaths. The CIA referred to these as "terminal experiments," those experiments in which the subject would be rendered incapacitated by massive injuries or would result in the subject's death. It is hardly secret knowledge that the CIA has intervened to suppress information regarding its activities.

> These activities and the accompanying mentality breed secrecy and deception not limited to CIA operators. Official lying, called "plausible denial," seems ubiquitous up the ranks to the president. Other government agencies and officials, Congress, and the public are told lies by omission or denial (Karolides, 103).

In fact, John Marks along with co-author Victor Marchetti had their book on the CIA seriously redacted before publication and legally blocked by the agency. Their book is titled *The CIA and the Cult of Intelligence* and was vigorously fought during the publishing process because of what it revealed about the CIA's covert activities.

Some of the actions carried-out by the CIA in the name of "national security" included covert para-military operations ranging from direct military interventions to terrorist-like force and violence, psychological warfare, espionage and counter-espionage all which bred secrecy and an "above the law" mentality. These activities were primarily international in nature as that was the original mandate of the CIA, but sometimes the agency was known to act domestically, and the Watergate scandal exposed this. This begs the question, what else could the agency have done within the borders of the United States or to Americans directly?

Very painful indeed it is to acknowledge that fellow Americans, even those government officials charged with national security concerns, could be involved in such clandestine domestic activities against the American population. But not to acknowledge it is dangerously, if treacherously, naïve. And as we shall see in the following two chapters, such naïveté provides opportunity to those political elites who can benefit.

231

ANOMALIES of the EVENT

The specific forensic details of any given event must constitute the building blocks of any theory or investigative angle into the nature of the event. Even if not initially thoroughly understood, only by holding the forensic evidence up for examination can any useful theorizing be developed. So, for example, when it is learned that *the very land* that Jim Jones would lease in 1976 and use for his Jonestown agricultural compound in Guyana, South America was obtained through contacts implicating government and military channels, this must be factored-in to any theoretical model of what was Jonestown (Meiers, 77-88; also footnote 124). The Guyanese military were a familiar presence at and in the vicinity of Jonestown.

In this case of the Jonestown massacre, three anomalous characteristics cast serious doubt upon the standard framing of events and point to motives and means well beyond the reach of Jim Jones:

a) Constant presence of military-style armed guards at, and surrounding Jonestown was a frequent observation made and attested to by survivors and anyone who had visited the site. In addition, a cache of 32 guns and thousands of rounds of ammunition found at the site was in keeping with military-style operations and guard duties associated with absolute control of the comings and goings of residents and visitors; a separate building at the Jonestown compound was designated as "ammunition storage";

b) Disproportionate numbers of psychotropic medications kept and discovered at the Jonestown compound defy any logical use for the population of what was believed to be as many as 1,200 residents. These drugs are the same as those used in the MKULTRA mind control experiments known to have been conducted by the CIA; and

c) Unexplained slow-rise of the body-count and subsequent mishandling of cadavers (i.e., lack of determination to find out what actually happened) by the U.S. government frustrated and disgusted surviving family members of the deceased. Over 400 Jonestown bodies were buried in a mass grave in Oakland, California.

U.S. and Guyanese governments' and militaries' presences along the way

Aside from the American political connections and infiltrations (e.g., school systems, welfare department, law enforcement agencies, SF housing authority, and a grand jury) the PT was able to cultivate back in California, governmental shielding facilitated and privileged Jones reaching down into South America. American television news would report

"After the killings the Guyanese authorities impounded the first tapes and notes made by the NBC crew" (Conspiratus, 7:44:30).

The presence of Richard Dwyer during the final White Night[13] as mentioned by Jones on the Q042 Death Tape is also an unacknowledged, and certainly unclarified, government connection. Dwyer was known to be both a CIA station chief and operative *and* a State Department official, which was the capacity he was working in while on the visit with Ryan. The tape made during the final White Night incriminates Dwyer's presence during the event:

> **JONES**: Take Dwyer on down to the east house. Take Dwyer.
>
> **WOMAN**: Everybody be quiet please.
>
> **MAN**: That means sit down, sit down. Sit down.
>
> **JONES**: They know. I tried so very, very hard. They're trying over here to see what's going to happen in Los Angeles. Who is he?
>
> [Voices]
>
> **JONES**: Get Dwyer out of here before something happens to him. Dwyer, I'm not talking about Ejar. I said Dwyer. Ain't nobody gonna take Ejar. I'm not lettin' 'em take Ejar (Q042).

What Dwyer's role was cannot be known with absolute certainty, but it must be deliberated, or at least pondered. The first reports out of Jonestown of 180-200 bodies came from a radio transmitter and on a frequency that only the CIA possessed, and that message likely came from Dwyer. He had previously, however, survived the shooting-spree at the Port Kaituma airstrip where Congressman Ryan and four others were killed and numerous injured earlier in the day. At some point, and for whatever reason, Dwyer made his way back to the agricultural compound.[14]

Guns were also a common presence at Jonestown and the community was accused of gun-running, if not gun-stockpiling. That only 32 guns were found at the Jonestown compound, along with several thousand

---

13   "White Night" is the term used by Jones for rehearsed suicide drills that he had his congregation practice in the years before the final event. This psychological conditioning, whatever its stated purpose may have been (loyalty test to Jones, demonstrating fearlessness in the face of death), is evidence of the sinister control over his people Jones cultivated. No legitimate religious worldview requires such a test and reveals the congregants of PT meant to the leadership far more than strictly a religious community.
14   For clarification, to reach Jonestown one had to fly by small aircraft to the remote airstrip at Port Kaituma 135 miles from the capital city Georgetown. Once in Port Kaituma, there were only secondary roads, if that, they were more like trails cut through the jungle, to the Jonestown site which was approximately thirteen miles away and took anywhere from two-to-three hours to reach by slow-moving tractor. The Jonestown compound was extremely isolated.

rounds of ammunition, tells only part of a story we may never fully know. A statement by a PT member back in the USA that she possessed 170 firearms to be shipped to Guyana alludes to activities certainly beyond missionary and agricultural work (Investigation of Bureau of Alcohol, Tobacco and Firearms, webpage at *ACJPT*). Also, "Desmond Roberts, one of the Guyanese military men at the meeting, had warned the prime minister and his staff for months that Peoples Temple was probably smuggling guns into Jonestown, but Burnham [the Guyanese Prime Minister] refused to investigate" (Guinn, 3).

The Guyanese military took control of Jonestown in the immediate aftermath of the massacre.

Some reports of Jonestown survivors state that fleeing Jonestown members were hunted in the jungle and many more people were shot than were initially reported (Lane, 176; Treaster). This would be consistent with the placement of bodies in rows as can be seen in virtually all of the stock film footage of the aftermath of the carnage.

Excessive quantities of psychotropic medications on site

The verbal, physical, sexual and financial abuse and intimidation by Jones of his PT congregation are all hallmarks of the psychological control by one person of a group. These together with the suicide drills called White Nights indicate that Jones was consciously attempting to control his flock using nefarious means. But none of these reveal the presence of an undercover medical and psychological/psychiatric operation being conducted in Jonestown. However, those controlling actions coupled with the forced or surreptitious use of pharmaceuticals creates a different picture.

The inordinate numbers of medications found at the Jonestown site, and their very advanced, for a jungle compound anyway, medical clinic, indicate something much more was taking place at Jonestown than merely agricultural endeavors. Jim Jones boasted, and it was a notable feature of the Jonestown agricultural project, that the on-site clinic was top-of-the-line and according Joseph Holsinger (Leo Ryan's Congressional Assistant in Washington, D.C.) many residents had *daily medical examinations*! (Conspiratus, 7:52:16-7:52:50).

The presence of this clinic is only circumstantial to a psychiatric medical experiment being conducted, but the following evidence is not.

Reporting in 1978 as the tragedy was unfolding, Peter King writing for the *San Francisco Examiner* put it this way: (I've stitched together select passages from King's report)

Potential troublemakers or defectors from the Peoples Temple flock in Jonestown were kept under tight control in a special "extended-care unit" where they were heavily drugged, according to former residents of the jungle compound.

There were enough dangerous drugs at the remote compound – thousands of doses of anti-depressants and downers – to treat each of the 900 cultists who lived there hundreds of times.

During a joint two-week investigation by *The Examiner* and *Associated Press*, a *partial* [emphasis mine] drug inventory was obtained. It revealed that the drugs in the Jonestown warehouse included thousands of doses of Quaaludes, Demerol, Seconal, Valium and morphine, plus 11,000 doses of two drugs used to control the behavior of manic depressives and others with extreme psychotic problems [Thorazine, Vistaril].

...many of the cultists might have been under the influence of drugs when they drank the deadly cyanide-grape punch.

Sources also named a temple member in San Francisco who is a registered nurse as the person in charge of procuring the drugs. They couldn't explain how the woman did it (King, 1978).

In the lead-up to the final White Night, Jones himself can be seen in the video clips under the influence of some kind of psychotropic. He displays the smacking-dry mouth so characteristic a side-effect of these kinds of medications. Jones was known for some time to be drug-dependent (Reiterman, 446), and it was something of an open secret among the Planning Commission.

Also, in the videos of Congressman Leo Ryan's visit, the camera often pans the audience of Jonestown residents in the main pavilion where the administration of the cyanide would begin, and the faces of some of the residents look blighted and without much affect. This too is an indication of someone under the influence of a psychotropic drug. I suspect it would have been these folks, many elderly, who would have been among the original death-count of 180-200 bodies first reported.

These folks would have indeed taken the medicine willfully, though not necessarily willingly, at the point of a gun or bayonet. Some mothers would not have been able to flee if they had young children, and with whom the poisonings began. Those who witnessed the beginning of the White Night stated that women with children were called to come to the front first to receive their drink.

PARTIAL LIST OF PSYCHOTROPIC DRUGS FOUND AT JONESTOWN

How Jones Used Drugs	FRONT PAGE
by Peter King	©1978, San Francisco Examiner

Caption under a photograph of seized drugs reads:
Some of the thousands of drugs smuggled into Guyana. The cult had
enough for hundreds of doses for each member.

Thorazine (chlorpromazine), 10,000 injectable doses and 1,000 tablets in a size normally given only "for severe neuropsychiatric conditions." The drug acts "at all levels of the central nervous system." It is effective for the "management of the manifestations of psychotic disorders" and for control of the manic depressive.

Quaaludes, 1,000 doses of the sedative-hypnotic drug frequently used in suicide attempts.

Vistaril, 1,000 doses. Used for total management of anxiety, tension and psychomotor agitation; can render the disturbed patient more amenable to psychotherapy in long-term treatment of neurotics and psychotics.

Noludar, 1,000 pills. A sleeping aid that produces both physiological and psychological dependence. Moderate overdoses can produce delirium and confusion; large overdoses, stupor leading to coma.

Valium injectable, 3,000 doses. Useful in treating neurotic states manifested by tension, anxiety, apprehension, fatigue, depressive symptoms or agitation.

Valium tablets, 2,000. An overdose of Valium in either form tends to make suicidal patients more likely to make a death attempt.

Morphine sulphate, injectable, 200 vials. This strong pain killer can be habit-forming and have complex psychological effects.

Demerol, 20,000 doses. A narcotic analgesic, it should be used with great caution and has multiple reactions similar to those of morphine.

Talwin, 1,150 doses. Similar to Demerol in morphine-like actions. The drug has a history of creating psychological and physical dependence.

Seconal, 1,000 pills. An extremely dangerous sedative and hypnotic that can be habit-forming. Must be used under medical supervision.

Under what conceivable and legitimate medical circumstances would such a pharmacopeia be required for up to 1,200 people, nearly 300 of whom are children? There can be *no credible medical reason* for the existence of this advanced clinic and its contents unless there is an unspoken or unrevealed operation underway.

Drugs and medications kept under such conditions of a communal living arrangement would be oriented mostly towards First Aid, perhaps malaria prevention if applicable (in East Africa where I lived for two years from 1984-1986 the standard medication was Chloroquine; in the event of contracting malaria the remedy was simply to increase the dose), and the other general needs of a diverse-in-age population such as insulin, pain-killers, aspirin, sleep aids, hydrogen peroxide, and other infection treating remedies such as antibiotics.

The idea is clear here: the inventory that was confiscated is far more in keeping with a psychiatric clinical trial or control group being conducted and monitored. While this is not conclusive proof of a CIA-run medical experiment, especially in the absence of complete and thorough autopsies and a paper trail, the evidence points in that direction.

Such evidence cannot be ignored or explained-away because it is difficult to account for or points in an undesirable, if intimidating, direction. To ignore the possibility that people may have been drugged into submission is in direct contradiction to the myth that they were brainwashed with religion and also it is in direct contradiction to what survivors have claimed they saw. Specifically, the testimony by the first medical examiner on the scene, Guyanese Dr. Leslie Mootoo who states that 70-80 percent of the bodies he examined had an injection mark in the back scapula indicating poisoning by injection rather than oral consumption (*New York Times* December 17, 1978: Most Jonestown Deaths Not Suicide, Doctor Says).

The methods employed by Jim Jones (threats, humiliations, repetitious playing of his sermons and voice over loud-speakers, working long hours, denial of sufficient sleep) all point more in the direction of the military-style psychological torturing of people in order to bring them to their breaking point. Add to these pharmacologicals, and all the necessary ingredients are in place for the extreme manipulation of a community.

Slow-to-develop body-count and mishandling of bodies – too few autopsies

909 people died at the Jonestown agricultural compound; 5 died at the Port Kaituma airstrip shooting; and 4 died at the Peoples Temple

compound in Georgetown.[15] This would give the impression that on the morning of November the 19th, the final and total tally of dead was the same number: 918. But this was not the case. It took a full SIX DAYS for the body count to reach 909 at the Jonestown site!

What could account for the slow-to-develop body count?

The total body count is not the result of a mass suicide done all at once over several hours. The White Night was finished by midnight on the 18th and those who had died by then numbered 180-200. Sometime around 3:00am a radio call on a CIA channel is received by the National Command Center in Washington, D.C. This is the single-most incriminating piece of information, along with the presence of Richard Dwyer, that the CIA is involved in the project. The cover story of their involvement is that they were "monitoring" Jonestown and the comings and goings of certain residents. But this is insufficient explanation given what proceeded to take place after that first night – namely, the body count steadily growing over the following days. If the CIA were only monitoring, out of benevolent concern, and not directly involved and seeking to conceal their presence, then they could have acted to intervene and prevent the deaths beyond the initial 200.

Of course, this is an assertion only based upon *observable facts* and what one would *reasonably expect* to happen under the stated circumstances. Unfortunately, circumstances are not always what they are stated to be.

Among these 180-200 deceased would have been the most vulnerable in the community. These people would not have had an opportunity to flee the pavilion and take their chances in the jungle – being either too old, too young, or a mother with one or more young children. Some mothers did run into the jungle with their children, only to be hunted down and retrieved back to the pavilion. Armed guards surrounding the pavilion threatened members with gunshot or crossbow if they tried to escape. It would have been a horrifying decision. Many were also elderly – 200 people at Jonestown were Social Security recipients. There were approximately 300 children under the age of sixteen.

Listening to the televised report of Air Force Captain John Moscatelli as he describes the body-count, his voice betrays a certain unease (Con-

---

15   This last incident in Georgetown speaks to the complicity of actors and actresses with motives beyond Jones' hypnotism. The circumstances in which the Georgetown deaths took place are bizarre indeed and the reader will likely find it incredulous, as I did, to learn that a mother (Sharon Amos, who had claimed to know Charles Manson no less) slit the throats of her 10, 11, and 21-year-old children, then proceeded to slit her own throat. All the while ex-Marine Charles Beikman was present in the house. Jim Jones' surviving son Stephan, in an odd and cynical twist, would confess to the killings, much to the surprise of the court during Beikman's trial. He was not taken seriously. Beikman was acquitted.

spiratus, 7:42:44-7:43:37). At the time he is speaking the body count is at 780. This would have been on Thursday, November 23. There would still be 129 bodies to account for.

November 1978						
Sunday	Monday	Tuesday	Wednes-day	Thursday	Friday	Saturday
			1	2	3	4
5	6	7	8	9	10	11
12	13	14	15	16	17 Ryan's visit and over-night stay	18 5:00pm White Night begins at Pavilion
19 3:00am CIA Radio channel reports 180-200 dead in mass suicide	20 First news reporters allowed in; 380-400 reported dead	21 480 reported dead	22	23 780 total reported dead	24	25 909 total reported dead at Jonestown
26	27	28	29	30		

An obvious question then is, what happened in the time since his report when the body-count continued to climb by those other 129 bodies? He said they already turned the bodies over by that Thursday. The testimonies simply don't fit the forensics.

The placement of the bodies in rows is not what one would expect to see in the aftermath of a mass-suicide as reported. The deaths would not have been serene, but rather an excruciating and painful death given to convulsions. Most if not all of the bodies can be seen lying face-down and with arms extended around people presumably their loved ones with whom they died.

But is this the posture of a death by cyanide? The answer is no.

Tim Carter describes watching his own wife and son die and states "my son was dead and he was frothing at the mouth. You know cyanide makes you froth at the mouth" (Nelson, 1:17:20-1:18:00). It is no serene death as the poison does its neurological damage there is extreme distress and discomposure coupled with convulsions. Certainly not the group deaths of families embracing one another as they "step-over" to the other side. The body arrangements seen in all the photographs bear resemblance to those having been dragged to the location as the feet are positioned with toes pointing away from the body.

Furthermore, all the bodies are lying more-or-less in the same position! They have been placed there.

On the topic of the handling of the deceased and subsequent investigation by autopsies, the scenario becomes one of inferences only. But this can also be telling of motives. Given the slow access to the site granted by the Guyanese and American officials, the removal of bodies chronicled by Rebecca Moore (2009, 105-106) where she describes the overall "failure to perform meaningful autopsies" – only seven autopsies were performed for over 900 deaths! – there just seemed little desire by government officials to get to the bottom of things. American officials could have spirited some cadavers out of the country early in the week to perform autopsies – they had knowledge and means to do so. They simply did not.

About all one can infer from this is, what did they *not* want to find out? Or did they already know?

After all the bodies had been removed and American officials were done with their "clean-up" of the site, the entire compound was turned back over to the Guyanese government, specifically in the control of Prime Minister Burnham, who "ordered all the personal effects, even the mattresses, burned, as if he feared contamination" (Meiers, 382).

Perhaps the researcher is not to make much of these actions, but a thorough, honest and humane inquiry would insist upon all of these effects being, first, examined as evidence and, second, returned to the families. It was a complaint among the family members that they were not allowed access to the bodies of their loved ones and/or were unable to obtain their personal belongings. This should not have been the case and cannot simply be characterized as mishandling. These personal effects could have contained valuable information about what was transpiring inside Jonestown. This *potential alone* for containing any clues warrants their preservation and examination. But alas, this was not done. Or did they already know?

What we are witnessing is the pattern when a cover-up is in progress: forensic information must be lost and/or destroyed, this is an imperative in a cover-up.

The body count continued to climb with the February 26, 1980 assassination-style murder (all were shot in the head) of the Mills family in the wake of, and presumably because of, Jeannie publishing her book *Six Years With God*. Though the murders are officially unsolved, they had an enormous impact on surviving members and defectors. Given that Jeannie's book was an insider's critical view of the temple, and that she along with her husband were the most vocal in their opposition to the Peoples Temple via their Concerned Relatives organization, their deaths could only serve to dissuade anyone else from further writing about their own experiences or the things they had witnessed first-hand. It apparently worked.

By and large the popular and even academic books and movies the public was subjected to range from the lurid and sensational to the point of being indistinguishable from fiction, to the theological and spiritual wherein demonic forces take hold of a man and his community. While these make entertaining reading and films, they are the material of (American) culture. *They are cultural creations, not sociological facts.*

MEDIA and the EVENT

In all of the mass media productions, in print and on the screen, what is missing about Jones' life-history includes his connection to some of the most clandestine activities of the government and its intelligence agencies. He would repeatedly claim that he was the object of attack by government forces and that his congregation, due to their race, were especially targeted. There *are* published accounts that include this history, but they are very few and not mass-produced (Meiers' excessively expensive book – currently listing at 399.95 dollars at the publisher's website – and Conspiratus Ubiquitus' documentary film by far do the best research in highlighting these connections of Jones). The systematic omission of this side of Jones' life is itself revealing of the intentions of officially and mass-produced narratives and constitutes part of a broader pattern of deception on a more systematic scale. This history is significant enough to provide an entirely new perspective upon who Jones was and it helps explain some of the otherwise inexplicable elements of the unfolding of the tragedy itself and its aftermath

Instead the public was subjected to a barrage of cult-scare literature in the popular press and anti-cult propaganda among academics. Cult de-programming also became something of a cottage industry, and not without its critics and controversy (Bromley/Richardson).

This media-driven formation of opinion is not restricted to the nightly news. The media conglomerates soon went into movie-making mode recreating the tragedy and its cult leader along thematic lines of a previously entrenched character in American culture, the *lone gunman*. Jim Jones would emerge from these theatrical releases as a madman of gargantuan proportions.

Two films, one a made-for-TV production, were particularly hastily done and released. Their quality attests to this as they seem almost farcical when viewed today. The 1979-produced *Guyana: Crime of the Century/ Cult of the Damned* was the first to be released in January of 1980. And then in April 1980 *Guyana Tragedy: the Story of Jim Jones* (which at various times may also have gone by the title *The Mad Messiah: the Story of Jim Jones*) aired on American television on CBS. Reiterman's assessment of these films is best repeated here: "such partially fictionalized and sensationalized accounts reinforced myths about the Temple and created new ones, and they retarded public understanding of Peoples Temple" (575).

But since the evidence suggests it was a massacre, a mass-murder not a mass-suicide, it is particularly distressful (and painful for surviving family members) to read representations of Jonestown portrayed in such a distorted manner by eminent American psychiatrist Rollo May:

> We cannot wipe from our memories the gruesome logic in the mass-suicide in Guyana in the summer of 1980 [*sic*], when 980 [*sic*] of the people belonging to this cult, all those present in the camp, who had come from America, committed suicide because Jim Jones, their leader, ordered them to do so. That is the logical climax of the activity of all cults which deny the conflict between good and evil (274).

This quote, by the way, is that of a *psychiatrist* and the Peoples Temple and Jonestown phenomena were both *psychologically-driven* as even the most casual observers whether religious or journalistic noted at the time. May's understanding and discussion of the Jonestown event are nothing more than American political folklore and mythology masquerading as history, sociology and psychology and they are delusions through and through.

Instant mass-market publishing blitz after Jonestown
Dates from copyright page

| 1978 | Dec 78 | Dec 78 | 1978 |

Before the year was even over the above four mass-market paperback books were available at grocery store check-outs. Keep in mind "the event" had only transpired beginning November 18 and the body count was not totaled until November 25.

On a personal level, my first acquaintance with the Jonestown incident was from a distance and in another country, Canada. It had an impact, albeit some years later, upon my own experience of religion as a young man having left home and moved to the city for work and joining a Pentecostalism congregation as part of integrating into my new surroundings and making new friends. It was the summer of 1982 in southern Ontario, Canada. Upon joining the Pentecostal church, I brought home some of their literature to my Anglican parents (Episcopalian Church in the U.S.). They in turn, being unfamiliar with Pentecostalism, brought this literature to their minister to see if I had joined a "religious cult." Their concerns were not unjustified given what had happened in the U.S. fewer than four years earlier. My own family's knowledge of JJ-PT-Jonestown would have come from books such as those in the photo above.

With the understanding of the events of Jonestown presented here, we are quite far-removed from the image of 900+ people willingly and robotically lining-up in a hypnotized state to accept their glass of poison Kool-Aid and then lying down to die. By now it should be clear that much, much more went on at the Jonestown compound than *we, the public at large,* have been told to believe, or more accurately *brainwashed* to believe.

The effect of this mass-media brainwashing on the broader population also encouraged the mostly-conservative Christian communities' own partisan exclusivity and anti-pluralistic worldview. One book that has gained unwarranted legitimacy is the odious work of Walter Martin titled *The Kingdom of the Cults*. Written more than two decades before Jonestown, it is a raw polemical attack on anything other than evangelical-fundamentalist style Protestant Christianity. When academics fail to represent an incident like Jonestown accurately, they feed these polemic monsters within our own society giving the likes of Martin the ammunition he needs to imbibe into his readers' minds the idea that the various "cults" he covers in his own "definitive work on the subject" share the same "cultic psychological patterns evidenced in manic proportions at Jonestown and in Waco [and] are present to some degree in each and every cult" (Martin, 38). This is undermining the health of civic pluralism and well-being of civil society, not to mention fostering terrible social science and the bad practice of the humanities.

It should come as no surprise then that the American evangelical-Christian community, having been sufficiently prepared through books like Martin's, were targeted among the media campaigners for the myths of Jonestown in a book written just for them, *People's Temple – People's Tomb* and co-authored by Doug Wead. Published every bit as hastily as those in the photo (1979), it does however give insightful clues from the perspective of a family member back home in America while the tragedy is unfolding. It is a religious book making frequent references to God and the "demonic" nature of Jim Jones. One cannot hold a harsh opinion of someone referring to Jim Jones by such terms, but this provides no physical explanation for what we are trying to unravel in this chapter.

Curiously enough, the book does make reference to "nagging question" about the fact that "several days" into the event, the body count was "over 400" (199). As already discussed, this number proved to be a grossly inadequate estimate as they would report finding bodies under bodies with an end number of "912" (202). The book ultimately accepts, in spite of the nagging questions, the explanation of bodies under bodies. Another curious mention is the "bizarre twist" of two temple members being sent with a large amount of cash in a briefcase and told, apparently upon Jones' instructions, to go to the embassy, presumably the American embassy (203). When the suitcase was later opened there was 500,000 U.S. dollars and a note to the Soviet Embassy. No explanation was given to the couriers of the suitcase.

In mentioning the nagging question and bizarre twist, among other statements of incredulity, *People's Temple – People's Tomb* at least points to the possibility that there is more to the story than has been told. In the desire to understand the deaths of his sister and mother as more than simply those who were subservient to a deranged and controlling cult leader, and to some degree defend the Christian religion, co-author Phil Kerns raises valid suspicions. Though he does not deny that control and subservience were factors, they are simply not the sum total of factors to account for all the forensic realities of the event. And he watched live and in real-time with about the maximum amount of concern anybody could possess: a concerned relative. He even includes his phone bill for part of November 1978 as evidence of his reaching-out to Washington officials in the immediate days after the reporting of the deaths reached the United States (108-109).

Furthermore, I make mention of this book mostly here as an example of the targeting of particular audiences. The co-author Doug Wead (Kerns lost family in the massacre) is the person of my interest here. He is a serial-writer for conservative religion and Republican Party causes and he is addressing the evangelical-Christian community with fears of the dangers of religious cults.

> While legal minds began trying to ascertain the consequences of cult investigations, America was confronted head-on with figures that said up to 10 percent of Americans may be involved in fringe cults whose doctrines involve everything from Satan worship to

UFO idolatry. Up to 5,000 new cults may have been organized in the last decade, and scholars estimate the number of adherents at between twenty and twenty-six million (Kerns/Wead, 213-214).

These statements, in addition to being unjustifiably sensationalistic, are wildly irresponsible and to no small degree shame the victims in their death. It is just this kind of portrayal of historical events that informs the thinking that has also infected academic fields.

Along this same line of observation of the interplay between these events and the myths that are created around them and *the role of certain writers* in propagating the delusions on behalf of the political elite, consider John G. Fuller's books first mentioned in the previous chapter on UFOs. In addition to the book cited there about the Betty and Barney Hill story in New England he also wrote *Incident at Exeter* about another New Hampshire sighting. Both of these books were published in 1966 and mass-marketed through the 1970s.

In 1968 Fuller switches topics and writes a book about a wild hallucinogenic experience that took place in the small French town of Pont-Saint-Esprit in 1951 and which had turned deadly (Samuel). That book was titled *The Day of St. Anthony's Fire* and represents, in light of the research presented here, something of a cynical public relations twist to nefarious government activities. Seventeen years after the event Fuller is providing cultural cover for

> A special procedure, designated MKDELTA, was established to govern the use of MKULTRA materials abroad. Such materials were used on a number of occasions. Because MKULTRA records were destroyed, it is impossible to reconstruct the operation us of MKULTRA materials by the CIA overseas; it has been determined that the use of these materials abroad began in 1953, and possibly as early as 1950 (U.S. GPO, 1976: 391).

The various materials alluded to are the psychotropic drugs believed to assist in mind control, among which was LSD (see drug list insert above). The congressional document also reads:

> LSD was one of the materials tested in the MKUTRA program. The final phase of LSD testing involved surreptitious administration to unwitting non-volunteer subjects in normal life settings by undercover officers of the Bureau of Narcotics acting for the CIA – [which] had developed six drugs for operational use and they had

been used in six different operations on a total of thirty-three subjects. By 1963 the number of operations and subjects had increased substantially (391-392).

Of course, there was at the time of Fuller's research no way to be certain the source of the Pont-Saint-Esprit hallucinations, but where else would one look? Perhaps details remained hidden and was since "greater care seems to have taken for the safety of foreign nationals against whom LSD was used abroad" (U.S. GPO, 1976: 400). Fuller alludes to as much at the close of his book and after a 270-page commemoration of personal testimony to the human drama and speculation about the source. He closes

> Dr. Giraud was kind enough to give me the full medical reports prepared for the Academy, and I took them back to my hotel in Nîmes to study. I had already prepared the basic outline for the book, which would lead naturally from the ergot theory, and conclude with the mercury theory. But it was then that I discovered the section in the report of LSD-25.
> Suddenly the story had twisted back to the premise that had stirred my interest.
> Whatever is the true answer to the mystery will probably never be known. The fact remains that the doctors and the toxicologist remain locked in an impasse.
> But as one doctor expressed his opinion: "There is one and only one cause of the tragedy: Some form of ergot, and that form has logically got to be akin to LSD" (271).

No mention is ever made about the origin of the LSD-25. That would be for later history to reveal (Samuel).

The COLD WAR and LIBERAL RELIGION

As covered in chapter three, the theological-political climate of the Cold War pitted atheists against believers, and in this Land of the Free communism implied atheism and vice versa. The Pentecostal roots of Jim Jones' theology were soon jettisoned, or at least watered-down, in favor of a more liberal-style of religion better in line with the *social gospel* quite prevalent in liberal Christianity at the time and characterized by such books titled as *The Death of God*. In fact, within liberal Christianity a so-called "death of God" movement had emerged and Jim Jones would harness it masterfully.[16] This movement that was extolled by liberal theo-

---

16   This movement is epitomized by such books as *The Death of God: The Culture of Our*

logians was much maligned by the conservative religious forces within the democratic-capitalistic American model and the Jonestown "suicides" facilitated that maligning.

The focus of the liberal theologians was upon the inequities of capitalism more so than the virtues of communism, or in critiquing various communist regimes' evils – which, incidentally, are manifold. Nevertheless, during the 1970s and against a backdrop of South American anti-communist "interventions" (adventures), the American political establishment and its proxies in conservative Christianity would make it a matter of American patriotism to denounce those liberal-leaning theologians and socialist regimes.

Jones would label his theology "Apostolic Socialism" and it is this rather clever fusing of the two traditions in American Christianity that would appeal both to Black Americans' Pentecostal/traditional theological ideas and couple these with the fight for civil rights that his Black congregation would have had strong consciousness of. Jones' theology perfectly incorporated and ministered to the racial tensions between Black and White Americans and represented a complex mixture of "strands of the black Christian tradition" (Moore, et al: xii), as well as non-Christian expressions of Black religion such as the Nation of Islam and Malcolm X. The rhetoric of the Black Panthers was also exploited (Moore, et al: 110-121) as was the philosophy of Angela Davis (prominent communist Black activist).

These ideological fusions allowed Jones to play fast-and-loose with traditional religious imagery and theology. He would sometimes slam the Bible to the floor and step on it. He would declare himself to be God. He was ever the showman and, often sporting dark sunglasses and white flowing robe, he would rail against the "Sky God," whom for Jones was a symbol of the "dead god" of traditional theology. His congregation would roar in approval.

With this dualistic – actually it was multi-ideological – configuration of American politico-religious discourse resonating in Jones' sermons and taped lectures and in which he sometimes used the terms "revolutionary suicide" and "suicide for socialism," the post-Jonestown massacre story played well into American anti-communist rhetoric, in addition to anti-cult rhetoric. The political capital gained on the behalf of rightist and more conservative elements of American religion against liberalism, socialism and other "lefty" ideologies was very successfully harnessed. Simply put, Jim Jones' life and "ministry" were copiously scrutinized by

---

Post-Christian Era by Gabriel Vahanian (1957), *Honest to God* by John A.T. Robinson (1963), *The Secular Meaning of the Gospel* by Paul M. van Buren (1963), *The Secular City* by Harvey Cox (1965), and of course *A Theology of Liberation* by Gustavo Gutiérrez (1973).

clergy, media, and politicians such that his demise was posthumously useful to apologists of conservative religion and politics. Facilitating these would be the rise in the early 1980s of cable television and politically-conservative televangelists – already noted herein to be so influential in the American political landscape.

Understandably, the left was quick to repudiate Jones and his movement downplaying his association with very high-profile liberal leaders associated with San Francisco politics – Democrat mayor George Moscone and gay activist Harvey Milk are notable examples.

In addition, Jones' anti-American theological-political statements gave him a cover-story to use against his people by making wild accusations that the CIA, State Department, or other government agencies were out to bring him and the Peoples Temple down. This was part of a broader fear strategy, coupled with the techniques of pharmaceutical and financial control already mentioned. When the massacre was over, the media's portrayal of rows of bodies lying arm-in-arm as a liberal-Christian, indeed communist, protest against the evils of a racist capitalist monster could appear as nothing but pure derangement to the average American onlooker. As Jones put it that final White Night and which closes the so-called "Death Tape": "Take our life from us. We laid it down. We got tired. We didn't commit suicide, we committed an act of revolutionary suicide protesting the conditions of an inhumane world" (Q042).

As psychological propaganda the massacre was very effective in forming a generation of Americans' opinions along the politico-religious lines suggested. The scale of death (900+ people) and images of bodies strewn about the Jonestown compound coupled with the reach of the media via television to large swaths of the public had a profound impact upon the consciousness of viewers. The ghastliness of the tragedy was horrifying – women, children, babies, even pets all lying about as though the grim-reaper himself had paid the compound a visit. And in one sense, he had. It was a "pornographic" site of carnage unimaginable to a healthy mind and righteous spirit and to this day resonates through the meme of "drinking the Kool-Aid" and the myth of the dangerous religious cult.

Alas, the academic field of Religious Studies would do little to clarify what had happened, in fact, it accomplished the opposite using rhetoric that merely fueled the horror. The imagery of the "pornography of Jonestown" is used repeatedly in one of academia's famed tomes on the subject, *Imagining Religion: From Babylon to Jonestown* (Smith: 109, 111, 112), and surveying Religious Studies' accounts of JJ-PT-Jonestown there is little to wonder about why the general populations' abysmal, if sensationalistic, understanding of events is so crippled and politically-charged.

In researching the topics for this book, it was made glaringly apparent that academics are among the easiest to dupe (see Quotes four through six preceding the Conclusion). Perhaps by virtue of their positions within the establishment, and their consequent livelihood so dependent, presenting research implicating government officials who are available for prosecution comes with chilling implications, both politically and legally. Even if the First Amendment protects speech that is solidly fact-based and not mere slander and libel, the pressure to suppress the facts is enormous, and yet it must be resisted. No less than the integrity of the historical record depends upon it.

The ABJECT FAILURE of RELIGIOUS STUDIES

The academic field of Religious Studies is thoroughly derelict in its research of Jim Jones, the Peoples Temple, and the Jonestown massacre – in fact, it is wretched.

Most certainly unwittingly, though not by accident, academe in this case has functioned as an unofficial flack for, by all appearances and likelihood, the CIA's mind control operation against PT members (medically) and the public (in propaganda). It was the *public* who was the target of the *brainwashing*, that is, the controlling of their thoughts. Less so the population of the Peoples Temple or Jonestown – they were drugged or coerced by other means. Jones' victims were psychologically, physically, sexually, and economically abused by the leadership of the Peoples Temple and deceived about the nature of just who Jim Jones was. This reaches far beyond mere manipulating people's thoughts. These are sociological and criminal acts of aggression and intimidation, pure and simple.

But is Religious Studies aware of these facts which have been long-available to the public? It appears not. These elements remain elusive to academe, and to its own impairment.

Jason Dikes gives a (partial) chronological outline of the historiography of Jonestown and the Peoples Temple as it has evolved over the past forty years (*ACJPT*). *Initially* after the event, the writings were sensational, lurid and exploitive of the events (see photo above of mass-marketing publishing blitz). The *second* type of literature is historiographic and academic. *Thirdly*, Jonestown and everything, both fact and fancy, that has come to represent it, has secreted into the broader culture – think only of the drinking the Kool-Aid meme.

Examples are legion in the field of Religious Studies wherein reference to JJ-PT-Jonestown are given light treatment and taken for granted as what the first category of historiography describes: a sensationalistic example of evil. The final quote at the beginning of this chapter is taken from Charles Kimball's *When Religion Becomes Evil* (2002). He demonstrates no awareness of the historical elements presented here. "They were blindly obedient to a charismatic leader whose journey... would seem to an outside observer too implausible to carry the story line of a fictional book or Hollywood screenplay" (90). So too with Steve Bruce's *Religion in the Modern World: From Cathedrals to Cults* (1996) which unquestioningly accepts the Jonestown deaths as mass suicides with no qualification (191). Mark Juergensmeyer in his *Terror in the Mind of God* (2000), though without going into any depth on the JJ-PT-Jonestown subject, ascribes the "suicidal act of violence" to what Jones thought "would elevate the struggle to the level of cosmic war" and so he chose to "escape what he feared would be capture and defeat" (165). In Derek Daschke and W. Michael Ashcroft's *New Religious Movements: A Documentary Reader* (2005) they include an edited version of the so-called "death tape" (a tape-recording made during the final hours of the massacre) where the reference to Richard Dwyer is removed and they conclude "918 people, including Jones, died, mainly by the self-inflicted cyanide poisoning, though some had been shot or had their throats slit" (243). George Chryssides' *Exploring New Religions* (1999) states the

> event was so extraordinary that some commentators have – perhaps understandably – resorted to conspiracy theories: Jones, they argue, was no mere clergyman, but a CIA agent commissioned to conduct an experiment in thought control. The most commonly offered theory, however, is that the group was an example of religion gone wrong, a fanatical group into which its members were brainwashed, and would do anything that Jim Jones, its authoritarian 'messianic' leader, commanded (34).

I wish that as much had been acknowledged in Jonathan Z. Smith's *Imagining Religion: From Babylon to Jonestown* (1982) which on this issue is, very regrettably, a work of theoretical imagination as suggested by the chapter titled "The Devil in Mr. Jones." Though not mentioned specifically in Dikes' historiography, *Imagining Religion* falls squarely in the first school (lurid and exploitive) while claiming to be in the second (academic and historical). Smith's is a work of, at times, garish exploitation (he includes as an appendix the final "death tape" transcript!) while present-ing itself as an academic examination and interpretation of Jonestown in which "most apparently died willingly" (108).

It is anything but.

His choice of references, though much more limited at his time of writ-ing, are represented in the photo on page 242. *Hold Hands and Die, The Suicide Cult,* and *Guyana Massacre* all appeared before the end of the year of the tragedy and hardly constitute reflective research. In fact, Smith ad-ditionally asserts that "Despite a number of more recent works, published since 1980, I have not seen cause to alter this essay in either matters of fact or, especially, in conclusions" (Smith, 162).

Unfortunate indeed. I will use his own words to make an appeal:

> As students of religion, we have become stubbornly committed to making the attempt (even if we fail) at achieving intelligibility. We must accept the burden of the long, hard road of understand-ing. To do less is to forfeit our license to practice in the academy, to leave the study of religion open to the charge of incivility and intolerance. Against this backdrop, I have deliberately chosen for my topic and event which is a scandal in the original sense of the word.... For those of us committed to the academic study of re-ligion, a comparable scandal is that series of events which began at approximately 5:00 P.M., on 18 November 1978 in Jonestown, Guyana. From one point of view, one might claim that Jonestown was the most important single event in the history of religions, for if we continue, as a profession, to leave it ununderstandable, then we will have surrendered our rights to the academy (104).

I would suggest, instead, academia has surrendered its responsibilities to the political elites and so have lost their nerve in the face of the elites' political means of coercion.

Smith's is an otherwise esteemed career in the field of Religious Stud-ies and which has received due recognition thus making it that much more imperative for his body of work to be corrected. He notes the "daily revisions of the body count" (109) but infers nothing from them. Hid-den in plain sight, in the death tape appendix, are the incriminating words "Get Dwyer out of here before something happens to him. Dwyer. I'm not talking about Ejar. I said Dwyer" (130). Any number of contemporane-ous newspaper accounts call into serious question the official version of events – some can be found in the References to this chapter. But not a peep from Smith. There is simply no explaining it. I cannot reconcile the 1978 news report by Peter King (cited above) describing the psychotropic pharmacopeia found at the Jonestown site and Smith's assertion that "most apparently died willingly."

It appears that currently Religious Studies as an academic field is simply unable to metabolize the forensic information presented in the research here. And this portends a very bleak future for the accuracy and efficacy of subsequent religious and political analyses and how they come to bear upon public policy as it will be hampered with severely tainted information. This will inevitably thwart and corrupt academic research and theorizing as has been noted already (Bainbridge, 359; cited above in chapter three). The melding of academic discourse with the political elites'/ establishment's (including military's) concerns is alarming. This is a very degrading dynamic in current American academic life and is something of an indication of a societal drift away from democratic institutions and toward fascism. More will be covered on this dynamic in the Conclusion.

Despite the current state of affairs in academia, I find it fitting, if respectful, to give the now-late Jonathan Z. Smith another hearing on the matter:

> It is now for others to continue the task, with Jonestown, or wherever the question of understanding human activities and expression is raised. For if we do not persist in the quest for intelligibility, there can be no human sciences, let alone, any place for the study of religion within them (120).

ANOTHER WARNING from the PAST

The warning at this juncture is that the *political capital gained by the meme of "Jonestown as suicide cult"* would make it easier for law enforcement to dupe the population against subsequent religious groups such as the Branch Davidians in 1993, almost fifteen years after Jonestown. The myth of Jonestown was used to justify the use of force against the Branch Davidians and for officials to save the Branch Davidian children from abusive adults. The mere mention of the possibility of a group-suicide seemed sufficient to intervene (Moore, 2009: 117).

But this was wildly overblown both in the case of the Branch Davidians specifically, and against religious groups generally. Chryssides said it best in concluding a section on Jonestown:

> The anti-cult prediction of a wave of suicide cults simply did not materialize. Years passed without any similar incident, and no

NRM (New Religious Movement) has ever led to a mass-suicide on that scale since Jonestown. It was not until 1993 – nearly fifteen years later – that 82 Branch Davidians died at Waco, Texas (46).

The facts surrounding the stand-off at Waco, Texas are as badly distorted as those of Jonestown and will be the subject of the next chapter and provide an instructive moment for our field of study. And that Chryssides' observation holds should not be surprising. People are not inclined toward mass-suicide. The very notion is rather absurd on its face, but the political capital embedded in such a narrative has already had tremendous effect in this regard. And while this has not gone unnoticed, it has gone mostly un-remedied – even in the field of Religious Studies.

The teaching of Religious Studies, as well as instructors in a variety of cognate academic fields, must be very cautious in their representations of groups like Peoples Temple and Jonestown otherwise the very establishment (academe) designed to promote accurate knowledge about the world becomes an unwitting purveyor of false information and historical distortions. This has an intellectually and socially degrading outcome upon those who consume this information.

Consider the assessment of the sociologist Williams Sims Bainbridge of the mindset of the agents and officials overseeing the Branch Davidian stand-off at Waco. Bainbridge's characterization of the mentality of the agents is that they thought of Koresh as a deranged man on the order of Jim Jones and as one "who possessed diabolical power over his brainwashed followers" (116). I agree there is little doubt the federal agents *thought that*, which is in keeping with the narrative about Jonestown and constitutes the cultural symptom within which there is much political capital (i.e., justification for a raid). But the federal agents' thoughts and assumptions about the Branch Davidians were purely delusional.

Hence, my use of the term *event horizon*.

Furthermore, it is *Bainbridge's comments* that most trouble me here, and which reflect his failure to recognize the forensic realities about the Waco event. He states most confidently that these agents

> could not recognize that charisma and an alternative symbolic world can be created through intensive interactions among members, in which the leader plays a key role but is far from a dictator. Put another way, the law enforcement agencies never seriously recognized that *religion* was the motive behind the actions of the branch [*sic*] Davidians" (italics mine; 116).

253

Whether intended as such or not, and I suspect not, this is a demagogic statement being both inflammatory and unjustified. *Religion was not the cause of their deaths, government action was.* No amount of inflammatory rhetoric, academic or political, will alter what can be seen in the FLIR (forward-looking infrared) video footage and observed in the behavior of officials.

Religion as the source of the tragedy at Waco is a false narrative and it amounts to a strategy of creating *otherness* (they are not us), or the *pathos of distancing.* As will become apparent in the forensic evidence which contradicts Bainbridge, and to put it into "conspiratorial" terms; media and academia never seriously recognized that the *activities of government officials rather than religion,* was the motive behind the actions of the Branch Davidians.

A reader could not be faulted for thinking he or she is reading from Bainbridge a passage better-suited from *People's Temple – People's Tomb* or other polemic off a Christian press in an attempt to deflect responsibility and blame away from orthodox or mainstream Christian beliefs and onto beliefs of a more "cultic" nature. As a researcher, this is distressing and I'm afraid that a modern sociologist referring to "symbolic systems" in the case of the deaths of the Branch Davidians has no more explanatory value and is tantamount to the spiritual explanations offered by conservative Christian apologists and authors such as Kerns-Wead. Mel White in *Deceived* seeks to, however empathetically and compassionately, distance mainline Protestant Christian religion and beliefs from Jones' activities. Similarly, *Jesus and Jim Jones* by Steve Rose also does this but from a more liberal and ecumenical Christian point of view wherein Jones had "largely rejected Christianity for Communism" (60). These literary responses are understandably concerned with the Christian religion and its appearance to the general public.

With the prevailing corrupted narrative placing the source of death squarely in the hands of a cultic religious leader and his pathological behaviors, the demagogic possibilities are potentially rich for both academic-theorist and defensive Christian-believer alike.

But this demagoguery has no place in scholarship, even that which is unwittingly perpetuated, and must be pushed-back for the sakes of *civil society, civic pluralism,* and *the historical record.* The social price paid for such corrupted myths is far too steep. Political powers feed off of these distortions and it is high time we recognize this both as scholars and citizens. Also, the line between scholarship and activism becomes somewhat blurred in the process. It is not easily avoidable that a scholar may experience a *moral compunction* to make others aware of this situation and to seek to disseminate a more fact-based explanation of events, which in turn has political capital vested in it. The *degree* to which one does so may initiate labels upon her or his scholarship that, in turn, can be exposed as polemic. When in the media a scholar is labelled as a "conspiracy theorist" or "activist," this only serves to denigrate the research conclusions and to treat them and the scholar in a dismissive manner.

Suspiciously, no similar protest is launched by the media when the *government* makes claims or files charges consistent with "conspiracy theory." George Orwell can only be summoned here, as noted in the Introduction – these are the Principles of Newspeak.

If scholars are condemned for holding conspiratorial theories when presenting their peer-reviewed conclusions, and yet political officials (including the legal apparatus) are heralded as truth-speakers, then the intellectual degradation of society is well underway, if not fully completed. It is nothing short of a direct assault against reason and research to demagogue these topics, and history has shown and continues to reveal just what the political and power elites are willing to do by way of their cultural means of coercion.

In the end, Jonestown is one of those instances wherein the governments' tight control of the forensic evidence, the absence/destruction of any relevant the paper trail and related documentation, the plausible deniability of officials, and the straight-up nefarious tendencies of certain human beings all collude to cast a long grey shadow over the iron-clad certainty of claiming direct and active government involvement through one of its MKULTRA-MKDELTA programs.

But common sense and past experience tell us where there is smoke there is usually fire.

For my part, having left home in Canada to be a missionary in Africa and join a group of unknown people whom, I took it by faith, shared my views, I feel a certain empathy for the residents of Jonestown. So much about other people we associate with in life we take on faith, especially in the social groups outside our families. Belonging to a community of like-minded people is one of the strongest and most fundamental characteristics a person can display. Manipulating this characteristic with intent for social and political control would be empowering to governments and their operatives, e.g., the intelligence services.

Consider the fourth quote opening this chapter. It describes a CIA *modus operandi* identical to that of Jim Jones' story.

At what point does it become irresponsible more so than prudent for the scholar to deny when faced with forensic evidence the involvement of government agencies? When does it cease to be naïveté and become *complicity with altering the historical record,* and worse, denying justice for the abused and deceased? Even though she may be exempt of criminality, the scholar, much like the investigative journalist, bears a certain accountability for the status of knowledge in the broader culture.

Fortunately, it is in the power of human reason and decency coupled with courage of convictions that the hidden and suppressed truths can be discerned. The *Critical Theory of Religion's* quest to understand the root of human suffering demands the *evidence fit the agony.* Jonestown was the source of much agony. On this count, tepid though it may be, John R. Hall and Lorne Dawson give affirmation to the possibility of government complicity in the essay "The Apocalypse at Jonestown" wherein they state,

> Because the United States government might have been able to prevent the tragedy, and also because government officials and representatives may have acted in ways that propelled it, there has been considerable speculation about the government's role.... Whatever the truth of the matter, such accounts cannot be easily assessed because the U.S. government has suppressed information about its dealings with Peoples Temple, partly on the basis of the sensitivity of its geopolitical interests. If remaining government files on Peoples Temple can be examined, they may well yield significant reassessments of its history (same holds for the NBC video "outakes" from its Jonestown coverage, which the network has refused to make public). Whatever comes of the search for more information, causal [*sic,* casual?] analysis of available evidence substantially revises the popular myth of Jonestown (Dawson, 205).

Scholars need find it their purview to sensitize readers to these realities of officials' malpractice when the evidence leads in that direction. Doing so will require a certain amount of nerve that must not fail. And to avoid doing so is dereliction of responsibility. Marginalizing information in this way fosters the degradation of language itself. The term "conspiracy theory" is a case in point. The historical record depends upon the human fortitude to seek and acknowledge *all* relevant facts which help explain the phenomenon under scrutiny. Human decency demands it. Science demands it. And the health of civil society and civic pluralism require it. In addition, it just may be that *by voicing our awareness, their hands may be stayed.* Call me an optimist.

REFERENCES
Books/Essays

Bainbridge, William Sims (1997). *The Sociology of Religious Movements.* New York: Routledge.

Bromley, David G. and James T. Richardson, eds. (1983). *The Brainwashing/Deprogramming Controversy: Sociological, Psychological, Legal and Historical Perspectives.* Lewiston, New York: Edwin Mellen Press.

Bromley, David G. and Anson D. Shupe, Jr. (1981). *Strange Gods: The Great American Cult Scare.* Boston: Beacon Press.

Bruce, Steve (1996). *Religion in the Modern World: From Cathedrals to Cults.* Oxford: Oxford University Press, 1997.

Chryssides, George D. (1999). *Exploring New Religions.* London: Cassell.

Daschke, Dereck and W. Michael Aschraft, eds. (2005). *New Religious Movements: A Documentary Reader.* New York: New York University Press.

Dawson, Lorne L. (2003). *Cults and New Religious Movements: A Reader.* Malden, Massachusetts: Blackwell Publishing.

Dikes, Jason (2013). A Brief and General Overview of Jonestown Historiography. *The Jonestown Report.* Vol. 15. http://jonestown.sdsu.edu/?page_id=40219 (accessed March 2019).

Fuller, John G. (1968). *The Day of St. Anthony's Fire.* New York: Signet, 1969.

Guinn, Jeff (2017). *The Road to Jonestown: Jim Jones and Peoples Temple.* New York: Simon & Schuster.

Jacobs, John (1977). CIA Papers Detail Secret Experiments on Behavior Control. *The Washington Post.* July 21.

Judge, John (1985). The Black Hole of Guyana: The Untold Story of the Jonestown Massacre. http://www.ratical.org/ratville/JFK/JohnJudge/Jonestown.html (accessed March 2019).

Juergensmeyer, Mark (2003). *Terror in the Mind of God: The Global Rise of Religious Violence.* 3rd ed. Berkeley: University of California Press. [Original edition, 2000].

Karolides, Nicholas J. (2006). *Banned Books: Literature Suppressed on Political Grounds.* Revised Edition. New York: Facts on File.

Kerns, Phil with Doug Wead (1979). *People's Temple – People's Tomb.* Plainfield, New Jersey: Logos International.

Kimball, Charles (2002). *When Religion Becomes Evil: Five Warning Signs.* Revised edition. New York: HarperCollins, 2003.

King, Peter (1978). How Jones Used Drugs. *San Francisco Examiner.* Dec. 28. Front Page.

Kinsolving, Lester (1978). Indianapolis, Ukiah Women Praised for Fight Against Jones. *Ukiah Daily Journal.* December 26.

Lane, Mark (1980). *The Strongest Poison.* New York: Hawthorn Books.

Marks, John (1979). *The Search for the Manchurian Candidate: The CIA and Mind Control.* New York: Times Books.

Martin, Walter (1965). *The Kingdom of the Cults.* Rev. Ed. Minneapolis, Minnesota: Bethany House Publishers, 1997.[17]

May, Rollo (1992). *The Cry for Myth.* New York: Dell.

McCoy, Alan W. (1988). *The Guyana Murders.* San Francisco: Highland House.

Meiers, Michael (1988). Was Jonestown a CIA Medical Experiment? A Review of the Evidence. *Studies in American Religions*, Volume 35. Lewiston, New York: Edwin Mellen Press.

> • A work of investigative journalism that presents the theory that the Central Intelligence Agency employed the Reverend Jim Jones to administer a pharmaceutical field test in mind control and ethnic weaponry to a large test group, namely the membership of the Peoples Temple. Proposes that Dr. Laurence Layton (Former Chief of the U.S. Army's Chemical and Biological Warfare Division) cultured the AIDS virus to be tested and deployed in a CIA-backed experiment in Jonestown, Guyana. (From the publisher's website)

Mills, Jeannie (1979). *Six Years With God: Life Inside Reverend Jim Jones's Peoples Temple.* New York: A&W Publishers, Inc.

Moore, Rebecca (2002). Reconstructing Reality: Conspiracy Theories About Jonestown. *Journal of Popular Culture.* Vol. 36, no. 2: 200-220.

Moore, Rebecca (2009). *Understanding Jonestown and Peoples Temple.* Westport, Connecticut: Praeger.

Moore, Rebecca, Anthony B. Pinn and Marry R. Sawyer, eds. (2004). *Peoples Temple and Black Religion in America.* Bloomington: University of Indiana Press.

New York Times (1978). Most Jonestown Deaths Not Suicide, Doctor Says. December 17. No author listed.

Ostrander, Sheila and Lynn Schroeder (1970). *Psychic Discoveries Behind the Iron Curtain.* New York: Bantam Books, 1971.

Price, David H. (2007). Buying a Piece of Anthropology, Part 1: Human Ecology and Unwitting Anthropological Research for the CIA. *Anthropology Today.* Vol. 23, No. 3: 8-13. June 2007.

---

17   Meiers notes that one of the characters in Jim Jones' life while he was living in Brazil in 1962-63 was Bonnie Malmin [Burnham Thielmann], whom he describes as "one of the few people to witness the public career [of Jim Jones] from beginning to end (166). At one point, she left Jones employ in South America in a time of personal crisis and came to the USA to spend time at the "Bethany Fellowship Training Center in Minneapolis" (145). See also Reiterman, 80. This same ministry is responsible for publishing *Kingdom of the Cults*, a book that is one of the most notorious works of demagoguery the Christian community has been subjected to in the past two generations. If a single book could be called a tool of brainwashing targeting evangelical and fundamentalist Christians, this is it!

Q042 Transcript prepared by Fielding M. McGehee III. Alternative Considerations of Jonestown & Peoples Temple. https://jonestown.sdsu.edu/?page_id=29079 (accessed March 2019). This is the same transcript that was also prepared by Stephen [sic] Rose found at ACJPT and published in his book.

Reiterman, Tim with John Jacobs (1982). *Raven: The Untold Story of the Rev. Jim Jones and His People.* New York: Tarcher/Penguin, 2008.

Rose, Steve (1979). *Jesus and Jim Jones.* New York: The Pilgrim Press.

Ross, Colin A. (2000). *The C.I.A. Doctors: Human Rights Violations by American Psychiatrists.* Richardson, Texas: Manitou Communications. 2006.

Rubin, Zick and Elton B. McNeil (1985). *Psychology: Being Human.* 4th ed. New York: Harper & Row.

Samuel, Henry (2010). French Bread Spiked with LSD in CIA Experiment. *Telegraph.* 11 March. https://www.telegraph.co.uk/news/worldnews/europe/france/7415082/French-bread-spiked-with-LSD-in-CIA-experiment.html (accessed 3/19).

San Jose Mercury (1978). Jones Lived Well, Kept to Himself During Mysterious Brazil Stay. November 27. No author listed.

Shenon, Philip (1988). C.I.A. Near Settlement of Lawsuit By Subjects of Mind-Control Tests. *New York Times.* October 6. https://www.nytimes.com/1988/10/06/world/cia-near-settlement-of-lawsuit-by-subjects-of-mind-control-tests.html (accessed March 2019).

Singer, Margaret Thaler with Janja Lalich (1995). *Cults in Our Midst: The Hidden Menace in Our Everyday Lives.* San Francisco: Jossey-Bass, 1996.

Smith, Jonathan Z. (1982). *Imagining Religion: From Babylon to Jonestown.* Chicago: University of Chicago Press.

Thielmann, Bonnie with Dean Merrill (1979). *The Broken God.* Elgin, Illinois: David C. Cook Publishing.

Thomas, Gordon (1989). *Journey into Madness: The True Story of Secret CIA Mind Control and Medical Abuse.* New York: Bantam Books, 1990.

Treaster, Joseph B. (1978). Survivor Says He Heard 'Cheers' and Gunshots After Cult Deaths. Special to the *New York Times.* December 17.

White, Mel (1979). *Deceived.* Old Tappan, New Jersey: Spire Books.

Witten, Manley (1979). Guyana: Autopsy of Disbelief. *Lab World.* (March) 30:3, Pgs. 14-19. Quoted in Meiers, pgs. 530-531.

Government Documents

U.S Government Printing Office (1975). Report to the President by the Commission on CIA Activities Within the United States. Washington, D.C.: June. https://archive.org/details/reporttopresiden01unit (accessed March 2019).

U.S. Government Printing Office (1976). Foreign and Military Intelligence, Book I: Final Report of the Select Committee to Study Governmental Operation with Respect to Intelligence Activities. United States Senate together with Additional, Supplemental, and Separate Views.

Washington, D.C. April 26. (A.k.a. The Church Committee). https://www.senate. gov/artandhistory/history/common/investigations/ChurchCommittee. htm (accessed March 2019).

Films/Documentaries

Conspiratus Ubiquitus (2008). *Evidence of Revision: The Assassination of America.* Etymon Productions. "History may be revised even as it is being written." Available for viewing at Top Documentary Films: https://topdocumentary-films.com/evidence-of-revision/ (accessed March 2019). Also available as a 3-DVD collection/set as of 2012. Produced by SOTT.net and Quantum Future Group, Inc. Published by Red Pill Press.

> • Posted 2008 at YouTube by *"Conspiratus Ubiquitus,"* this is an independent video-narrative that strings together snippets of various publicly available news and professionally-produced documentaries (e.g., *NBC, PBS, Superstation*) without commentary. The topics range from the assassinations of JFK, RFK, MLK and the Jonestown tragedy. It opens with the phrase: *This documentary series contains many historical video documents that have, in essence, been controlled. Documents which define history should belong to the public, not private interests.* At the link included here the JJ-PT-Jonestown story begins at 7:22:50 through 7:58:50.

History Channel (2000). *Mind Control: America's Secret War.* Documentary film in the series History's Mysteries for The History Channel and A&E Television Networks. Aired February 2011 on the Military Channel. https://www.you-tube.com/watch?v=bNv_VOn4puY (accessed March 2019).

Nelson, Stanley, producer/director (2007). *Jonestown: The Life and Death of Peoples Temple.* The American Experience. A Firelight Media production in association with the BBC. PBS Home Video.

Thalman, Tria (2007). *CIA Secret Experiments: Mind Control.* Produced by National Geographic Television for National Geographic Channel. Part of a series titled Undercover History: CIA. (Repeat aired February 15, 2011). A preview of the program can be found at YouTube: https://www.youtube. com/watch?v=NUW-frxo2X4 (accessed March 2019).

White, Mel (1979). *Deceived*: I. A Mel White Production. Gospel Films Video. (This is a two-part documentary made by a Christian minister before and after the Mills' 1980 assassination. Part II, 1983).

Internet Resource

Alternative Considerations of Jonestown & Peoples Temple. Sponsored by the Department of Religious Studies at San Diego State University. Site manager

Rebecca Moore. https://jonestown.sdsu.edu/ (accessed March 2019). (AC-JPT)

- This is an excellent resource for Peoples Temple and Jonestown research and is updated on an ongoing basis. To its credit, it does not appear (best that I can discern) to discriminate against researchers and evidence that point to U.S. government (CIA and State Department in this case) involvement in the crime and/or cover-up. And this in spite of being maintained by surviving family members of individuals involved in the Jonestown massacre. Their stated purpose: *This website is designed to give personal and scholarly perspectives on a major religious event in recent U.S. history. Its primary purpose is to present information about Peoples Temple as accurately and objectively as possible.* It is a MERLOT site (Multimedia Educational Resource for Learning and Online Teaching).

SOLILOQUY

A DEFIANT LAMENT

Where are the images?
Powerful images!
Images that have the ability to change one's understanding of events.
Moreover,
to change one's worldview.
Everyone, Everywhere,
needs to drop what they are doing to pause ... to watch ...

The most distressing element of this research has been
to witness the systematic
suppression of images.

In studies such as these the methodological process must be grounded in
forensics and physical reality if we are to maintain the scientific nature
of the discipline. I was trained in the methodologies of one of the found-
ing fathers of Religious Studies as a scientific discipline, C.P. Tiele, who
stated: "The object of our science is not the superhuman; and the task
of investigating religion as a historical-psychological, social, and wholly
human phenomenon undoubtedly belongs to the domain of science."[1]

Then science it is.

I will stake my thesis on the efficacy of the images referenced in the final
two chapters –
And challenge the reader to view widely-suppressed images in an ef-
fort to understand how we have been deceived, as a nation and a glob-
al body-politic.

THE IMAGES of WACO and SEPTEMBER 11
(Witnessing Sacred Place and Sacred Time)

Below are listed two documentaries of enormous historical importance to the United States of America and, as a result of America's
global reach, well beyond. These two documentary references (one for
the Branch Davidian-ATF/FBI stand-off in Waco, Texas in the spring of

---

1   See References to the Conclusion.

1993 and one for the September 11, 2001 terrorist attacks) stand together as providing sufficient forensic evidence undermining the official stories in both cases – stories in which religion plays a central and direct role in the narratives of the motives of the participants. These two references refute the claims given by our leaders and could serve as sufficient evidence to officially re-inquire into these events, if not re-litigate them.

In the case of the 1993 Branch Davidian compound destruction, the occupants were not suicidal as according to the myth of Jonestown, but were shot or gassed to death by federal agents. The documentary *Waco: The Rules of Engagement* produced in 1997 and even winning an Academy Award nomination (!) will provide all the forensic evidence needed to dispel the myths of who were these people called the Branch Davidians, and any supposed danger they posed to themselves or their community.[2]

&

In the case of September 11, 2001, controlled demolition brought down the three World Trade Center buildings, not the highjack-commandeering and impact of two planes by those with a theology of revenge. The information provided in *9/11 Blueprint for Truth: The Architecture of Destruction* produced in 2008 will also demonstrate that the very "collapses" of the three World Trade Center skyscrapers are themselves proof that the official document of the *9/11 Commission Report* is a whitewash and a cover-up because the collapses of the buildings are not collapses at all, but controlled demolitions.

Reason and common sense do not conflict with science, and should these two sources be consulted by the reader, *the lie that religion is implicated into the motives and causes of these events will be laid bare to the bone.* Exposing these *crimes of the state against citizens* (the Critical Theory) by way of religious engineering is a sacred duty of the scholar and activist.

Again, I here stake the credibility of my thesis on the information and images provided *in these two sources alone* and the reader's ability to discern the truth and facts of these events from the visual images and evidence provided therein.

The numbers appearing in brackets, for example (1:34:27), are the hour, minute and second in the documentary reference for that chapter. These final two chapters are best read in conjunction with viewing the documentaries which are both available (for now at least) for public viewing at numerous websites, perhaps most popular is YouTube. Precise times might vary depending upon whether one is watching the DVD or online.

---

2   Recent (as of 2017) postings of this documentary for the academic community contain a sanitized and redacted version omitting some of the most incriminating visual evidence.

7

ARMAGEDDON AT WACO, TEXAS: THE BRANCH DAVIDIANS

The delusion: *a group of apocalyptically-minded people called Branch Davidians – who are more-or-less religious cultists – living on a Texas ranch as followers of the messiah-like figure David Koresh who is also accused of illegal weapons-stockpiling and pedophilia, chose to resist government arrest and cling to their beliefs unto their deaths, if not by setting the blaze to their compound themselves then by their willingness to stay inside with their children in spite of the dangers, thereby dying in the fiery destruction of their Waco compound.*[1]

The correction: *fraudulent legal claims against David Koresh; evidence of foreknowledge by media of ATF military-style assault on compound; FLIR (Forward-Looking Infra-Red) video footage of FBI military-style raid on compound and assassination by gunfire of Branch Davidian members; subsequent scrubbing of site with destruction of vital forensic evidence coupled with no serious independent analysis of debris, all point to criminally aggressive, even murderous, ATF and FBI attacks upon the occupants resulting in the deaths of 80 people of whom 21 were children. This tragedy was then followed by an overtly-partisan investigation in Congress in which Republicans seek to gain political advantage over the bungled Clinton administration officials, and Democrats portray David Koresh in a caricatured manner and as a demon-possessed suicidal maniac on the order of Jim Jones and his Peoples Temple.*

---

1   This incident was also fueled in the public's mind by the stories of Jonestown suicide and represents how sinister these lies can become when they are used as historical distortion for other later incidents, thus compounding the obfuscation. This is one reason why it is imperative to deconstruct these lies.

Quotes

The Master said: "If you govern them with decrees and regulate them with punishments, the people will evade them but will have no sense of shame. If you govern them with virtue and regulate them with the rituals, they will have a sense of shame and flock to you."
— Confucius (551-479 B.C.E.) *The Analects: 2.4*[2]

In the case of the Branch Davidians, the news media were saturated with reports of gun stockpiling, sexual misconduct, and child abuse. Despite the alarm and hostility provoked by such reports and by popularly accepted notions of "cults" in general, we believe that an accurate, truthful portrayal of David Koresh and his follower and of the events surrounding the siege of their community in Waco is essential for understanding contemporary religious life in our country.
— James Tabor/Eugene Gallagher (1995), Preface to *Why Waco?*

By day the dead impaled on spikes along the road. What had they done? He thought that in the history of the world it might even be that there was more punishment than crime but he took small comfort from it.
— Cormac McCarthy (2006), *The Road*

A LOCAL APOCALYPSE

As with the Jonestown tragedy and suggested in the previous chapter, the Waco disaster is another incident which may still possess an *event horizon* for readers, in that it may influence the way we all continue to think about religious cults today and it provides something of a template for what constitutes a *religious cult*.

I can vividly recall for myself how I thought and felt about the situation unfolding ever so agonizingly over nearly two months at Waco. We talked about it at work; it was the subject of conversation with friends and family; and I formulated personal opinions about what ought to have been done. Of course, like everyone else, my opinions were based on what the news media reported was taking place out there in the Texan wilds, and what federal officials stated in their press releases.

These are very crucial elements (media and government officials) in fomenting and sustaining the delusions that this book asserts exist, and

---

2   Chichung Huang (1997). *The Analects of Confucius: A Literal Translation with an Introduction and Notes.* New York: Oxford University Press.

the associated autocratic tendencies required to obtaining the desired political or other social effect. The principal tendency being the news media is widely, if indirectly via corporate interests, controlled by government imperatives and their directives are what shape the public's mind as to the nature of the event in question. In this case, the demonization of David Koresh and his followers was instrumental to keeping the public mind focused upon the actions of the Branch Davidians (BDs) and not the actions of government agencies.

It was early 1993 and my wife and I had moved to Arizona from Massachusetts late in the previous year. I was still aghast at the "No Guns Allowed" sign (complete with the red circle and diagonal line over the image of a pistol) in the lobby of the local Post Office. Having moved from a state where gun regulations were much stricter, the feeling of having moved not only westward in location but also backward in time was hard to shake. The consciousness of the "Old West" is still very prevalent in southwestern culture. The country as a whole, however, including even right-leaning Arizona, had just elected Democrat Bill Clinton as President for his first of what would be two terms, and the nation seemed to be on something of a progressive trajectory.

Clinton had been inaugurated for little more than _one month_ when the Feb. 28–April 19, 51-day-long siege began in Waco.

The Branch Davidian siege first erupted, and then unfolded in a somewhat excruciating and drawn-out day-after-day saga. At the time, I personally understood the event more in terms of a geo-western-United States type of confrontation: law enforcement versus gun-toting Texan religious cultist. This seemed sufficient, for me at that time, to justify law enforcement pressing the confrontation to the end and storming the compound in order to save the inhabitants from David Koresh. But mine was a very convoluted understanding of what was taking place and based solely upon the television reports.

The media portrayed David Koresh as an unstable and polygamous "sinful messiah" who stockpiled gun parts that could be used to make illegal weapons such as machine guns and was a threat to the greater community. There was also the accusation that he was a pedophile. Once the Bureau of Alcohol, Tobacco and Firearms (ATF) had made the decision to go into the compound, it was clear they would be satisfied with nothing less than the complete surrender of the entire population hold-up inside. The level of force used upon the inhabitants in the initial February 28 raid provides the certainty that this was the ATF's end goal: *the seizure of the total population of cultists, preferably unharmed, but with whatever force was necessary.*

267

Upon closer examination, it becomes apparent that the initial raid need not have taken place at all, and was instead a misguided effort to bolster an agency, or agencies, whose reputation had suffered in the previous year's Ruby Ridge, Idaho fiasco against the Weaver family (37:15). In that incident, the FBI[3] was made to appear over-zealous, to put it mildly – having sniper-shot the wife of their target while she was holding her young child – in its approach to apprehending a suspect and the bureau had procured a reputation badly in need of refurbishing. Within a year of the Ruby Ridge incident, and perhaps expecting the ATF might come at his group similarly, on July 30 of 1992 David Koresh had *invited* the local office of the ATF through his gun dealer out to their Waco ranch to inspect his inventory (36:44).

Yes, that's correct, his *inventory*.

Koresh had knowledge that the ATF was investigating him and apparently wanted to satisfy their concerns. Koresh was licensed to purchase for re-sale guns and gun parts in the state of Texas (24:15). This is not the same thing as "stockpiling weapons."

Words *do* matter.

The testimony given before Congress suggests that David Koresh had plenty of weapons on site, some were in fact illegal and this could have been thoroughly investigated and likely resolved had the ATF visited Mt. Carmel (the name given to the BD compound/living quarters). The problem is that the search warrant for David's arrest consisted mostly of statutory rape allegations over which the ATF has no jurisdiction (28:00-32:06). Jack Harwell, Sheriff of McLennan County, states that their department of human services investigated allegations against David but could never obtain enough evidence to make an arrest.

Alas, the laws of Texas allowed for the marriage of minors with parental consent.

The media was responsible for the assertions of child molestation and sexual misconduct by David, but they failed to report that under Texas law, and with the parents' permission, girls as young as fourteen years-old can be wed. David Koresh likely *did* in fact sleep with a girl as young as fourteen years-old, but it appears as though she was a willing member of the community and with her parents' support (30:40).

As undesirable as this condition may be, it turns out to be a legal side issue – if not a full-blown distraction for public consumption. The ATF

---

3   At Ruby Ridge the U.S. Marshal Service, FBI, and ATF (albeit in a more legal and background role) were involved. The incident took place between August 21 and 31, 1992.

evidently had other motives for seizing the compound. Toward the end of the 51-day stand-off, and with the FBI now in charge, the offer by David Koresh to write about the Seven Seals and reinterpret the prophecies in a manner such that the group did not have to die as a fulfillment of prophesy was rejected by the FBI as merely a stalling tactic. The FBI would launch the final and catastrophic raid the next morning (1:24:15-1:25:30).

No government action of this consequence happens in a vacuum or without some intentionality on the part of properly-positioned individuals in authority, whether in the commission of the original act or in its subsequent cover-up. In this case the motive of the ATF is tarnished by its own incriminating behavior in seeking publicity for the agency ahead of the initial raid (37:50, 41:50) and being fully equipped with fax machines and media outreach capabilities, yet lacking communications equipment enough to call for 911 assistance for their own injured agents during the initial raid and resulting shoot-out (53:30, 54:13).

These facts pull back the veil concealing the *why* question of motive in addressing the military – in the commission of the original act or in its subsequent whitewashingstyle force used by the ATF in its initial raid, notwithstanding official statements to the contrary. Additionally, the FBI sought the Army's assistance and procured "250 rounds of high explosive, 40mm grenade launcher ammunition" according to a U.S. General Accounting Office memorandum dated August 21, 2000.

Grenade launchers needed to seize a civilian population?!?

Given that there were older, even elderly, people, women and children in the compound – what could possibly justify the tactics used against the Branch Davidians? The Waco disaster begs the question of why federal officials would behave this way. Why would U.S. law enforcement (initially in the February 28 raid the ATF, then the very next day, March 1, the FBI would assume control) take such aggressive and intentionally harmful action against a compound of women and children – even if they thought David Koresh was so wicked?

As for the manipulation of public perception, there is no way to know for certain how many times Jim Jones and the Jonestown mass-suicide myth (delusion) was invoked by the media in their broadcasts and in American conversations generally during the stand-off. But it is not unreasonable to expect that it did in fact happen, and frequently. Two references in this documentary alone do so: 21:00 and 2:13:10. With the Jonestown delusion resonating within the narratives of the unfolding drama at Mt. Carmel, the intellectual and political stages are set for government agencies to further shape public opinion about religion's role, the government's own motives, and, of course, the subsequent policies and commensurate funding that must be extracted from the taxpayer in order to "protect the American people" from such dangerous religious cultists.

On their part, eighty BDs lost their lives (in both the initial raid and final inferno) among whom were twenty-one children under the age of sixteen, thirty-one women, and at least four persons over fifty-five years of age. Several unidentifiable bodies were of indeterminable age. No government official or agency was held accountable and no one charged in the deaths.

RESUSCITATING SELF-DISGRACED LAW ENFORCEMENT INSTITUTIONS

According to their own testimony, the intent of the ATF was to sneak-up to the compound and catch the Branch Davidians by surprise with the hope of arresting David Koresh (40:00) and securing the surrounding community. Even though the element of surprise had been lost (41:00-43:00), the decision was made to go in anyway. The calculation must have been that they had come too far to retreat now. Yet, retreat the ATF would in the face of a very well-armed group of resisters. Retreating in humiliation, and four dead or dying, the ATF was again, along with other law enforcement agencies, in the spotlight as a dysfunctional institution and reviving justifiable questions about its competence and viability.

The issue becomes: what was so *urgent* to compel the ATF to raid the compound in the first place? There is no clear answer to that question beyond "saving the BDs from David Koresh," which in this case is also an attempt to "save them from themselves." Thirty-five BDs exited the compound during the stand-off: fourteen adults and twenty-one children. The rest presumably stayed in the compound of their own will. Sixty-two adults stayed within the compound of their own choice, along with them were twenty-one children, who would have had no choice in the matter remaining with and at the behest of their parents, in all likelihood.

Government institutions charged with protecting the lives and welfare of innocent people would not force a confrontation over the criminality of *one person* (David Koresh) only to risk endangering the lives of those *many other innocents* around Koresh – one would hope and expect (1:18:30-1:19:20). Nevertheless, the ATF went into the compound knowing fully the BDs knew they were coming. With the element of surprise lost, the only resolution at the time would have been to call-off the raid.

Since this did not happen, the issue then becomes, who shot first?

Crucial evidence is missing, and this is all but unexplained and unaccounted for. The key piece of forensic evidence to answer the question of who shot first was the front door of the compound. *A missing front door?* Again, this is a door that would prove once-and-for-all who shot first! But it's gone – missing completely from the forensic evidence that should have been meticulously scrutinized in the aftermath (45:00-45:30).

This is strong circumstantial evidence of a cover-up. Not only is there testimony by Texas Rangers that the FBI "scrubbed" the site (2:11:15-2:12:05) but journalists also had their tapes confiscated by the FBI and not returned, though they had been promised that they would be (2:09:30).

Once things spiraled out of control by the BDs firing back with unexpected force, the ATF was exhausted of ammunition and forced to stand down, then retreat (56:40-57:35). Thereafter would commence the stand-off between the eighty-three BDs remaining inside the compound and the surrounding FBI, who would obtain military hardware – tanks and helicopters – to intimidate and aggravate the BDs.

The FBI's behavior during the stand-off is inexcusable: agents bared their rear-ends "mooning" the BDs who could see from their windows (1:16:30-1:17:10). Tanks rampaged around the compound in an intimidating manner (1:17:20). The final military-style assault on the compound using CS gas and the resulting fire were over-the-top actions by rogue government actors against a civilian population that are more characteristic of the fascist control of society by oppressive ruling elites.

The destruction of evidence can be explained by only one motive: the desire to conceal what actually happened. It appears that the ATF's bungled attempt to refurbish their tarnished image was subsequently compounded by the FBI's crimes to "clean-up" after the ATF and by waging a long psychological battle again the BDs and then finally assaulting the compound military-style.

Rather than resuscitate a reputation tarnished the year earlier at Ruby Ridge, Idaho, the ATF/FBI only cast more doubt upon their motives, competency, validity of their chain-of-command, if not their very *raison d'être*.

PSYCHOLOGICAL OPERATIONS AGAINST the BRANCH DAVIDIANS and the PUBLIC

The tactics used by the FBI against both the BDs *and* the public (via the manipulation of the media) are characteristic of the fascist-style control over society. This is not hyperbole and should be considered in the context of other nations' known fascist and/or communist governments' absolute or near-absolute control of communications systems. The military control of civilian life is characterized by the tight control of media and the suppression of information about the physical and repressive violence used by the government and its officials against the citizenry.

To begin, the ATF[4] misled the military (by falsely alleging the BDs of harboring illegal drugs and making it thereby a justifiable drug-raid) in order to get military training, equipment and arms to assault the compound (38:40). In addition, the news media was kept back from the compound approximately one mile from the opposite side where the assault was being launched in an attempt to maintain FBI control of the story and the images to which the media had access (1:18:00-1:18:30). The FBI proceeded to use military-style psychological warfare tactics against the inhabitants of the compound after blocking the only road providing access to the compound (39:45).

Are these the types of tactics that a duly-elected government would take against civil society consisting of women, children, and elderly folks in order to "flush-out" one bad guy who is embraced among them? Do these actions reveal a government agency concerned for the well-being of the citizenry?

The answer is suggested in the following episode.

The negotiations between David Koresh (initially along with Steve Schneider who was on the phone with the FBI before turning it over to David) and FBI negotiator Jim Cavanaugh are most revealing of the FBI's mindset and intentions. Consider this exchange between them (1:04:30-1:06:27):

> JC: Well, I think we need to set the record straight, and that is that there was no guns on those helicopters. There was National Guard officers on those helicopters…
>
> SS: He says there were no guns on those helicopters.
>
> DK: That's a lie! That is a lie! He's a damn liar!
>
> SS: Did you hear that?
>
> JC: I know what he said but it's not true.
>
> SS: He wants to talk to you now.
>
> JC: Okay.
>
> DK: Now Jim, you're a damn liar. Now let's get real.

---

4   The Treasury Department was also implicated in these early phases to arrest David Koresh and in the cover-up report given to Congress (39:30).

JC: David, I...

DK: No! You listen to me! You're sittin' there and tellin' me that there were no guns on that helicopter!?

JC: I said they didn't shoot. There's no guns on...

DK: You are a damn liar!

JC: Well, you're wrong, David.

DK: You are a liar! [Screaming]

JC: Okay. Well, just calm down...

DK: No! Let me tell you something. That may be what you want the media to believe, but there's other people that saw too! Now, tell me Jim again. You're honestly going to say those helicopters didn't fire on any of us?

...Pause...

JC: David?

DK: I'm here.

JC: What I'm sayin' is that those helicopters didn't have mounted guns. Okay? I'm not disputing the fact that there might have been fire from the helicopters. If you say there was fire from the helicopters, and you were there that's okay with me. What I'm tellin' you is there was no mounted guns, ya know, outside mounted guns on those helicopters.

DK: I agree with you on that.

JC: Alright. Now, that's the only thing I'm sayin'. Now, the agents on the helicopters had guns.

DK: I agree with you on that!

JC: You understand what I'm sayin'?

DK: Well, no. What the dispute was over, I believe Jim, is that you said they didn't fire on us from the helicopters.

JC: Well, what I mean is a mounted gun...

DK: Yeah, But like that's beside the point. What they did have was machine guns.

JC: Okay, I don't know what they had. They were armed. The people inside had pistols or rifles...

DK: We agree then.

JC: Okay, alright, that's good. That's good. We agree, okay? Let's just leave it at that.

Considering this conversation, it is most difficult to see law enforcement officials as paragons of truth-telling. They instead appear to be much more intent on controlling the behavior of the BDs, that is, forcing them to surrender under questionable Constitutional authority.

What else could possibly explain the following military-style tactics, more precisely *psychological warfare* tactics, used against women and children:

-FBI snipers were located in positions such that no one could exit the compound (1:08:30);

-high-intensity bright lights shined into the compound at night instigating sleep deprivation (1:15:05);

-sounds of animals being slaughtered played loudly and during night-time hours (1:13:10; 1:15:20-1:15:35);

-loud music blared into the compound, also during sleep hours (1:13:30);

-tanks rolling around the perimeter of the compound bull-dozing everything in sight, even doing so repeatedly over a grave that the BDs had buried one of their own (Peter Gent) who had died during the initial shoot-out; this was done with the full knowledge of the FBI that the grave was present and the BDs could witness the disrespectful desecration of their friend's grave (1:17:30-1:19:00);

FBI spokesman Bob Ricks claims not to even know what psychological warfare is and states the chances were "minimal" that such tactics were used (1:14:30-1:15:05).

OUR WEAKENED (and WORSE) REGULATORY-LEGISLATIVE INSTITUTIONS

The inability of Congress to get to the bottom of the event and expose the nature of just what happened fits an historic pattern of Congressional Commissions that serve more as whitewashes and cover-ups rather than serious attempts to look at forensic evidence and to get to the facts. The decades-earlier Warren Commission investigating the 1963 assassination of President John F. Kennedy comes to mind. In time, and subsequent to the Branch Davidian tragedy, the 9/11 Commission would do exactly the same thing. This pattern of intentional-failure must be broken as it constitutes a key element in the *modus operandi* of forces and agents hostile to democracy (and the facts) and who are determined upon using government to further unrevealed agendas. This pattern is also the circumstantial evidence that the institutions of the democratic form of government can be manipulated by those same hostile forces.

Aiding and abetting a cover-up is no less a crime than the original criminal action.

In the case of the assault upon the BDs and resulting Congressional inquiry, partisanship would prevail in the hearings and this isn't difficult to detect. As the Reference documentary *Rules of Engagement* progresses this becomes very clear to the viewer. Seeing this example of public officials taking sides for or against the Clinton administration's handling of the incident over and above an honest attempt to hold the players accountable and to get to the truth of the criminal actions, signals a loss of the effectiveness of Constitutional law.

The enthusiasm of Republican Senators is to find fault with the Clinton administration's handling of the BDs is seen with the outrage by John Mica over the fact that children were left unprotected by gas masks, yet the FBI stormed the compound using CS gas (1:31:15-1:31:58). The backward bowed corpse of an eight-year-old girl is horrific evidence of the overkill used by the FBI against these harmless Americans[5] and a grim spectacle of the desperation that law enforcement can be capable of resorting to in order to preserve their existence (2:06:10). Republicans ultimately only expose the incompetence of the Clinton administration's Justice Department (Janet Reno) rather than holding the ATF and FBI accountable for their mishandling of the BD siege.

This amounts to pure politics.

The Democratic politicians, on the other hand, seem intent only upon demonizing David Koresh and the BDs. Representative Tom Lantos of California does a particularly histrionic performance before the Commission calling the "lunatic fringe" anyone who does not agree that it was "the apocalyptic vision of the criminally insane charismatic cult leader who was hell-bent on bringing-about this infernal nightmare in flames and the extermination of the children and the women and the other innocents" (4:10-5:10). Joseph Biden goes to the point of insinuating the BDs had suicidal tendencies by setting the fire themselves! Chuck Schumer also does great disservice to the hearings in defending the actions of the ATF and FBI against the testimonies of the defense lawyers (34:00-36:00) and does so with glaring ignorance not knowing the lethality of the projectiles used against the BDs. He engages in the worst sort of political melodrama thoroughly unbefitting a member of Congress.

---

5   There were not only Americans in the compound that day but also British, Australian, Canadian, Mexican, New Zealand, and at least one Filipino national.

Most inexcusable, if infuriating, is that Congress members had full access to the FLIR tapes discussed here (2:01:05-2:01:10) and yet persist to make these claims of guilt on the part of the BDs.

However, the political parties come together at one point and this is at the summation of the hearings when both Republican and Democrat politicians conspire against the American people by smearing the BDs. Perhaps most egregious are the final comments by high-ranking Senators, both Republican (Orin Hatch) and Democrat (Joseph Biden), that the BDs themselves started the fire in a mass-suicide (2:12:15-2:12:45). It was a despicable display of bipartisan contempt for, and collusion against, the American people.

These politicians' statements are observably false in light of the FLIR footage (1:50:00-1:55:00). Furthermore, adding to the obfuscation, and a pathetic attempt at that, James Quintiere (Congressional Fire Investigator) states that the flashes seen on the FLIR footage are reflections of sunlight and not flashes that caused the fire which destroyed the compound. This he states in contradiction to the other FLIR technologist's testimony and outside sources (Infraspection Institute).[6]

The failure of the political parties to get answers and accountability for the assassination-by-gunfire of the BDs demonstrates, to me at least, that political concerns were paramount, not justice for the BDs. One only has to see the contorted corpse of the backward-bowed body of an eight-year-old girl (2:06:09-2:06:30) to see the effects of cyanide on children. She had to have died an excruciating death as her muscles contracted her into this deformed position – *while she was still alive!*

In the case of the American-made apocalypse brought upon the Branch Davidians at Waco, Texas in 1993, it is accurate to say that the two-party system acted politically and legally as one party in *undermining justice for the victims.* Certainly, the two parties acted as *one party in deception* in their investigative and legislative roles in protecting the executive branch during the Congressional hearings and subsequently providing the whitewash of responsibility (i.e., the BDs themselves incinerated the compound) and bringing to an end any further legal proceedings. If this is does not represent a complete breakdown of our democratic institutions and the separation of powers, or presage something worse (which in fact did take place in the form of the September 11, 2001 terror attacks and the abysmal *9/11 Commission Report*), then there seems very little

---

6   CBS' news program 60 Minutes had hired Infraspection Institute to analyze the FLIR footage for their own investigation. Their analysis would never make it to air.

hope in the near future for the remedies to appear given the strident nature of the ATF's, FBI's, and Congress' collective behavior. This portends much more innocent suffering at the hands of government power and their officials.

Another level of outrage comes with the understanding that this criminal mayhem was all done at the expense of taxpayers – subsidized by us – the American people. Our paid-for-hire-officials are conspiring against us and this is an inauspicious, if gravely ominous, political reality of current American political life.

Watch the testimony of FBI Special Agent John Morrison (2:03:40-2:05:15) and ask yourself if his is the type of representation the citizens of this country deserve?

REFERENCE
Documentary Film

Gazecki, William, Dan Gifford and Michael McNulty, producers (1997). *Waco: The Rules of Engagement.* (136 minutes) Fifth Estate Productions. May be viewed in its entirety at: https://topdocumentaryfilms.com/waco-the-rules-of-engagement/ (accessed March 2019).

  • This is an *Emmy Award*-winning and *Academy Award*-nominated documentary that should be much more widely known about and understood by the American people. If every adult were made aware of its contents, and had it explained to them that this injustice could be remedied through Constitutional means, very possibly the character of our government and the media's role in society could be changed by this citizen awareness and activism. Even more to the point, the problems of the abusive rhetorical strategy of implicating religion in events that this book and its research seeks to address could be put to the full-light of day.

Additional References

Tabor, James D. and Eugene V. Gallagher (1995). *Why Waco? Cults and the Battle for Religious Freedom in America.* Berkeley: University of California Press.

U.S. General Accounting Office (2000). *Department of Defense: Military Assistance During the Branch Davidian Incident.* Chairman on the Committee of Government Reform. August 21. Washington, D.C.

U.S. Government Printing Office (1996). *Investigation into the Activities of Federal Law Enforcement Agencies Toward the Branch Davidians.* Thirteenth Report by the Committee on Government Reform and Oversite. House of Representatives. August 2. Washington, D.C.

8

ISLAM COMES TO THE HOMELAND ON A TUESDAY: 9/11

The delusion: *Nineteen Arab men with a radical interpretation of Islam hijack four aircrafts on September 11, 2001 crashing them into the <u>two</u> World Trade Center buildings in New York City, the Pentagon in Washington, D.C. with the fourth plane crashing in a field in Pennsylvania causing the deaths of nearly 3,000 people and compelling the U.S. into a "war on terror." They did so motivated by a hatred of American freedoms and the U.S.'s cultural influence which they deem insidious. Their ideology is rooted primarily within a theology of war referred to as 'jihadi Islam', which is, to be sure, but a fraction of Islam's worldwide population. Muslims number over one and a half billion across the globe, nevertheless, the religion provides the theological justification for waging such an attack and any disagreements to this can be attributed to the "war within Islam." The West and especially America, are the victims of this theology for which there is no meaningful way to rationalize or negotiate a compromise as its followers are intent upon establishing an Islamic Caliphate or state in as wide an area of the world as they can. September 11, 2001 was their greatest achievement and they and they alone are responsible.*

The correction: *Video and eyewitness testimony, physical samples in the dust, and forensic fingerprint of controlled demolition of <u>three</u> steel frame World Trade Center buildings (WTC1 and WTC2 in the morning with WTC7 coming down at 5:20PM) combine to render the two airline crashes <u>insufficient cause for the total damage sustained</u>; furthermore, the immediate military control and physical scrubbing of the site at Ground Zero, coupled with a blatantly-flawed analysis of the destroyed towers in the 9/11 Commission Report which initially ignored the third tower's destruction, implicate sources and actors within the U.S. Command were responsible for the terror attack and not external enemies. Jihadi Islam is but a convenient cover story that in historical-geopolitical ways can also be attributed to U.S. foreign policy interests in the Middle East dating back a century.*

Quotes

In regard to sentences with which we describe events, there can be questions at different levels. If the phenomenon described needs explanation, we demand a causal description that makes clear how the phenomenon in question comes to pass. If, by contrast, the description itself is incomprehensible, we demand an explication that makes clear what the observer meant by his utterance and how the symbolic expression in need of elucidation comes about.

– Jürgen Habermas, 1976 in *Communication and the Evolution of Society*, pgs. 10-1 (see Conclusion)

Is it not that there exists a government within the government in the United States? That secret government must be asked who carried out the attacks.

– Osama bin Laden, September 28, 2001 *The Daily Ummat,* Karachi, Pakistan

A lot of guys don't know if they're gonna do the job anymore. I know it's either this or the Army now, and I like saving lives, I don't like taking them. But after what I saw, if my country sends me to go kill…. I'll do it now.

– A young "ground zero" fireman being interviewed in *9/11,* a 2002 CBS documentary by Jules and Gedeon Naudet

Why did we not see the truth about 9/11? Well, it appears as if our government lied to us about the building collapses. The 9/11 Commission Report reinforced that lie. FEMA and NIST justified it. The corporate media repeated it, and they hammered it in. We really didn't have much of a chance.

– Richard Gage, founder Architects and Engineers for 9/11 Truth, 2008 in *9/11: Blueprint for Truth, the Architecture of Destruction* (52:50-53:13)

What about the 9/11 Commission? Its entire report is based on the unquestioned premise that bin Laden was behind the attacks. When we look closely, however, we see that the Commission's own co-chairs, Thomas Kean and Lee Hamilton, later admitted that this assumption was not supported by any reliable evidence.

– David Ray Griffin, 2011 in *9/11 Ten Years Later: When State Crimes Against Democracy Succeed,* pg. 9 (see insert in Conclusion, *Bibliography of David Ray Griffin on 9/11 Truth*)

The JOURNEY of MANY

As most Americans conscious of the events on the morning of September 11, 2001, the airborne terror attack upon the colossal and commanding World Trade Center towers was a huge surprise being both stunning by virtue of its spectacular nature and horrifying in its consequences for the country. Furthermore, visually and emotionally, it was overwhelming to witness the gaping and smoking holes in the sides of the towers where the planes had entered, and the sight of human beings falling or jumping to their deaths was devastating. Finally, and ultimately, the very buildings themselves transforming violently from shining glass and metal skyscrapers into expanding white dust clouds spreading out across Manhattan as though a volcano had erupted, provided the images of *shock and awe* that will forever influence all who witnessed them.

In preparing this book, it was a deeply personal struggle wrestling with the question as to what would be the best way to introduce the topic of the terror attack of 9/11 and the general propositions of *9/11 Truth*, as it has come to be called. This is the event/issue that has had the biggest personal impact upon me, my career, and my research and to which I had devoted the better part of two years in activism. I am not solely an objective observer and *Religious Delusions, American Style* is not intended as a purely academic work. It is also a polemical work with elements of my very struggle embedded in this narrative.

While the principal evidence offered here in this chapter is the physical destruction of the buildings themselves, the broader context for the attack is not so difficult to understand. It may be painful to understand, if rather shocking, but not difficult. This is otherwise known as dealing with the "why?" question.

Why would anybody in our own government want to do something like that?

Given that some readers alive near the publication date of this book will have for themselves living memory of the event, it also then becomes *personal*. Any one of us could have been in those towers on that day! I could have worked in them or stopped for breakfast at the "Windows on the World" restaurant on floor 106 of the tower that was struck by the first aircraft that morning. *Any one of us could have been there.* Why would anyone within the USA want to murder *me*? 9/11 is terribly personal for Americans who experienced it fully-consciously, that is, rivetted by events of the day and for whom the *why* questions can overshadow the forensics, and indeed, may render the forensics null-and-void, which is a pure act of delusion.

I was asked this *why* question frequently during my 9/11 Truth activism. The shortest and simplest way to answer it, I found, was that the attack was an act of *war-provocation*. In essence, it was to have the effect of frightening the American people and convincing them that the military adventure into Afghanistan was necessary lest the attack be repeated – the political capital gained from the 9/11 attack was reconstituted for the subsequent attack on Iraq and the false pretenses solicited for it (i.e., the non-existent weapons of mass destruction Saddam Hussein supposedly possessed).

The understanding of the 9/11 attack as war provocation conducted by elements *within* the American command, resolves and addresses, at least temporarily, the issue of "big picture" motives for why such an attack could be sought by military-elites. Almost anyone can rationalize the notion "war is profitable," even if it is difficult to emotionally accept such a rationalization. This temporary resolution, in turn and in order to make explanatory headway, must be exploited with additional facts that are themselves irrefutable in order to make the scientific case for 9/11 Truth. One simple question to pose is: *did and does the USA continue to have a* **stronger** *or* **weaker** *military presence on the world stage after and since 9/11?* This book answers the question with a resounding **stronger**. Mission accomplished, as they say.

But before this chapter begins referencing the scientific case for 9/11 Truth, the historical context and motivation can easily be referenced from observations made during the Cold War.

Recall the quote by George Kennan near the end of chapter three wherein he notes that upon the demise of the Soviet Union, the American military-industrial complex would be forced to invent a new enemy lest the economy sustain an unbearable blow. This is not a coincidence of geopolitics but a structural requirement of the American economy. Kennan made this statement in 1987, two years before the collapse of the Berlin Wall and the Iron Curtain.

The 1990s were, in retrospect, the transition years for the newly-invented enemy that would sustain the military-industrial complex for, at the time of this writing, what appears to be the foreseeable future: Middle East adventures for control of the region's oil reserves.

KEEPING a TRADITION ALIVE and WELL: The FALSE FLAG

As an act of war provocation, the terror attack of September 11, 2001 is best understood as being in the tradition of the bloody political *coup d'état*. In this case, a rogue troupe of actors embedded within the command structure of the United States military and intelligence establishments, the Pentagon, the Air Force, CIA and NSA and in some instances federal law enforcement, the FBI. This is a short-list and by far-and-away the best single resource covering these particular elements of the attack is Webster G. Tarpley's *9/11 Synthetic Terror: Made in USA* (see References to Conclusion).

With this coup[1] against President George W. Bush, whose very survival was not assured given certain events of the day, the coup-planners were able to get direct access to the military command structure and its vast power potential and thereby force their will upon the country.

There are precedents for such things. I suggested in the Introduction that Nero may have indulged in effectively the same type of political action in the 64 C.E. Rome fire scenario if it were in fact at his bidding that the fire began. And even if not directly responsible for the setting of the fire, his subsequent blaming of the Christians without evidence or proof is tantamount in bringing about his desired effect: the persecution of a group with questionable loyalties to his regime and the expansion of his palace. It was a win-win for old Nero.

In England, the 1605 "Gunpowder Plot" is commemorated as a foiled Roman Catholic plot against the crown and Parliament. In reality, among the plotters was Thomas Percy "double agent instigating the plot for the royal chancellor Lord Cecil." Among those blamed for the would-be attack was Guy Fawkes,

> a patsy, a dupe, ensnared by the chief minister himself in a mad scheme to blow up King and Parliament. The real plot was royally successful: to invent a pretext for war with Spain. This fraud was the foundation of the British Empire. In 1898, the American century was ushered in by a similar anti-Spanish hoax: the bombing of the USS *Maine* in Havana harbor (Tarpley, inside front cover).

The British, in the interest of their empire, have long been known to be complicit in deceptively fostering internal strife within the regions it occupied during the empire days and even using religion to do so. Think only of the founding of the American republic to recount a history of Brit-

---

1   A coup does not necessarily have to overthrow the government and replace the political leaders with their own operatives. In the American instances cited here, a coup takes place behind the scenes and utilizes the political entities contemporaneously in positions of power and exercises its will through them. Not infrequently do the publicly recognized powers co-operate with these behind the scenes power brokers, no less out of fear for their own existence. JFK may be the highest official to suffer retaliation for pushing back against the hidden forces of the power elites. This is how I understand the coup to have operated in the 9/11 attack, with President George W. Bush merely capitulating to their will, for fear of his own life of course.

ish insurgency against the rebel colonial states. In fact, the British may serve as the *big brother* in this regard – given that it is the largest and most recent European power to have spanned huge swathes of the planet.

Much of George Orwell's political imagination is rooted in his own experience of working with the imperial police in Burma. He understood the subversive techniques needed to politically control regions not always hospitable to British foreign rule. Some examples include the Mau Mau in Kenya, the Ahmadiyya Muslims in India-Pakistan, and to a lesser degree the Baha'i in Iran-Palestine, even the early American Mormons were favorably viewed by the British during a period of religious awakening in America and whom the British might cajole into anti-American federalist sentiments, which the early Saints held. Whether tribal or religious, these groups were used (to what degree is always the question) by British colonial powers under a "divide and conquer" strategy.

The logic is straightforward enough.

Creating a pretext for an attack is another common strategy to manipulate public opinion to assent to war. Intrigue around the December 1941 Japanese attack on Pearl Harbor in Hawaii is one example. Was it a complete surprise as the public was told? Or were there indications the Japanese were planning to launch the attack? Or perhaps *provocations* on the American side so that the Japanese *would* attack? Either way, the Japanese sent over 350 aircraft to make the bombing – a rather large fleet by which to be taken completely by surprise!

In effect, the 1962 Bay of Pigs fiasco was something of a coup, albeit a failed one, by the CIA against President John F. Kennedy. He was very suspicious of the CIA and afterwards had gone on record as wanting to "smash it into a thousand pieces." And of course, his death by assassination is itself a poorly covered-up conspiracy in which only the politico-media establishment continues to foster the myths about his death.

Finally, so-called "Gulf of Tonkin Incidents" provided the rationale for the deepening American involvement in the Vietnam War. In short, on August 2 and 4 of 1964 the Navy's *USS Maddox* engaged North Vietnamese torpedo boats and fired upon them. Questions surrounding the second incident and the subsequent admission by former Defense Secretary Robert McNamara that it never happened, even called into question the veracity of the first attack. President Lyndon Johnson addressed the nation on the basis of the second attack and espoused the U.S.'s escalation of the Vietnam War.[2]

---

2   The President's speech can be viewed here: https://www.youtube.com/watch?v=Dx8-ffi-YyzA (accessed April 2019).

ISLAM COMES TO THE HOMELAND ON A TUESDAY: 9/11

In the September 11, 2001 attack, and from the standpoint of the President *during* the coup/attack, G.W. Bush had every reason in the world to be afraid for his life and that of his family. There *were* terrorists who could kill him. They were simply domestic rather than foreign, contrary to the popularized myth that he himself was forced to propagate. One curious fact that indicates as much is that Crawford Elementary School in Texas was the only school in the United States to be evacuated on 9/11, other than, of course, schools and buildings in the vicinity of "ground zero" in Manhattan. The President's aircraft *Air Force One* had been threatened, also the White House in Washington, D.C., as well as the Bush family's Crawford ranch and hence the evacuation of the local elementary school.

During those frightful hours only Vice President Dick Cheney remained in the White House in the underground bunker called the Presidential Emergency Operations Center. The President, if you recall from the Introduction or indeed from that day, was not *allowed* to return to the White House until later in the afternoon. This alone ought to raise eyebrows and points us in the direction from where power is stemming.

SHAKING the FOUNDATIONS

The September 11, 2001 terrorist attack on the United States shook not only the foundations of the peaceful tranquility and sense of existential security felt here in continental North America from foreign invaders, but it shook also our worldview. Not only were we no longer physically invulnerable, but it seemed the very place of America in world affairs was being directly challenged. The fact that it came to us in the form of terrorist insurgents from the Middle East who are relatively weak compared to U.S. military might, and not a major world power, seemed even more humiliating. Delivered to us on that day was our own *nakba* (political disaster), much as the Palestinians had experienced in their unsuccessful battle against the Israelis.

But there was yet another foundation that was shaken.

It was the very foundation upon which the twin towers in New York were constructed. The cores of the WTC buildings were far stronger than we've been led to believe. They were constructed with the possibility in mind of an aircraft hitting them (58:00-59:30),[3] and there is no explanation for the destruction of the *three* WTC buildings other than that of controlled demolition and the use of explosive force.

---

3   Times here are from the Architects and Engineers for 9/11Truth's YouTube page.

Many many people heard the explosions as they escaped the towers after the airplane impacts. The reader can hear for him or herself a huge explosion at (1:04:15-1:04:20).

It was never fully explained as to why the public was denied the reports by firemen that the New York City Fire Department had collected. The NYFD had obtained *over 200 interviews* with firefighters immediately after the attack and with many of them stating openly that they heard numerous explosions during the course of their rescue efforts. When the *New York Times* sought access to these interview records, they were denied. The newspaper used the Freedom of Information Act (FOIA) to get them and ultimately did. What these interviews reveal is that the firemen felt directly threatened by the presence of explosives inside the towers. Their statements reveal this unequivocally.[4]

But even more dramatic than these, there were explosions in the basements of WTC1 or north tower, *the first building to be hit* by American Airlines FL11 at 8:46am. That's correct, huge explosions were reported *before* the plane hit. Consider that for a moment.

There is a man who saw and heard it all. A man who came to be known as "the Last Man Out" of WTC1. His name is William Rodriguez. He approached the 9/11 Commission to report what he witnessed, but his testimony would not be included in the final *9/11CR* when it was published.

What he experienced defies the mythology of that day. William was a long-time janitor in the north tower. In the two-to-three seconds prior to the impact, William heard, saw and felt an enormous explosion in the *basement* of the tower. It was so forceful that it had the ability to push William up from below. He was on the first level below ground of a total of six sub-level floors. *Then* came the more distant sound of American Airlines Flight 11 making impact some 90 stories above where William stood. He heard it as a distinct and separate sound. Then, another worker, Felipe David, came up from the second sub-level floor to the first crying "explosion, explosion." William says Felipe's skin was hanging from his arms and face as we was badly burned.

From his testimony before the 9/11 Commission:

---

4   The *New York Times* has archived: "A rich vein of city records from Sept. 11, including more than 12,000 pages of oral histories rendered in the voices of 503 firefighters, paramedics, and emergency medical technicians, were made public on Aug. 12. The *New York Times* has published all of them. The oral histories of dispatch transmissions are transcribed verbatim. They have not been edited to omit coarse language." https://archive.nytimes.com/www.nytimes.com/packages/html/nyregion/20050812_WTC_GRAPHIC/met_WTC_histories_full_01.html (accessed February 2019).

Rodriguez testified under oath that explosions were going off in the basement of the North Tower before the first plane impacted the building. He explained in great detail to the Commissioners the numerous cases of serious injuries he had personally witnessed that were caused by these explosions. He even provided the panel with a list of firsthand witnesses to the explosions, people who were ready to testify under oath. One of the individuals Rodriguez recommended the panel summon was his friend and fellow employee, John Mongello. Mongello was in the lobby of the neighboring South Tower when the first aircraft plowed into the North Tower where Rodriguez was located. It would be another sixteen minutes before the second aircraft would rip into the one Mongello was in. Yet, within a minute of the first plane hitting the North Tower, an elevator in the South Tower exploded to smithereens right before his eyes![5]

William Rodriguez and Felipe David were not the only WTC workers who experienced this pre-impact explosion and felt its power. Frank Morelli and Barry Jennings both heard explosions prior to the first impact. The Naudet brothers' video in the lobby of WTC1 revealed that there was such heavy damage in the lobby that one fireman states it looked as though "a bomb had gone-off in the lobby."

On that morning, I, too, recall hearing reports in the news of bombs going off at the WTC. It didn't seem surprising at the time given that in the previous 1993 attack at the WTC, a truck bomb was used. It made a certain amount of logical sense that terrorists might combine the two methods of crashing airplanes and vehicle bombs. The problem is, this suggestion soon falls under the weight of the evidence, which requires much deeper-access to the building's internal structure than bombs placed outside to account for the physical destruction of towers witnessed and recorded.

There is only one possible explanation for the destruction of the three WTC buildings, and that is the *controlled demolition hypothesis*. It is important to remember that not only were the buildings impacted by the airplanes that exploded, but a third tower – WTC7 – a building not hit by any aircraft whatsoever and imploding in upon itself in classic controlled demolition fashion at 5:22pm on the evening of September 11, 2001.

5   William Rodriguez's story would become quite well-known in the aftermath of the attack and in the country's need for heroic figures (he even met with President George W. Bush and Hillary Clinton), but his testimony about the explosions in the basement were ignored, much to his dismay. https://coto2.wordpress.com/2011/08/10/last-man-out-on-911-makes-shocking-disclosures/ (accessed April 2019). His story can also be viewed at YouTube "911 The Last Man Out – William Rodriguez." https://www.youtube.com/watch?v=_EEvJ-3SLAA (accessed April 2019).

Watch World Trade Center Building 7 implode – the image is widely available online

The Explosive Demolition Hypothesis contains the following ten points which constitute direct (if unimpeachable) evidence of explosive destruction (from Architects and Engineers for 9/11 Truth):

1. Sudden onset of destruction at location of *jet impacts,*

2. Straight-down, symmetrical progression *outside* footprint,

3. Squibs: explosive charges visible at *lower floors,*

4. Free-fall acceleration through path of *greatest* resistance,

5. *Near total* destruction of structural steel frame,

6. *Lateral ejection* of structural steel up to *600 feet,*

7. *Sounds and flashes* produced by explosions,

8. Enormous pyroclastic-like *clouds* of pulverized concrete,

9. *Iron microspheres* in dust and pools of molten iron,

10. *Chemical evidence* of thermite incendiaries.

These ten characteristics of a *typical controlled demolition* cannot be duplicated by the behavior of organic fires, regardless of ignition source (8:45-10:30; 28:30-29:00). Too often people are buffaloed by the assertion that there was 10,000 gallons of jet fuel on the planes and somehow that explains the disintegration of the buildings. This is a grotesque distortion and plainly absurd when given some critical reflection.

It is quite remarkable to hear the accusations directed at 9/11 Truth that it is not open to evidence other than what proves its own preconceived conclusions that the government was somehow involved. Important to point-out that all of the evidentiary information offered in this chapter (*9/11 Blueprint for Truth: The Architecture of Destruction*) is thoroughly and transparently open to public scrutiny and verification. The architects and engineers who are among the petition signatories are an international, degreed and vetted collection of certified professionals. This is called the peer-review process.

This is not the case, however, with the NIST and FEMA reports on the collapses of the buildings. Those reports were produced by *closed groups of scientists*[6] who feel no need to confront arguments presented by other scientists, eyewitnesses, and first-responders. The image of John Gross,

---

6   https://www.nist.gov/engineering-laboratory/final-reports-nist-world-trade-center-disaster-investigation (accessed January 2019).

Lead Engineer of the NIST Report, responding to questions about molten metal is revealing, if not disturbing (29:30-31:45).

If peer review means anything at all to scientific knowledge, then this alone discredits the NIST and FEMA reports as neither were subject whatsoever to peer review.

As Richard Gage points out in his presentation, the NIST report only discusses the conditions relevant up to the point of *initiation of collapse* (1:31:45-1:33:50). All of the visual and physical evidence *after* the beginning of the collapses is omitted from their scrutiny. The viewing public is forced to reconcile, and not without significant cognitive dissonance, these two realities: *the unanimity of politicians' and media's explanation for the cause of the buildings collapses* vs *the visceral fact of the implausibility of that explanation.*

The NIST and FEMA reports are frauds and a disgrace and betrayal to all citizens and the freedoms granted to us in this country. Those involved are worthy of investigation and prosecution if necessary. Wars have been started with these lies.

As if to underscore the egregious behavior of our political leaders and their appointees, the destruction of evidence afterwards is lamented by Bill Manning in the 125 year-old trade journal *Fire Engineering* magazine:

> Structural steel from the World Trade Center has been and continues to be cut up and sold for scrap. Crucial evidence that could answer many questions … is on the slow boat to China, perhaps never to be seen again in American until you buy your next car. Such destruction of evidence shows the astounding ignorance of government officials to the value of a thorough, scientific investigation (48:15-49:40).

So, as it turns out, it is the purveyors of the 9/11 delusion who are not open to the facts and scientific reasoning. To them I direct attention to the first quote at the beginning of this chapter by Habermas – don't give us symbolic expressions which do not relate to reality, but rather a causal explanation of what we actually see. If those who are hawking the 9/11 delusion believe 9/11 Truth is closed-minded, they are not only sorely mistaken, but are themselves guilty of their own accusations. I routinely hear on the news reference to "9/11 as an inside job" being nothing more than a "conspiracy theory." For whom do they speak? To those in the media and political world who continue to peddle the fear of terrorism, may they always remember, *those who cover-up a crime are themselves guilty of a crime, and just as guilty as the original perpetrators.* Such is a perilously-complicit position to be in, for sure.

Furthermore, this is so absolutely contrary to the facts as to be the reason for the dualistic-schizophrenic nature of the American political scene post-9/11 discussed at the end of this chapter. Tarpley asserts that these demonstrably-false claims channeled through the mass-media have the potential and intent to traumatize society and may in fact *induce* a mental breakdown in some individuals (see Conclusion; Tarpley, 348). This should not be surprising given the significant role of trauma in the human organism generally. What else is "shock-and-awe" supposed to activate but raw-organic trauma. And this was done by the state against its own citizens.

REFERENCE
Documentary Film

Gage, Richard (2008). *9/11: Blueprint for Truth, the Architecture of Destruction* (2008 Research Edition). Video lecture presentation by Architect Richard Gage, AIA (American Institute of Architects). (112 minutes) Produced by Architects and Engineers for 9/11 Truth.

- This presentation on the forensic evidence for the controlled demolition of the *three* World Trade Center buildings is the single most important bit of information Americans have not heard sufficiently. It has the scientific and professional credibility to cause any honestly-reasoning person to agree that the *9/11CR* could be nothing other than a whitewash and cover-up. This presentation is damning to the idea that *two aircraft* could have accomplished the physical destruction of *even* the <u>two</u> very large "twin towers," *never mind* a <u>third</u> tower, therefore, the role of the hijackers (and their motives … allegedly jihadi Islam) is insufficient as the explanations for the events of the day. This explanation is the one proposed in the *9/11CR* and is simply irreconcilable with the material evidence presented herein.

  This forensic evidence stands on its own and *must* be confronted by Religious Studies scholars, as it must by *all investigators* whose areas of expertise include research into or commentary upon the 9/11 attack, and whose analyses and subsequent narratives require an understanding of the *political nature* of the attack itself. A refusal to do so, in this researcher's opinion, undermines any attempt to explain the attack because of the resulting misappropriation of cause. This produces a *tainted historical record* which will thwart sound sociological research. The systemic and prevailing failure to confront and account for this information is the result of an intellectual and social degradation that is currently gripping American political-social-intellectual life. The outcomes speak for themselves (see Kishi in References to the Conclusion; also chapter one Mark Lewis Taylor).

View at the official website of Architects and Engineers for 9/11Truth: https://www.ae911truth.org/evidence/videos/video/5-9-11-blueprint-for-truth (accessed February 2019). Can also be viewed at Architects and Engineers for 9/11Truth's YouTube page: https://www.youtube.com/watch?v=O-QgVCj7q49o (accessed February 2019).

Additional Reference

Naudet, Gedeon and Jules (2002). *9/11*. Hosted by Robert DeNiro. CBS. Presented by Nextel. Aired March 10.

POSTSCRIPT: A NOTE on the DUALISTIC, PERHAPS SCHIZO-PHRENIC, NATURE of the NATIONAL PSYCHE at this TIME

There is a reason the term "fake news" which has surfaced in the most-recent election cycles has found a resonance with so much of the American population, irrespective of party affiliation. During the summer of 2008 when I was involved in 9/11Truth activism, this was one of the principal issues of the day: the news media seemed thoroughly derelict in its coverage of the 9/11 terror attack, and on so many other important issues. It appeared there was something of a paranoid toleration for the topic on the part of journalists who didn't want to contradict government officials, even on the most basic of questions or issues. One question that stood-out at the time, even prior to fully understanding the extent of American officials' complicity (i.e., controlled demolition of the buildings), was the issue of *where were the Air Force's defensive aircraft on that day?*

Even a casual perusal of the events as they unfolded exposes the glaringly obvious: depending upon how you parse it, as much as an hour and a half goes by in which the knowledge of the hijackings was out there floating in the FAA (Federal Aviation Administration – the folks working in the air traffic control tower at your local airport) and military surveillance systems.

Consider this timeline:

8:14 FAA made aware FL11 hijacked

8:42 FAA made aware FL175 hijacked

8:46 FL11 hits WTC1

8:50 FAA made aware FL77 hijacked

9:03 FL175 hits WTC2

9:28 FAA made aware FL93 hijacked

9:37 FL77 hits Pentagon

10:03 Passengers crash FL93

What the hell was the Air Force up to between 8:46 and 9:37AM? *That's nine minutes short of an hour with no Air Force response when the Pentagon got hit.* And this is being most generous with the timeline. If you think about it, the FAA was first aware something was wrong as early as 8:14 (give them a generous ten minutes to call it in) and the Pentagon was hit at 9:37. That's nearly an hour and a half with the Air Force asleep in the cockpit.

Or consider this timeline: *a full hour* elapses between 9:03 when the entire planet knew that hijackings were underway having watched FL175 hit the second tower and 10:03 when the passengers themselves crashed FL93 in a Pennsylvania field. The absence of a defensive presence by the Air Force is inconceivable but for some tampering with normal command and control procedures and protocols.

These timelines are as absurdly unacceptable as the prior insinuation that foreign terrorists could have rigged the buildings with explosives. The U.S. Air Force is far more competent than the abject failures in these timelines suggest. In fact, this is circumstantial evidence of moles and pre-planning *within* the command structure of the U.S. military (see Conclusion; Ryan, 119-141; Tarpley).

As if these weren't enough.

While events were unfolding in Washington, D.C., the Air Force's so-called Doomsday Plane, a Boeing E-4B, "the world's most advanced electronics platform [was] circling over the White House at the time of the Pentagon attack" (see References to Conclusion; Gaffney, back cover). There could be no aviation surprises with this piece of equipment in the air.

The suggestion is inescapable, and we are experiencing the *gaslighting* of a nation.

> gas·light·ing *v. 1. The act of causing a person to doubt his or her sanity through the use of psychological manipulation.*
> – Dictionary.com

Even to this day nearly twenty years since the attack, a low-level paranoid rejection prevails in most institutional settings to the information contained within 9/11Truth arguments. It is palpable and visible. Yet the facts persist in reason and experience.

Two aircraft cannot knock straight-down three buildings no matter the religion of the pilots

I attribute this condition to what Loewen discussed in his *Lies My Teacher Told Me* in which only a generation's forgetfulness allows history and facts to be reinterpreted and recontextualized and thereby given new meaning, or in the case of power, re-appropriated for political ends. He references the Swahili culture of east Africa in which a distinction is made between *sasha* and *zamani* in the historical memory of the population. Essentially, *zamani* is a history in which people live through themselves and is more difficult to write about by professional authors without criticism. Sasha on the other hand, is that history beyond the living memory of the consumers (listeners, readers) of that same history. Loewen assesses textbooks' treatment of recent American history compared to the history of the periods before readers would have any personal recollection (see chapter one; Loewen, 259-260).

His revelations are quite dismaying.

These textbooks' collective failure to discuss accurately and honestly any number of historical facts regarding America's past (from the Europeans' treatment of the Native Americans to the role of the FBI in subverting the civil rights movement) have set the conditions for the population's current state wherein *in the absence of the living memory of events, the education-media systems can massage and rewrite history to their own design. Furthermore, with the political elites in control of the mainstream media and the overall message, deception about facts is easily harnessed as a cultural means of coercion via the suppression of images and resulting manipulation of public opinion.*

In the case of 9/11, not *enough time* has elapsed for *enough people* to dissociate from the event and so discussing it beyond the commonly-accepted narrative remains difficult as many people still have the initial imprint and all the associated trauma, anger, and rationale for the attack, etc., vested in the initial *shock and awe*. Considering alternatives to the original is psychologically more traumatic. Suggesting the American Air Force had properly-placed moles who enabled, indeed conducted, the airborne attacks on that morning remains near-unfathomable, and understandably so, for many Americans to this day. Be that as it may, the forensics of the attack suggest this to be the case.

There are consequences for allowing distortions to prevail in the media and political spheres. The incident – discussed in the Conclusion – of the senseless murder of an elderly Sikh man gardening outside of his business establishment by the vengeful Frank Roque in the days after September 11 is a lesson to be learned that I trace directly back to the trauma caused by the attack and the delusions fostered as to its cause. It turns out, modern society is not immune from acting-out its deepest fears and the health of civil society and civic pluralism are directly threatened.

Yet, there exists in American culture another reality. A parallel reality that is even better-oriented to the historical facts – though it is largely unacknowledged in the mass mainstream news media, political discourse, and educational systems. It is the forensic-conspiratorial reality which has all but been erased from public discourse except for where it can be tarnished as fake news and thereby undermined of its credibility.

Nevertheless, when in a large American metropolis – New York City – a billboard with a 9/11Truth message can be on full display (see insert below), while at the same time the political establishment and media conglomerate continue to uphold the contradictory position, then, I observe and attest that there is a certain schizophrenia in the psyche of Americans' social consciousness.

There are many thousands of Americans (and those of other nationalities) who understand events as they truly are, as State Crimes Against Democracy, and the advertisement below is evidence of this. Regardless of what demagogic pundits say about the mind and character of those labeled as "conspiracy theorists," the existence of billboards as the one below reveals a dualism to American social and political life.

The billboard is fundraising for an advertising campaign to spread the word about *World Trade Center Building Seven*, the third tower to collapse on September 11, 2001, this at 5:20 pm and straight down in on itself and into its own footprint. Quite an accomplishment for foreign terrorists given the building had the Mayor's secure bunker in the form of the Office of Emergency Management, a CIA field office, and two U.S. Secret Service floors in it.

Building What? advertising campaign

The **Building What?** *campaign is pleased to announce beginning today, December 29, through December 31, NFL great (name deleted by author) will match,* <u>*up to $10,000,*</u> *all donations made to the next TV ad campaign.*

Thanks to your generous support, the **BuildingWhat?** *campaign has raised over $27,000 since the launch of the new fundraising drive on December 5. We are thrilled and grateful that two-time Superbowl champion (name deleted by author) has so generously stepped forward to spur us toward the $50,000-milestone. Between now and the end of the year, (name deleted by author) will match every dollar you donate; and just a reminder, every dollar you do give in 2010 will be fully tax-deductible when you file your taxes in the coming months!*

For more information on the next round of TV spots, please go to BuildingWhat.org. *To donate, simply click below:*
(29/12/2010 – website no longer accessible)

An *announcement by AE911Truth.org of fund-raising campaign. Especially note the tax-deductible eligibility of donations to this organization that exposes the cover-up of the "building-collapse" myth. This indicates that it is not yet too late for the Republic.*

Given that the attack of Sept. 11 is still a part of many readers' living memory (zamani), it is far more difficult to articulate relatively novel understandings about it without generating some type of emotional reaction – hence the paranoid rejection. Complete avoidance of the topic of 9/11Truth is the most characteristic response within academe and this is most revealing.

The best scientific and most authoritative resource the reader can associate with is the website www.AE911Truth.org and the more than 3000 (as of January 2019)[7] vetted-credentialed professionals (degreed and licensed architects and/or engineers) who have signed the petition demanding a new 9/11 investigation with subpoena power. The evidence they bring forth is impeccable beyond refute and the only reason it is not being confronted by the authorities is that it leads to very high-level leaders incriminating them in a conspiracy. Their evidence is presented in the two-hour discussion titled *9/11 Blueprint for Truth: The Architecture of Destruction* which convinces most "everyone who sees it that all three buildings were brought down by incendiaries and explosives" (see References in Conclusion to David Ray Griffin, 2011a: 112).

Working backwards from controlled demolition, as *9/11 Blueprint for Truth* points out, it required a certain level of access to the building that was simply not available to the general public. The list of possible candidates with access is highly restricted and secure. Certainly, foreign terrorists would have been unable to access the interior of the building sufficiently to perform work consistent with a controlled demolition. The assertion that they could have is absurd.

Alas, the logic is clear enough. Ask yourself why the mainstream media has not brought this information to the wider American public. Certainly *60 Minutes* could devote a twenty-minute segment to Richard Gage's presentation; he has produced a ten-minute version, after all!

The answer is, there is simply *no* reason *but* for political-corporate and vested interests that must keep the story smothered, marginalized and away from public view lest it accumulate political momentum and evolve into a concrete political movement with individuals of power held ac-

7   The scientific evidence presented by AE911Truth settles the discussion in an empirical way.

countable. That, in all likelihood, would result in a crisis of confidence in the nation's government and perhaps necessitating a Constitutional convention or crisis in order to rebuild the basic integrity of the nation's institutions. We should be so fortunate. Instead, they gave us the "Wars against Islam" which it appears the warlords have been planning for some time.

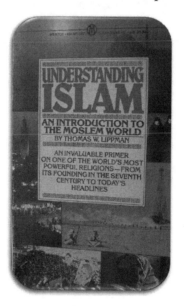

Conditioning the American people for the coming "Islamic wars" Book cover of the 1982 Understanding Islam: An Introduction to the Moslem World by Thomas W. Lippman announcing Islam as "one of the world's most <u>powerful</u> religions" – evidently powerful enough to collapse-straight-down <u>three</u> steel-framed buildings with <u>two</u> jets! The American general public had begun to be conditioned about the coming threat of Islam as early as the mid-to-late 1970s.

CONCLUSION

THE POLITICO-MEDIA ESTABLISH- MENT, SCHOLARSHIP, AND ACTIVISM

The delusions: *In contemporary USA there is a free and independent press which keeps close eye and scrutiny on the activities of elected politicians, administration officials, bureaucrats, and any-and-all government representatives in its effort to serve as a "forth estate" in the democracy; the first three estates consist of the tripartite division of powers demanded by the Constitutional form of government: executive, legislative and judicial. The effectiveness of media's oversight of government is evidenced by such scandals as WikiLeaks and the "Snowden affair." The government simply cannot keep secrets, no matter how benign or egregious the deed. In addition, academia is fully-independent to pursue all manner of research projects without limitation or interference from government agencies/entities in the interest of free conscience, thought, and speech protected by the U.S. Constitution. Consequently, there is no restriction to political activism within the bounds of the law. Activists are free to state their cases in whatever manner they choose without interference from government which would never suppress the media's willingness to cover topical and newsworthy stories.*

The corrections: *Media, most specifically the mass-mainstream news media, is anything but free from political influence and control. In fact, it serves as the unacknowledged-outlet for government policies offering only the most watered-down criticisms of questionable, indeed nefarious, even illegal, activities and then almost exclusively from a partisan political perspective. Very-little-to-nothing that amounts to aggressive, independent, crime-seeking investigative journalism exists in the USA today (other than that concerned with civilian misdeeds rather than upon the misdeeds of political-financial elites), except for on the Internet, and from which information is easily marginalized by the demagoguery of that same mass-mainstream news media or suppressed using technical capabilities. In addition, research in academia is badly corrupted by the mythologies of current political expediency, which often include predetermined villains and plotlines, but also the academic funding mechanisms that provide incentive to develop (a priori) investigations and inquiries that serve politically-established narratives. This is very easily exposed with historical and empirical* *research. Though little-advertised and understood by the public, the very structural conditions of academic financing expose conflicts of interest that would not sustain even the most rudimentary of ethical evaluations.*

Quotes

You cannot wake a man who is only pretending to be asleep.
– Navajo proverb

The number of propaganda campaigns in the West which have first taken hold in cultured settings is remarkable. Because he is convinced of his own superiority, the intellectual is much more vulnerable than anybody else to this maneuver.
– Jacques Ellul, 1965 in *Propaganda: The Formation Of Men's Attitudes*

[T]he investigative journalist is the propagandist's natural enemy, as the former serves the public interest, while the latter tends to work against it.
– Mark Crispin Miller, 2005 in the Introduction to Edward Bernays' 1928 book *Propaganda*

Intellectuals internalize the conception that they have to make things look complicated. Otherwise, what are they around for?
– Noam Chomsky, 2005 in *Imperial Ambitions: Conversations on the Post-9/11 World*, Disc 2, Track 6

I'm astounded there aren't more American political films. I'm amazed, when you can make movies for nothing, there are not people out there making these incredibly angry anti-war movies. How come?
– Brian De Palma, 2006, quoted at the IMDb website

If the past is any guide, we would benefit from scrutinizing how the intelligence community interfaced with academia to get what they want.
– David H. Price, 2007 in *Buying a Piece of Anthropology*

In any case, it was a corrupt society in which he no longer felt any interest. "People get the government they deserve," the Professor said once.
– James E. Gunn (American novelist), 1977 in his book *Kampus*

SOCIAL CONSEQUENCES of POLITICO-MEDIA-DRIVEN DELUSIONS

The previous chapter and final example of what I have termed *religious delusions* is also the issue I have invested the most research-time and energy into. It is the one delusion to which I have applied my efforts as an activist to dispelling – that is, 9/11 Truth activism via a hunger strike which lasted seventeen days in 2008 drawing attention to the fact that Senator John McCain had written the Foreword to *Debunking 9/11 Myths: Why Conspiracy Theories Can't Stand Up to the Facts*. It was *Popular Mechanics'* book version of their rebuttal to 9/11 Truth research and it did an appalling job of refuting 9/11 Truth's propositions and which resorted to the label "conspiracy theory." My Senator at that time was running a Presidential campaign along with Sarah Palin and his Phoenix office seemed a legitimate venue to pursue the political issues I was raising, even beyond his direct after-the-fact participation[1] by writing the Foreword (Gadsby, 2008).

I wanted him to see the video of WTC7 coming down and how it so obviously appears as a controlled demolition. I wanted to see *his* reaction. But it was not to be.

In addition to a challenge to Senator McCain, the hunger strike was a way to test the condition of local news media and get a sense of their tolerance for the subject of 9/11 Truth. The finding was that there is very little-to-no tolerance for the subject. It will take yet more time, decades perhaps if JFK's assassination is any comparison, for these difficult political historical facts to be assimilated into conventional American history.

---

1   I am working with the assumption that his "participation" was completely unwitting and that he, like the rest of the nation, was deceived about the nature of the 9/11 attack/operation. One objective and factual clue suggesting as much is the omission of McCain's Foreword in the 2011 edition of the same book (see photo insert under McCain in References for this chapter). Though never confirmed to me directly why the omission in the second edition, I can only infer from facts. But the logic seems clear enough: if the issues I was raising in the 2008 hunger-strike were clearly and obviously foolish and refutable, then Senator McCain would/could have left his Foreword stand, and confidently so. Since this was not the case, I take it he was persuaded by the facts presented to him, and so quietly removed his endorsement (power is best exercised discreetly). I refuse to pass judgement upon Mr. Cain's failure to push the matter beyond removal of his Foreword. If the late Senator understood matters of internal American political life along the lines presented in this volume, then he knew full-well the consequences of speaking-out (e.g., JFK, MLK, and RFK) and challenging that political system on such a weighty matter as 9/11. Doing so is for citizens of relative unimportance such as myself, and so can go mostly ignored. Incidentally, not one television network in the Phoenix metropolitan area reported my concerns, which were accompanied by appeals of hundreds of supporters over the seventeen-days. Just the same, I feel compelled to acknowledge Senator McCain's bravery and willingness to not only fight for the country in the military sense, but also in the political, which between the two may be the far longer and more persistent battle. Rest in peace, Senator McCain.

In the meantime, however, I see no intrinsic conflict-of-interest with this activism of my past and my now writing about it in an historical manner. It is no mere academic issue when one comprehends in real-time his government generating and sustaining a war provocation and in so doing, re-writing history accordingly. This is a crisis that must be addressed on two fronts: the *political* and *historical*. It is no exaggeration to say that the very health of civil society and the success of civic/religious pluralism, upon which American democracy and individual rights depend, are at stake with the issues raised herein. Lives in the wars will be wasted – foreign lives and domestic lives. There will also be unpredicted outcomes for scaring the citizens.

These manipulations on behalf of war provocations will have *no good outcome*.

One troubling consequence of frightening the citizens is that certain among the population will react irrationally and violently when prodded in such a manner. A certain segment of people can, in fact, be counted upon to do so, almost without exception as though it were a natural law of the human constitution. This is a dangerous latent potential that leaders must take care not to activate, or worse, exploit.[2]

It is this very natural and organic law that is selected and manipulated by the political elites in order to guide public opinion and the war effort that is afoot. When this manipulation includes religion, the stakes can be even higher. E.R. Dodds reminded us that within Greek history, those much-esteemed founders of our own heritage:

> To offend the gods by doubting their existence, or by calling the sun a stone, was risky enough in peacetime; but in war it was practically treason – it amounted to helping the enemy ... [t]hat, I think, is part of the explanation – superstitious terror based on the solidarity of the city-state. I should like to believe that it was the whole explanation. But it would be dishonest not to recognise that the new rationalism carried with it real as well as imaginary dangers for the social order (191).[3]

Arizona, the state where I reside, has been affected in no small way by the events of September 11, 2001. In addition to the nearly 200 deaths

---

2   As of the time of this writing in early 2019, we are approaching the twenty-fifth anniversary of the 1994 Rwanda genocide in which approximately 800,000 people were violently murdered, mostly by machete, upon the scurrilous political claims made by government officials over radio that one tribe posed a threat to another. Previously, many of those incited to violence by the demagoguery were the neighbors of those whom they would later murder.

3   Recall quote by Jerry Falwell and Pat Roberston prior to the Introduction

of soldiers[4] in the wars, the personal-individual citizen's psyche has been violated, and the social consequences of interpersonal relations damaged by mistrust. These have been witnessed in dramatic ways within our relatively small state. The result is a certain social barbarism and political primitivism that does not bode well for the health of civil society and success of civic pluralism – which are the ultimate concerns of and hoped-for outcomes of this book.

Sadly, we've seen here in Arizona anti-Islam rallies most recently in 2015 (González) and again in 2017. Mosques have been threatened (Merrill and Mitchell) and at times physically vandalized (Huff-Post). Perhaps the reader recalls that "hate crimes against Arabs and Muslims in the U.S. increased by 1,700% in 2001 according to crime statistics compiled by the FBI. In 2000, the FBI received reports of 28 hate crimes against Muslims and Arabs in the US. In 2001, that number increased to 481" (BBC News, 2003).

In the nineteen years since 9/11 the social conditions and political climate for Muslims, and those perceived to be Muslims – very often Sikhs are mistaken for Muslims – have not improved (Kishi). The 2016 Trump campaign brought its own challenges with its rhetoric high against Muslim refugees dislocated from the Syrian, Libyan, and Iraqi conflicts. Even as the images of fleeing Middle Eastern refugees under the most extreme conditions of hardship made their way to the American people, the U.S. hardened its political rhetorical position against the desperate migrants.

I would suggest that this is a very direct consequence not only of the narratives of Islam and Muslims as perpetrators of 9/11, but is also the consequence of, and perhaps a climax of sorts, of a multiple-generations-long and generalized anti-Arab-Islam public opinion (brainwashing/*religious engineering ATOR*, Def. 78: 173/329) campaign in popular culture against the American people. Arguably, it may have begun with Sirhan's Manchurian Candidate assassination of RFK in 1968 (see chapter four, Issenberg, also Shaheen). And though this is a matter of longer historical consequence, it does, however, help contextualize the individual events covered in chapters four and eight wherein developing Middle East policy is the actualized end result.

And so, it was in the Middle East, Afghanistan specifically, where in 2004 Arizona paid yet another of the human consequences of the *war on terror delusion* in the person of Pat Tillman. He was killed by fratricide – his mother's terminology – and in the aftermath of the military

4   Arizona War Dead: Casualties in Iraq and Afghanistan. *AZ Central.com*. Part of the *USA Today Network*. https://www.azcentral.com/story/news/local/arizona/2016/05/13/arizona-war-dead-casualties-iraq-and-afghanistan/84257852/ (accessed January 2019).

investigation, the family was left with the feeling that the military had gone to great lengths and at the highest levels to foster disinformation about their son's killing.[5] Pat's signing-up for the military was a complete act of patriotism some few months after 9/11. His death was treated by officials as an opportunity to promote the smooth functioning of the war machine. *To the state*, his death was to be that of a hero, dying for the cause of freedom and all its glory – a G.I. Messiah, as one academic put it. *To Pat's family*, his death was an utterly shameless exploitation and deception going to the top of the chain of command. *To academe*, his death is another opportunity to reinforce and exploit cultural perceptions,[6] or at its critical-best, to explain them, while simultaneously never coming close to addressing the stated concerns of those involved and who have challenged the state (i.e., Pat Tillman's own concerns about how "fucking illegal" the war was, or the family's quest for answers and the cover-up by Pentagon officials).

By all appearances, this is the condition of early twenty-first century American academe – it is working in full synergy with the political power of the state to the point of colluding with empire and serving as one arm in the cultural means of coercion by the state.

Sadly, and tragically, there was another cost to be wrested from Arizona: the ruthless and senseless murder of Balbir Singh Sodhi, an elderly Indian-Sikh man gardening on the property of his small business establishment – a gas station – here in Mesa, east of Phoenix. This became known as the "9/11 revenge killing." The gunman's motive was revealed when he stated at a local bar that he was intent on killing a "towel head." His actions and this story of murder are the outcome of the dangerous risks to the general population who is being fed inflammatory lies about religion. It is no matter of speculation that people *will* react in prejudicial ways toward those who resemble the ones who are fearfully perceived.

---

5   The official military investigation of Pat Tillman's death was accompanied by high-level Pentagon contradictions, concealments, and stone-walling, foot-dragging, and flag-waving memorials such that Pat's family rebelled. Their story alone is yet another case study in officials' malfeasance and where the mainstream media misses the story altogether. See *The Tillman Story*.

6   As one advertisement reads for a discussion by Dr. Jonathan Ebel titled "Safety, Soldier, Scapegoat: Pat Tillman and American Civil Religion" (sponsored by Arizona State University's Center for the Study of Religion and Conflict), Tillman should be seen "as the twenty-first century embodiment of a figure, the G.I. Messiah, who has loomed large in American perception of the soldier since the early twentieth century." Whatever the merits of Ebel's thesis, his opinions are rather quite ironic given that Tillman was a most vocal opponent to religious ideas. This type of academic gibberish does little to help the citizen or student understand reality. https://csrc.asu.edu/programs/conversations-center/safety-soldier-scapegoat-pat-tillman-and-american-civil-religion (accessed April 2018). Discussion can be watched in the Vimeo archive: https://vimeo.com/91731736 (accessed April 2018).

Teaching at community college near where the 9/11 revenge killing occurred, when I first heard about it, it was particularly distressing. On the surface it was easy to rationalize the revenge motive. But beyond that, who or what was the assailant looking for when he sought-out his victims? The entire nation was traumatized and was told they were Arab-Muslim hijackers, but who and what was the would-be killer looking for? And how would he identify him/them? It seemed imperative, I thought, to speak with this person who now sat on federal death row. His name is Frank Roque and below is a segment of our conversation conducted five years after the 2001 murder:

> **BG**: My next question is a two-part question. What did you know at the time, on September 15, about Muslims and compare that to what you feel you know today about Muslims? And I mean just generally.

> **FR**: At the time of September fifteenth, all I would see on the TV, lot of hatred, lot of uhh … lot of hatred, lot of anger toward us. Not just burning flags and stuff, but saying, you know, they want to kill all Americans. Everything I knew about Muslims at the time and prior to that was from what I saw them do, you know what they reported on the news, on the TV, or I happen to read in the newspaper that somebody else had bought and I just found it and read it, or something. But everything after, the only thing I've learned, is that, you know there are different categories, like, you know the Hindus or whatever, they wear turbans but, and other Muslims wear turbans, but they don't have the same religion or something.

> **BG**: That was going to be my next question, to ask you basically the same question but about Sikhs. What did you know at the time about Sikhs and what do you feel you know today about Sikhs?

> **FR**: *Yea, I knew nothing at the time about Sikhs, or Indian, or Hindus or Sikhs. I just viewed them all as just hateful Muslims.*

> **BG**: *Kind of all the same.*

> **FR**: *Yea, I viewed them all the same. I viewed them all as hateful only because of the words they would speak on international television. Their leaders* (Roque, December 2006).

Roque's words speak for themselves, but in conversing with him I could not help but sense a sinking feeling that somehow Roque was a victim of media-driven delusions. Not to excuse his actions whatsoever, he is fully responsible and accountable, yet, the indisputable fact remains that

303

flying *two airplanes* into *two buildings* does not account for the destruction of the *three World Trade Center towers*, regardless of who is piloting them, turbaned or otherwise.

Who fed Frank Roque his religious delusions?

This American-educated high school graduate was unaware of any differences between Muslims and Sikhs such that he could not distinguish one from the other. Since these communities are relatively unknown (marginalized in the case of Islam) or new in the American experience, a certain ignorance on the part of the general population is understandable. However, there is no excuse for the American education system for gaps such as this. It requires only minimal familiarity with the clothing of a Sikh to learn the difference between one and a Muslim. This visual information is broadly lacking in the population and can easily be corrected within the school system, popular culture and media, not to mention a deliberate campaign by governments at all levels would not be unjustified.

This oversight and knowledge deficit are facilitating the political exploitation of Islam and the use of religion as a cultural means of coercion against the population in order to manipulate public opinion. In this way, American politics itself demonstrates cultic qualities that sustain and propagate it.

AMERICAN POLITICS as NATIONAL CIVIC CULT: RELIGION as CULTURAL MEANS of COERCION, *AGAIN*

Def. 67 *Cults* are social enterprises primarily engaged in the generation and exchange of novel compensators (*ATOR*, 157/329).

Def. 100 *Politics* is the cultural specialty dedicated to negotiation of power relationships among groups in society (*ATOR*, 280/330).

The current American political and media systems are in the business of creating cults. By creating and perpetuating religious delusions the political system generates social enterprises, in both the community and in academia, in which the discourse is replete with the exchange ratios of the novel compensators, i.e., the religious delusions. The discourse in society focused upon "Islamic terrorism" is the contemporary novel compensator of the exchange ratios taking place in society, and in a variety of spheres of life such as law enforcement efforts, interfaith dialogue in the community, academic output, or any and all social activities or exchanges working in symbiosis with the political, social, cultural, education, and economic systems.

One Arizona example of an educational deficiency that could easily be rectified here within the community college system's curriculum is teaching the course Introduction to Islam. The MCCCD system includes the course in its line-up of Religious Studies courses, though it is, in fact, rarely taught – let alone promoted. Up until the fall semester of 2017 the course was granted *no* General Education Designations (GEDs) which are education categories for fulfilling the core requirements of a degree.[7] Individual courses are granted "designations" from among these categories which provide incentives for students to take the course in order to fulfill his or her requirements. For sixteen years students were given an *unnecessary disincentive* to take a course that could have familiarized them with a rudimentary knowledge of Islam. Workforce development is a key part of our educational mission and seeding this general knowledge into the workforce, which itself is made-up of members of that same religion, can only have a positive social outcome for the local workforce. This situation needs some explaining, by someone.

The greater Phoenix area is a diverse city with many immigrant populations, Muslims not least among them. It seems profoundly obvious that *Introduction to Islam* ought to be granted the maximum number of GEDs possible to foster the health of civil society and promote civic pluralism. When students return to their homes, families and friends with the basic knowledge of history and beliefs of Islam (as with any other unfamiliar religion), this goes a long way to mitigating the falsehoods propagated in mass media and providing citizens with defenses against these morally destructive, intellectually dishonest, and socially divisive *memes*.

In community college we prepare the workforce with everyone from the air-conditioner technician who walks-up to a stranger's home on a call to be greeted by a dark-skinned elderly man with a brightly-colored turban and the scent of incense heavy in the air, to the medical technician who will encounter a young Muslim woman whose modesty must be navigated in her reluctance to remove her hijab in public. Or in my case as a nursing aide, who, in preparing an elderly Alzheimer's man for bed by gesturing to him to take-off his underpants only to have him vociferously react to the removal of his undergarment, which I only later discovered

---

7   In addition to Composition, Critical Reading, and Mathematics students must take a selection of courses from among Humanities, Arts and Designs, Social Behavioral Sciences, Natural Sciences, and Literary and Critical Inquiry for examples. These are designed to balance a student's exposure to knowledge and sharpen critical skills needed across life's occupational demands. The community college plays a vital role in bridging young people to the community's workforce and in keeping mid-career students current in their skills, both technical and social. In our case, in the Phoenix area, the Maricopa County Community College District (MCCCD) serves a large urban population in a county of over four million and growing steadily.

was his Mormon clothing. Familiarity with these images of lifestyle differences in the classroom will dispel so many distortions hurled by the mass media and political establishment.

The 9/11 revenge killing ought to be sufficient justification to put Introduction to Islam on the roster. Besides, students *are* interested in the course (I informally poll them every semester), but they must be practical first. Sadly, as I write this, for the full calendar year of 2019, two semesters and the summer sessions, there is but *one section* of Introduction to Islam offered across the MCCCD system (ten campuses city-wide) with a total of 15 courses and 263 classes in Religious Studies on the roster. One in 263! There is no excuse for this.

I can only state that I am confounded at this condition. From the education perspective, mitigating anti-Islamic rhetoric for the sake of workplace harmony in a cosmopolitan setting seems an obvious enough goal. The social consequences are simply too great, and the health of civil society is at risk.

In any case, this oversight is easily correctable .

Education *about religion* is essential in this pluralistic and increasingly diversifying population. Religious Studies has the conceptual tools and vocabulary at its disposal to discuss Islam to a general American audience and with the ability to mitigate the very dangerous demagoguery coming out of the mainstream culture (Gadsby, 2006a). I am *not* referring to 9/11 Truth and inserting it into a general educational or classroom audience. Doing so would be inappropriate on a number of levels, at least for the foreseeable future. That being said, the inflammatory way most news is covered when implicating Muslims such that their religion is cited as the source of misdeeds must be pushed-back against by providing comparative examples of human behavior in and outside of Islam specifically and religion generally.

The biased reporting in the news is latent and insidious and is not difficult to disclose.

Again, unhappily, Arizona provides an excellent case study. Consider the news-reporting on these dual family tragedies which took place here in the greater Phoenix area. The headlines read as follows:

Muslim man guilty of "Honor Killing'"in Daughter's Death
(Schabner and Netter, 2011),
and
Mesa wife gets 3.5 years for running over husband after '12 election
(Mahoney, 2015).

306

These two headlines bring into sharp relief the manipulations to which Americans are subjected. People are products of their cultural, political, and media systems and a citizen doesn't have much choice of motive in the daughter's death at the hands of her own father. It is clearly religious.

Yet the husband, though surviving his wife's assault, was victimized as a result of her mental state. There can be no doubt that this is the case. But what of the mental state of the father? Is there a medical diagnosis for excessive anger and loss of control? No mention was made if alcohol was a factor, further complicating his state of mind. The answer seemed clear, he is a Muslim and he stated he did not like his daughter's westernized lifestyle. His beliefs alone were sufficient to compel him to his actions, we were told.

But what of the right-wing rhetoric espoused by the wife that was responsible for triggering her mental illness? There is a specific source for anti-Obama rhetoric: FOX News and various "conservative" national radio broadcasts. These outlets were never singled-out and implicated as the source of the wife's actions and were instead granted a pass in the shadows of the myths of Islam.

Of course, the irony revealed in the research presented here is that the original event garnering Islam its notorious status, the 9/11 attack, is itself a lie. The 9/11 *myths of Islam* have been used to religiously engineer public opinion along these lines in order to sustain war provocations, i.e., the war on terror. In this way the religious delusion of 9/11 serves as a theological creed in the national civic cult. The role of Islam in that cult is an example of religion (being used) as a cultural means of coercion to manipulate Americans' minds and extract from them the blood and treasure required to accomplish the goals of the political elites (empire).

This is blatant religious engineering.

The damage to civic pluralism and the health of civil society has been duly documented. Violence against minority groups is again on the rise after a lull since 9/11, and not coincidentally as result of American election cycles. Even in this charged political environment remedies are readily available, if one is seeking them.

What prohibits a show such as *Little Mosque on the Prairie* from wide distribution as a public service across the mass communications spectrum?

That's right, *Little Mosque on the Prairie.*

Each semester I show an episode of this Canadian-made sitcom to my World Religions class (it is produced by the *Canadian Broadcasting Cor-*

poration, or CBC – equivalent to America's *PBS* – *Public Broadcasting System* which means federal government funds underwrite the program). It doesn't require much imagination to discern the intent behind the show: to provide non-Muslim Canadians with a view of Muslims from a setting and perspective Canadians across generations can relate to. The show ran from 2005 through 2012 over which it found a loyal following.

> **Wikipedia reads**: The series premiere drew an audience of 2.1 million, an exceptionally strong rating for domestic programming in the Canadian television market, and on par with Canadian ratings for popular American series. It was, in fact, the largest audience the CBC had achieved in a decade for an entertainment program;
>
> **IMDb reads**: When the series finale aired in April 2012, the CBC negotiated distribution deals in 92 countries including Israel. Ironically, at that time, it did not air on any television outlet within the United States, Canada's next door neighbor. It has now been made available streaming over the Internet for American customers on the *Hulu* network.

The show won a humanitarian award. The point here is that there is some measure of cultural benefit to be gained by society in promoting these images. However, these images are not useful to a national civic cult where Islam must be positioned as mortal enemy and something to be resisted. This message consistently comes through in the news reporting where the delusions are best-perpetuated. As a result, the news itself is delivered in a politically-charged and very partisan configuration. This environment is indicative of a competitive news media intent on ratings and profits, but more than that, serving specific political interest. The absence of independence of politics and profit motives have perpetuated a marked decline in the quality of American news. One analyst puts it this way:

> Tabloid television has been big business, of course, for well over a quarter-century. Its rise was fueled by a number of factors, not least of which was the launch in 1980 of CNN, the first 24-hour news channel ... FOX News Channel was launched in 1996, underscoring the fact that cable news – and even network news – was there to make money. It hardly mattered that everything broadcast on TV jumbled into one big spectacle, whether it was a celebrity murder trial or a presidential address. Minute-by-minute competition among network newscasts and among news-magazine shows such as *60 Minutes* and *A Current Affair* led to a sort of programming arms race, and an inexorable slide

into the softer, more salacious – and more popular – "infotainment" that now fills prime-time hours (Kolhatkar, 78).

This bleak indictment upon the American news and entertainment landscape reflects today's equivalent of the Roman Empire's *bread and circuses*. Our leaders proceed upon a path for the nation with little awareness let alone input from the masses whom will pay the price of the policies of the leaders. The masses are literally being abused by the political system.

How often have we heard one or another version of the following clichés: *religion is a powerful force in society*, or *religion affects everybody's lives whether one is religious or not*, or maybe, *everyone is religious in some way, even if not a believer in traditional religions*? Every American understands how, similar to free speech, the right to freedom of religion is so important that there is special mention of its protection in the form of the First Amendment to the U.S. Constitution, reading thus:

> Congress shall make no law respecting an establishment of religion, or prohibiting the free exercise thereof; or abridging the freedom of speech, or of the press, or the right of the people peaceably to assemble, and petition the Government for redress of grievances.

This leaves broad latitude for the citizens to practice their religions both privately and in the public square. This latitude, we have witnessed, gives ample opportunity for individuals in official capacities to exploit religion for some political goal. This has taken the form of a civic religion with its own unofficial national creed and fanaticism (see chapter one; Stein, 11-12).

The current political structures and climate are producing their own tensions, much in the same way that religious cults are in a state of tension with their surrounding socio-cultural environment, so too American politics cultivates charismatic leaders delivered to us through standardized and more-or-less homogeneous and/or politically-bifurcated media presentations.

One observation notes:

> [L]ate twentieth-century civil religion asserted itself with the brazenness of a newly fashioned fundamentalism. Further exacerbated by September 11, U.S. civil religion in the early twenty-first century risks degenerating into a national cult (Hecht/Biondo, 45).

Based upon the research here, I suggest that the American political system is already, *de facto*, a socio-political cult, with elements of traditional religion embedded throughout. It is replete with supernaturalism[8] and

---

8   Examples of supernaturalism are memes like "magic bullet" and "collapsing buildings" in the JFK and 9/11 conspiracies respectively.

creedal fidelity, the two hallmarks of fundamentalist-style religion. The current American political climate has devolved and degenerated into a highly partisan and polarized bifurcation incapable of empathetic compromise.

The same dualistic pattern holds true for much of the news reporting with the news delivered from either the left or the right of the political spectrum. Coupled with this is a certain introversion, if self-absorption, to American news that denies the public a more global perspective on world events. Reporting seems mostly concerned with issues that are of direct (storms and weather), and mostly trivial (good deeds or animal stories), significance to an American audience. And while this may seem appropriate, if they are not balanced by a worldlier outlook, it will result in a form of unhealthy introversion that is crippling to the American cultural mind (see Terms of Delusion, American Exceptionalism).

In some respects, living within the United States today displays characteristics popularly associated with participation in a religious cult. If *control of the minds* of the followers is a variable, there is sufficient evidence that the mass media is performing precisely that function. American political and celebrity life fulfills the demands for heroes and idols. *Cut-off from the factual world* by the degraded condition of the news media, the American citizen and public opinion in general are ever-more vanquished by the political elites who control the mechanisms of power.

As promised in the Introduction, more comments by one of America's preeminent sociologists, C. Wright Mills, who noted the trend over half a century ago. He writes in the immediate post-WWII period, a period we now understand to be the Project Paperclip era. It is the mid-1950s when he notes:

> public opinion has become the object of intensive efforts to control, manage, manipulate, and increasingly intimidate. In political, military, economic realms, power becomes, in varying degrees, uneasy before the suspected opinions of masses, and, accordingly, opinion-making becomes an accepted technique of power-holding and power-getting (310).

The omnipresent reach of the U.S. military hegemony around the globe has put enormous pressures upon the political and financial elites to manage the homeland. It turns out that it is not difficult to find partners across the social and capitalist spectrum to collaborate. The mass-market published *Trading with the Enemy: An Expose of the Nazi-American Money Plot 1933-1949* showed the degree to which American industrialists and capitalists were willing to collude with Hitler, and how much the American reader wanted to know about it! That there were academics (Norwood) and even religious figures and institutions (Heschel) to collude with the Nazi empire against the citizens should not surprise us by this late stage of the research presented here.

In the case of book publishing and movies, the author of *The Business of Books* who worked in the industry notes,

> During World War II ... I can think of no book that was published that discussed the Holocaust or criticized American foreign policy toward the Jews or others who were being exterminated. As in Hollywood, where not a single film even mentioning these issues appeared until well after the war, publishing was extraordinarily silent (chapter 3; Shiffrin, 62).

The pattern repeats itself.

Consider the twin publishing efforts by Margaret Singer and Steve Emerson. They echo each other in their respective topics with titles *Cults in Our Midst: The Hidden Menace in Our Everyday Lives* and *American Jihad: The Terrorists Living Among Us*. Theirs is a terrifying world indeed. These two authors can be considered part of an official brainwashing campaign in their subject areas.

Peddlers of Fear

1995   2002

These two books are oriented for a popular audience and appeal to hyperbole (the fear factor) in order to make their cases. The existential threat posited by both is fiction; in fact, both are government-fabricated myths used to socially-engineer American public opinion and domestic and foreign policy. Books such as these introduce a most primitive and noxious element into politics by lowering the bar to a very crude level

> *rooted in fear-based discourse and an oversimplification of facts. Citizens are encouraged to go along with whatever government policies are conjured in the name of keeping them "safe."*

The activism of four 9/11 widows, the so-called "Jersey Girls," produced a better piece of investigative journalism, indeed scholarship, than not only the *9/11CR* but a good deal of the polemics produced by academe, and certainly by popular writers, that has been published and foisted upon the public since 9/11. A documentary film based on the efforts of these New Jersey widows titled *Press for Truth* reveals what citizens are faced with when confronting the bureaucracy of the U.S. federal government.

They had a total of 318 questions for the 9/11 Commission:

28 or 9% were satisfactorily answered;
73 or 23% were addressed but not adequately answered;
191 or 60% were generally ignored or omitted from the report;
26 or 8% were unclear (Kleinberg/Van Auken, 2004).

The tightly-controlled 9/11 Commission stonewalled the families in order to prop-up the *9/11 myths of Islam* and the war provocations which had already been implemented (in the form of the War on Terror and the Afghanistan invasion) by 2003 when the commission was established.

It is a dishonor to see university presses and New York publishing houses churn-out volumes on terror analysis with no reference to the empirical, verifiable information presented here and that is widely available, in spite of having been suppressed in the mass media. It is beyond scandalous and is evidence of religious engineering taking place in current American political and cultural life! Academia is complicit in this state of affairs – and to its shame.

Today sympathy toward Islam may garner one a second look by the federal intelligence services, much in the same way atheistic sympathies would have warranted a second look by Hoover's FBI under McCarthy's witch-hunt of the 1950s. Under such circumstances, activism can be an appropriate response to empirical research when that same research reveals an existential threat to society, and thereby one's own perceived welfare. As stated in the Preface, these delusions spanning America's history have come at "deep costs to human dignity and welfare, and to the much-cherished American way of life."

To examine how one's own field has perpetuated these delusions seems then an appropriate task for all relevant disciplines.

RELIGIOUS STUDIES as CULTURAL MEANS of COERCION and the ABJECT FAILURE of ACADEME, *AGAIN*

Very alarming is Religious Studies' role in perpetuating these religious delusions and political myths. The field stands to be reprimanded for doing such, and it will forever be a stain upon it. Should political conditions change, and it seems unlikely that they cannot given enough time, the academic field of Religious Studies (along with numerous others, Political Science to be sure) will stand condemned and humiliated for demonstrating not even a flicker of consciousness about the issues raised here. Failure of nerve, referring to a-now-recurring problem in the field, doesn't begin to describe the current state of academic affairs (Wiebe).

Let me recount a certain exchange between myself and Peter Bergen whose career reveals the cross-over between academia and mass media. Bergen is faculty at Arizona State University's School of Politics and Global Studies in addition to a National Security Analyst at CNN. He comes to the topic with a certain "street cred" in that he had interviewed Osama bin Laden prior to the 9/11 attack. At a public lecture in 2013 while promoting his most recent book *Manhunt: The Ten-Year Search for Bin Laden from 9/11 to Abbottabad*, I asked him if during his 1997 interview whether bin Laden himself ever used the term *al-Qaeda* in their discussion. Bergen answered no, the term was largely a "secret" and rarely if ever used by bin Laden. While this may have been true, bin Laden openly used other names to refer to his followers and the term *al-Qaeda* during this period was more likely to be used by U.S. officials in preparing their dossier for the villain they would ultimately accuse for 9/11.

In searching for news articles wherein the term *al-Qaeda* was used prior to 9/11/01, there were and are very few to be found, and those where the term is used, it is used by American sources, e.g., "US federal prosecutors have been building a case against Osama bin Laden and his al Queda organization since at least 1995" (BBC, 1998b). Often bin Laden is reported-on with no reference to *al-Qaeda* (BBC, 1998a).

To an American an *al-Qaeda* rebel-fighter would appear similar to a *mujahedeen*, a rebel Muslim fighter of any of a number of nationalities from Africa or western Asia, whom U.S. intelligence and military agencies had mobilized for various conflicts – in Afghanistan against the Soviets most especially. Bergen had written that bin Laden had created *al-Qaeda* back in 1988 and so the term should have been in known usage by 1997, but it was not (Gunaratna, 3; 246).

313

The term comes into widespread use only after 9/11/01 when all parties, bin Laden included, would adopt it once the global-reaching and over-arching structure of the myth was established. Bin Laden at first denied he had any involvement in the attack, only to say otherwise within a couple months, according to a video release. The term *al-Qaeda* has a generalized meaning *the base* or *the foundation* in Arabic, and so is not inappropriately used for the fighters in this context. Historically, the city of Mecca was *al-Qaeda* for the early community of Muslims, or *ummah*; the base from which they would spread the word of their God. Curiously, in a 2005 *Guardian* article, British Labour Party member and Foreign Secretary Robin Cook wrote:

> Bin Laden was, though, a product of a monumental miscalculation by western security agencies. Throughout the 80s he was armed by the CIA and funded by the Saudis to wage jihad against the Russian occupation of Afghanistan. Al-Qaida, literally "the database," was originally the computer file of the thousands of mujahideen who were recruited and trained with the help from the CIA to defeat the Russians. Inexplicably, and with disastrous consequences, it never appears to have occurred to Washington that once Russia was out of the way, Bin Laden's organization would turn its attention to the west (Cook).

Or, would these mujahedeen be those who provide the personnel and the cover-story for the next phase of Middle East engagement?

In one sense, all of this historical conjecture about the use of the term *al-Qaeda* means laughably little in light of the proposition that *two airplanes cannot knock straight-down three buildings*. Perhaps unexpectedly, this proposition now helps guide and ground the researcher through the mists of official obfuscations and tangential facts.

Peter Bergen's role in propagating the myths is most transparently that of purveyor of official delusions to the upper-middle classes of educated American society and culture. He cannot escape the accusation in light of forensics and history, whether he is witting or unwitting. The concern here is the influence *within* academe that seamlessly segues with that from the politico-media establishment.

Religious Studies research on 9/11 has been abysmal and its near unanimous chorus of blaming radical Muslims for the attack has been deafening. No doubt academic specialization and balkanization is part of the problem. What cause would a Religious Studies researcher have to read *Fire Engineering*, or *Elevator World*, the respective trade journals of these fields? None at all, really! Yet, both of these magazines, when taken in the context of a broader research Religious Studies agenda, contain very important glimpses into the bigger picture of the event's overall scope than what is widely portrayed within the field – and they provide forensics – i.e., science.

It is important to remember that Religious Studies has also been victimized by the absence of investigative journalism in the USA. Academe is but one of society's institutions dependent upon a certain degree of journalistic input and reporting from foreign regions. The universal silence of Religious Studies scholars on 9/11 Truth, however, reveals and unwillingness, fear, and general reluctance of academia to countenance 9/11 Truth propositions – their veracity notwithstanding.

There is pandemic rejection of the information that leads to the conclusion of 9/11 being an inside job. Most egregious in this way are Mark Juergensmeyer's *Terror in the Mind of God* (2000 and 2003) and Bruce Lincoln's *Holy Terrors: Thinking about Religion after September 11* (2003 and 2006) both are in a second edition or beyond. I use the term "egregious" to highlight that they take uncritically statements by government officials, and then proceed to create research agendas based upon those "facts" or "evidences" provided by government – all the while only having the effect of corrupting the very field they seek to advance, and further reinforcing a tainted historical record.

Juergensmeyer is most eager to rephrase his research to make it toe-the-political-line. I noted in 2008:

The two editions of this book provide a revealing insight into the nature of the academic study of Islamic-based terrorism. Juergensmeyer is a noted authority on religiously-inspired violence and has studied numerous cults or sects of different religions and he was researching this topic long before 9/11. In a version of his book written prior to 9/11 he discusses OBL and some of those with whom he associated. Juergensmeyer does not use the designation "Al Qaeda" in referring OBL, et al. in the 2000 edition. Yet, in the 2003 edition, the third edition, the author has included Al Qaeda in the index and sprinkled the text with references to it and even more-emphasized OBL's role in and among Islamic-based activities. Most curious is a shift in emphasis seen on pages 179/182, in the respective editions. In the latter edition OBL is cited as the one who "regards America as a worldwide enemy. One of the members of a movement associated with the al Qaeda network explained why." But in the earlier edition Juergensmeyer writes, "Mahmud

Abouhalima has said that he regards America as a worldwide enemy" (Gadsby, 2008: 165-166).

This is nothing less than an act of academic ventriloquism.

Bruce Lincoln, on the other hand, is mesmerized by what he considers a "document of extraordinary historic importance: the set of instructions Mohamed Atta left in his luggage on the morning of September 11, 2001, along with his last will and testament, apparently intending that these papers be found after his death (appendix A)" (Lincoln, 8). Since we cannot be certain about the authenticity of the luggage, it explains nothing by way of the 9/11 attack. In fact, that luggage, it should be noted, was left at the Portland, Maine airport where Atta began his journey. Given that it was a common occurrence for luggage to miss a connecting flight, no alarms were raised until after the attack and the luggage was subsequently connected to Atta, who could not have known his luggage was lagging behind having checked it in at Maine's airport. The question is, if Atta wanted his luggage to be found, he would not have checked it in given that he was planning to crash the airplane into a building. Something doesn't add-up. Ultimately, what Lincoln considers so very important provides little explanatory value given the events of the day.

Just as none of the psychological analyses and theories of dependency and control can account for the copious medications found on-site and slow body-count anomalies at Jonestown; and no amount of apocalyptic-theological speculations account for the FLIR-captured sniper-fire directed at the Branch Davidians; so too, no amount of Islamic rage done in the name of *al-Qaeda* or otherwise, directed toward the United States can account for the controlled demolitions of *three* World Trade Center buildings on 9/11. No academic treatises about obtuse, if peripheral, topics account for one shred of the forensics presented here in the previous chapters.

The MILITARY-POLITICAL USE of ACADEMIA, or the DEFENSE DEPARTMENT'S DEPARTMENT of RELIGIOUS STUDIES

[On political language] As soon as certain topics are raised, the concrete melts into the abstract and no one seems able to think of turns of speech that are not hackneyed.
— George Orwell in *Why I Write*, p. 105

Throughout the topics of this book, general education (public and private) has been utilized to promote government goals and policies to the youth in grade school and high school (chapter one in promoting

316

the founding myths of the nation over-and-above and to-the-exclusion-of – or worse – of the indigenous population; chapter two in maintaining the Bible vs evolution/religion vs science myths; and in chapter three by perpetuating the communist fear and its predatory ideology of atheism). In post-secondary education, the universities and academic scholarship have been unanimous in preserving the myth of the dangerous religious cult (chapters six and seven) and carrying right on through to the war on terrorism, Islamic radicalism, etc. *ad nauseam* (chapter eight).

In addition, there is long-standing controversy in the area of government and military funding for research done within universities (see chapter three Christopher Simpson; also chapter four Bettina Arnold; and Brian Bogart, and David H. Price below). University research and science in general depend upon the free exploration of knowledge without political concerns or hindrances from special interests. Is this even possible with the state overseeing the direction of the research agendas? It seems highly unlikely.

Religious Studies, to its credit, has been sensitive and self-reflective to the political ramifications of the influence upon and subsequent use of its scholarship by officials (see chapter three Iva Doležalová (*et al*); Russell McCutcheon 2004, and Donald Wiebe 1998 below). However, to its shame, Religious Studies has hitched its wagon to official narratives and buffered government assertions about "radical Islamic terrorism." As formidable as it may seem to a contemporary Religious Studies practitioner (scholar and student alike) to confront such politically explosive and controversial material, the failure to acknowledge its existence results in a degradation of the historical record such that accurate social-scientific theorizing is thwarted (see chapter three; Bainbridge, 1997: 359).

Put up against the forensic material present in chapter eight, the motives for the Department of Defense[9] to actively manipulate the research agendas of universities churning-out the literatures of political science, international relations, war studies, global religions, and many other departments and themes, become quite obvious. In order to maintain the war budgets, the threats must be manufactured and promoted and public opinion of the majority of the population best be on board since they are providing the funding through their taxes. With the stakes being so high, little wonder that an outgoing President with much experience with war left something of an ominous warning. In examining that "complex" the President was so very concerned about, intrepid young scholar of military history Nick Turse notes,

9   DOD – moniker for all Pentagon operations: army, navy, air force and each's intelligence service in coordination with the National Security Agency (NSA).

A few years after President Eisenhower pointed to the "unwarranted influence" of the military-industrial complex, Democratic senator J. William Fulbright of Arkansas spoke out against the militarization of academia, warning that, "in lending itself too much to the purposes of government, a university fails its higher purpose." He drew attention to the existence of what he called the military-industrial-academic complex, or what historian Stuart W. Leslie has since termed the "golden triangle" of "military agencies, the high technology industry, and research universities" (32).

I think the reader can see immediately the conflict of interest between the Pentagon and the results of the research presented here.

The dereliction of modern intellectual and academic life has been the most dispiriting of this entire decade-long quest. Scholarship today, if it is to have any relevance whatsoever beyond its own self-serving career-based interests, cannot sit idly-by and allow the conditions that prevailed described by Chadwick in the Introduction, or more pertinent, the narratives that continue to prevail in the political-media culture and promoted by government officials. This is precisely what is happening. Wars are being waged in the name of enemies that do not exist in the manner in which our leaders present them to us, and the threats posed by those enemies are so conflated to the desired effect, regardless of the technical capabilities of the alleged terrorists. This is what makes this research possible and not difficult to expose.

It appears as though we have made no progress in the past 2,000 years. To this stagnation, recognition must be given to the contribution of scholars of the academic field of religion. Religious Studies scholars are literally standing by while fires are lighted to engulf groups who pose no particular threat except to an established narrative that serves the purposes only of the privileged elite. Worse yet, they are contributing to the mass delusional state of affairs that enables this condition to persist.

If this is not a corruption of the field then what is? In part, it is the academic and legitimating institution for war-making. What we have currently is scholarship for war. This is very dangerous.

I can only plead along with George Orwell from his *1984*,

But when war becomes literally continuous, it also ceases to be dangerous. When war is continuous there is no such thing as military necessity. Technical progress can cease and the most palpable facts can be denied or disregarded. As we have seen, researches that could be called scientific are still carried out for the purposes of war, but they are essentially a kind of daydreaming, and their failure to show results is not important. Efficiency, even military efficiency, is no longer needed. Nothing is efficient in Oceana except the Thought Police (see Introduction; Orwell, 1949: 163).

Is this more-or-less not the same condition we currently find ourselves in regarding American wars in the Middle East? Again, Arizona provides a case study with Arizona State University (ASU – which is currently *the* largest state university in the USA) providing research on "radical Islam" to the military. But ASU is not to be singled-out for special criticism. This is simply the current structure of academic financing, and it must be assumed that the entire list of some 533 institutions cited by Bogart are in the same predicament. Below is how ASU publicly described their grant from the Department of Defense.

Pentagon-Commissioned Academic Research on Islam

Finding Allies: Mapping Counter-Radical Muslim Discourse

<u>Funder</u>: Minerva Research Initiative/ONR-DOD [Office of Naval Research-Department of Defense]

The rise of Muslim extremism is among the most critical issues facing the global community in the twenty-first century. The diffusion of exclusivist, extremist interpretations of Islam is not just a threat to non-Muslims but to Muslim communities as well. In addition to the violence perpetrated by extremists, they seek to effect cultural change across the Muslim world to facilitate their agendas, in areas ranging from ritual to gender relations. Although there is a substantial literature on Muslim extremists, very little is known about the counter-extremist discourses and networks that are critical to their containment and eventual defeat.

This research agenda sets all the parameters of the discourse within a pre-existing framework of historical events. This is music to the military's ears in that it assumes the enemy's existence and seeks to find (create?) the responses to it. But to academic research, it is a version of "Religious Studies Taps" in which it may literally represent the funeral of independent, institutionally-autonomous and critical scholarship. This rivals the situation in Germany under fascism (see Heschel; and Norwood) wherein scholarship became complicit with the state. If Joseph Goebbels can declare "Jewish intellectualism is dead" amidst book-burnings on university campuses (Norwood, 75), in what way is "Islamic intellectualism" or "Palestinian intellectualism" not also moribund in contemporary politico-academic life given the marginalization of Islamic scholars? (See Gordon, footnote 144). Religious Studies segues seamlessly with these efforts and one can find among 9/11 studies tome-after-tome of "academic research" propping-up the Islamic threat.

Consider the conflicts of interest of the "Pentagon Commissioned Academic Research on Islam" funded by the Minerva Research Initiative: *the nation's military complex is directing the course of academic research*. This situation is so blatantly-corrupted that it is no wonder certain elements of American history are pure hagiography (myths) including items and events as *magic bullets, suicidal children,* and *implausibly collapsing buildings.*

For an overview of the academic issues raised by government funding for research see "The Minerva Controversy." In military parlance, what we are faced with is a *full-spectrum-dominance* of the mechanisms of control with intent of democratic subversion wherein a staged-event is then seized-upon for propaganda purposes to then manipulate the political capital gained from the subsequent fear generated by the staged-event. This can only be achieved by the resources accessible to state actors and their apparatuses of control (*ATOR*, D42 & D43: 80/327).

It is important to keep in mind that this is the strategy of empire. In order to maintain control of a region distant from the source of power, instability of indigenous forces must be harnessed from which social and political instability can be managed/manipulated. The British precedent for this type of political and psychological subversion can be found in Frank Kitson's *Low Intensity Operations* where he discusses "one of the most remarkable instances of a cause being manipulated, if not invented, to make a wide appeal is afforded by the Mau Mau movement in Kenya" (31). By getting the masses of the Mau Mau supporters to be mobilized by a relatively minor, if incidental grievance, "thousands gave their lives for it, neither knowing nor caring that the original area concerned only extended to a few square miles." As Kitson shrewdly reminds us "it is in men's minds that wars of subversion have to be fought and decided" (31).

It appears little brother (U.S.A.) has learned well from big brother (U.K.). In a sense, the discussion at this point has circled back around to that of chapter three and America's inheriting the mantle of empire after WWII and the implementation of techniques necessary to maintain that global position.

SOLUTIONS from RELIGIOUS STUDIES?

For all the criticism that this book and its research has leveled at the field of Religious Studies, a curious contradiction has persisted. There is no reason to believe the field is so badly adrift in the sea of conformity that it is beyond the point of no return. There is *always* a corrective moment that can be seized. The knowledge that is produced by this field has the potential to build a new critical analysis and to change the historical record and contribute greatly to the health of civil society and the promotion of civic pluralism. This could be one such moment.

The testimony of Nancy T. Ammerman in the *Waco: Rules of Engagement* documentary (13:58 and 32:40) is an excellent example of where our field merits its existence. She provides valuable insight to the Congressional inquiry into the nature of apocalyptic groups and had her general advice been heeded, it is highly unlikely the compound would ever have been stormed and overcome with such tragic consequences. In her estimation, there was just no need for it. The people inside were *not a threat* to their neighbors. After seeing *Waco: The Rules of Engagement*, the reader can decide for herself or himself whether this is so.

The desire to represent facts honestly (truthfully) must always be at the forefront of education. Only in doing so will a society be built that is both healthy and vibrant with civic pluralism. Those of us engaged as teachers, instructors, researchers, and others involved in public education have this solemn responsibility: to strengthen civil society. *Genuine religious pluralism is a stabilizing force within the context of a healthy civil society.* When religious groups are singled-out for scrutiny by the political forces, this becomes a destabilizing social factor and history provides a number of warnings. From *Lies My Teacher Told Me*:

> Philosopher Martin Heidegger once defined truth as "that which makes a people certain, clear, and strong," and publishers of American history textbooks apparently intend to do just that, avoiding topics that superficially might seem to divide Americans. Before we abandon the old "correspondence to fact" sense of truth in favor of Heidegger's more useful definition, however, we may want to recall that he gave it in the service of Adolf Hitler (chapter one; Loewen, 338-339).

Before the field of Religious Studies can begin to correct the historical record, it must first cease being under attack directly by political demagogues. When Islamic scholars are singled-out and scrutinized by political operatives using independent academic and bureaucratic venues, then we have a condition that harkens back to the days of the preeminence of the intelligence services and their "buying a piece" of the academic action. The persecution of Islamic scholars in U.S. universities by none other than Lynne Cheney, wife of the Vice President, along with Joseph Lieberman, running-mate to Democratic Presidential-hopeful Al Gore in 2000, coupled with the academic chilling-effect the news media and the political system generally promoted through *think tanks* whose representatives appear on television news, all combine to stifle any objective representation of Islam and its history by those who are specialists in the subject.

This is an act of political intimidation and coercion (*ATOR*, Def. 38: 78/326) by the apparatus of the state. How on earth are scholars supposed to feel free to scrutinize geo-political conditions under the watchful eyes of the Vice President's wife? Is this not state-sponsored Islamophobia? The state is acting as a religious cult, creating tensions and schisms. Religious Studies cannot provide solutions under the political conditions of coercion.

Once academics unshackle themselves from undue influence of a political nature on what is supposed to be intellectually free thought and research, only then can they begin to reassemble the historical record minus the errors of state deception. Once this hidden history is exposed for what it is, a series of State Crimes Against Democracy (SCADs), then the historical record can begin to take shape (Introduction; deHaven-Smith, 9).

When the facts of the demolition of the twin towers, as revealed by credentialed and respected architects and engineers, are pitted against the various definitions of *jihad* by Religious Studies scholars in attempting to account for September 11, 2001, the "discourse" on the Religious Studies side becomes an exercise in futility. In fact, it's embarrassing. No wonder those of us in academia have been referred to as "quackademics" (Webster G. Tarpley, various lectures).

If Religious Studies (as any other academic field) is to maintain its relevance within the modern, free and democratic state and its contributions useful to an academic and thoroughly scientific understanding of religion, then the field should be able to offer-up analyses leading to potential solutions to issues facing the day. If religion is as potent a force in human life as I suspect it is, then to elaborate upon its true nature is an effort worthwhile. Currently, it appears that religion is being implicated into events where instead political operatives are at work, and the academic field that ought best to redress the historical record is impotent at best and complicit at worst.

Further complicating the discourse, so long as our *political, economic,* and *intellectual* lives remain in a state of division on the first two and disorientation regarding global issues and international political affairs on the last, then the political elites of this nation will have their way with both the political and economic directions of the nation.

In a final reference to Snow's *Two Cultures* (at end of Acknowledgments) wherein he warned of the failure of the two intellectual groups, the scientific and the humanities, to sit down and discuss their common concerns would have grave consequences for society as a whole. I believe we are witnessing this happening today. Within the research of the humanities including Religious Studies there is no cross-over into the fields trodden here (architectural science, fire engineering, deep politics, military war games/drills). This is to be expected generally, but not specifically. Academic fields must break-out of their cocoons to venture into territories untypical when relevant. The oversight of this crippled epistemology (the theory of how we *know*) results in a distorted ontology (the theory of what *exists*). The hidden, thus novel, element to history is the cause of the dilemma. What has been named "unspeakable" must be discussed for the benefit of our collective future which is depend upon the health of civil society and the success of civic pluralism.

American society is breaking down not only between the technological and the uneducated, but also the political left and the political right and the economically impoverished and the economic elite. The media reinforces and perpetuates the divisions. Snow's analysis was confined to the two intellectual classes, but with increased access to information provided by the Internet, his analogy can be extended to the generally-informed public.

> In western society there has been lost even the pretence of common culture. Persons educated with the greatest intensity we know can no longer communicate with each other on the plane of their major intellectual concern. This is serious for our creative, intellectual and, above all, our normal life. It is leading us to interpret the past wrongly, to misjudge the present, and to deny our hopes of the future. It is making it difficult or impossible for us to take good action (chapter two; Snow, 60).

In agreement with Edward Bernays' account that "Social progress is simply the progressive education and enlightenment of the public mind in regard to its immediate and distant social problems" (151), the concern remains that in this sophisticated world of technology the public's mind may be deceived as to where and what are its actual and existential social problems, both immediate and distant, and these will be hijacked by the social engineers on behalf of the political elite. The writing career of one of the earliest and most authoritative 9/11 Truth authors provides a case-study in the hijacking of a message and the near-absolute censorship and suppression of the broader perspective of that message. That literary career is discussed below.

Graeme MacQueen, writing initially in the field of Religious Studies then as an independent scholar, is well aware of the potential of myth and religion to be abused by power. MacQueen has also shown his courage by publicly speaking-out on the now mostly-forgotten anthrax terrorism in the days after 9/11 (MacQueen, 2014).

The blatant abuse of religion in the form of a disparaged Islam caricatured by American political elites is an abuse the field of Religious Studies ought to rightly call-out. This has been established forensically with the explosions and implosion of the three WTC buildings, and politically, though woefully-inadequately legally and institutionally. All the while, but for the unintimidated voices of David Ray Griffin and Graeme MacQueen, the academic field of Religious Studies stands idly by as though nothing is amiss. Such is the current state of affairs for academia in the world of politics, the high-stakes game of global dominance, and the use and abuse of religion.

In Europe, scholars in the post-Nazi era would go to great lengths to de-Nazify Biblical and New Testament studies and German theology which had seen the Jewishness of Jesus purged in Aryan academic discourse. An entire bureaucracy had been created in the form of the Institute for the Study and Eradication of Jewish Influence of German Church Life which was devoted to the cause of "draining Jesus of his Jewishness" (Heschel). Jesus would regain his Jewish race and heritage with post-WWII scholars such as Rudolph Bultmann and Martin Hengel in Germany and Geza Vermes in England.

But as always, timing is everything. Once the war was over, it became an academic not political issue to give Jesus back his Jewishness. When the Nazis were in power, this would have been an act of subversion. It would have taken incredible nerve to speak against Nazi ideology while they were in power and so academe conformed.

Alas, failures of nerve are nothing new.

American Religious Studies and Islamic Studies desperately need to reevaluate its positions on Islam's role in the modern world. Religious

Studies needs to help *de-terrorize Islam* and give it back its actual histo-riography and *decouple it from the hagiography of 9/11* and the *mythology of the war on terror* with their socially destructive consequences. And even if the political and formal educational systems cannot yet incorporate 9/11 Truth into the mix, there is plenty of corrective education that can be done in the meantime until political conditions can sustain the expo-sure of certain delusions.

As for Christianity fit for modern pluralistic America in the twenty-first century, nothing less than a messiah who is reconnected to both his Jewish (Jesus) and Greek (Christ) roots and universalized for a global humanity will meet the needs of a rapidly diversifying nation. This de-capitalized and de-imperialized yet authentically re-Americanized Jesus would max-imize the health of civil society and promote civic pluralism in the hopes of a more peaceful and inclusive vision of the future for all. The United States is in need of a Christianity that fosters the diversity of the popula-tion rather than seeking to dominate in the world of geopolitics.

The CURIOUS CASE of DAVID RAY GRIFFIN

The treatment and handling (or lack thereof) in the mainstream liter-ary world of the writings of David Ray Griffin (DRG), an impeccable and prolific scholar, is most illuminating of our current times. He early-on spearheaded the literary base of the 9/11 Truth movement with the book *The New Pearl Harbor* in 2004 which provides the big-picture geopolitical context for the 9/11 attack. His intellectual output on the 9/11 topic is largely unacknowledged in the mainstream of media literary culture (e.g., *New York Times Book Review*, *New York Review of Books*) as the informa-tion he presents remains taboo and simply indigestible by the majority of society's contemporary institutions. This *will* change, but it will take time, and probably lots of it. We stand today a full fifty-five years after the John F. Kennedy assassination and in-spite of *all* the material publicly available, virtually *all* the mainstream news outlets continue to perpetuate the myth of the lone-gunman.

It would be farcical were it not so tragic.

One thing is for certain, the freedoms of speech and the press grant-ed in the U.S. Constitution are still able to have their effect and with-out them the writings of dissenters such as DRG may never see the light of day.

Griffin also continues, despite being retired, to be an active author in the field of theology and the natural sciences and the philosophical effort to reconcile the two views. His analyses of these superficially conflicting worldviews have always been ones of moderation and clear consideration of the limits of the respective positions. He is no reactionary and solidly maintains a scientific orientation in all his academic work, even when discussing matters of a religious-theological nature, to which he is not dismissive.

The humanities and the sciences really do have much to say to each other by way of positive contributions. The worldview presented in the theological writings of DRG is that of pluralism with mutual understanding and a reconciling of what, all too frequently, are presented as antagonistic viewpoints (e.g., science vs religion; or religion vs no religion, theism vs atheism). His career represents our culture's best attempts from within academe to achieve the goals I stipulated in the Preface to this book: that is, debate about the existence of God or gods, as a cultural *meme*,[10] should be used with intent to be *morally instructive, intellectually nourishing and socially uniting, rather than allowing it to be used in ways that are morally destructive, intellectually dishonest, and socially divisive – partisan, in other words*. I'm afraid the partisans have been the ones wielding the power and positions to themselves create the memes and to frame the issues and debates, and provide the definitive and official stories and thereby control all political potential, i.e., public policy.

The case of DRG is a precise example of the meaning of George Orwell's warning from *1984*: "*Who controls the past controls the future. Who controls the present controls the past*" We are witnessing live and in real-time a transparent display of *A Theory of Religion*'s model of the *repressive state*. The relative tight control of the exposure of DRG's work in the mainstream media *must* have an explanation as it is unjustified in light of its social and political importance and the unimpeachable nature of the scientific evidence he presents. That *not one of these books* has been reviewed with any seriousness and thoroughness in the national establishment press, for example *The New York Times, Wall Street Journal*, and/or *Washington Post*,[11] might seem blatantly obvious

---

10   A meme is simply what we pass on culturally to our children from generation to generation and what is spread within and across cultures through language and other means of communication. Memes, like genes, are conceived as "replicators," little bundles of cultural information that get transmitted from person to person and carry-on doing so taking on lives of their own as they get shaped and reshaped from person to person in the transmission process. "We might call this thing an idea, an instruction, a behaviour, a piece of information" (see chapter two; Blackmore, 4). In this sense, religion and no religion, and all the various dimensions of the debate about God or gods, are themselves memes.

11   However, *The New Pearl Harbor Revisited: 9/11, the Cover-Up, and the Exposé* did receive mention as "Pick of the Week" by Publishers Weekly in November 2008.

based upon the research presented herein since they collectively poses a direct challenge to official narratives. Does the existence of this research, then, provide an *explanation* for the silence on these topics by the political elites and their media? If so, it should then be of interest to academics. But we find a similar condition of silence there also.

Bibliography of David Ray Griffin on 9/11 Truth

- *The New Pearl Harbor: Disturbing Questions about the Bush Administration and 9/11*. Northampton, Massachusetts: Olive Branch Press, 2004.

- *The 9/11 Commission Report: Omissions and Distortions*. (OBP-Same as above) 2005.

- *Christian Faith and the Truth Behind 9/11*. Louisville, Kentucky: Westminster John Knox Press, 2006.

- With John B. Cobb, Richard A. Falk and Catherine Keller. *The American Empire and the Commonwealth of God: A Political, Economic, and Religious Statement*. Louisville, Kentucky: WJK Press, 2006.

- *Debunking 9/11 Debunking*. OBP, 2007.

- *9/11 and American Empire: Intellectuals Speak Out*. With Peter Dale Scott, eds. OBP, 2007.

- *9/11 Contradictions: An Open Letter to Congress and the Press*. OBP, 2008.

- *The New Pearl Harbor Revisited: 9/11, the Cover-Up, and the Exposé*. OBP, 2008.

- *Osama Bin Laden: Dead or Alive?* OBP, 2009.

- *The Mysterious Collapse of World Trade Center 7: Why the Final Official Report about 9/11 is Unscientific and False*. OBP, 2010.

- *Cognitive Infiltration: An Obama Appointee's Plan to Undermine 9/11 Conspiracy Theory*. OBP, 2011.

- *9/11 Ten Years Later: When State Crimes against Democracy Succeed*. OBP, 2011.

Religious Studies does not refer to Griffin and his overwhelmingly-relevant-to-the-field books in any of its major journals. None have reviewed his volumes and their historical importance in the book reviews sections of, for examples, *Journal of the American Academy of Religion, The Journal of Religion, Religious Studies Review,* or the *Bulletin for the Study of Religion.* Architects and Engineers for 9/11 Truth simply does not exist in these intellectual environments.

On one hand it is mystifying, but by now the reader must have an inkling as to why this condition prevails. The implications for the official story of the *9/11CR* would incriminate deep political costs and demand a realignment of

327

our national security priorities. It is astonishing to the critical and investigating mind that this research is ignored – but then again, under social and political conditions that are most achievable in the current *American model and practice of a repressive state,* one could rightly ask, should we be so astonished?

Whether or not the national psyche would react sufficiently enough to force the political system to alter under the strain of the awareness of these officially-promoted religious delusions, is yet to be known. Is there enough empathy within the national psyche to demand that officials be held accountable? Or does the corporate-capitalist system have the populace sufficiently distracted by entertainment or forced by need to focus upon more immediate concerns, such as maintain access to adequate non-financial-devastating healthcare, not to mention a living wage?

The prospects seem daunting for the success of activism in the current social-political climate. Awareness may be the best one can hope for. Incidentally, *A Theory of Religion* demonstrates these social and political conditions referred to above, are also observable by their characteristics and demarcated as Axioms, Definitions, and Propositions.

I suggest citizens see themselves as the targets of *coercion* via an elaborate brainwashing campaign conducted by a *state* increasingly characterized by a *political elite* using the *cultural means of coercion* at its disposal by engaging in *deception* and *religious engineering* for the sake of the financial *elites* and their control of American civil society which they operate as a *cult movement* in the form of a national civic political cult – the two-party system, i.e., a *repressive state.* The humility required to recognize such a deliberate manipulation of public opinion is itself a first step to dispelling the delusions that enable and facilitate that manipulation.

The state has promoted any number of religious delusions such that we can no longer render ourselves *detached* from the experience. The victims are no longer the *other – they are us.* As we've seen, victims of these state-sponsored delusions may not even be afforded the basic rights due all citizens. Recall the abysmal number of autopsies (only seven) done in the aftermath of Jonestown relative to the total number of victims (918). Or that it took 444 days and the efforts of several grieving New Jersey widows to initiate the 9/11 Commission as the federal government made no efforts to that end as the Vice President at that time, Dick Cheney, pushed-back against any investigation.

What can possibly explain the absence of determination to find out what happened? Intentionality is at work in these instances, not failed oversight, neglect, or incompetence. One can only wish these latter were so, but they are not. The victims were marginalized and ultimately buried in mass graves along with the truth of the matters and the hope of any semblance of justice coming forth. The victims' truths were intentionally lost to history.

Upon hearing such news of overt deception and religious engineering, most citizens would want to believe that they would or could *never* be brainwashed in such a manner – either by a charlatan or the government. Living with this *pathos of distance*, it then becomes easy to accept the official stories. These official stories, with the aid of the media, then take hold in the popular culture and civic imagination and subsequently become narratives loaded with political capital dependent upon *otherness*, e.g., cult members, terrorists, or similar "othering" trait.

Only empathetic and courageous research can rupture these strategies of cultural coercion.

Withholding information that would potential change perceptions is instrumental to the control of people. It is what enables history to be "revised even as it is being written," as one dissident filmmaker put it. The systematic suppression/oversight of DRG's work in the academy is blatant and inexcusable revealing a *position to be maintained* rather than a *factual explanation of events to be sought*. Our field, then, becomes an extension of the political, and by implication, military apparatuses. That is why the funding source is so overt. Scholars are doing the bidding of the military.

This is nothing less than the intellectual degradation of the field and it is to be fought against and reversed. It is impossible to be truly independent scholars within such an environment. To argue that it is somehow fundamentally different than the academic conditions preceding and during the Third Reich is an intellectually dangerous self-delusion rendering us impotent as an academic field of inquiry incapable of describing history as it was experienced (see chapter four References, Arnold).

We are currently experiencing the scenario wherein the news media is so thoroughly watered-down with the interests of the ruling class that there is little of significant critical value in an evening newscast. An awareness of this reality has entered the public consciousness in the most recent election cycle (2016) in the form of *fake news* and that it lurks among the authentic news. The problem, however, is though the masses are aware of it, its roots and content are themselves the material of disinformation by those same elites[12] (see The Terms of Delusion footnote to Propaganda

---

12   Just as with the use of the term "conspiracy theory," recently the "deep state" has been

entry). When political leaders toss-about terms such as "the deep state" or "enemy of the people" or even "fake news" without solid-factual context, then the leaders' use of these terms becomes yet another tool in their methods of the deception.

Recall Jürgen Habermas' quote from the beginning of chapter eight? It was particularly applicable to the deceptive descriptions given to us by government officials for the "collapses" of the World Trade Center towers, which were in fact explosions. If this is not a revealing and glaring example of Habermas' use of terminology, what could be? It is worth repeating here because it applies to any number of the chapters in this book:

> In regard to sentences with which we describe events, there can be questions at different levels. If the phenomenon described needs explanation, we demand a causal description that makes clear how the phenomenon in question comes to pass. If, by contrast, the description itself is incomprehensible, we demand an explication that makes clear *what the observer meant* by his utterance and how the symbolic expression in need of elucidation comes about (italics mine).

It has become the domain of (some few) late-night comedians to deliver the harshest criticisms against politicians. McLuhan recognized as much when he stated that "Humor as a system of communications and as a probe of our environment – is often the best guide to changing perceptions" (92). Yet the most urgent of the topics delivered in this book have yet to find their way into the comedian's notebook, though let it be said there is nothing to be made fun of, but for the ridiculous responses by government officials, journalists, and "scientists" to questions posed by researchers of 9/11, the Branch Davidians, or the Jonestown massacre. To this day all remain in the realm of conspiracies when drifting away from official narratives. In the terminology of JKF assassination author James Douglass, these topics remain "unspeakable."

The jury is still out and only future-history will determine the verdicts on the topics raised here. Perhaps one day we will know exactly what has been flying over the skies of the U.S. and other parts of the world – because the

---

the open subject of obfuscation. Where the President would insinuate the deep state was *attacking him* (in the form of the FBI investigations and scandals), my own understanding would be that the deep state put the President *into power* (in the form of billions of dollars of free campaign airtime – whether pro or con for candidate Trump) only to then use him, for better or for worse, to his credit or discredit. Weaknesses and vulnerabilities come in many forms and decisions made by the deep state, are just that, *deep* – we, the public at large, don't get to examine them but must infer them from forensic research, historical context, considering motive, and an understanding of who had technical capabilities to accomplish what is verifiably knowable.

leaders will tell us the honest truth. Maybe one day the official record will read the truth about just what happened in Jonestown in 1978, or Waco in 1993, and on the morning of September 11, 2001. Each of these along with the previous topics has become a narrative that is part of America's mythological past and serves its current geo-political purposes. It appears most accurate to say that as myths, they are "systems of social significance, encoded within narratives of the epic past and the anticipated future, coordinated within behavioral and institutional systems of cognitive and social control, [and] characterize our responses to the various *incongruities* and *disruptions* that come with historical existence" (italics mine; McCutcheon, 1998: 71). Along with historical *incongruities* and *disruptions* just mentioned, I would here add *manipulations*. In short, the power we give to these myths (delusions) is equal to the power the ruling political elites will possess in using them against us and for their own novel, and mostly concealed, purposes and for a *future* for us of *their* choosing.

We could learn from the Puritans of early New England: once spectral evidence was turned on those ruling authorities (elites) of their day, it suddenly lost its power over the courts. History seems to record that only when the power structure itself begins to lose its grip do these deceptive and destructive myths lose theirs. This will require significant political realignment. Future history should be interesting indeed.

The good news is that the *future* is in our hands (*ATOR*; Def. 2: 27/325).

It seems appropriate to end this Conclusion and this volume with words from the book that informed chapter one on the Salem Witch Trials of 1692. At the close of her Preface, Marion Starkey recognizes that the delusional hysteria of days-of-old is not absent in the modern era. She, and now I join her, "would like to believe that leaders of the modern world can in the end deal with delusion as sanely and courageously as the men of old Massachusetts dealt with theirs" (15).

REFERENCES

Books/Essays

Ahmed, Nafeez Mosaddeq (2002). *The War On Freedom: How and Why America was Attacked September 11, 2001.* Joshua Tree, California: Tree of Life Publications.

Ahmed, Nafeez Mosaddeq (2005). *The War On Truth: 9/11, Disinformation, and the Anatomy of Terrorism.* Northampton, Massachusetts: Olive Branch Press.

BBC News (1998a). U.S. 'Charged' bin Laden Before Bombings. August 25. http://news.bbc.co.uk/2/hi/africa/157902.stm (accessed April 2019).

BBC News (1998b). Bin Laden: 'No Hand' in Embassy Bombing. December 25. http://news.bbc.co.uk/2/hi/south_asia/242155.stm (accessed April 2019).

BBC News (2003). US 9/11 Revenge Killer Convicted. 1 October. http://news.bbc.co.uk/2/hi/americas/3154170.stm (accessed January 2019).

Bernays, Edward (1928). *Propaganda*. Brooklyn, New York: Ig Publishing, 2006.

Bogart, Brian (2007). Unwarranted Influence: Chronicling the Rise of US Government Dependence on Conflict. M.A. Candidate Advanced Strategies for Peace & Diversity, University of Oregon. http://nwopc.org/files/PentaVersitiesByState.pdf (accessed January 2019).

CBC News (2007). Little Mosque wins Humanitarian Award. CBC Arts. October 9. http://www.cbc.ca/news/entertainment/little-mosque-wins-humanitarian-award-1.663430 (accessed January 2019).

Chomsky, Noam (2005). *Imperial Ambitions: Conversations on the Post-9/11 World*. Interviews with David Barsamian. 4 CDs. New York: Henry Holt and Company.

Cook, Robin (2005). The Struggle Against Terrorism Cannot be Won by Military Means. *Guardian*. July 8. https://www.theguardian.com/uk/2005/jul/08/july7.development (accessed April 2019).

Dodds, E.R. (1951). *The Greeks and the Irrational*. Berkeley: University of California Press.

Douglass, James W. (2008). *JFK and the Unspeakable: Why He Died and Why it Matters*. Maryknoll, New York: Orbis Books.

Ellul. Jacques (1965). *Propaganda: The Formation of Men's Attitudes*. Trans. Konrad Kellen and Jean Lerner. New York: Vintage Books, 1973.

Emerson, Steven (2002). *American Jihad: The Terrorists Living Among Us*. New York: The Free Press.

Gadsby, Blair Alan (2006a). Teaching *Religion(s)* in the Community College: Students Can Handle Theory Early. *Bulletin of the Council of Societies for the Study of Religion*. November. 35: 4, 92-95.

Gadsby, Blair Alan (2006b). Interview with Frank Roque. Unpublished transcript, December 21.

Gadsby, Blair Alan (2008). *Hungry for Truth: One Man's Struggle to Confront September 11, 2001*. Scottsdale, Arizona: Hungry4Truth Books.

González, Daniel (2015). Muslims brace for series of anti-Islam protests in Phoenix, around U.S. The Republic/AZCentral.com. October 9. https://www.azcentral.com/story/news/local/phoenix/2015/10/09/anti-islam-protests-phoenix-muslims-safety-precautions/73597738/ (accessed January 2019).

Gordon, Lewis R. (2008). From the Editor. *The Temple University Faculty Herald.* Philadelphia, Pennsylvania: Temple University. Vol. 38: 3.

Griffin, David Ray (2011a). *Cognitive Infiltration: An Obama Appointee's Plan to Undermine the 9/11 Conspiracy Theory.* Northampton, Massachusetts: Olive Branch Press.

Griffin, David Ray (2011b). *9/11 Ten Years Later: When State Crimes Against Democracy Succeed.* Northampton, Massachusetts: Olive Branch Press.

Gunaratna, Rohan (2002). *Inside Al Qaeda: Global Network of Terror.* New York: Berkley Books.

Gusterson, Hugh (2008). The Minerva Controversy: Unveiling Minerva. The Social Science Research Council. October 9. http://essays.ssrc.org/minerva/2008/10/09/gusterson/ (accessed January 2019).

Habermas, Jürgen (1979). *Communication and the Evolution of Society.* Trans. Thomas McCarthy. Boston: Beacon Press. [Original German, 1976]

Hayes, Christopher (2006). The 9/11 Truth Movement's Dangers. CBS News/*The Nation.* https://www.cbsnews.com/news/the-9-11-truth-movements-dangers/2/ (accessed January 2019).

Hecht, Richard D. and Vincent F. Biondo III, eds. (2012). *Religion and Culture: Contemporary Practices and Perspectives.* Minneapolis: Fortress Press.

Heschel, Susannah (2008). *The Aryan Jesus: Christian Theologians and the Bible in Nazi Germany.* Princeton, New Jersey: Princeton University Press.

Huffington Post (2018). Mosque-Vandalizing Mom Arrested. https://www.huffingtonpost.com/entry/disturbing-footage-shows-mother-teaching-kids-anti-islamic-racism_us_5aaaac0be4b0bb0accaaf859 (accessed January 2019).

Juergensmeyer, Mark (2000). *Terror in the Mind of God: The Global Rise of Religious Violence.* Berkeley: University of California Press.

Juergensmeyer, Mark (2003). *Terror in the Mind of God: The Global Rise of Religious Violence.* 3rd ed. Berkeley: University of California Press.

Kishi, Katayoun (2017). Anti-Muslim Assaults Exceed 2001 Total. Pew Research Center. November 14. http://www.pewresearch.org/fact-tank/2017/11/15/assaults-against-muslims-in-u-s-surpass-2001-level/ (accessed January 2019).

Kitson, Frank (1971). *Low Intensity Operations: Subversion, Insurgency and Peace-keeping.* Harrison, Pennsylvania: Stackpole Books.

Kleinberg, Mindy and Lauri Van Auken (2004). FSC Questions to the 9/11 Commission with Ratings of its Performance in Providing Answers. Members of the Family Steering Committee for the 9/11 Independent Commission. https://911independentcommission.org/ (accessed January 2019).

Kolhatkar, Sheelah (2010). The News Merchant. *The Atlantic.* September. Pgs. 76-84. Summary: "The inside story of how tabloid TV news is made, bought, and paid for – and its implications for the news industry and our society."

Lincoln, Bruce (2006). *Holy Terrors: Thinking About Religion after September 11.* 2nd ed. Chicago: University of Chicago Press. Original edition 2003.

MacQueen, Graeme (1988). *Whose* Sacred History? Reflections on Myth and Dominance. *Studies in Religion/Sciences Religieuses,* 17: 143-157.

MacQueen, Graeme (2014). *The 2001 Anthrax Deception: The Case for a Domestic Conspiracy.* Atlanta, Georgia: Clarity Press.

Mahoney, Emily (2015). Mesa Wife Gets 3.5 Years for Running Over Husband After '12 Election. Arizona Republic. May 21. https://www.azcentral.com/story/news/local/mesa/2015/05/21/mesa-woman-ran-over-husband-abrk/27710635/ (accessed January 2019).

Manning, Bill (2002). Selling Out the Investigation. *Fire Engineering.* January 1. Vol. 155, Issue 1. http://www.fireengineering.com/articles/print/volume-155/issue-1/departments/editors-opinion/elling-out-the-investigation.html (accessed January 2019).

Martin, Luther H. and Donald Wiebe (2012). Religious Studies as a Scientific Discipline: The Persistence of a Delusion. *Journal of the American Academy of Religion.* Vol. 80. No.3. September. 587-597.

McCain, John (2006). Foreword. In *Debunking 9/11 Myths: Why Conspiracy Theories Can't Stand Up to the Facts.* Edited by David Dunbar and Brad Reagan for *Popular Mechanics.* New York: Hearst Books.

2006   2008   2011

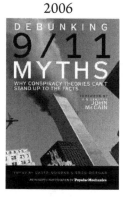  

The 2006 edition of Popular Mechanics' pathetic attempt to discredit 9/11 Truth and its research had Senator John McCain's endorsement. Not so in the 2011 edition. Did the 2008 public hunger strike have an effect on McCain's thinking?

McCutcheon, Russell T. (1998). *Redescribing 'Religion' as Social Formation: Toward a Social Theory of Religion. In What is Religion? Origins, Definitions, and Explanations.* Leiden: E.J. Brill. Edited by Thomas Idinopulos and Brian C. Wilson.

McCutcheon, Russell T. (2004). 'Just Follow the Money': The Cold War, The Humanistic Study of Religion, and the Fallacy of Insufficient Cynicism. *Culture and Religion.* Vol. 5, No. 1: 41-69.

McCutcheon, Russell T. (2005). *Religion and the Domestication of Dissent, or, How to Live in a Less than Perfect Nation.* London: Equinox.

McLuhan, Marshall and Quentin Fiore (1967). *The Medium is the Massage.* New York: Bantam Books.

Merrill, Laurie and Garrett Mitchell (2015). Phoenix-area mosques receive threatening letters, Muslim group says. May 25. AZCentral.com/Part of *USA Today* Network. https://www.azcentral.com/story/news/local/phoenix/2015/05/25/2-arizona-mosques-receive-threatening-letters-a-muslim-group-says/27932381/ (accessed January 2019).

Mills, C. Wright (1956). *The Power Elite.* London: Oxford University Press.

Norwood, Stephen H. (2009). *The Third Reich in the Ivory Tower: Complicity and Conflict on American Campuses.* Cambridge: Cambridge University Press.

Price, David H. (2007). Buying a Piece of Anthropology, Part 1: Human Ecology and Unwitting Anthropological Research for the CIA. *Anthropology Today.* Vol. 23, No. 3: 8-13. June edition.

Price, David H. (2007). Buying a Piece of Anthropology, Part 2: The CIA and Our Tortured Past. *Anthropology Today.* Vol. 23, No. 5: 17-22. October edition.

Roque, Frank (2006). Taken from transcript notes of author telephone interview with federal death row inmate. Arizona Department of Corrections. December 21, unpublished.

Ryan, Kevin Robert (2013). *Another Nineteen: Investigating Legitimate 9/11 Suspects.* USA: Mircrobloom.

Schabner, Dean and Sarah Netter (2011). Muslim Man Guilty of 'Honor Killing' in Daughter's Death. ABC News. February 22. http://abcnews.go.com/US/muslim-man-guilty-honor-killing-daughters-death/story?id=12975396 (accessed January 2019).

Schall, Lars (2014). *The Sound of Silence in Academia Connected to 9/11.* February 21. http://www.larsschall.com/2014/02/21/the-sound-of-silence-in-academia-connected-to-911-2/ (accessed January 2019).

Seigel, Jessica (2004). Ms. Women of the Year: Jersey Girls. Winter edition. http://www.msmagazine.com/winter2004/womenoftheyear.asp (accessed January 2019).

Shenon, Philip (2008). *The Commission: The Uncensored History of the 9/11 Investigation.* New York: Twelve/Hachette Book Group.

Singer, Margaret Thaler with Janja Lalich (1995). *Cults in Our Midst: The Hidden Menace in Our Everyday Lives.* San Francisco: Jossey-Bass, 1996.

Smith, Jonathan Z. (1982). *Imagining Religion: From Babylon to Jonestown.* Chicago: University of Chicago Press, 1988.

Stark, Rodney (2000). On Theory-Driven Methods. In Jon Stone, ed. *The Craft of Religious Studies.* New York: Palgrave. Pgs. 175-196.

Stark, Rodney and William Sims Bainbridge (1987). *A Theory of Religion.* New Brunswick, New Jersey: Rutgers University Press, 1996.

In order of appearance in this Conclusion are the following Definitions from *ATOR*:

Def. 78 *Religious engineering* is the conscious design of compensator packages and other elements of culture for use in cults.

Def. 67 *Cults* are social enterprises primarily engaged in the generation and exchange of novel compensators.

Def. 100 *Politics* is the cultural specialty dedicated to negotiation of power relationships among groups in society.

Def. 42 Those who monopolize the means of coercion are the *political elite.*

Def. 43 A *repressive state* exists when the political elite use their monopoly on the cultural means of coercion to impose below market exchange ratios on non-elite members of the society.

Def. 38 *Coercion* is the interaction strategy of threatening to inflict great costs on others, thereby imposing on them exchange rations which are below market value.

Def. 41 The *state* is the monopoly of the cultural means of coercion by a clearly differentiated group of specialists.

Def. 40 *Cultural means of coercion* refers to knowledge, capabilities, and technologies that can inflict unbearable costs on the human organism.

Def. 79 *Deception* is any interaction strategy that intentionally leads other people to accept explanations which one privately rejects.

Def. 51 An *elite* is a group with great control over its exchange ratio.

Def. 58 A *cult movement* is a deviant religious organization with novel beliefs and practices.

Def. 2 The *future* consists of the universe of conditions which can be influenced but not known.

Sunstein, Cass R. and Adrian Vermeule (2008). *Conspiracy Theories.* Harvard University Law School and University of Chicago Law School. Public Law & Legal Theory Research Paper Series. No. 199. https://papers.ssrn.com/sol3/papers.cfm?abstract_id=1084585 (accessed January 2019).

Tarpley, Webster Griffin (2006). *9/11 Synthetic Terror: Made in USA.* 3rd ed. Joshua Tree, California: Progressive Press. [5th Edition, 2011]

Tarpley, Webster Griffin (2011). *The 46 Drills, War Games, and Operations that Made It All Happen.* Chart in PDF. http://tarpley.net/docs/drills_of_911.pdf (accessed March 2019).

Thompson, Paul (2004). *The Terror Timeline: Year by Year, Day by Day, Minute By Minute: A Comprehensive Chronicle of the Road to 9/11 – and America's Response.* New York: Regan/HarperCollins.

Tiele, C.P. (1897). *Elements of the Science of Religion: Morphological.* Vol. 1. Edinburgh: William Blackwell and Sons.

Turse, Nick (2008). *The Complex: How the Military Invades our Everyday Lives.* New York: Metropolitan Books.

Wiebe, Donald (1984). The Failure of Nerve in the Academic Study of Religion. *Studies in Religion/Sciences Religieuses.* 13: 401-422. Reprinted in *The Politics of Religious Studies: The Continuing Conflict with Theology in the Academy.* (1998). New York: St. Martin's Press, pgs.141-162.

Winn Leith, Mary Joan (2012). The Bible Divide: The Difference Between Theology and Religious Studies. *Biblical Archaeology Review.* March/April. Vol. 38 No. 2. Pg. 24. http://www.biblicalarchaeology.org/daily/biblical-topics/archaeologists-biblical-scholars-works/the-difference-between-theology-and-religious-studies/?mqsc=E3103350 (accessed January 2019).

Films/Documentaries/Lectures-Discussions

Battsek, John (2011). *The Tillman Story.* Directed by Amir Bar-Lev. Narrated by Josh Brolin. (95 minutes) The Weinstein Company and A&E Indiefilms in association with Diamond Docs and Embassy Row.

Greenwald, Robert (2004). *Outfoxed: Rupert Murdoch's War on Journalism.* The Disinformation Company. (80 minutes) https://www.bravenewfilms.org/outfoxed_educators (accessed January 2019). May be available for viewing at YouTube.

Nowosielski, Ray, et al. (2006). *Press for Truth.* A film based in part on Paul Thompson's *The Terror Timeline.* (85 minutes) Banded Artists Productions and GlobalVision. http://topdocumentaryfilms.com/911-press-for-truth/ (accessed January 2019).

• Chronicles the efforts of the "Jersey Girls" who were the force behind pushing Congress to investigate the 9/11 attack – it is remarkable that our elected officials needed the goading in the first place! Ms. Magazine profiled the widows in the winter of 2004 and honored them as "Women of the Year" for their determination and for successfully petitioning Congress to create the 9/11 Commission (above, Seigel). In spite of their very heroic efforts, it still took 444 days to open the investigation, almost unthinkable under any other circumstances and itself provides powerful circumstantial evidence of a cover-up.

Tarpley, Webster G. (2011). The Last Secret of 9/11 Truth: The 46 Drills, War Games, and Operations that Made it all Happen. The Kevin Barrett Show. August 24. http://tarpley.net/2011/08/24/the-last-secret-of-911-truth/ (accessed March 2019).

THE TERMS OF DELUSION

The following terms within the popular American lexicon are used by the media and political spokespersons and their systems of communication to reinforce the delusions that have been discussed in the previous topical chapters. This is not to say that everyone who uses them from these systems is intentionally trying to delude the American and other people. Rather, they are used perfunctorily without critical examination or reflection. To be sure, however, there are those who use them for just such reasons. Consequently, Americans (the principal target audience) carry about in their minds seriously distorted concepts that cloud their understanding of any number of given historical facts/events as they have happened and current events as they arise.

American Exceptionalism: this doctrine has been the single biggest contributor to the American mind's deprecating attitude to the rest of the world and has bred a certain intellectual apathy in the population. With this understanding of oneself and the nation, there is little to hold in high regard of other peoples and nations. It breeds a needless and unjustified sense of superiority, or at worst, contempt for the ways that others practice their lives and cultures. Nothing, the reasoning goes, can compare to the way America does things. *AE* is insidious and should be purged from the thought-life and vocabulary of every American. In its own way, it serves as a secular yet parallel philosophy to that espoused by the religious fundamentalists-evangelicals on the order of Falwell-Roberston on the *700 Club* cited in the Quotes Over the Centuries on page three. Consult John T. Bookman's *The Mythology of American Politics* pages 95-97, for an historical overview of "*American Exceptionalism*" (see References to Introduction).

Biblical Literalism: the belief in the uniqueness of the Bible as a text revealed by God to the ancient Israelite people, but for whom, ultimately, he intended *all of mankind* to find guidance and salvation therein. Among Christian believers there is a wide array of ideas about the nature of the Bible's uniqueness spanning everything from a generalized inspiration-al-spirituality of the text (non-literalist, metaphorical, or liberal readings) to the fully-divinely-revealed "word of God" belief wherein every injunction must be applied as directly as the text states with no revisions or modernist interpretations (hermeneutics). This latter view is that of the fundamentalists, Pentecostals, and many evangelicals and identified as *BL*. The degree of authority given to the book coupled with a literal reading of certain passages with political implications, or seemingly so (e.g., access to abortion or opposition to gay marriage), give great potential for religious and political leaders to direct certain and sizeable segments of public opinion. The American people would be well-served if educated in the manner of Religious Studies regarding the historical-sociological nature of "sacred texts" so as to identify when a public statement ought to be taken as rhetoric and not a prescription for law. *BL* is also identified as *Divine Revelation* or the doctrine that the Bible is the *Word of God*.

Conservative: this is one half of a false-dichotomy that has duped the American public for at least a half-dozen generations. In American parlance, conservatism connotes a small-government posture that does not interfere with individuals' private activities, or at least purports to be so, and therefore is minimalist in the lives of the people. This includes everything from lower taxes to minimal regulatory authority in business and civilian personal life to a "strong defense" *vis-à-vis* a sustained military. In reality, contemporary American conservatism is a contradiction in practice. On the one hand it asserts minimal government involvement in the lives of its citizens while on the other hand seeking to regulate reproductive practices (abortion), marriage partner choices (opposition to gay marriage), limiting free speech (anti-flag burning amendments to the U.S. Constitution), and inserting prayers in schools (primarily Christian prayers thus dictating, or at least guiding and encouraging, religious choices) to name four examples. Simply, American conservatism as it is currently practiced is a cover for partisan politics that are decidedly Republican Party-political positions as outlined in the RNC platform (Republican National Committee) and are anything but conservative.

Conspiracy Theory: this term is so misleadingly-used in public discourse, and yet its manipulation so transparently obvious (rhetorically and historically), that it stands out as a principal case study of the semantic obfuscation foisted upon the American people by the corporate, political and social elites. The distorted way it is used in media and by politicians is widely-pervasive as to serve as something of a template of the strategy of state propaganda. For example, in what sense of the term is the official government story of the *9/11CR not* a conspiracy (theory)? The nineteen suicide hijackers claimed to be responsible for September 11 is, of course, a conspiracy – a conspiracy consisting of at least these nineteen plus, we are told, Osama bin Laden, Ayman Al Zawahiri, Khalid Sheik Mohammed, among others. The legal system uses the term for a precise definition, i.e., as in a "conspiracy to commit fraud" or murder, or some other criminal act. To apply the term *CT* only to those allegations that challenge a state-sponsored official story, as the media and politicians routinely do, is a gross misuse and inaccuracy of the term and circumstantial evidence of a whitewash in progress. The very important book by Lance de-Haven Smith *Conspiracy Theory in America*, referenced in the Introduction, noted the term's first use (*insertion* is a better term than *use* as it was a very deliberate act on the part of government officials) in media originated in early 1967 with CIA's efforts to discredit criticism of the Warren Commission Report (21).

Cult (religious): this term is particularly useful when stoking-up public opinion and sentiments against a group. This was successfully accomplished during the Branch Davidian siege by the FBI by associating the group with the Jonestown population. The two groups and their leaders were, in fact, worlds apart, but this did not stop the demagoguery centering on the term *cult*, especially *suicidal religious cult*, and the ensuing, reportedly-justified, provocation against the Branch Davidians by the ATF. The term should be used with awareness that there is an academic and sociological meaning and use of the term, and then there is also a popular use of it. Complicating the popular understanding is a religious and mostly inflammatory use of the term that is applied in the distorting manner in mainstream documentaries and news broadcasts. In this way, mainstream media present what is consider *normal* vs *cultic* religious behavior. The vested interests of the dominant religious group's (Euro-centric Christianity) use of the term is never called into question. Mostly negative political consequences result when the dominant religious groups' use of the terms of religious legitimation goes unchallenged, and that of differing or minority religious groups goes unheard. The chapters of this book are submitted as evidence.

Free Press: in a democratic republic or free society access to information is critical to the political process. Informed voters are theoretically and necessarily part of the entire process by selecting their leaders in a meaningful and constitutional authorization of power. It is more-or-less assumed in the U.S. today that the fourth estate operates independently from the other three estates, which in this country consists of the three branches of power: executive, legislative, and judicial. The fourth estate is not to be subject to restrictions by the other three estates and is restrained only by its ability to serve the overall process of constitutional democracy. It is self-regulated in that it is held to the standards of objective truth as discernable in a free and open society. In this way, there is no need for government regulation of the news-gathering process as it is self-regulating, self-correcting and self-validating as well as self-discrediting and self-de-legitimizing if it produces bad information.

Liberal: this is the second half of the false-dichotomy referred to above as *conservative.* It is used to refer to Democratic Party philosophy and politics primarily and includes more progressive views on social/cultural issues such as access to abortion, gay rights, free speech (though this is always relative), and with an economic and tax policy more generous toward the poor and lower income citizens. Liberal policies typically stand for a more aggressive government posture on regulations with more oversight on the economy and greater enforcement of environmental issues, healthcare, or other social concerns. Involvement in these areas of political, economic, and social life are not confined to political party platforms and the term can be used as adjectives for views within a party. For example, a liberal leaning Republican may be in favor of legal gay marriage but not abortion rights, and also remain conservative with fiscal policy.

Lone Gunman, lone wolf: the myth of the lone gunman has been one of the most useful terms in covering-up criminal conspiracies. With the lone gunman all further inquiry is stopped in its tracks once he or she is apprehended. What need is there for ongoing investigation when all the criminality can be laid at the feet of a single person? Hitler is a case in point. When one considers the atrocities of the Nazis, it is unthinkable that Hitler could have been in any way *solely* responsible for the degree and extent of their crimes. Undoubtedly, a few additional names come to mind as his henchmen, but all too often Hitler is tagged with the force behind the Nazis' evil deeds and sheer logistics make this implausible. This is also the case with characters like Lee Harvey Oswald and Osama bin Laden who are cited as the prime movers of the deeds that traumatized the nation.[1]

---

[1] In considering how Hollywood movies play a role in disinformation and reinforcing po-

Propaganda: since WWII this term has not been applied to the American political or educational systems or to Hollywood film production and other sources that purportedly inform the public such as print, radio or television news. The horrific outcomes of propaganda overtly utilized by the Nazi regime by Joseph Goebbels make it a term of noxious intent that no one today would ever want to apply to his own government's activities. In so far as propaganda is a systematic effort, implying the collusion of agencies both private and public, it is very difficult to understanding the handling of the official versions of Jonestown, Waco, and September 11 as anything other than the result of concerted propaganda efforts. The assassination of JFK would also fall into this category. The reader is encouraged to look at Edward Bernays' book *Propaganda* for a clearer understanding of how "society consents to have its choice narrowed to ideas and objects brought to it [*sic*] attention through propaganda of all sorts" (39).

---

litical myths and delusions, it is instructive to view a scene in the 1973 film *Executive Action* starring Burt Lancaster which purported to be, and advertised itself as, the first movie to deal with "conspiracy theories" and the JFK assassination. Using original footage of the president's motorcade rolling down the streets of Dallas on its way to Dealey Plaza and the fateful moment, at 1:11:24 the movie cuts-away from the motorcade shot. Yet, today in a clip readily available for viewing at YouTube under "JFK assassination secret service stand down," the film-clip continues to roll beyond the point shown in the movie and to where the viewer watches incredulously as agent Emory P. Roberts Secret Service agent standing in the car behind JFK's waves-off two body guards standing on the back of JFK's limousine and whom would have afforded the president protection from the rear. The official explanation for the waving-off of these guards was so onlookers could get a better view of the president. Really!?! Hardly a convincing answer, but that's what we've been given (see Conclusion; Douglass, 271). In any case, the filmmakers did not deem it necessary to pursue a Secret Service conspiracy angle. Nor could they have envisioned a day in which public access to the original footage would be so readily available! Had they any inkling that the general public would get to see the footage *they had access to* at the time in 1973, they would have been pressed to address, or at least include, somehow, the incriminating image. But who could have foretold, after all, that the Internet would be invented? (See References in Conclusion to *ATOR* Def. 2: 27/325). The interpretation of Hollywood's film is clear: its intent is upon diverting attention *away from* the Secret Service and the role of moles *within* the government acting as subversives. As Douglass in the above reference notes, "The House Select Committee on Assassinations drew the reluctant conclusion: it may well be that by altering Dallas Police Department Captain Lawrence's original motorcycle plan, the Secret Service deprived Kennedy of security in Dallas that it had provided a mere day before in Houston" (Douglass, ibid.). In the end, the film *does* challenge the lone gunman mythology, but it does so with more distortions and confusion – mission accomplished.

Acknowledgments

(And one final warning)

A research project such as this would be impossible were it not for courageous investigative journalists, whistleblowers, insiders, and other "leakers" of information who take the risks necessary for the truth to be known. And for the scholars and researchers, degreed and un-degreed, who are willing to discuss these topics amidst their peers and to the public. It is rare these days that a scholar will stick his or her neck out and state what *can be* so obviously established true yet remains "unspeakable."

The dissident press in combination with the Internet are the last bastions of fully-free (albeit manipulable) speech as the mass-mainstream and highly commercialized-politicized media have crowded out all resonances of alternative narratives of history and current events that challenge the power and financial structures which have developed in (and enveloped) the globe since the end of WWII. One need only think of "embedded journalists" in the most recent wars to interpret what is happening – the message *is* massaged.

This condition is one of the early steps in a drift away from democracy and representative government – the systematic and official silencing of the opposition. Today this is done in the most sophisticated of manners, which helps disguise its true potential and capabilities and perhaps even the intentions behind it, and makes it appear less than something oppressive.

But this condition is oppressive just the same. If knowledge is power, then withholding accurate information from "we the people" is tantamount to stripping us of our power.

The Internet has been indispensable for pulling it all together and threading it into a narrative. This community of resources we call the World Wide Web should never be taken for granted. I have included the availability dates last known as of this writing for video documentary references posted at public forums. There is no guarantee that this information will always be available, and the online resources included are the most vulnerable in their accessibility due to their reliance on the maintenance of the Internet itself. These should be given priority when checking my sources and references. Evaluate them for yourself.

There is a very good reason, as I have lamented, that certain images are withheld from the public...*they are powerful!* And what gives these images their power? It is their ability to conform to our reason, previous experience, and common sense and this renders them far more persuasive in shaping our worldview than the strained statements of our leader, those demagogues, despite the high offices from which they speak. In those references where the video can be viewed, the date was included of my last access to it; where the reference cannot be viewed but its source is archived only, this was noted with the date.

To *ASK QUESTIONS* and to *DEMAND ANSWERS* is not only the clarion call of activists seeking to bring-about change, or the driving impulse of journalists to break the next important investigative story. It is also the labor of scholars. And when answers are provided to our questions may we find honesty *in those answers*, and boldness *in ourselves* when confronting them should we suspect dishonesty. Furthermore, it is the duty and imperative of our politicians, most especially the elected ones of Congress, to ask the hard questions and demand the answers fitting to the facts. Their collective failure in recent years has left the country weakened and on a perilous course wherein the future is decided in places and by individuals who do not represent the *People*.

And finally, I end with a thought from C.P. Snow, whom I've followed as something of an intellectual compass in navigating through the mists of contemporary religious-political knowledge: *for the sake of the intellectual life, for the sake of this country's (U.K. of 1950-60s) special danger, for the sake of the western society living precariously rich among the poor, for the sake of the poor who needn't be poor if there is intelligence in the world, it is obligatory for us and the Americans and the whole West to look at our education with fresh eyes* (see chapter two; Snow, 50).

Visit **Blair's Blog** for a digital and updated assemblage of resources related to those topics covered herein; http://bgadsby.wixsite.com/blairs-blog (accessed March 2019).

Index